POSTMODERNISM

POSTMODERNISM

A READER

Patricia Waugh
Lecturer in English, University of Durham

Edward Arnold
A division of Hodder & Stoughton
LONDON   NEW YORK   MELBOURNE   AUCKLAND

© 1992 Selection and editorial matter Patricia Waugh

First published in Great Britain 1992
Reprinted 1993 (with minor corrections)

Distributed in the USA by Routledge, Chapman and Hall, Inc.
29 West 35th Street, New York, NY 10001

British Library Cataloguing in Publication Data

Postmodernism: Reader
  I. Waugh, Patricia
  809

  ISBN 0–340–57380–5 (hbk)
  ISBN 0–340–57381–3 (pbk)

Typeset in Helvetica and Times by Rowland Phototypesetting Ltd,
Bury St Edmunds, Suffolk
Printed and bound in Great Britain for Edward Arnold,
a division of Hodder and Stoughton Ltd,
Mill Road, Dunton Green, Sevenoaks, Kent TN13 2YA
by Biddles Ltd, Guildford and King's Lynn

Contents

Acknowledgements

I would like to thank all those friends and colleagues who have contributed in a variety of ways to this book: for conversations with and suggestions from Jo Catlin, Andrew Crisell, Peter Dempsey, David Fuller, Barry Lewis, Lynne Pearce, Stephen Regan and Richard Terry. I am very grateful to Irving Velody and Jim Goode for organising the excellent History of the Human Science lecture programme at Durham University on Modernity and Postmodernity and to Irving for his knowledge of postmodern social theory. Denise Brown's friendship has helped to make my own postmodern condition bearable (but that would need another book) and even, on occasion, telling ourselves the right stories at the right times, positively celebratory and hilarious! Many thanks also to Durham University for granting me a term of research leave, likewise to Alec Waugh, Jane Lewis and Robert, Eileen and Eric Kirkham for their unfailing help and care, and to Christopher Wheeler at Edward Arnold for his support and enthusiasm for this project.

The editor and publishers would like to thank the following for permission to use copyright material in this book:

Cambridge University Press for the extracts from Immanuel Kant, 'An Answer to the Question: What is Enlightenment?', reprinted from David Simpson, ed., *German Aesthetic and Literary Criticism*, (1984) and Richard Rorty, *Contingency, Irony and Solidarity* (1989); 'Against Interpretation' from *Against Interpretation* by Susan Sontag. Copyright © 1964, 1966 by Susan Sontag. Reprinted by permission of Farrar Straus & Giroux, Inc.; Manchester University Press for Jean-François Lyotard, 'Answering the Question: What is postmodernism?', from *The Postmodern Condition: A Report on Knowledge*, (1986); New Left Review for the extract from Terry Eagleton, 'Capitalism, Modernism and Postmodernism; from *New Left Review*, 152 (1985); the extract from *The Sense of An Ending: Studies in the Theory of Fiction* by Frank Kermode. Copyright © 1967 by Oxford University Press, Inc. Reprinted by permission; the author and Partisan Review for the extract from Irving Howe, 'Mass Society and Postmodern Fiction', *Partisan Review*, 26 (1959); Penguin Books Ltd for the extract from *Twilight of the Idols* by Friedrich Nietzsche, translated by R.J. Hollingdale (Penguin Classics, Second Edition 1990), Translation and Translator's Note copyright © R.J. Hollingdale, 1969; Routledge for the extracts from Linda Hutcheon, *A Poetics of Postmodernism* (1988) and Brian McHale, *Postmodernist Fiction* (1987); Telos Press Ltd for Anthony Giddens, 'Modernism and Postmodernism', *New German Critique*,

22 (1981) and Jürgen Habermas, 'Modernity versus Postmodernity' *New German Critique*, 22 (1981), reprinted as 'Modernity – an incomplete project' in *Postmodern Culture*, ed., Hal Foster (1985), Pluto Press; the author and the University of Illinois Press for the extract from Ihab Hassan, *Paracriticisms* (1975), © 1975 by the Board of Trustees of the University of Illinois; the author and the University of Minnesota Press for Fredric Jameson, 'Periodizing the Sixties', from *The Sixties Without Apology*, eds., S. Sayres et al., copyright © 1984 by *Social Text*; the University of Pennsylvania Press for the extract from Alan Wilde, *Horizons of Assent* (1987).

Every effort has been made to trace copyright holders of material produced in this book. Any rights not acknowledged here will be acknowledged in subsequent printings if notice is given to the publisher.

Introduction

For over a decade, Postmodernism has been a key term in the vocabularies not only of literary theorists but also political scientists, philosophers, geographers, media theorists and sociologists. It is beginning to appear more frequently in feminist debates, government papers on education and even in tabloid newspapers. Yet over ten years ago, the American writer John Barth had declared it to be a term: 'awkward and faintly epigonic, suggestive less of a vigorous or even interesting new direction in the old art of storytelling than of something anticlimactic, feebly following a very hard act to follow' (Barth, 1980, 66). In 1980, the term was only just beginning to enter the full range of the human sciences. It still carried emphatically *aesthetic* connotations: for Barth it is a continuation but modification of cultural Modernism, a way of 'telling stories'. Interestingly, by 1990, although 'Postmodernism' as a concept has emphatically spilled out of the boundaries of literary critical debate, it still carries with it, wherever it goes, the idea of 'telling stories'. But the stories are now indistinguishable from what was once assumed to be knowledge: scientific 'truth', ethics, law, history. Postmodernism had by this time also invented the story of its own genealogy, returning to earlier thinkers such as Nietzsche, Bataille, Artaud and even de Sade, as well as more recent theorists such as Barthes, Foucault, Derrida and Lacan. Or rather, I would say, it had constructed *genealogies*. It was becoming evident that just as there were many Postmodernisms, so must there be a variety of theoretical precursors and historical trajectories.

This Reader has its own sense of the identity of Postmodernism. I have regarded Postmodernism as a theoretical and representational 'mood', developing over the last twenty years and characterised by an extension of what had previously been purely *aesthetic* concerns into the demesne of what Kant had called the spheres of the 'cognitive' or scientific and the 'practical' or moral. For this reason, it seems useful to place the current theoretical debate about the validity of such practices in a context which acknowledges the roots of postmodern strategies in a history of aesthetic thought that can be traced back at least as far as European Romanticism. Even in terms of *immediate* history, Postmodernism was first used extensively in a literary critical context. It entered American criticism in the fifties to describe Charles Olson's attempt to define the existence of a new non-anthropocentric poetry whose Heideggerian anti-humanism was directed at seeing 'man' as a being in the world, as radically situated as any other object. A similar tendency appeared at around the same time in the French New Novel, particularly in the anti-humanist aesthetics of Alain Robbe-Grillet and in Susan Sontag's rejection of an 'intellectualised' depth/surface model of interpretation for an acceptance of the experience of art as sensuous surface, what she referred to as an 'erotics' of literature.

What these rather different critical positions share is a suspicion of subject-centred reason or philosophies of consciousness and they can now be seen as part of a gathering critique of modernity which has developed into a major tendency in current postmodern thought. The specific 'postmodern' tendencies in the writers mentioned above have their roots most obviously in the philosophical thought of Martin Heidegger. From his first major work, *Being and Time* (1927) and more insistently in later essays collected in *The Question Concerning Technology* or *Poetry, Language, Thought*, Heidegger developed a critique of Cartesianism as the founding methodology of modernity: one which he saw as productive of the violences of the West and inadequate as a ground for knowledge. For Heidegger, the Cartesian assumption of a radical split between knowing subject and inert object of knowledge has led to a world in which the detached superiority of the scientist becomes the model and ground of all existence. Instead of experiencing world as a texture through which we come to be, world is observed as an inert material body to be manipulated through a series of dualisms generated by the subject-object split (mind/body, spirit/matter, reason/emotion, masculinity/femininity). Modernity is thus a condition defined by a characteristic denial or disavowal of Being-in-the-world. A detached subjectivity has come to stand over an inert nature, speculating, observing, judging and manipulating it for its own ends. All relations become instrumental. Behind each is an empty subjectivity swallowed up in calculative thinking, radically disembedded from world: a Being-in-the-world founded on the denial of world through its subjugation to a technological will. Heidegger advocates instead a return to a sense of situatedness in a world which pre-exists us and cannot be consciously manipulated or defined, but through which we come into being as it 'worlds' through us. We can only come to be what we are within the world and through the textures of understanding which it provides, but we can strive to retrieve what is unsaid by recognising that Cartesian 'presence' is only one form of relationship. For Heidegger, the aesthetic provides an alternative to Cartesian logic or method because poetry allows a radically ontogenetic 'showing forth' which refuses that mode of conceptualisation which divides us from the world. Poetry reminds us that we come to be through others and in language. It can teach us humility. It asks us to *listen* and to suspend the imperial activity of looking.

Other 'postmodern' tendencies began to emerge from the sixties onwards with a variety of philosophical orientations. Leslie Fiedler talked of a new democratic art which would bridge the gap between high and mass culture and undo the elitist 'autonomy' of Modernism. Others decried this tendency (Irving Howe, for example) as a debased commodification of the aesthetic. John Barth talked of abandoning the 'literature of exhaustion' for a recognition of the essentially parodic literature of replenishment: the aestheticist recognition that everything has always already been said before and that parody 'replenishes' through a self-conscious recognition that implication in a prior discourse does not entail exhaustion and inert imitation. Ihab Hassan developed an 'aesthetics of silence' similar to Sontag's. Both advocate art made opaque and resistant to the consumption which is interpretation: art existing in the world as a sensuous surface. To look back on these early literary critical discussions of Postmodernism may seem to involve a return to a remote history which has very little to do with the current mood of the postmodern. Certainly, by the early eighties, the term has shifted from a description of a range of aesthetic practices involving playful irony, parody, parataxis, self-consciousness, frag- mentation, to a use which encompasses a more general shift in thought and seems to register a pervasive loss of faith in the progressivist and speculative discourses of modernity. Postmodernism is now used to express the sense of a new cultural epoch in which distinctions between critical and functional knowledge break down as capitalism, in its latest consumerist phase, invades everything including the aesthetic, the post-colonial world and the uncon- scious, leaving no remaining oppositional space. Postmodern art or postmodern thought may now be seen as a symptom of wider cultural changes: either complicit with what is viewed as a change for the worst, or a possible mode of liberation from or insight into the blindnesses of modernity and Modernism.

By the eighties, therefore, Postmodernism tends to be used in three broad senses: as a term to designate the cultural epoch through which we are living and largely viewed in apocalyptic terms; as an aesthetic practice which is seen variously as co-extensive with the commodified surfaces of this culture or as a disruption of its assumptions from within through a 'micropolitics' or 'politics of desire'; and as a development in thought which represents a thorough-going critique of the assumptions of Enlightenment or the discourses of modernity and their foundation in notions of universal reason. The specifically literary critical debate began to be dissolved into the larger theoretical and cultural one with the publication of Jean-François Lyotard's *The Postmodern Condition* in 1979 (translated into English in 1984). It is clear, however, that Lyotard's declaration of the collapse of grand narratives and metanarratives (the focus of this later debate) was always implicit in the earlier discussions. This theme became more insistent as post-structuralist textualism displaced the holistic certainties of structuralist thought, that last defence of universal System and logically deducible depth/surface relation. What began to emerge was a tendency or mood across a range of disciplines which involved an intense sense of dissatisfaction or loss of faith in the forms of representation, the political and cultural practices, associated with Modernism and modernity. Because this mood is complex and variously focussed there is no one 'Postmodernism', but it could be argued that Postmodernism is a 'structure of feeling' which is certainly dominant for many intellectuals and emergent, at the very least, for others. Some commentators (Callinicos, 1989) have viewed it purely as a construction of disaffected radicals, seeking alternative significance for their own intellectual activity after the failure of the political idealism of 1968. There is probably much truth in this, but it is not sufficient to explain the full complexity of the postmodern 'mood'. Certainly, I would agree that Postmodernism foregrounds the aesthetic, but that does not necessarily entail that it is a withdrawal from political commitment or ethical concern.

The aestheticism of the postmodern takes a variety of forms. It produces that confusing sense that Postmodernism is an invention of theorists who then project their own construction upon the world and find all around them confirmation of what they have assumed the postmodern to be. Postmodernism is always involved in 'bootstrapping' circularities of knowledge and experience and in performative self-contradictions where it discovers itself forever implicated in that which it seeks to proclaim as inauthentic and exhausted. Viewed simply as a term to describe a cultural epoch, it clearly contradicts its own premises. In postmodern terms, totalities such as 'periods' simply do not exist outside the inventive minds of philosophers and historians. But one can begin to offer a tentative genealogy of the postmodern by examining its range of orientations and responses to the sense of failure of Enlightenment. All Postmodernisms foreground the aesthetic, but in different ways. Some develop a 'politics of desire', in order to proclaim a sense that Reason has failed and that a return to the body is long overdue. Others prefer to respond to the perceived collapse of the grand narratives of history, justice, equality, founded on the concept of universal reason, by developing context-specific strategies or local interventions which draw on the concept of 'language games' in the later thought of Ludwig Wittgenstein. In this version, not only is *truth* abandoned, but also the desire to retain *truth-effect*. Dissensus entirely displaces the ideal of consensus. Alternatively, philosophers such as Alisdair MacIntyre develop an interest in resisting the potential nihilism of late modernity by returning to pre-modern definitions of 'virtue' through a hermeneutic notion of cultural situatedness. We can resist the fragmentation of the modern if we reformulate the narratives of the past within the historically constituted practices and traditions which we inherit as part of a cultural community. Writers like Foucault return to a Greek concept of 'techne', of existence as an aesthetic practice, which takes up many of the ideas of the philosopher Friedrich Nietzsche (who, with Heidegger, can be seen as the major precursor of much postmodern thought). If these foci seem diverse, they derive, however, from a common source: a sense of the inadequacy of Enlightenment theories of knowledge and traditional rationalist or empiricist methodologies and a shift towards the *aesthetic* as a means of discovering an alternative to Cartesianism and Kantian Reason. It is not surprising, therefore, that Postmodernism was first widely discussed in a specifically literary critical context. By returning to this context in this Reader, I hope to show how a re-examination of these early discussions may help to unravel the current confusion about the use of the term. Postmodernism can be understood, in my view, as the culmination of an aestheticist tradition deriving from Romantic thought and beginning with writers such as Schiller. This tradition has consistently viewed Enlightenment reason as complicit in its instrumentalism with industrial modernity and has turned to the aesthetic as a type of practice which can resist the potentially 'totalising' violence of the concept (the 'logic of the same'). It has drawn on the aesthetic in order to offer both a critique of social rationalisation and the restriction of definitions of knowledge to what can be consciously and conceptually formulated. What is new is its current pervasiveness: Postmodernism is the aesthetic spilled over into the moral and cognitive. These tendencies have been understood in terms of materialist accounts of economic change, but also through an examination of the perceived limitations and failures of the philosophical discourses of modernity.

First let us look at the dissatisfactions and discontents of postmodernity before we consider more closely the centrality of the aesthetic in the alternatives proposed in postmodern theory. Though there are many forms of Postmodernism, they all express the sense that our inherited forms of knowledge and representation are undergoing some fundamental shift: modernity may be coming to an end, strangled by its own logic, or rendered exhausted by economic changes which have propelled us into a new age of information technology, consumerism and global economics which erode the stability of concepts such as nation, state or essential human nature. The historian Arnold Toynbee was the first to develop this sense of the contemporary world. His six volume *A Study of History* appeared in 1947. R.C. Somerville suggested 'postmodern' to describe Toynbee's focus, and Toynbee himself subsequently took up the term in his later writing, using it in much the way that Spengler had talked of the modern in his earlier *Decline of the West*. For Toynbee, the postmodern age would be the fourth and final phase of Western history and one dominated by anxiety, irrationalism and helplessness. In such a world, consciousness is adrift, unable to anchor itself to any universal ground of justice, truth or reason on which the ideals of modernity had been founded in the past. Consciousness itself is thus 'decentred': no longer agent of action in the world, but a function through which impersonal forces pass and intersect. Art becomes not so much an expression of human spirit, but another commodity. Like knowledge, therefore, it can no longer be critical but only functional. Moreover, we are in the postmodern condition and, implicated in a culture where all knowledge is produced through discourse, we can no longer seek transcendence. There is no position outside of culture from which to view culture. There is no Kantian 'view from nowhere', no conceptual space not already implicated in that which it seeks to contest. There can only be disruption from within: micropolitics, language games, parodic skirmishes, irony, fragmentation.

Central to the 'postmodern condition' therefore, is a recognition and account of the way in which the 'grand narratives' of Western history and, in particular, enlightened modernity, have broken down. Counter-Enlightenment, of course, is as old as Enlightenment itself, but whereas in the past (in Romantic thought, for example), the critique of reason was accompanied by an alternative foundationalism (of the Imagination), Postmodernism tends to claim an abandonment of all metanarratives which could legitimate foundations for truth. And more than this, it claims that we neither need them, nor are they any longer desirable. We have witnessed the terror produced through the instrumental modes of universal reason, the generalising violence of the concept, and discovered that we no longer want 'truth' and we do not even require 'truth-effect'. In fact, as we shall see, there is often an alternative foundationalism lurking in many postmodern arguments (of desire, language, art, the body) and in those of its aestheticist and philosophical precursors. The collapse of Enlightenment 'grand narratives' was famously proclaimed by Lyotard in *The Postmodern Condition*, but was already familiar in the thought of Nietzsche, Wittgenstein and Foucault amongst others. The immediate intellectual context for Lyotard's book (1979) was the demise of Structuralism and the development of a post-structuralist critique of systems of knowledge which assume a stable depth/surface relation such that a hidden 'core' of truth may be archaeologically uncovered with the appropriate tools of excavation and causally related to an apparently contingent surface. In this, in the work of Derrida, Lacan and the later Barthes, for example, the signifier was given priority over the signified, meaning shown to be radically indeterminate, all texts implicated in an endless intertextuality so there could be no space outside of text; no origin or source of meaning. This theory produced a number of radical critiques of traditional philosophy and, in particular, of the notion of 'foundationalism': the idea that knowledge is the reflection of truth and that we can discover a stable foundation for it in God, History or Reason. History becomes a plurality of 'islands of discourse', a series of metaphors which cannot be detached from the institutionally produced languages which we bring to bear on it. Alternatively, history is a network of agonistic language games where the criterion for success is performance not truth. The implication of this is that 'truth' cannot be distinguished from 'fiction' and that the aesthetic has thus incorporated all. Lyotard's book argued for an acknowledgement of the exhaustion of metanarratives claiming to legitimate foundationalist claims, and advocated context-specific agreements, heterogeneity, pragmatism, incommensurability. Totalities are equated with totalitarianism and terror: we must renounce our nostalgia for them and instead embrace the aesthetic pleasure of local games with language instead of the imperialist pleasure of the universal concept. Foucault's work has much in common with this emphasis. Although his writing shifts from an early focus on the way in which subjectivities are institutionally constructed to a final (post-Nietzschean) emphasis on the capacity of the subject to shape itself aesthetically, his work has been consistently critical of the 'totalities' of Enlightenment universalism. Whereas Lyotard approaches this through Wittgenstein, however, Foucault develops a counter-Enlightenment tradition which has always been interested in that which reason excludes and which has tended, therefore, to privilege the aesthetic. The focus of Foucault's critique is the Enlightenment equation of Reason with progress, knowledge and emancipation. He turns to thinkers such as Bataille and Nietzsche in order to examine ways in which a pervasive will to power is enacted through formations of knowledge where the former is rationalised and disguised as a will-to-truth. Like Lyotard, Foucault is critical of 'total theories': theories which claim to account for all aspects of human existence. His procedure has been to focus attention on the 'other' excluded by and constructed through such theories: desire, the body, madness, multiplicity, sexuality, and to show how so-called transcendent theories arise out of institutional discourses constructed through this process of exclusion.

What Lyotard and Foucault share in their critique of Enlightenment is a sense that there cannot be a view from nowhere, that knowledge always arises out of embodiment, cultural and biological. Not surprisingly, therefore, Postmodernism seems to represent a shift from the conceptual absolutes of philosophy to the contingencies and ironies of literature as a form of non-conceptual embodied representation which can avoid the violent totalisations of abstract thought. So, a philosopher like Richard Rorty suggests that philosophers should turn to literary criticism. Only by abandoning altogether the outworn rhetoric of metaphysical truth, can we embrace the potential offered to us currently to reshape existence through aesthetic activity. Rorty argues that there are no real walls, only painted ones. We should therefore abandon the attempt to rebuild foundations and instead focus attention on 'style' and embodied particularity. For this reason, he sees poets and novelists as the philosophers of the future. Poetic irony and contingency may come to provide the possibility of imaginative expansion of human sympathy and empathy as a basis for that social and political solidarity no longer available in the terms of the grand narratives of Enlightenment.

Although each of these versions of the postmodern represents a departure from the norms of an analytic tradition of philosophy or political science, none of them is at all new within a specifically *aesthetic* context. In many ways, Postmodernism can be seen as the latest version of a long-standing attempt to address social and political issues through an aestheticised understanding of the world, though it may be more thoroughly and pervasively aestheticising than any previous body of thought. This tradition has a long history with which literary critics, rather than political theorists, are likely to be familiar. In this Reader, therefore, I have tried to return the postmodern debate to a specifically aesthetic tradition, for its discussion within the human sciences generally often marginalises the implications of viewing it in such a context. Although the most obvious aestheticist source for Postmodernism is the writing of Nietzsche and Heidegger, their critique of modernity as an over-extension of a Cartesian subject-centred Reason was prefigured throughout Romantic theory and practice. Schiller's *On the Aesthetic Education of Man* (1797), written during the reign of Terror after the French Revolution, expresses a belief in the aesthetic as the redemptive hope for an age of increasingly instrumental rationality. He saw that the reproduction of a culture must involve the life of the senses as well as that of reason or consciousness. His letters propose an aesthetic solution to the intractable problems thrown up by the failure of the totalising and abstract logic evident in the political vocabularies of his time. Although Schiller advocates aesthetic autonomy, it is in order that art may effect an existential reconciliation with world, free us from the violences and habits of ratiocinative thought. Schiller does not advocate a 'politics of desire' in the style of *one* of the modes of the postmodern (the Deleuzian), but he does initiate a critique of Enlightenment grand narratives to which Postmodernism can be seen to be heir.

This foregrounding of art develops through various philosophical orientations into a full-blown postmodern aestheticism. One branch develops a hermeneutic notion of *sensus communis* from Heideggerian thought and appears in a postmodern concern with context-specific consensus as an alternative to abstract Enlightenment universalism (Rorty, MacIntyre). Another develops the Nietzschean sense of truth as a form of radical fictionality arising out of embodiment and appears in the postmodern form of a politics of desire (Deleuze, Guattari) or an aesthetics of existence (late Foucault). Nietzsche had argued in his 1873 essay 'On Truth and Lie in an Extramoral Sense' that every concept is necessarily a falsification of what it purports to represent, for the world is radically fragmentary and contingent. The only authentic reconciliation is not that which claims to reunite us with the world at some higher level of spirit, but that aesthetic shaping which knows itself, self-consciously, to be a provisional fiction. Here lies Nietzsche's legacy both to postmodern theories of desire and to those of radical fictionality. The late

Romantic Nietzsche, proponent of Dionysian intensity, is also the postmodern Nietzsche, advocating life as aesthetic shaping or 'techne'. In both modes, he recognises human longing for immediacy and tempers it with the ironic recognition of the inevitability of mediation. In aesthetic experience, however, there is some escape from the tyranny of the conceptual and the abstract. Aesthetic activity allows us the biological delight of experiencing the ultimate impulse of the will to power as chaos coming into form: Dionysian fragmentation of energy willing itself into coherence. Order must be created out of oneself for the gods have fled, metaphysical certainties are in disarray and only one's own bodily desire, disciplined and aesthetically shaped, may provide a foundation for truth. Life is the supreme artistic challenge and the human body both the material to be shaped and the source of shaping energy. Self is an endless gathering and interpretation of fragments of experience: this is a postmodern self which is still recognisably a Romantic one.

Both the Heideggerian and the Nietzschean legacy to Postmodernism represent a critique of consciousness as subject-centred reason. In neither can one continue to look within and through a rational process, purged of internal or external distraction, come to know the categories which can ground universal theories of truth or justice. The legacy has produced a variety of Postmodernisms. On the one hand are those thinkers such as Rorty and, in a different way, MacIntyre, for example, who develop the hermeneutic idea of *sensus communis*. In *Truth and Method*, Gadamer drew on Heideggerian thought to offer a defence of interpretation intended to affirm why truth cannot be limited to method. No method can be foundational because we always understand the world before we begin to reflect upon it. We are always in a situatedness in world where knowledge can never be absolute because the object of knowledge is always expanded by the attempt to know it. Objectivity always arrives too late. Prejudice is a necessary precondition of enlightenment, rather than its negation, for only if we are interested can our prejudices be challenged. Only as we are expanded out of them can we know what they are. Immediacy is dependent upon mediation. Knowledge of the world cannot be divorced from being in the world and neither self nor world can be foundationally conceptualised: knowledge and experience are inextricably bound up with each other and always culturally located. Again, the 'post' of the Postmodernism which develops out of this broadly hermeneutic tradition, implies that there can be no position from outside culture from which to offer a critique of it. Implication is all.

Other Postmodernisms, whilst recognising this, also develop strategies of internal disruption: parody, dissensual language games, metafiction, varieties of aesthetic play. An extreme form of this is represented by what I have referred to as the 'politics of desire'. This is a liberatory as opposed to a culturally pessimistic mode of the postmodern. It is most closely associated with Gilles Deleuze and Felix Guattari, the former a philosopher and the latter a psychoanalyst, and with their book *Anti-Oedipus* (1972). In effect, this work extends the concerns of earlier writers such as Norman O'Brown and Herbert Marcuse with the political possibilities of liberation of desire through a Nietzschean challenge to subject-centred reason through the body. The Kantian ideal of a unified rational subject is displaced by one of liberation as the release of multiple desiring intensities which are normally restricted and controlled through the orders of modernity. Desire is seen to be constructive of social reality, Bataille-style excess the means of liberation from capitalist economy. As with much postmodern thought, however, it is unclear how this solution is not utterly complicit with its object of critique. Capitalism has already fragmented the self, consumerism stimulated a never-to-be satisfied desire. Equally, it is unclear how the substitution of desire for reason as the basis of ideal human activity does not replace Enlightenment universalism with a new foundationalism of the body which is just as reductive of human potential.

It is already apparent that any attempt to 'map' the postmodern will encounter endless contradictions. Finally, it must accept its own self-contradictions: this Reader, like all accounts of Postmodernism, conceptualises it in ways which run counter to the alleged spirit of Postmodernism. I have chosen to foreground 'aesthetic' dimensions because my own understanding of Postmodernism has arisen out of such a context. It is one perspective on the postmodern, but 'truth', of a kind, in that although it cannot be verified it is capable of carrying the investments of human belief. To argue at a theoretical level that all assertions are the fictions of incommensurable language games is to deny the fact that most people do, indeed, continue to invest in 'truth-effects'. If we continue to invest in 'grand narratives', such narratives can be said to exist. Grand narratives can be seen to be ways of formulating fundamental human needs and their 'grandness' is a measure of the urgency and intensity of the need. They are unlikely, therefore, simply to die, though they may need to be profoundly transformed. I suspect that Postmodernism will increasingly come to be seen as a strategy for exposing oppressive contradictions in modernity, but I would wish to resist the idea that we have all embraced it as an inevitable condition. We can work with it, I would suggest, in some contexts shaping our behaviour through universal emancipatory ideals, in others recognising the lurking cultural imperialism potentially involved in any such position and thus drawing on the postmodern as a strategy of disruption. Freud argued that maturity is the ability to live with hesitation, ambiguity and contradiction. Perhaps to grow up is to live suspended between the modern and the postmodern, resisting the temptation for resolution in one direction or the other.

The material in the Reader has been organised according to the logic of this argument. This introduction is augmented (in Section One) by a short piece offering a view of modernity and postmodernity from a sociologist, Anthony Giddens, who has professed a Habermasian-style desire to see Enlightenment as unfinished, not exhausted. In order to suggest ways in which one might begin to think about relations between cultural Modernism and Postmodernism, it is complemented by an extract from the work of a literary critic, Alan Wilde, whose book *Horizons of Assent* appeared in 1987. In this book, Wilde attempted to view Modernism and Postmodernism, respectively, in terms of two varieties of irony: the 'disjunctive' and the 'suspensive'. Disjunctive irony portrays the world as fragmented but is propelled by an impulse towards resolution, transcendence and coherence which can exist simultaneously with the acknowledgement of fragmentation. Suspensive irony intensifies fragmentation and suspends the impulse towards coherence. In literary critical terms, it represents a fairly common way of understanding differences between Modernism and Postmodernism (see Kermode, 1968; Lodge, 1977; for a critique of this perception see Waugh, 1992).

SECTION ONE

Modernism and Postmodernism

1   Anthony Giddens

From *Modernism and Post-Modernism*

New German Critique, volume 22, 1981, pp 15–18.

There are three comments I should like to make about the content of Jürgen Habermas's interesting and provocative paper. One concerns the further development of a point that is a key theme in what he has to say; the second of my remarks is in some part critical of Habermas's arguments; and the final one is really a question, an enquiry about the differences between Habermas's views and those of Adorno.

1   Habermas raises an issue both of great importance and of formidable complexity in suggesting that certain transformations of time-experience are intrinsically involved with so-called 'modernism' in art. He concentrates his discussion upon the 'secret' appeal to the classical buried in modernism, and upon the temporal self-destructiveness of the *avant-garde* which is constantly implicated in the moment of its own dissolution. This theme undeniably connects with a fondness for the scandalous, a distaste for all convention which however acknowledges that today's scandals are tomorrow's conventions – and hence is perhaps unable in fact to realise the impact of that very 'negation' which it seeks. I find Habermas's analysis of these matters both subtle and thought-provoking. But I think it is possible to connect them more directly than Habermas does, in this particular paper at least, with transformations of time-space relations introduced by the spread of industrial capitalism in the late 18th and 19th centuries. I am impressed by a convergence of recent work in the philosophy of time, social history, and urban theory, upon what can be called the *commodification of time-space* with the formation of industrial capitalism; this work, I think, can be directly connected with Marx's classical characterisation of the 'commodity.'[1] In capitalism, Marx makes clear, time – as quantified form – becomes fundamental to the intersection of class relations within the

---

[1] cf. Anthony Giddens, *A Contemporary Critique of Historical Materialism* (California, 1981).

labour-process. The quantification of time is the medium of the exploitative generation of surplus-value, in contrast to the 'direct' appropriation of surplus production or labour in agrarian class-divided civilisations.

Of course, there is an abundance of historical material documenting the diffusion of clocks, the technology for the quantification of time, in post-feudal Europe; Mumford, among others, has argued that the clock, rather than power-machinery as such, is the prime element in modern mechanical culture. But it takes a good deal of theoretical analysis to connect such materials to a more penetrating understanding of time and space as themselves commodified forms. As Marx shows, all commodities have a 'double existence,' as both substance and form. A good or product has qualities of its own; but these are complemented, in a capitalist economy, by the 'pure form' of exchange-value. As exchange-value, commodities have nothing in common as regards their substance: anything can be exchanged for anything else, via money. Simmel is wrong, however, to regard money as the prime exemplar of the commodification of social relations. More elemental, as Marx indicates especially in certain sections of the *Grundrisse*, is 'commodified time' (or, as I prefer to say, commodified time-space). Two connected social transformations are involved: time acquires a 'double existence'; and commodified time becomes detached from the commodification of space.

Commodified time has become so much an inherent part of our experience in contemporary capitalism, I think, that Heidegger was forced to introduce the most tortuous neologisms in order to recover a philosophical sense of time (time-space). The 'substance' of time-space is what Heidegger refers to as 'prescencing,' the constitution of Being in its fading into nothingness. But in our society, the 'substance' of time-space has become overshadowed by time as quantified form, and space as quantifiable extension. The consequences bite very deeply into the character of our daily lives, and help create that distinctively modern 'everyday life' of which Lefèbvre speaks. The differentiation of commodified time from commodified space is integrally related to the coordination of activity involved in labour discipline in the workplace; to the severance of work from 'free time' as sequential segments of a life governed by routine rather than by tradition; and to the severance of human beings from nature through the transformation of urban space through the prevalence of the 'created environment' of contemporary urbanism.

The profound – and perhaps in some respects irreversible – character of these transmutations were barely understood by those who experienced the first force of their impact in the 19th century. In art as in the social sciences one can readily discern a split between an essentially Romantic conservatism and a progressivism that puts its weight behind science and technology. I would interpret 'modernism' in art (insofar as the term has a clear designation at all) as a break with *both* of these types of standpoint. Modernism is neither only a protest against lost traditions, nor an endorsement of their dissolution, but in some degree an accurate expression of the 'emptying' of time-space.

2   These considerations lead me to take a more positive attitude towards certain developments in art which Habermas treats rather dismissively. Perhaps surrealism, for example, was a failure as an emancipatory project, as contributing to a recovery of a rational basis for the normative character of 'everyday life.' But I think this is still to see surrealism within the confines of the

residual opposition between Romanticism and progressivism noted above. For surrealism belonged to currents of change in modern culture that stretch well beyond what had become a separated sphere of 'art.' In literature, in linguistics, in philosophy, in science, we find parallel modes of transfiguration. The fact that they do occur suggests that some strikingly similar developments in European culture in the early years of the 20th century, might have a good deal to do with Kuhn's 'scientific revolutions.' Such 'revolutions' may be less a generic part of the development of science, stimulated by changes internal to science itself, than features of relatively uncommon, but more embracing, cultural transitions (cf. Bachelard). The common element in the transformations occurring subsequent to the turn of the 20th century is a concern to elucidate the asymmetry of substance and form. The emergence of structuralist linguistics is exemplary in this respect; latter-day syntheses of structuralism and psychoanalysis rest upon deeper conceptual affinities than sceptics may suspect.

However all this may be, I would be inclined to see in surrealism an exploration of substance and form that was by no means just an abortive experiment. Of course, it is hard to say in a cursory way anything that would do justice to a complicated subject. But I think it possible to see in surrealism an investigation of the generative principles that create the 'observable' characteristics of the object-world; and at the same time a sublation of that object-world, as commodified time-space.

3   Habermas distinguishes two senses of 'modernism,' the broader sense referring to the project of Enlightenment. He wishes to affirm a defence of 'modernism' in this more general sense, whatever may have been the shortcomings of artistic 'modernism,' against the attacks of neo-conservatism today. I fully share his worries about the rise of 'new conservatisms,' in various guises and contexts. And I would also accept his view, if I understand it correctly, that the 'new conservatisms' cannot just be combatted by established orthodoxies of the Left. The critique of Enlightenment has to be part of the intellectual endeavours of the Left today, not simply the monopoly of the Right. Such a view was, of course, already well-developed in the writings of Adorno and Horkheimer. This brings me to my point of interrogation about Habermas's discussion. He several times refers approvingly to Adorno, and evidently endorses some main elements of the ideas of that author, particularly in respect of the relation between the two types of 'modernism.' At the same time, however, he appears rather strongly to reaffirm the principles of Enlightenment almost without qualification. What view does he take of the position advanced by Horkheimer and Adorno in *Dialectic of Enlightenment*? One can recognise without difficulty that Habermas's views have always differed considerably from those of the 'older generation' of the 'Frankfurt School.' But is there any sense in which he is prepared to admit that Enlightenment thought and practice (mirroring on a general plane the fate of the *avant-garde* in the short-term) contained, at source, the seeds of its own dissolution?

2   Alan Wilde

From *Modernism and the Aesthetics of Crisis*

Horizons of Assent, John Hopkins University Press, 1987, pp 41–9.

No movement terminates abruptly, least of all modernism, and crisis, in any case, is not termination, in literary periods any more than in drama. So it is hardly surprising that modernism continues on – not only in isolated pockets, as it does today – but, at least until the Second World War, as a definable (if increasingly unstable) movement with its own special characteristics, most notably in England in the nineteen thirties among the members of the so-called Auden Group. The fact is that the major preoccupations of the earlier decade are still visible in the late modernism of its successor, and the writers of the thirties reveal themselves to be, if anything, still more self-conscious, yet more aware of the rift between self and world than their elders. But differences there are, and for my purposes it will be most illuminating to focus on one in particular.

The thirties, a decade on an altogether smaller scale than its predecessor – though a noisier one perhaps – is, fully as much as the twenties, a time of paradoxes. Indeed, external events forced on the thirties writers a series of troubling contradictions, centering in particular on the rival claims of artistic vocation and political commitment, which they then proceeded to debate publicly in the endless manifestos and declarations of those years. But whether arguing art and politics, exploring the contrary tugs of past and future (C. Day Lewis's 'In Me Two Worlds'), investigating the mysterious inconsistencies of personality (Isherwood's Truly Weak Man), or tracking down the sources of perverse and destructive evasions (Auden's negative inversion of the will), in all these cases the writers disclose their faith that contradictions are susceptible of resolution. The genuine paradox of the twenties gives way to apparent paradox, metaphysics to social science. Consciousness, no less initially confused and divided against itself, marches behind the banners of Marx or Freud (or both), trampling down in the process all of the mythical monsters of the decade: the old gang and the wicked mothers, the politicians and the clergy, and not least the craven doubts and hesitations of the self. So Auden, in a poem called 'Crisis' (in the *Collected Poetry* of 1945), answers his opening question – 'Where do They come from? Those whom we so much dread' – by demonstrating not only that we are ourselves responsible for the horrible anxieties, fears, and neuroses that afflict us, but, in addition, that we have 'failed as their pupils,' that in continuing, however obliquely and ruinously, to resist the 'Terrible Presences' we create, we open ourselves to a better future. So, first awareness, and then action and choice: the proper exercise of the will. It is the age's formula and its promise of relief. The aesthetics of crisis yields, in the decade's most characteristic metaphor, to the image of travel and to the resolving vision of a 'New Country.'

But this is to make things too simple. From the start, the decade's enthusiasm for change rings a bit hollow. Auden's *Paid on Both Sides* counsels love and migration: the difficult journey to a new life (New Country again) undertaken in a spirit of active but not histrionic commitment. But from time to time, the Chorus belies the social hope, shifting its attention from the local feud that is the major subject of the charade to the unchangeable human condition: the sense of 'Man divided always and restless always,' to quote from *The Dog Beneath the Skin*, in which the same call to choose another life is undermined by the same covert intuition of the hopelessness and uselessness of choice. In *Paid on Both Sides*, Anne Shaw expresses, while rejecting, the thought of 'divided days / When we shall choose from ways, / All of them evil, one' (p. 14). And throughout Auden's (and Isherwood's) work in the thirties – from '1929,' where 'a sudden shower / Fell willing into grass,' symbolizing the unthinking natural world and 'making choice seem a necessary error' (p. 37), to *The Ascent of F 6*, where the Abbot recommends, mysteriously, given the general direction of the play, 'the complete abnegation of the will' (p. 154) – there runs the belief that any choice, because conscious, implies division and is therefore evil. I'm suggesting, in other words, that, in addition to the apparent paradoxes the decade traffics in, there are genuine paradoxes as well, but that these, half buried and contravened by the bugle calls to action, work not to define a present crisis, as among the earlier modernists, but to intimate the inevitability of one in the future.

Of course, the decade was in any case moving, thanks to the economic and political events of the time, to its own more public crisis, but I doubt that the Auden Generation would, in the long run, have made substantively different decisions or expressed substantively different attitudes had events been otherwise. In retrospect at least, modernism appears to have been sliding toward a state of exhaustion and impasse. Jogged from the heights their elders held, defensively and with a kind of aesthetic bravado, the writers of the thirties, and particularly the decade's ironists, found themselves more bewildered than heartened by their frequently superficial involvements: troubled by the detachment that, as they recognized, still afflicted them but uneasy in their demand for participation in a world whispering, beneath the shrill slogans and hopeful therapies, of disaster beyond the reach of politics and psychology and of disorder not to be stabilized by the symmetries of art. The chief paradox of the decade – the inevitable but unintended subversion of depth through a relentless attention to surface, undertaken in an attempt to change both self and world by rendering language transparent – this paradox marks the effective end of modernism and of the attitudes that made absolute irony possible. Symptomatically, perhaps, Auden and Isherwood turned to religion in the forties, seeking a final resolution of modernist paradox, intractable now to art as well as to politics. In the philosophic city of Auden's 'Spring 1940' man's doubleness is recognized and, sub specie aeternitatis, accepted. New Country has been transvalued and left behind.

Younger writers have turned elsewhere, in so many directions, in fact, that it sometimes seems impossible to identify the goal because of the superabundance of movement. What can be said with some assurance is that postmodernism tries in any number of ways to refute – or simply rejects – the very bases of modernist beliefs. Distance, detachment, depth, essentialism, anthropomorphism, humanism, analogies, and the privileging of sight have all been anathematized, most famously perhaps by Robbe-Grillet in *Pour un nouveau roman* (though I don't mean to attribute all of these rejections to him) and more recently by writers like Raymond Federman, Ronald Sukenick, and other participators in the 'literary disruptions' described in Jerome Klinkowitz's book of that title. Most important may be what Erich Kahler views, with considerable asperity, as 'the disintegration of form in the arts.' Given Kahler's examples, there is much to be said for his diatribe, but it is possible too to speak, with Venturi, of an expanding, more comprehensive form, aiming, as he says, to fulfill through contradiction and complexity 'the obligation toward the difficult whole' (pp. 89–103). Symmetry, shapeliness, and binary oppositions (*pace* Lévi-Strauss and the structuralists) are clearly at a discount; and if Derrida is right in asserting that, since all oppositions are implicitly hierarchical, one of the two terms is always more valued, then still more so is the notion of genuine paradox.

We begin, then, with an antipathy to at least certain kinds of order. But that is only the beginning – or only the manifestation – of the change. Modernism reaches through order toward stability, and in Derrida's antimetaphysics the very idea of presence undergoes increasing deconstruction, revealing only and always an elusive absence. The high modernists, it should be said, had themselves begun to dismantle the infrastructures of their universe, making visible everywhere the shadow of the abyss, but what is at issue here is as much an attitude as a vision. In the movement from depth to surface, from an orderliness defined in terms of harmony or stasis to a more kinetic sense of order, from the high seriousness of the modernists (even at their most whimsical or witty) to contemporary ideals of play, there is a further and more basic shift. To speak metaphorically first, paradise, once lost, is now abandoned: Dowell's desperate desire not to concede the passing of the 'true sunshine; the true music' is transformed, more or less cheerfully, into an antiessentialist *je m'en foutisme*. The modernist nostalgia over origins is replaced by a dismissal of them; the frustration of being unable to resolve a dilemma gives way to an acceptance of the impossibility of making any sense whatever of the world as a whole. Acceptance is the key word here. Modernist irony, absolute and equivocal, expresses a resolute consciousness of different and equal possibilities so ranged as to defy solution. Postmodern irony, by contrast, is suspensive: an indecision about the meanings or relations of things is matched by a willingness to live with uncertainty, to tolerate and, in some cases, to welcome a world seen as random and multiple, even, at times, absurd. Forster's vision of simple contiguity has been naturalized, so to speak, transformed from a bleak intimation of unbearable meaninglessness into an acceptance of life as sometimes messy and vital, sometimes more prosaically quotidian, and, at worst, as manageably chaotic. The last phrase is possibly too self-contradictory to pass without comment. I mean simply that, at the least, postmodernism has managed to establish enclaves of occasionally odd and curious pleasures, 'the smaller pleasures,' Forster calls them in *The Life to Come*, while continuing (in some cases) to acknowledge, if only covertly, the confusion that attends and surrounds them.

All of this is to say that the conditions that made possible the modernist imagination of crisis have now gone by the board. Yeats was righter than he knew. The center has indeed not held – and for a good reason: to all intents and purposes, it has disappeared, taking with it the fulcrum on which the modernist dilemma turned or, rather, supported itself. Paradox has become quandary, the scales have been unbalanced, and we have come, depending upon how one chooses to read the present, either to what Spanos calls 'this silent realm of dreadful uncertainty,' where and only where we are 'likely to discover the ontological and aesthetic possibilities of generosity' (pp. 167–68) or, according to Kahler, to 'the triumph of incoherence' (pp. 73–109). Neither alternative is all that joyful, though Spanos at any rate sees hope in the break from the modernist tradition. I don't think it would be inaccurate to assert that, as the large, imposing structures that embody the modernist crisis become, from the thirties onward, increasingly modest and various, crisis itself, redefined as an almost continuous response to a decentered or uncentered world turns, quite simply, into anxiety, that uneasy burden of contingent existence. And for Spanos, anxiety is exactly what the postmodern artist ought to be aiming at, as a way 'of undermining the detective-like expectations of the positivistic mind, of unhoming Western man' (p. 167). Barthelme's Thomas puts the case more lightly but with similar intent in *The Dead Father*: 'Things are not simple. . . . Things are not done right. Right things are not done. There are cases which are not clear. You must be able to tolerate the anxiety. To do otherwise is to jump ship, ethics-wise' (p. 93).

Tolerating the anxiety. It is a reasonable, if not complete, definition of the postmodern sensibility, in any case of its ironic wing. And there, for the moment, I want to leave that sensibility, at least as something to be contemplated for its own sake. It is time to focus backward again, using the present as a vantage point from which to survey the past more accurately. The question that remains (it is the one I posed at the outset and left hanging) is this: how are we to evaluate and respond to the practitioners of absolute irony, the modernist masters whose reputations are in many cases currently under siege? For the response, Barthelme's portrait of the Dead Father once more comes neatly to hand. As I suggested earlier, that colossal relic of the past is Barthelme's myth of modernism: imperious (his murderous temper); commanding (his 'Authority. Fragile, yet present' [p. 67] and his fondness for issuing ukases); aesthetic (he is an art connoisseur manqué and the novel's most spacious and rhetorical speaker); a devotee of organization and order ('What purpose? What entelechy?' [p. 168] is his question to two of his children); and, finally, someone who, as he admits, enjoys 'having it both ways' (p. 15). Certainly, it is a comprehensive, if parodic, account of the modernist myth, critical but not without humorous sympathy; and it is wholly appropriate the Barthelme's postmodern version of *The Waste Land* discovers the possibility of redemption in the death of its Fisher King. But though Thomas oversees the burial with which the book closes, as the Dead Father descends still unwillingly into his grave, he disclaims responsibility: 'Processes are killing you,' he says, 'not we. Inexorable processes' (p. 158). The remark echoes what may be the novel's central comment, which appears at the end of the interpolated book within the book, 'A Manual for Sons.' 'Patricide,' the anonymous author of the 'Manual' writes, 'is a bad idea. . . . It is not necessary to slay your father, time will slay him, that is a virtual certainty. Your true task lies elsewhere. Your true task, as a son, is to reproduce every one of the enormities touched upon in this manual, but in attenuated form. You must become your father, but a paler, weaker version of him. . . . Your contribution will not be a small one, but "small" is one of the concepts you should shoot for. . . . *Fatherhood can be, if not conquered, at least "turned down" in this generation* – by the combined efforts of all of us together' (p. 145).

The strategy is typically Barthelmean: the small-scale effort to disenchant or demystify inherited beliefs and imperatives informs all of his work. And typical too is the novel's climactic revelation. In its final chapter, where, unequivocally now, the rains do fall, the Dead Father learns that the Golden Fleece he has all along been seeking (for him the journey is a quest to recover his youth) does not exist – or not in the shape or place he had imagined:

No Fleece? asked the Dead Father.
Thomas looked at Julie.
She has it?
Julie lifted her skirt.
Quite golden, said the Dead Father. Quite ample. That's it?
All there is, Julie said. Unfortunately. But this much. This where life lives.

(pp. 174–75)

Together with the antipatricidal message of the 'Manual for Sons,' this interchange makes Barthelme's related points: the value of a not too vigorous stand against the largeness of absolute values; the effort to participate in an admittedly confused world; and the acceptance of life, however drab, as the only source of the smaller pleasures. So then, the largely ritual nature of the journey that loosely structures the book suggests a debunking of the insistent modernist quest, in *The Waste Land* and elsewhere. What you find, the novel implies, is what you already have under your nose – or, in this case, under Julie's skirt. As a low-keyed restatement of the anxiety of influence, *The Dead Father* contrasts a modest present with a too solid past, all moral bluster and aesthetic retreat, and proceeds, in a final parody of Eliot, to its own 'burial of the dead'. Allowing for rather too much and too derivative artfulness of its own, a sometimes numbing indulgence in nonreferential play, the novel succeeds wonderfully well in dramatizing its refusal of the sustained, the coherent, and the organic and, equally, its affirmation of the provisional and suspensive – in asserting, in short, the validity of local, uncoordinated pleasures against the claims of entelechy. But does the portrait of the Dead Father stand up to the facts of modernism? If I'm right in what I've been saying all along, then the answer is no, although Barthelme's summons to smallness provides a helpful clue to the truth. What is required, I think, is less a 'turning down' in the present of modernism's overwhelming fatherhood, as the novel conceives it, than a recognition that the modernists were themselves somewhat less monumental than they are now taken to be.

Earlier, rejecting Brooks's criterion of maturity, I described the modernists as heroic, but that word may be as inadequate as the other for the scale and condition I'm trying to suggest. Isherwood's phrase 'the anti-heroic hero' (used to describe Forster) comes closer to the mark perhaps, but even qualified, the idea of heroism is not likely to sit well with an age like the present, so resolutely seeking, exceptions like Pynchon notwithstanding, to miniaturize both its aspirations and its forms. No, not even the antiheroic hero: it is too easy to conjure up an endlessly receding line of statues, their heads drooping disconsolately but each upper lip still defiantly stiff. What word will do then? To find it we need to recognize in the unresolved quality of modernist irony (to return to the essential mode of its art) a refusal of easy answers and, at the same time, to acknowledge in its absolute poise not confidence and rest but crisis and arrest – to concede, that is, the *humanity* of the modernist enterprise. At the heart of that enterprise one discerns the intense need to shape a disordered world – not, in the first instance, either to reform or escape it but, instead, to establish, if only negatively, a relationship with it. The search for relationship is what links the modernist attempt with the postmodern effort now in process; and if the latter has, by reformulating the problem, brought the specifically modernist crisis to an end and opened the door to new solutions, it has sometimes succeeded only too well in packaging them in severely attenuated containers. I'm not sure that anyone can declare today what the mainstream of postmodernism is, but it is at least possible to discern, here and there within the movement, the danger on the one hand of a too flaccid acceptance of disorder and, on the other, of a too easy retreat into a reductive, minimalist aestheticism that makes Clive Bell's pronouncements seem hardy by comparison. For what characterizes the modernist consciousness above all is the energy of its desire. And where postmodernism succeeds, it does so by embodying that energy, though, to be sure, on a less heroic scale. In these cases, the sons have become the fathers, as Barthelme says, their achievement, as he also implies, not only a weakening of the originals but a redirection of their energy, so that the sons manage, in the unobtrusively symbolic phrase of *Between the Acts*, to 'touch earth,' as the modernist ironists, for all their perfervid primitivism, ultimately failed to do.

Between the Acts, odd though it may sound to say so, seems to me still the most impressive of *postmodern* novels, and all the more interesting for representing an awareness of and a response to the crisis I've described, not by a later generation but by one of the major modernists reacting to the dead end her own earlier work reveals. For the awareness and the response seem to me unquestionably deliberate. Far more fluid and open in its form than novels like *To the Lighthouse* and *The Waves*, Woolf's final work contrives nonetheless to allude to the paradoxes of absolute irony. Throughout the book, we are presented with an insistent structure of opposites, which culminates in the contrasting *'Unity–Dispersity'* (p. 235) the pageant ends with. (The reference at one point to 'the donkey who couldn't choose between hay and turnips and so starved' [p. 74] neatly summarizes the inevitable consequences of absolute irony's arrested poise.) But the oppositions, the novel makes clear, are *thematic* – merely conceptualizations of life's ineradicable ambiguities; and to that degree, equally true or equally false or – and this is the most accurate way of viewing them – equally irrelevant: '"Yes," Isa answered, "No," she added. It was Yes, No. Yes, yes, yes, the tide rushed out embracing. No, no, no, it contracted' (p. 251). What we have here is not modernism's balanced 'either-

or' but, as contemporary critics are fond of saying, postmodernism's more comprehensive 'both-and.'

In any case, it is not on the level of theme but of texture that the novel's final vision asserts itself: in its enormous density, its heterogeneous materials, its constant reference to the absolute dailiness – the 'Monday or Tuesday' – of the life it presents. Within the context of its omnipresent noise – and its silences ('We are always in a plenum, in being,' Merleau-Ponty writes, '. . . just as silence is still a modality of the world of sound' [p. 352]) – things seem to exist, as they do not in the earlier novels, in their own right; not simply as avenues to transcendent vision but, like the animals passing in and out of the barn or the fish swimming 'in their self-centered world' (p. 55), as themselves. For *Between the Acts* maintains and expresses a contact with things as they are: the world as perceived. The reference to touching earth derives from an allusion to Antaeus, and Antaeus is precisely the right emblem for Woolf's novel and for the postmodern imagination as well. Thus, later in the book, starlings attack the tree behind which Miss La Trobe, the exhausted author of the pageant, has been concealed, and she witnesses 'a quivering cacophony . . . birds syllabling discordantly life, life, life, without measure' (p. 245). There is nothing placid about the scene, as the world (the starlings) imposes itself on Miss La Trobe's being (her consciousness incarnated in the tree), but that is the point. The unsought activation of perception begins again the process of vision, and 'from the *earth* green waters seemed to rise over her'; 'words of one syllable sank down into the *mud*. She drowsed; she nodded. The *mud* became fertile' (pp. 246, 247–48; my italics). What *we* witness is the affirmation of the *Lebenswelt*, or, rather, we are given an image of vision arising out of and rooted in it: an acceptance of the gaps and discontinuities that were once, for Woolf and other modernists, the source of horror and now, between the acts, become the basis of life and creation.

If Woolf's affirmation defines the nature of postmodern irony, it also releases the energy of desire contained in the earlier novels and in 'Monday or Tuesday.' And so too, it seems to me, postmodernism in general – or at its best – fulfills the blocked energies inscribed in the modernist crisis. Thus Ferguson, the narrator of Max Apple's 'Vegetable Love,' failing in his modernist attempt to discover depth (his center) and his late modernist effort to become transparent (the name he assumes is Glass), realizes that 'starting from himself and stretching right to the farthest astronaut hitting a golf ball on the moon, there was a line of chaos as direct as the plumb line that went through Ferguson.' 'Who had absolutes?' he asks himself, and answers, simply, as he prepares for a new life, 'I have tried.' The tone resembles nothing we associate with modernism, and no more do Ferguson's final attitudes: the rejection of certainty and the acceptance of chaos – the attainment, in other words, of suspensiveness. But the roots of his quest point backward as surely as his solution points ahead. The breaking up of paradox, then, can be interpreted not as the discrediting of modernism but as the release of its humanity; and, retrospectively, we can now see, in distance and detachment, in the search for order and its creation through absolute irony, not moral smugness and aesthetic complacency but, to say it one last time, the dynamics of consciousness in crisis. By humanity I intend, I should say, not whatever may result from the personal revelations about Woolf and Strachey, Forster and Eliot, and the rest, which, in exposing clay feet that leave prints no different from our own, threaten, in some instances at least, to simplify the problematics of their work. The evidence I'm referring to, the case against the dehumanizing and dismissal of modernism, exists in the texts themselves. Biography will shed its light no doubt, but all the rest – and it is what counts, after all: the still vital legacy of modernism to its rebellious sons and daughters, inevitably attempting once again to make it new – all the rest is literature.

SECTION TWO

Postmodernism and Literary History

This section offers material which illustrates the short overview of the literary history of Postmodernism outlined in the general introduction. Most of it is self-explanatory, but some contextualisation may be helpful. Leslie Fiedler's essay was published in 1969 and looks forward to later debates about the extent to which postmodern artefacts are simply complicit with the commodified surfaces of mass culture or instead represent a genuinely democratic attempt to extend art out of the confines of an elite modernist autonomy. Fiedler takes the view that Modernism attempted to protect the aesthetic by withdrawing from what its practitioners regarded as a debased mass culture. Of course, one can challenge the assumption both that Postmodernism is any more accessible than Modernism simply because it incorporates elements of mass culture and, indeed, whether Modernism itself actually represented such a withdrawn aesthetic autonomy in the first place. The essay was indicative of a new counter-Modernism, however, which resisted the parochialisms and anti-pathetical attitude to technical virtuosity of the British 'Movement' of the fifties and sixties but nevertheless prompted a desire to re-evaluate modernist writing.

Sontag and Olson represent an early Heideggerian-style resistance to interpretation which also began to develop in the late fifties and early sixties. Throughout the sixties, Sontag was interested in the idea of an 'aesthetics of silence': art which could resist the instrumental modes of Western logic by refusing to accommodate interpretation as the imposition on its body of an intellectual will. By the seventies, she had developed a critique of over-aestheticisation, however, and had returned, if problematically, to a notion of the autonomy of art normally associated with Modernism. Sontag was one of the first to recognise, in the attempt to aestheticise culture, not only the dangers of accommodation to consumer stylisation of life, but also the latent compatibility of some versions of this with the ideologies of Fascism. She is perhaps most appropriately to be regarded as a 'late modernist', but her work conveys a sense of the development throughout the sixties of a new, apocalyptic 'postmodern' sensibility. Kermode's *A Sense of an Ending* (1966), can also be situated here, though its orientation is Nietzschean rather than Heideggerian, developing ideas of the philosopher H. Vaihinger (*The Philosophy of As If*) and those of the poet Wallace Stevens. Kermode effectively reads Nietzsche as a last ditch Romantic humanist asserting the necessity for the human imagination, arising out of desire, to create orders in a world which is either alien and indifferent or simply a 'chaos of sensation'. For Kermode, like later postmodernists such as Lyotard, reality exists outside our fictions. His argument, however, is that we can only ever approach it if we become as self-conscious as possible about the fiction-making process. Fiction must be metafiction or it may collapse into a dangerous mythology where subjective and provisional fictions are taken to be absolute realities. Self-consciousness is necessary for the preservation of and respect for otherness.

Both Ihab Hassan, in a series of books published throughout the seventies and eighties, and William Spanos, through the journal *Boundary 2*, did much to develop a postmodern aesthetic. Hassan consciously worked within a Nietzschean paradigm of knowledge and art, Spanos within a Heideggerian one. In *The Right Promethean Fire* (1980), Hassan talked of a 'posthumanism' involving a re-vision of the human form and of human destiny brought about through the development of new technologies and new conceptualisations of the subject arising out of post-structuralism. His work is often written in a playful and aphoristic Nietzschean style, and like the earlier philosopher, he too recognises that the intractibility of the body must always condition the forms of the human imagination. His work illustrates very clearly the debt of Postmodernism to Romanticism, developing a Nietzschean understanding of the self as a fiction and working within a dialectic of post-Romantic Imagination and irony: desiring immediacy but recognising the inevitability of mediation. Spanos' work similarly developed an interest in immanence and temporality, suggesting that postmodern art represents a new existential aesthetic which he opposes to the spatial fixity of Modernism. Perhaps one of the major problems with this approach, and with most articulations of Modernism, is that it often conflates the *critical construction* of Modernism with the texts themselves. Simply because Stephen Dedalus articulates an aesthetics of impersonality and stasis at the end of *A Portrait of the Artist as a Young Man* (1916), for example, the novel itself does not have to be read in such terms. Paradoxically, one of the problems in all discussions of Postmodernism which attempt to define it against Modernism is that critical constructions themselves may be invested in as if they were truths. Spanos is perhaps not so much talking about Modernism as the New Critical construction of it in terms of a particular theory of linguistic autonomy. If Modernism is read in this way, it is not difficult to view Postmodernism as an 'existential' departure. Like Sontag and Hassan, however, he is concerned to challenge the 'will-to-power' of interpretative criticism and to develop a hermeneutic relation where criticism acknowledges its own temporality and strenuously avoids promulgating a 'view from nowhere'. His writing represents a further mode of the gathering critique of Cartesianism.

3 Irving Howe

From *Mass Society and Postmodern Fiction*

Partisan Review, volume 26, 1959, pp 426–36.

In the last two decades there has occurred a series of changes in American life, the extent, durability and significance of which no one has yet measured. No one can. We speak of the growth of a 'mass society,' a term I shall try to define in a moment; but at best this is merely a useful hypothesis, not an accredited description. It is a notion that lacks common consent, for it does not yet merit common consent. Still, one can say with some assurance that the more sensitive among the younger writers, those who feel that at whatever peril to their work and careers they must grapple with something new in contemporary experience, even if, like everyone else, they find it extremely hard to say what that 'newness' consists of – such writers recognize that the once familiar social categories and place-marks have now become as uncertain and elusive as the moral imperatives of the nineteenth century seemed to novelists of fifty years ago. And the something new which they notice or stumble against is, I would suggest, the mass society.

By the mass society we mean a relatively comfortable, half welfare and half garrison society in which the population grows passive, indifferent and atomized; in which traditional loyalties, ties and associations become lax or dissolve entirely; in which coherent publics based on definite interests and opinions gradually fall apart; and in which man becomes a consumer, himself mass-produced like the products, diversions and values that he absorbs.

No social scientist has yet come up with a theory of mass society that is entirely satisfying; no novelist has quite captured its still amorphous symptoms – a peculiar blend of frenzy and sluggishness, amiability and meanness. I would venture the guess that a novelist unaware of the changes in our experience to which the theory of mass society points, is a novelist unable to deal successfully with recent American life; while one who focussed only upon those changes would be unable to give his work an adequate sense of historical depth.

This bare description of the mass society can be extended by noting a few traits or symptoms:

1 Social classes continue to exist, and the society cannot be understood without reference to them; yet the visible tokens of class are less obvious than in earlier decades and the correlations between class status and personal condition, assumed both by the older sociologists and the older novelists, become elusive and problematic – which is not, however, to say that such correlations no longer exist.

2 Traditional centers of authority, like the family, tend to lose some of their binding-power upon human beings; vast numbers of people now float through life with a burden of freedom they can neither sustain nor legitimately abandon to social or religious groups.

3 Traditional ceremonies that have previously marked moments of crisis and transition in human life, thereby helping men to accept such moments, are now either neglected or debased into mere occasions for public display.
4 Passivity becomes a widespread social attitude: the feeling that life is a drift over which one has little control and that even when men do have shared autonomous opinions they cannot act them out in common.
5 As perhaps never before, opinion is manufactured systematically and 'scientifically.'
6 Opinion tends to flow unilaterally, from the top down, in measured quantities: it becomes a market commodity.
7 Disagreement, controversy, polemic are felt to be in bad taste; issues are 'ironed out' or 'smoothed away'; reflection upon the nature of society is replaced by observation of its mechanics.
8 The era of 'causes,' good or bad, comes to an end; strong beliefs seem anachronistic; and as a result, agnostics have even been known to feel a certain nostalgia for the rigors of belief.
9 Direct and first-hand experience seems to evade human beings, though the quantity of busy-ness keeps increasing and the number of events multiplies with bewildering speed.
10 The pressure of material need visibly decreases, yet there follows neither a sense of social release nor a feeling of personal joy; instead, people become increasingly aware of their social dependence and powerlessness.

Now this is a social cartoon and not a description of American society; but it is a cartoon that isolates an aspect of our experience with a suggestiveness that no other mode of analysis is likely to match. Nor does it matter that no actual society may ever reach the extreme condition of a 'pure' mass society; the value of the theory lies in bringing to our attention a major historical drift.

If there is any truth at all in these speculations, they should help illuminate the problems faced by the novelists whose work began to appear shortly after the Second World War. They had to confront not merely the chronic confusion of values which has gripped our civilization for decades. In a sense they were quite prepared for that – the whole of modern literature taught them to expect little else. But they had also to face a problem which, in actually composing a novel, must have been still more troublesome: our society no longer lent itself to assured definition, one could no longer assume as quickly as in the recent past that a spiritual or moral difficulty could find a precise embodiment in a social conflict. Raskolnikov, fellowship in hand, might still be troubled by the metaphysical question of what a human being can allow himself; but Raskolnikov as a graduate student with an anxious young wife and a two-year-old baby – what was the novelist to make of him? Something fresh and valuable, no doubt; but only if he were aware that this new Raskolnikov had to be seen in ways significantly different from those of the traditional modern novelists.

How to give shape to a world increasingly shapeless and an experience increasingly fluid; how to reclaim the central assumption of the novel that telling relationships can be discovered between a style of social behavior and a code of moral judgment, or if that proves impossible, to find ways of imaginatively projecting the code in its own right – these were the difficulties that faced the young novelists. It was as if the guidelines of both our social thought and literary conventions were being erased. Or as a young German writer has recently remarked:

> There's no longer a society to write about. In former years you knew where you stood: the peasants read the Bible; the maniacs read *Mein Kampf*. Now people no longer have any opinions; they have refrigerators. Instead of illusions we have television, instead of tradition, the Volkswagon. The only way to catch the spirit of the times is to write a handbook on home appliances.

Taken literally, this is close to absurd; taken as half-comic hyperbole, it reaches a genuine problem.

The problem, in part, is the relationship between the writer and his materials. Some years ago Van Wyck Brooks had spoken of the conflict between the life of the spirit and the life of commerce, and had called upon American writers to make their choice. Most of them did. Almost every important writer in twentieth century America, whether or not he read Brooks, implicitly accepted his statement as the truth and chose, with whatever lapses or qualifications, to speak for the life of the Spirit.

But was the conflict between spirit and commerce, between culture and society still so acute during the postwar years? Was not a continued belief in this conflict a stale and profitless hangover from the ideologies of the Thirties? Might there not be ground for feeling, among the visible signs of our careless postwar prosperity, that a new and more moderate vision of society should inform the work of our novelists? It hardly matters which answers individual writers gave to these questions; the mere fact that they were now being seriously raised had a profound impact upon their work.

Those few who favored a bluntly 'positive' approach to American society found it hard to embody their sentiments in vibrant – or even credible – fictional situations. The values of accommodation were there for the asking, but they seemed, perversely, to resist creative use. For almost two decades now there has been an outpouring of 'affirmative' novels about American businessmen – Executive Suites in various shades; but I do not know of a single serious critic who finds these books anything but dull and mediocre. At least in our time, the novel seems to lend itself irrevocably to the spirit of criticism; as the Camus has remarked, it 'is born simultaneously with the spirit of rebellion and expresses, on the esthetic plane, the same ambition.'

But what has been so remarkable and disconcerting is that those writers who wished to preserve the spirit of rebellion also found it extremely hard to realize their sentiments in novels dealing with contemporary life. Most of them were unable, or perhaps too shrewd, to deal with the postwar experience directly; they preferred tangents of suggestion to frontal representation; they could express their passionate, though often amorphous, criticism of American life not through realistic portraiture but through fable, picaresque, prophecy and nostalgia.

Morally the young novelists were often more secure than their predecessors. Few of them were as susceptible to money and glitter as Fitzgerald; few had Hemingway's weakness for bravado and swagger; few succumbed to hallucinatory rhetoric in the manner of Faulkner. Yet, as novelists, they were less happily 'placed' than the writers who began to publish in the Twenties and early Thirties. They lacked the pressure of inevitable subjects as these take shape in situations and locales. They lacked equivalents of Fitzgerald's absorption with social distinctions, Hemingway's identification with expatriates, Faulkner's mourning over the old South. Sentiments they had in abundance and often fine ones; but to twist a remark of Gertrude Stein's, literature is not made of sentiments.

Literature is not made of sentiments; yet a good portion of what is most fresh in recent American fiction derives from sentiments. Better than any other group of literate Americans, our novelists resisted the mood of facile self-congratulation which came upon us during the postwar years. To be novelists at all, they had to look upon our life without ideological delusions; and they saw – *often better than they could say* – the hovering sickness of soul, the despairing contentment, the prosperous malaise. They were not, be it said to their credit, taken in. Yet the problem remained: how can one represent malaise, which by its nature is vague and without shape? It can be done, we know. But to do it one needs to be Chekhov; and that is hard.

My point, let me hasten to add, is not that novelists need social theories or philosophical systems. They do, however, need to live in an environment about which they can make economical assumptions that, in some ultimate way, are related to the ideas of speculative thinkers. Let me borrow a useful distinction that C. Wright Mills makes between troubles and issues. Troubles signify a strong but unfocussed sense of disturbance and pain, while issues refer to troubles that have been articulated as general statements. Novelists, as a rule, concern themselves with troubles, not issues. But to write with assurance and economy about troubles, they need to be working in a milieu where there is at least some awareness of issues. And in the troubled years after the Second World War it was precisely this awareness that was often lacking.

A few serious writers did try to fix in their novels the amorphous 'troubled-ness' of postwar American experience. In *The Violated*, an enormous realistic narrative about some ordinary people who reach adulthood during the war, Vance Bourjaily seemed consciously to be dramatizing a view of American society quite similar to the one I have sketched here. He chose to write one of those full-scale narratives composed of parallel strands of plot – a technique which assumes that society is distinctly articulated, that its classes are both sharply visible and intrinsically interesting, and that a novelist can arrange a conflict between members of these classes which will be dramatic in its own right and emblematic of larger issues. But for the material Bourjaily chose – the lives of bewildered yet not uncharacteristic drifters during the past two decades – these assumptions could not operate with sufficient force; and as his characters, in the sameness of their misery, melted into one another, so the strands of his narrative, also having no inevitable reason for separate existence, collapsed into one another.

Norman Mailer, trying in *The Deer Park* to compose a novel about the malaise of our years, avoided the cumbersomeness of the traditional social novel but could find no other structure that would give coherence to his perceptions. Mailer tried to embody his keen if unstable vision in a narrative about people whose extreme dislocation of experience and feeling would, by the very fact of their extreme dislocation, come to seem significant. But in its effort to portray our drifting and boredom full-face, in its fierce loyalty to the terms of its own conception, *The Deer Park* tended to become a claustrophobic work, driving attention inward, toward its own tonal peculiarities, rather than outward, as an extending parable. Throughout the novel Mailer had to fall back upon his protagonist, through whom he tried to say that which he found hard to show.

A whole group of novelists, among the best of recent years, has found itself responding to immediate American experience by choosing subjects and locales that are apparently far removed from that experience yet, through their inner quality, very close to it. These writers are sensitive to the moods and tones of postwar American life; they know that something new, different and extremely hard to describe has been happening to us. Yet they do not usually write about postwar experience *per se*: they do not confront it as much as they try to ambush it. The film critic Stanley Kaufmann has noted a similar phenomenon:

> When Vittorio de Sica was asked why so many of his films deal with adultery, he is said to have replied, 'But if you take adultery out of the lives of the bourgeoisie, what drama is left?' It is perhaps this belief that has impelled Tennessee Williams into the areas that his art inhabits. He has recognized that most of contemporary life offers limited dramatic opportunities . . . so he has left 'normal' life to investigate the highly neurotic, the violent and the grimy. It is the continuing problem of the contemporary writer who looks for great emotional issues to move him greatly. The anguish of the advertising executive struggling to keep his job is anguish indeed, but its possibilities in art are not large-scale. The writer who wants to 'let go' has figuratively to leave the urban and suburban and either go abroad, go into the past, or go into those few pockets of elemental emotional life left in this country.

Abroad, the past, or the few pockets of elemental emotional life: – many of our best writers have pursued exactly these strategies in order to suggest their attitudes toward contemporary experience. In *The Assistant* Bernard Malamud has written a somber story about a Jewish family during the Depression years, yet it soon becomes clear that one of his impelling motives is a wish to recapture intensities of feeling we have apparently lost but take to be characteristic of an earlier decade. Herbert Gold's *The Man Who Was Not With It* is an account of marginal figures in a circus as they teeter on the edge of *lumpen* life; but soon one realizes that he means his story to indicate possibilities for personal survival in a world increasingly compressed. The precocious and bewildered boy in J.D. Salinger's *The Catcher in the Rye* expresses something of the moral condition of adolescents today – or so they tell us; but clearly his troubles are not meant to refer to his generation alone. In *A Walk on the Wild Side* Nelson Algren turns to down-and-outers characteristic of an earlier social moment, but if we look to the psychic pressures breaking through the novel we see that he is really searching for a perspective for estrangement that will be relevant to our day. In *The Field of Vision* Wright Morris moves not backward in time but sideways in space: he contrives to bring a dreary Nebraskan middle-class family to a Mexican bull-fight so that the excitement of the blood and ritual will stir it to self-awareness. And while, on the face of it, Saul Bellow's *The Adventures of Augie March* is a picaresque tale about a cocky Jewish boy moving almost magically past the barriers in American society, it is also a kind of paean to the idea of personal freedom in hostile circumstances. Bellow's most recent novel *Henderson the Rain King* seems an even wilder tale about an American millionaire venturing into deepest Africa, in part, the deepest Africa of boy's books; but when he writes that men need a shattering experience to 'wake the spirit's sleep' we soon realize that his ultimate reference is to America, where many spirits sleep.

Though vastly different in quality, these novels have in common a certain obliqueness of approach. They do not represent directly the postwar American experience, yet refer to it constantly. They tell us rather little about the surface tone, the manners, the social patterns of recent American life, yet are constantly projecting moral criticisms of its essential quality. They approach that experience on the sly, yet are colored and shaped by it throughout. And they gain from it their true subject: the recurrent search – in America, almost a national obsession – for personal identity and freedom. In their distance from fixed social categories and their concern with the metaphysical implications of that distance, these novels constitute what I would call 'post-modern' fiction.

But the theme of personal identity, if it is to take on fictional substance, needs some kind of placement, a setting in the world of practical affairs. And it is here that the 'post-modern' novelists run into serious troubles: the connection between subject and setting cannot always be made, and the 'individual' of their novels, because he lacks social definition and is sometimes a creature of literary or even ideological fiat, tends to be not very individualized. Some of the best postwar novels, like *The Invisible Man* and *The Adventures of Augie March*, are deeply concerned with the fate of freedom in a mass society; but the assertiveness of idea and vanity of style which creep into such books are the result, I think, of willing a subject onto a novel rather than allowing it to grow out of a sure sense of a particular moment and place. These novels merit admiration for defending the uniqueness of man's life, but they suffer from having to improvise the terms of this uniqueness. It is a difficulty that seems, at the moment, unavoidable and I have no wish to disparage writers who face it courageously. Still, it had better be said that the proclamation of personal identity in recent American fiction tends, if I may use a fashionable phrase, to be more a product of the will than of the imagination.

It may help to strengthen my point – critics ought not to strengthen such points too much – if I turn for a moment to the two most-discussed literary groups of the last few years: the 'angry young men' in England and the 'beat generation' writers of San Francisco.

Partly because they write in and about England, Kingsley Amis, John Braine and John Wain are blessed with something utterly precious to a writer: a subject urgently, relentlessly imposing itself upon their imaginations. They have earned the scorn of a good many American critics – notable, of course, for asceticism – who point out that it is not clear whether it is a better or just bigger share of the material and cultural goods in contemporary England that these writers want. But while you can feel righteous or even hostile towards Amis and Braine, you can hardly deny that in their novels one finds something of the focussed desire, the quick apprehension and notation of contemporary life which, for reasons I have tried to suggest, has become somewhat rare in serious American fiction. These English writers face a predicament of the welfare state: it rouses legitimate desires in people of the 'lower orders'; it partly satisfies these desires; but it satisfies them only to the point of arousing new demands beyond its power of meeting. For society this may be irksome; for writers it is exhilarating. Gripes can be transformed into causes, ambitions cloaked as ideals. And the 'angry young men' are particularly fortunate in that their complaints lead them to deal with some of the traditional materials of the novel: frustrated ambition, frozen snobbery, fake culture, decaying gentility. Through comedy they are able to *structure* their complaints. Their work touches upon sore spots in English life, hurting some people and delighting others. It threatens the Establishment, perhaps its survival, more likely its present leaders. It creates tension, opposition, a dialectic of interests. All of which is to say: it rests upon an articulated, coherent though limited vision of English social relations.

By contrast, the young men in San Francisco seem largely a reflex of the circumstances of mass society. They are suffering from psychic and social disturbance: and as far as that goes, they are right – there is much in American life to give one a pain. But they have no clear sense of why or how they are troubled, and some of them seem opposed in principle to a clear sense of anything. The 'angry young men' in England, even if their protest will prove to be entirely opportunistic and momentary, can say what it is that hurts. The San Francisco writers fail to understand, as Paul Goodman has remarked, that

> It is necessary to have some contact with institutions and people in order to be frustrated and angry. They [the San Francisco writers] have the theory that to be affectless, not to care, is the ultimate rebellion, but this is a fantasy; for right under the surface is burning shame, hurt feelings, fear of impotence, speechless and powerless tantrum, cowering before papa, being rebuffed by mama; and it is these anxieties that dictate their behaviour in every crisis.

These writers, I would content, illustrate the painful, though not inevitable, predicament of rebellion in a mass society: they are the other side of the American hollow. In their contempt for mind, they are at one with the middle class suburbia they think they scorn. In their incoherence of feeling and statement, they mirror the incoherent society that clings to them like a mocking shadow. In their yearning to keep 'cool' they sing out an eternal fantasy of the shop-keeper. Feeling themselves lonely and estranged, they huddle together in gangs, create a Brook Farm of Know-Nothings, and send back ecstatic reports to the squares: Having a Wonderful Time, Having Wonderful Kicks! But alas, all the while it is clear that they are terribly lost, and what is more pitiable, that they don't even have the capacity for improvising vivid fantasies. As they race meaninglessly back and forth across the continent, veritable mimics of the American tourist, they do not have a Wonderful Time. They do not get happily drunk, many of them preferring milk shakes and tea; and their sexual revelations, particularly in Kerouac's *The Subterraneans*, are as sad as they are unintentional. They can't, that is, dream themselves out of the shapeless nightmare of California; and for that, perhaps, we should not blame them, since it is not certain that anyone can.

No wonder, then, that in Kerouac's novels one is vaguely aware that somewhere, in the unmapped beyond, a society does exist: a society with forms, requirements, burdens, injustices, duties and pleasures; but that in the space of the novels themselves we can only find a series of distraught and compulsive motions. The themes of what I have called 'post-modern' fiction are reflected in the San Francisco writers as caricature and symptom; for if you shun consciousness as if it were a plague, then a predicament may ravage you but you cannot cope with it.

Where finally does this leave us? In the midst, I hope, of the promise and confusion of American writing today. No settled ending is possible here, because the tendencies I have been noticing are still in flux, still open to many pressures and possibilities. But it may not be too rash to say that the more serious of the 'post-modern' novelists – those who grapple with problems rather than merely betraying their effects – have begun to envisage that we may be on the threshhold of enormous changes in human history. These changes, merely glanced by the idea of the 'mass society,' fill our novelists with a sense of foreboding; and through the strategy of obliqueness, they bring to bear a barrage of moral criticisms, reminders of human potentiality, and tacit exhortations.

The possibilities that appear to them are those which struck at T.E. Lawrence when he returned from Arabia and discovered that he did not know how or why to live. One such possibility is that we are moving toward a quiet desert of moderation where men will forget the passion of moral and spiritual restlessness that has characterized Western society. That the human creature, no longer a Quixote or a Faust, will become a docile attendent to an automated civilization. That the 'aura of the human' will be replaced by the nihilism of satiety. That the main question will no longer be the conditions of existence but existence itself. That high culture as we understand it will become increasingly problematical and perhaps reach some point of obsolescence.

But before such prospects – they form the bad dreams of thoughtful men, the nightmares our 'post-modern' novelists are trying to exorcise – the mind grows dizzy and recalcitrant. It begins to solace itself with rumblings about eternal truths, and like the exacerbated judge in Faulkner's *The Hamlet*, cries out, 'I can't stand no more . . . This case is adjourned!'

4   Leslie Fiedler

From *Cross the Border – Close the Gap*

Cross the Border – Close the Gap, Stein and Day: New York, 1972, pp 61–85.

To describe the situation of American letters at the end of the sixties is difficult indeed, almost impossible, since the language available to critics at this point is totally inappropriate to the best work of the artists who give the period its special flavor, its essential life. But precisely here is a clue, a way to begin: not with some presumed crisis of poetry or fiction, but with the unconfessed scandal of contemporary literary criticism, which for three or four decades now has vainly attempted to deal in terms invented to explain, defend, and evaluate one kind of book with *another* kind of book – so radically different that it calls the very assumptions underlying those terms into question. Established critics may think that they have been judging recent literature; but, in fact, recent literature has been judging them.

Almost all living readers and writers are aware of a fact which they have no adequate words to express, not in English certainly, nor even in American. We are living, have been living for two decades – and have become acutely conscious of the fact since 1955 – through the death throes of Modernism and the birth pangs of Post-Modernism. The kind of literature which had arrogated to itself the name Modern (with the presumption that it represented the ultimate advance in sensibility and form, that beyond it newness was not possible), and whose moment of triumph lasted from a point just before World War I until one just after World War II, is *dead*, i.e., belongs to history not actuality. In the field of the novel, this means that the age of Proust, Mann, and Joyce is over; just as in verse that of T.S. Eliot, Paul Valéry, Montale and Seferis is done with.

Obviously, *this* fact has not remained secret: and some critics have, indeed, been attempting to deal with its implications. But they have been trying to do it in a language and with methods which are singularly inappropriate, since both method and language were invented by the defunct Modernists themselves to apologize for their own work and the work of their preferred literary ancestors (John Donne, for instance, or the *symbolistes*), and to educate an audience capable of responding to them. Naturally, this will not do at all; and so the second or third generation New Critics in America, like the spiritual descendants of F.R. Leavis in England (or the neo-neo-Hegelians in Germany, the belated Croceans in Italy), end by proving themselves imbeciles and naïfs when confronted by, say, a poem of Allen Ginsberg, a new novel by John Barth.

Why not, then, invent a New New Criticism, a Post-Modernist criticism appropriate to Post-Modernist fiction and verse? It sounds simple enough – quite as simple as imperative – but it is, in fact, much simpler to say than do; for the question which arises immediately is whether there can be *any* criticism adequate to Post-Modernism. The Age of T.S. Eliot, after all, was the age of a literature essentially self-aware, a literature dedicated, in avowed intent, to analysis, rationality, anti-Romantic dialectic – and consequently aimed at eventual respectability, gentility, even, at last, academicism. Criticism is natural, even essential to such an age; and to no one's surprise (though finally there were some voices crying out in dismay), the period of early twentieth-century Modernism became, as it was doomed to do, an Age of Criticism: an age in which criticism began by invading the novel, verse, drama, and ended by threatening to swallow up all other forms of literature. Certainly, it seems, looking back from this point, as if many of the best books of the period were critical books (by T.S. Eliot and Ezra Pound and I.A. Richards, by John Crowe Ransom and Kenneth Burke and R.P. Blackmur, to mention only a few particularly eminent names); and its second-best, novels and poems eminently suited to critical analysis, particularly in schools and universities: the works of

Proust-Mann-and-Joyce, for instance, to evoke a trilogy which seems at the moment more the name of a single college course than a list of three authors.

We have, however, entered quite another time, apocalyptic, antirational, blatantly romantic and sentimental; an age dedicated to joyous misology and prophetic irresponsibility; one, at any rate, distrustful of self-protective irony and too great self-awareness. If criticism is to survive at all, therefore, which is to say, if criticism is to remain or become useful, viable, relevant, it must be radically altered from the models provided by Croce or Leavis or Eliot or Erich Auerbach, or whoever; though not in the direction indicated by Marxist critics, however subtle and refined. The Marxists are last-ditch defenders of rationality and the primacy of political fact, intrinsically hostile to an age of myth and passion, sentimentality and fantasy.

On the other hand, a renewed criticism certainly will no longer be formalist or intrinsic; it will be contextual rather than textual, not primarily concerned with structure or diction or syntax, all of which assumes that the work of art 'really' exists on the page rather than in a reader's passionate apprehension and response. Not words-on-the-page but words-in-the-world or rather words-in-the-head, which is to say, at the private juncture of a thousand contexts, social, psychological, historical, biographical, geographical, in the consciousness of the lonely reader (delivered for an instant, but an instant only, from all of those contexts by the *ekstasis* of reading): this will be the proper concern of the critics to come. Certain older critics have already begun to provide examples of this sort of criticism by turning their backs on their teachers and even their own earlier practices. Norman O. Brown, for instance, who began with scholarly, somewhat Marxian studies of Classic Literature has moved on to metapsychology in *Life Against Death* and *Love's Body*; while Marshall McLuhan, who made his debut with formalist examinations of texts by Joyce and Gerard Manley Hopkins, has shifted to metasociological analyses of the mass media in *Understanding Media*, and finally to a kind of pictographic shorthand, half put-on and half serious emulation of advertising style in *The Medium is the Message*.

The voice as well as the approach is important in each case, since neither in Brown nor McLuhan does one hear the cadence and tone proper to 'scientific' criticism of culture, normative psychology or sociology attached to literary texts. No, the pitch, the rhythms, the dynamics of both are mantic, magical, more than a little *mad* (it is a word, a concept that one desiring to deal with contemporary literature must learn to regard as more honorific than pejorative). In McLuhan and Brown – as in D.H. Lawrence earlier, Charles Olson when he first wrote on Melville – a not so secret fact recently hushed up in an age of science and positivism is candidly confessed once more: criticism is literature or it is nothing. Not amateur philosophy or objective analysis, it differs from other forms of literary art in that it starts not with the world in general but the world of art itself, in short, that it uses one work of art as an occasion to make another.

There have been, of course, many such meditating works of art in the past, both fairly recent (Nietzsche's *Birth of Tragedy*) and quite remote (Longinus *On The Sublime*), which make it clear that the authority of the critic is based not only on his skills in research or his collection of texts but on his ability to find words and rhythms and images appropriate to his ecstatic vision of, say, the plays of Euripides or the opening verses of *Genesis*. To evoke Longinus or even Nietzsche, however, is in a sense misleading, suggesting models too grandiose and solemn. To be sure, the newest criticism must be aesthetic, poetic in form as well as substance; but it must also be, in light of where we are, comical, irreverent, vulgar. Models have appeared everywhere in recent years but tentatively, inadvertently as it were – as in the case of Angus Wilson, who began a review of *City of Night* some years ago (in the pages of an ephemeral little magazine), by writing quite matter-of-factly, 'Everyone knows John Rechy is a little shit.' And all at once we are out of the Eliotic church, whose dogmas, delivered *ex cathedra*, two generations of students were expected to learn by heart: 'Honest criticism and sensitive appreciation are directed not upon the poet but upon the poetry. . . . The mind of the mature poet differs from that of the immature one not precisely on any valuation of personality, not by being necessarily more interesting, or having "more to say," but rather by being a more finely perfected medium in which etc., etc.'

Unless criticism refuses to take itself quite so seriously or at least to permit its readers not to, it will inevitably continue to reflect the finicky canons of the genteel tradition and the depressing pieties of the Culture Religion of Modernism, from which Eliot thought he had escaped – but which in fact he only succeeded in giving a High Anglican tone: 'It is our business as readers of literature, to know what we like. It is our business, as Christians, *as well as* readers of literature, to know what we ought to like.' But not to know that such stuff is funny is to be imprisoned in Church, cut off from the liberating privilege of comic sacrilege. It is high time, however, for such sacrilege rather than such piety; as some poets have known really ever since Dada, without knowing how to keep their sacrilege from becoming itself sacred; as the dearest obscenities of Dada were sanctified into the social 'art' of Surrealism under the fell influence of Freud and Marx.

The kind of criticism which the age demands is, then Death-of-Art Criticism, which is most naturally practised by those who have come of age since the death of the 'New Poetry' and the 'New Criticism.' But it ought to be possible under certain conditions to some of us oldsters as well, even those of us whose own youth was coincident with the freezing of all the madness of *symbolisme-Dada-surréalisme* into the rigidities of academic *avant-garde*. In this sense, the problem of the aging contemporary critic is quite like that of the no-longer-young contemporary novelist, which one necessarily begins to define even as he defines the dilemma of the critic.

In any case, it seems evident that writers not blessed enough to be under thirty (or thirty-five, or whatever the critical age is these days) must be reborn in order to seem relevant to the moment, and those who inhabit it most comfortably, i.e., the young. But no one has even the hope of being reborn unless he knows first that he is dead – dead, to be sure, for someone else; but the writer exists as a writer precisely for someone else. More specifically, no novelist can be reborn until he knows that insofar as he remains a novelist in the traditional sense, he is dead; since the traditional novel is dead – not dying, but dead. What was up to only a few years ago a diagnosis, a predication (made, to be sure, almost from the moment of the invention of the novel: first form of pop literature, and therefore conscious that as compared to classic forms like epic or tragedy its life span was necessarily short) is now a fact. As certainly as God, i.e., the Old God, is dead, so the Novel, i.e., the Old Novel, is dead. To be sure, certain writers, still alive and productive (Saul Bellow, for instance, or John Updike, Mary McCathy or James Baldwin), continue to write Old Novels, and certain readers, often with a sense of being quite up-to-date, continue to read them. But so do preachers continue to preach in the Old Churches, and congregations gather to hear them.

It is *not* a matter of assuming, like Marshall McLuhan, that the printed book is about to disappear, taking with it the novel – first form invented for print; only of realizing that in all of its forms – and most notably, perhaps, the novel – the printed book is being radically, functionally altered. No medium of communication ever disappears merely because a new and more efficient one is invented. One thinks, for instance of the lecture, presumably superannuated by the invention of moveable type, yet flourishing still after more than five centuries of obsolescence. What is demanded by functional obsolescence is learning to be less serious, more frivolous, a form of *entertainment*. Indeed, it could be argued that a medium begins to be felt as entertainment only at the point where it ceases to be a necessary or primary means of communication, as recent developments in radio (the total disappearance, for instance, of all high-minded commentators and pretentious playwrights) sufficiently indicates. Students at any rate are well aware of this truth in regard to the university lecture, and woe to the lecturer (of whom, alas, there are many) who does not know it!

In any event, even as the 'serious' lecture was doomed by the technology of the fifteenth century, and the 'serious' church service by the philology of the eighteenth and nineteenth – so is the 'serious' novel, and 'serious' criticism as well, by the technology and philology of the twentieth. Like the lecture and Christian church services, its self-awareness must now include the perception of its own absurdity, even impossibility. Since, however, the serious novel of our time is the Art Novel as practiced by Proust, Mann, and Joyce and imitated by their epigones, it is that odd blend of poetry, psychology, and documentation, whose real though not always avowed end was to make itself canonical, that we must disavow. Matthew Arnold may have been quite correct in foreseeing the emergence of literature as scripture in a world which was forsaking the Old Time Religion: but the life of the New Scriptures and the New Time Religion was briefer than he could have guessed.

Before the bible of the Christians and Jews ceased to be central to the concerns of men in Western society, it had become merely a 'book' among others; and this, indeed, may have misled the Arnoldians, who could not believe that a time might come when not merely *the* Book ceased to move men, but even books in general. Such, however, is the case – certainly as far as all books which consider themselves 'art,' i.e. scripture once removed, are concerned; and for this reason the reborn novel, the truly new New Novel must be anti-art as well as antiserious. But this means, after all, that it must become more like what it was in the beginning, more what it seemed when Samuel Richardson could not be taken *quite* seriously, and what it remained in England (as opposed to France, for instance) until Henry James had justified himself as an artist against such self-declared 'entertainers' as Charles Dickens and Robert Louis Stevenson: popular, not quite reputable, a little dangerous – the one his loved and rejected cultural father, the other his sibling rival in art. The critical interchange on the nature of the novel to which James contributed 'The Art of Fiction' and Stevenson 'A Humble Remonstrance' memorializes their debate – which in the thirties most readers believed had been won hands down by James's defense of the novel as art; but which in the dawning seventies we are not sure about at all – having reached a time when *Treasure Island* seems somehow more to the point and the heart's delight than, say, *The Princess Casamassima*.

This popular tradition the French may have understood once (in the days when Diderot praised Richardson extravagantly, and the Marquis de Sade emulated him in a dirtier book than the Englishman dared) but they long ago lost sight of it. And certainly the so-called '*nouveau roman*' is in its deadly earnest almost the opposite of anything truly new, which is to say, anti-art. Robbe-Grillet, for example, is still the prisoner of dying notions of the *avant-garde*; and though he is aware of half of what the new novelist must do (destroy the Old, destroy Marcel Proust), he is unaware of what he must create in its place. His kind of antinovel is finally too arty and serious: a kind of neo-neo-classicism, as if to illustrate once more that in the end this is all the French can invent no matter how hard they try. Re-imagined on film by Alain Resnais, *Last Year at Marienbad* speaks to the young; but in print it remains merely *chic*, which is to say, a fashionable and temporary error of taste. Better by far, and by the same token infinitely more pertinent is Samuel Beckett, who having been born Irish rather than French, finds it hard to escape being (what some of his readers choose to ignore) compulsively and hilariously funny.

Best of all, however, and therefore totally isolated on the recent French scene (except for the perceptive comments of that equally ambiguous figure, Raymond Queneau) is Boris Vian, especially in his most successful work of fiction, *L'écume des jours*, recently translated into English as *Mood Indigo*. Indeed, Boris Vian is in many ways a prototype of the New Novelist, though he has been dead for a decade or so and his most characteristic work belongs to the years just after World War II. He was, first of all, an Imaginary American (as even writers born in the United States must be these days), who found himself in total opposition to the politics of America at the very moment he was most completely immersed in its popular culture – actually writing a detective novel called *I Will Spit On Your Grave* under the pen name of Vernon Sullivan, but pretending that he was only its translator into French. In fact, by virtue of this peculiar brand of mythological Americanism he managed to straddle the border, if not quite close the gap between high culture and low, belles-lettres and pop art. On the one hand, he was the writer of pop songs and a jazz trumpeter much influenced by New Orleans style; and on the other, the author of novels in which the thinly disguised figures of such standard French intellectuals as Jean Paul Sartre and Simone de Beauvoir are satirized. But even in his fiction, which seems at first glance quite traditional or, at any rate, conventionally *avant-garde*, the characters move toward their fates through an imaginary city whose main thoroughfare is called Boulevard Louis Armstrong.

Only now, however, has Vian won the audience he all along deserved, finding it first among the young of Paris, who know like their American counterparts that such a closing of the gap between elite and mass culture is precisely the function of the Novel Now – not merely optional as in Vian's day, but necessary. And though most of the younger American authors who follow a similar course follow it without ever having known him, by a shared concern rather than direct emulation, he seems more like them than such eminent American forerunners of theirs as Faulkner or Hemingway (except perhaps in Hemingway's neglected early burlesque, *Torrents of Spring*, and Faulkner's self-styled 'pot-boiler,' *Sanctuary*.) Vian, unfortunately, turned to the form of the Pop Novel only for the work of his left hand, to which he was not willing even to sign his own name, writing in *L'écume des jours* what seems superficially a traditional enough love story to disarm the conventional critics; though it is finally undercut by a sentimentality which redeems its irony, and reflects a mythology too Pop and American for neo-neo-Classicists to bear.

The young Americans who have succeeded Vian, on the other hand, have abandoned all concealment, and when they are most themselves, nearest to their central concerns, turn frankly to Pop forms – though not, to be sure, the detective story which has by our time become hopelessly compromised by middlebrow condescension: an affectation of college professors and presidents. The forms of the novel which they prefer are those which seem now what the hard-boiled detective story once seemed to Vian: at the furthest possible remove from art and *avant-garde*, the greatest distance from inwardness, analysis, and pretension; and, therefore, immune to lyricism, on the one hand, or righteous social commentary, on the other. It is not compromise by the market place they fear; on the contrary, they choose the genre most associated with exploitation by the mass media: notably, the Western, Science Fiction, and Pornography.

Most congenial of all is the Western, precisely because it has for many decades now seemed to belong exclusively to pulp magazines, run-of-the-mill TV series and Class B movies, which is to say, has been experienced almost purely as myth and entertainment rather than as 'literature' at all – and its sentimentality has, therefore, come to possess our minds so completely that it can now be mitigated without essential loss by parody, irony – and even critical analysis. In a sense, our mythological innocence has been preserved in the Western, awaiting the day when, no longer believing ourselves innocent in fact, we could decently return to claim it in fantasy. But such a return to the Western represents, of course, a rejection of laureates of the loss of innocence like Henry James and Hawthorne: those particular favorites of the forties, who despite their real virtues turn out to have been too committed to the notion of European high art to survive as major influences in an age of Pop. And it implies as well momentarily turning aside from our beloved Herman Melville (compromised by his New Critical admirers and the countless Ph.D. dissertations they prompted), and even from Mark Twain. To Hemingway, Twain could still seem central to a living tradition, the Father of us all, but being Folk rather than Pop in essence, he has become ever more remote from an urban, industrialized world, for which any evocation of pre-Civil War, rural America seems a kind of pastoralism which complements rather than challenges the Art Religion. Folk Art knows and accepts its place in a class-structured world which Pop blows up, whatever its avowed intentions. What remains are only the possibilities of something closer to travesty than emulation – such a grotesque neo-Huck, for instance, as the foulmouthed D.J. in Norman Mailer's *Why Are We in Vietnam*, who, it is wickedly suggested, may *really* be a Black joker in Harlem pretending to be the White refugee from respectability.

And, quite recently, Twain's book itself has been rewritten to please and mock its exegetes in John Seelye's *Huck Finn for The Critics*, which lops off the whole silly-happy ending, the deliverance of Nigger Jim (in which Hemingway, for instance, never believed) and puts back into the tale the cussing and sex presumably excised by the least authentic part of Samuel Clemens' mind – as well as the revelation at long last, that what Huck and Jim were smoking on the raft was not tobacco but 'hemp,' which is to say, marijuana. Despite all, however, Huck seems for the moment to belong not to the childhood we all continue to live, but to the one we have left behind.

Natty Bumppo, on the other hand, dreamed originally in the suburbs of New York City and in Paris, oddly survives along with his author. Contrary to what we had long believed, it is James Fenimore Cooper who now remains alive, or rather who has been reborn, perhaps not so much as he saw himself as in the form D.H. Lawrence re-imagined him en route to America; for Cooper understood that the dream which does not fade with the building of cities, but assumes in their concrete and steel environment the compelling vividness of a waking hallucination, is the encounter of Old World men and New in the wilderness, the meeting of the transplanted European and the Red Indian. No wonder Lawrence spoke of himself as 'Kindled by Fenimore Cooper.'

The Return of the Redskin to the center of our art and our deep imagination, as we all of us have retraced Lawrence's trip to the mythical America, is based not merely on the revival of the oldest and most authentic of American Pop forms, but also projects certain meanings of our lives in terms more metapoliti-cal than political, which is to say, meanings valid as myth is valid rather than as history. Writers of Westerns have traditionally taken sides for or against the Indians; and unlike the authors of the movies which set the kids to cheering at the Saturday matinees of the twenties and thirties, the new novelists have taken a clear stand with the Red Man. In this act of mythological renegacy they have not only implicitly declared themselves enemies of the Christian Humanism, but they have also rejected the act of genocide with which our nation began – and whose last reflection, perhaps, is to be found in the War in Vietnam.

It is impossible to write any Western which does not in some sense glorify violence; but the violence celebrated in the anti-White Western is guerrilla violence: the sneak attack on 'civilization' as practised first by Geronimo and Cochise and other Indian warrior chiefs, and more latterly apologized for by Ché Guevara or the spokesman for North Vietnam. Warfare, however, is not the final vision implicit in the New Western, which is motivated on a deeper level by a nostalgia for the Tribe: a form of social organization thought of as preferable both to the tight two-generation bourgeois family, from which its authors come, and the soulless out-of-human-scale bureaucratic state, into which they are initiated via schools and universities. In the end, of course, both the dream of violence in the woods and the vision of tribal life, rendered in terms of a genre that has long been the preferred reading of boys, seems juvenile, even infantile. But this is precisely the point; for what recommends the Western to the New Novelist is pre-eminently its association with children and the kind of books superciliously identified with their limited and special needs.

For the German, brought up on Karl May, the situation is quite similar to that in which the American, who grew up with Cooper or his native imitators, finds himself. What has Old Shatterhand to do with Art, asks the one, even as the other asks the same of Chingachgook. And the answer is *nothing*. The legendary Indians have nothing to do with Art in the traditional sense, everything to do with joining boy to man, childhood to adulthood, immaturity to maturity. They preside over the closing of the Gap which aristocratic conceptions of art have opened between what fulfills us at eight or ten or twelve and what satisfies us at forty or fifty or sixty.

In light of all this, it is perhaps time to look again at the much-discussed 'immaturity' of American literature, the notorious fact that our classic books are boy's books – our greatest novels at home in the Children's Section of libraries; in short, that they are all in some sense 'Westerns': accounts of an idyllic encounter between White man and Non-White in one or another variety of wilderness setting. But suddenly this fact – once read as a 'flaw' or 'failure' or 'lack' (it implies, after all, the absence in our books of heterosexual love and of the elaborate analysis of social relations central to the Continental novel) – seems evidence of a real advantage, a clue to why the Gap we now want to close opened so late and so unconvincingly, as it were, in American letters. Before Henry James, none of our novelists felt himself cut off from the world of magic and wonder; he had only to go to sea or, especially, to cross our own particular Border, the Frontier, to inhabit a region where adults and children, educated and uneducated, shared a common enchantment.

How different the plight of mid-nineteenth-century English writers, like Lewis Carroll or Edward Lear or George Macdonald, who had to pretend that they were writing exclusively for the nursery in order to enter the deep wonderland of their own imaginations. Even in our own time, a writer like J.R.R. Tolkien found it necessary to invent the Hobbits in a book specifically aimed at children, before he could release the fearful scholarship (another device foreign to American mythologies) and presumably adult magic of the Rings Triology. It makes a difference, after all, whether one thinks of the World Across The Border as Faerie or Frontier, fantasy or history. It has been so long since Europeans lived their deepest dreams – but only yesterday for us. And this is why even now, when we are at last sundered from those dreams, we can turn rotten-ripe without loss of essential innocence, be (what has become a model for the young of all the world, as Godard's *Weekend* testifies) decadent children playing Indians; which is to say, imaginary Americans, all of us, whether native to this land or not. But to be an American (unlike being English or French or whatever) is precisely to *imagine* a destiny rather than to inherit one; since we have always been, insofar as we are Americans at all, inhabitants of myth rather than history – and have now come to know it.

In any case, our best writers have been able to take up the Western again – playfully and seriously at once, quite like their ancestors who began the Revolution which made us a country by playing Indians in deadly earnest and dumping all that English Tea into the salt sea that sundered them from their King. There are many writers still under forty, among them the most distinguished of their generation, who have written New Westerns which have found the hearts of the young, particularly in paperback form; since to these young readers, for reasons psychological as well as economic, the hardcover book with its aspiration to immortality in libraries begins to look obsolete. John Barth's *The Sotweed Factor* represents the beginning of the wave that has been cresting ever since 1960 and that has carried with it not only Barth's near contemporaries like Thomas Berger (in *Little Big Man*), Ken Kesey (in both *One Flew Over the Cuckoo's Nest* and *Sometimes a Great Notion*), and most recently Leonard Cohen (in his extraordinarily gross and elegant *Beautiful Losers*) – but has won over older and more established writers like Norman Mailer whose newest novel, *Why Are We in Vietnam?*, is not as its title seems to promise a book about a War in the East as much as a book about the idea of the West. Even William Burroughs, expert in drug fantasies and homosexual paranoia, keeps promising to turn to the genre, though so far he has contented himself with another popular form, another way of escaping from personal to public or popular myth, of using dreams to close rather than open a gap: Science Fiction.

Science Fiction does not seem at first glance to have as wide and universal appeal as the Western, in book form at least, though perhaps it is too soon to judge, for it is a very young genre, indeed, having found itself (after tentative beginnings in Jules Verne, H.G. Wells etc.), its real meaning and scope, only after World War II. At that point, two things become clear: first, that the Future was upon us, that the pace of technological advance had become so swift that a distinction between Present and Future would get harder and harder to maintain; and second, that the End of Man, by annihilation or mutation, was a real, even an immediate possibility. But these are the two proper subjects of Science Fiction: the Present Future and the End of Man – not time travel or the penetration of outer space, except as the latter somehow symbolize the former.

Perhaps only in quite advanced technologies which also have a tradition of self-examination and analysis, bred by Puritanism or Marxism or whatever, can Science Fiction at its most explicit, which is to say, expressed in words on the page, really flourish. In any case, only in America, England, and the Soviet Union does the Science Fiction Novel or Post-Novel seem to thrive, though Science Fiction cartoon strips and comic books, as well as Science Fiction TV programs and especially films (where the basic imagery is blissfully wed to electronic music, and words are kept a minimum) penetrate everywhere. In England and America, at any rate, the prestige and influence of the genre are sufficient not only to allure Burroughs (in *Nova Express*), but also to provide a model for William Golding (in *Lord of the Flies*), Anthony Burgess (in *The Clockwork Orange*), and John Barth (whose second major book, *Giles Goat-boy*, abandoned the Indian in favor of the Future).

Quite unlike the Western, which asserts the difference between England and America, Science Fiction reflects what still makes the two mutually distrustful communities one; as, for instance, a joint effort (an English author, an American director) like the movie *2001: A Space Odyssey* testifies. If there is still a common 'Anglo-Saxon' form, it is Science Fiction. Yet even here, the American case is a little different from the English; for only in the United States is there a writer of first rank whose preferred mode has been from the first Science Fiction in its unmitigated Pop form. Kurt Vonnegut, Jr., did not begin by making some sort of traditional bid for literary fame and then shift to Science Fiction, but was so closely identified with that popular, not-quite-respectable form from the first, that the established critics were still ignoring him completely at a time when younger readers, attuned to the new rhythm of events by Marshall McLuhan or Buckminster Fuller, had already made underground favorites of his *The Sirens of Titan* and *Cat's Cradle*. That Vonnegut now, after years of neglect, teaches writing in a famous American university and is hailed in lead reviews in the popular press is a tribute not to the critics' acuity but to the persuasive powers of the young.

The revival of pornography in recent days, its moving from the periphery to the center of the literary scene, is best understood in this context, too; for it, like the Western and Science Fiction, is a form of Pop Art – ever since Victorian times, indeed, the *essential* form of Pop Art, which is to say, the most unredeemable of all kinds of subliterature, understood as a sort of entertainment closer to the pole of Vice than that of Art. Many of the more notable recent works of the genre have tended to conceal this fact, often because the authors themselves did not understand what they were after, and have tried to disguise their work as earnest morality (Herbert Selby's *Last Exit to Brooklyn*, for instance) or parody (Terry Southern's *Candy*). But whatever the author's conscious intent, all those writers who have helped move Porn from the underground to the foreground have in fact been working towards the liquidation of the very conception of pornography; since the end of Art on one side means the end of Porn on the other. And that end is now in sight, in the area of films and Pop songs and poetry, but especially in that of the novel which seemed, initially at least, more congenial than other later Pop Art forms to the sort of private masturbatory reverie which is essential to pornography.

It is instructive in this regard to reflect on the careers of two publishers who have flourished extraordinarily because somehow they sensed early on that a mass society can no longer endure the distinction between low literature and a high, especially in the area of sex; and that the line drawn early in the century between serious, 'artistic' exploitation of pornography (e.g. *Lady Chatterley's Lover*), and so-called 'hard-core' pornography was bound to be blurred away. Even the classics of the genre straddle the line: *Fanny Hill*, for example, and de Sade's *Justine*, as do more recent works like John Rechy's *City of Night* or Stephen Schneck's *The Night Clerk*, whose sheer dirtiness may be adulterated by sentiment or irony but remains a chief appeal. This, at any rate, Maurice Girodias and Barney Rosset appear to have sensed; and from both sides of the Atlantic they have, through the Olympia Press and Grove Press, supplied the American reading public, chiefly but not exclusively the young, with books (including, let it be noted, Nabokov's *Lolita*, the sole work in which the pursuit of Porn enabled that emigré writer to escape the limitations of early twentieth-century *avant-garde*) exploiting, often in contempt of art and seriousness, not just Good Clean Sex, but sadism, masochism, homosexuality, coprophilia, necrophilia, etc. etc.

The standard forms of heterosexual copulation, standardly or 'poetically' recorded, seem oddly old-fashioned, even a little ridiculous; it is *fellatio*, buggery, flagellation that we demand in order to be sure that we are not reading Love Stories but Pornography. A special beneficiary of this trend has been Norman Mailer, whose first novel, *The Naked and the Dead*, emulated the dying tradition of the anti-war art novel, with occasional obscenities thrown in, presumably in the interest of verisimilitude. But more and more, Mailer has come to move the obscenity to the center, the social commentary to the periphery, ending in *Why Are We in Vietnam?* with an insistence on foul language and an obsession with scatology which are obviously ends in themselves, too unremitting to be felt as merely an assault on old-fashioned sensibility and taste. And even in his earlier Pop Novel, *An American Dream*, which marked his emergence from ten years in which he produced no major fiction, he had committed himself to Porn as a way into the region to which his title alludes: the place where in darkness and filth all men are alike – the Harvard graduate and the reader of the *Daily News*, joined in fantasies of murdering their wives and buggering their maids. To talk of such books in terms of Dostoevski, as certain baffled critics have felt obliged to do, is absurd; James Bond is more to the point. But to confess this would be to confess that the old distinctions are no longer valid, and that critics will have to find another claim to authority more appropriate to our times than the outmoded ability to discriminate between High and Low.

Even more disconcertingly than Mailer, Philip Roth has with *Portnoy's Complaint* raised the question of whether 'pornography,' even what was called until only yesterday 'hard-core pornography' any longer exists. Explicit, vulgar, joyous, gross and pathetic all at once, Roth has established himself not only as the laureate of masturbation and oral-genital lovemaking but also as a master of the 'thin' novel, the novel with minimum inwardness – ironically presented as a confession to a psychiatrist. Without its sexual interest, therefore, the continual balancing off of titillation and burlesque – his book has no meaning at all, no more than any other dirty joke, to which genre it quite clearly belongs. There is pathos, even terror in great plenty, to be sure, but it is everywhere dependent on, subservient to the dirty jokes about mothers, Jews, shrinks, potency, impotency; and Roth is, consequently, quite correct when he asserts that he is less like such more solemn and pious Jewish-American writers as Saul Bellow and Bernard Malamud, than he is like the half-mad pop singer Tiny Tim (himself actually half-Arab and half-Jew).

'I am a Jew Freak,' Roth has insisted, 'not a Jewish Sage' – and one is reminded of Lennie Bruce, who was there first, occupying the dangerous DMZ between the world of the stand-up comedian and that of the proper maker of fictions. But Bruce made no claim to being a novelist and therefore neither disturbed the critics nor opened up new possibilities for prose narrative. Indeed, before *Portnoy's Complaint*, the Jewish-American novel had come to seem an especially egregious example of the death of belles-lettres, having become smug, established, repetitive and sterile. But *Portnoy* marks the passage of that genre into the new world of Porn and Pop, as Roth's booming sales (even in hardcover!) perhaps sufficiently attest.

It is, of course, the middle-aged and well-heeled who buy the hardcover editions of the book; yet their children apparently are picking it up, too, for once not even waiting for the paperback edition. They know it is a subversive book, as their parents do not (convinced that a boy who loves his mother can't be all bad), and as Roth himself perhaps was not at first quite aware either. Before its publication, he had been at least equivocal on the subject of frankly disruptive literature; full of distrust, for instance, for Norman Mailer – and appears therefore to have become a Pop rebel despite himself, driven less by principle than by a saving hunger for the great audience, quite like that which moved John Updike recently out of his elitist exile towards best-sellerdom and relevance in *Couples*.

There is, however, no doubt in the minds of most other writers whom the young especially prize at the moment that their essential task is to destroy once and for all – by parody or exaggeration or grotesque emulation of the classic past, as well as by the adaptation and 'camping' of Pop forms just such distinctions and discriminations. But to turn High Art into vaudeville and burlesque at the same moment that Mass Art is being irreverently introduced into museums and libraries is to perform an act which has political as well as aesthetic implications: an act which closes a class, as well as a generation gap. The notion of one art for the 'cultural,' i.e., the favored few in any given society and in another subart for the 'uncultured,' i.e., an excluded majority as deficient in Gutenberg skills as they are untutored in 'taste,' in fact represents the last survival in mass industrial societies (capitalist, socialist, communist – it makes no difference in this regard) of an invidious distinction proper only to a class-structured community. Precisely because it carries on, as it has carried on ever since the middle of the eighteenth century, a war against that anachronistic survival, Pop Art is, whatever its overt politics, *subversive*: a threat to all hierarchies insofar as it is hostile to order and ordering in its own realm. What the final intrusion of Pop into the citadels of High Art provides, therefore, for the critic is the exhilarating new possibility of making judgments about the 'goodness' and 'badness' of art quite separated from distinctions between 'high' and 'low' with their concealed class bias.

But the new audience has not waited for new critics to guide them in this direction. Reversing the process typical of Modernism – under whose aegis an unwilling, aging elite audience was bullied and cajoled slowly, slowly, into accepting the most vital art of its time – Post-Modernism provides an example of a young, mass audience urging certain aging, reluctant critics onward toward the abandonment of their former elite status in return for a freedom the prospect of which more terrifies than elates them. In fact, Post-Modernism implies the closing of the gap between critic and audience, too, if by critic one understands 'leader of taste' and by audience 'follower'. But most importantly of all, it implies the closing of the gap between artist and audience, or at any rate, between professional and amateur in the realm of art.

The jack of all arts is master of none – professional in none, and therefore no better than any man jack among the rest of us, formerly safely penned off from the practitioners we most admire by our status as 'audience.' It all follows logically enough. On the one hand, a poet like Ed Sanders, or a novelist like Leonard Cohen grows weary of his confinement in the realm of traditional high art; and the former organizes a musical Pop Group called the Fugs, while the latter makes recordings of his own Pop songs to his own guitar accompaniment. There are precedents for this, after all, not only as in the case of Boris Vian, which we have already noticed, but closer to home: in the career, for instance, of Richard Farina, who died very young, but not before he had written that imperfect, deeply moving novel, *Been Down So Long It Looks Like Up to Me*, and had recorded a song or two for the popular audience.

Meanwhile, even more surprisingly some who had begun, or whom we had begun to think of, as mere 'entertainers,' Pop performers without loftier pretensions, were crossing the line from their direction. Frank Zappa, for example, has in interviews and in a forthcoming book insisted on being taken seriously as poet and satirist, suggesting that the music of his own group, The Mothers of Invention, has been all along more a deliberate parody of Pop than an extension of it in psychedelic directions; while Bob Dylan, who began by abandoning Folk Music with left-wing protest overtones in favor of electronic Rock and Roll, finally succeeded in creating inside that form a kind of Pop surrealist poetry, passionate, mysterious, and quite complex; complex enough, in fact, to prompt a score of scholarly articles on his 'art.' Most recently, however, he has returned to 'acoustic' instruments and to the most naïve traditions of country music – apparently out of a sense that he had grown too 'arty,' and had once more to close the gap by back-tracking across the border he had earlier lost his first audience by crossing. It is a spectacular case of the new artist as Double Agent.

Even more spectacular, however, is that of John Lennon, who coming into view first as merely one of the Beatles, then still just another rock group from Liverpool, has revealed himself stage by stage as novelist, playwright, movie maker, guru, sculptor, etc., etc. There is a special pathos in his example since, though initially inspired by American models, he has tried to work out his essentially American strategies in English idioms and in growing isolation on the generally dismal English scene. He has refused to become the prisoner of his special talent as a musician, venturing into other realms where he has, initially at least, as little authority as anyone else; and thus provides one more model for the young who, without any special gift or calling, in the name of mere possibility insist on making all up and down America, and, more tentatively perhaps, everywhere else in the world, tens of thousands of records, movies, collections of verse, paintings, junk sculptures, even novels, in complete contempt of professional 'standards.' Perhaps, though, the novel is the most unpromising form for an amateur age (it is easier to learn the guitar or make a two-minute eight-millimeter film), and it may be doomed to become less and less important, less and less central, no matter how it is altered. But for the moment at least, on the border between the world of Art and that of non-Art, it flourishes with especial vigor in proportion as it realizes its transitional status, and is willing to surrender the kind of 'realism' and analysis it once thought its special province in quest of the marvelous and magical it began by disavowing.

Samuel Richardson may have believed that when he wrote *Pamela* and *Clarissa* he was delivering prose fiction from that bondage to the *merveilleux* which characterized the old Romances; but it is clear now that he was merely translating the Marvelous into new terms, specifically, into bourgeois English. It is time, at any rate, to be through with pretenses; for to Close the Gap means also to Cross the Border between the Marvelous and the Probable, the Real and the Mythical, the world of the boudoir and the counting house and the realm of what used to be called Faerie, but has for so long been designated mere madness. Certainly the basic images of Pop forms like the Western, Science Fiction and Pornography suggest mythological as well as political or metapolitical meanings. The passage into Indian Territory, the flight into Outer Space, the ecstatic release into the fantasy world of the orgy: all these are analogues for what has traditionally been described as a Journey or Pilgrimage (recently we have been more likely to say 'Trip' without altering the significance) towards a transcendent goal, a moment of Vision.

But the mythologies of Voyage and Vision which the late Middle Ages and the Renaissance inherited from the Classical World and the Judaeo-Christian tradition, and which froze into pedanticism and academicism in the eighteenth and nineteenth century, have not survived their last ironical uses in the earlier part of the twentieth: those burlesque-pathetic evocations in Joyce's *Ulysses*, Eliot's *The Waste Land*, Mann's *Joseph and His Brothers*, or the *Cantos* of Ezra Pound. If they are not quite dead, they should be, *need* be for the health of post-Art – as, indeed, Walt Whitman foresaw, anticipating the twenty-first century from the vantage point of his peculiar vision more than a hundred years ago.

> Come Muse migrate from Greece and Ionia,
> Cross out please those immensely overpaid accounts,
> That matter of Troy and Achilles' Wrath, and Aeneas'
>   Odysseus' wanderings,
> Place 'Removed' and 'To Let' on the rocks of your
>   snowy Parnassus,
> Repeat at Jerusalem . . .

Pop Art, however, can no more abide a mythological vacuum than can High Art: and into the space left vacant by the disappearance of the Matter of Troy and the myths of the ancient Middle East has rushed, first of all, the Matter of Childhood: the stuff of traditional fairy tales out of the Black Forest, which seems to the present generation especially attractive, perhaps, because their 'progressive' parents tended to distrust it. But something much more radically new has appeared as well: the matter of Metropolis and the myths of the Present Future, in which the nonhuman world about us, hostile or benign, is rendered not in the guise of elves or dwarfs or witches or even Gods, but of Machines quite as uncanny as any Elemental or Olympian – and apparently as immortal. Machines and the mythological figures appropriate to the media mass-produced and mass-distributed by machines: the newsboy who, saying SHAZAM in an abandoned subway tunnel, becomes Captain Marvel; the reporter (with glasses), who shucking his civilian garb in a telephone booth is revealed as Superman, immune to all but Kryptonite – these are the appropriate images of power and grace for an urban, industrial world busy manufacturing the Future.

But the Comic Book heroes do not stand alone. Out of the world of Jazz and Rock, of newspaper headlines and political cartoons, of old movies immortalized on TV and idiot talk shows carried on car radios, new anti-Gods and anti-Heroes arrive, endless wave after wave of them: 'Bluff'd not a bit by drainpipe, gasometer, artificial fertilizers,' (the appropriate commentary is Whitman's), 'smiling and pleas'd with palpable intent to stay' – in our Imaginary America, of course. In the hands of our new writers, they live a secondary life, begin to realize their immortality: not only Jean Harlow and Marilyn Monroe and Humphrey Bogart, Charlie Parker and Louis Armstrong and Lennie Bruce, Geronimo and Billy the Kid, the Lone Ranger and Fu Manchu and the Bride of Frankenstein, but Hitler and Stalin, John F. Kennedy and Lee Oswald and Jack Ruby as well; for the press mythologizes certain public figures, the actors of Pop History, even before they are dead – making a doomed President one with Superman in the Supermarket of Pop Culture, as Norman Mailer perceived so accurately and reported so movingly in an essay on John F. Kennedy.

But the secret he told was already known to scores of younger writers at least, and recorded in the text and texture of their work. In the deep memory of Leonard Cohen writing *Beautiful Losers*, or Richard Farina composing *Been Down So Long It Looks Like Up to Me*, or Ken Kesey making *Sometimes a Great Notion*, there stir to life not archetypal images out of books read in school or at the urging of parents; but those out of comic books forbidden in schools, or radio and TV programs banned or condescendingly endured by parents. From the taboo underground culture of the kids of just after World War II comes the essential mythology which informs the literature of right now. As early as T.S. Eliot, to be sure, jazz rhythms had been evoked, as in 'O O O O that Shakesperherian Rag – It's so elegant, So intelligent . . .,' but Eliot is mocking a world he resents; and even in Brecht's *Three Penny Opera*, the emulation of Pop music seems still largely 'slumming.' In the newest writers, however, mockery and condescension alike are absent, since they are not slumming; they are living in the only world in which they feel at home. They are able, therefore, to recapture a certain rude magic in its authentic context, by seizing on myths not as stored in encyclopedias or preserved in certain beloved ancient works – but as apprehended at their moment of making, which is to say, at a moment when they are not yet labeled 'myths.'

In some ways the present movement not only in its quest for myths, but also in its preference for sentimentality over irony, and especially in its dedication to the Primitive, resembles the beginnings of Romanticism, with its yearning for the Naïve, and its attempt to find authentic sources for poetry in folk forms like the *Märchen* or the ballads. But the Romantics returned exclusively toward the Past in the hope of renewal – to a dream of the Past, which they knew they could only write, not actually live. And, indeed, there persists in the post-Modernists some of that old nostalgia for folk ways and folk-rhythms, curiously tempered by the realization that the 'folk songs' of an electronic age are made not in rural loneliness or in sylvan retreats, but in superstudios by boys singing into the sensitive ear of machines – or even by those machines themselves editing, blending, making out of imperfect scraps of human song an artifice of simplicity only possible on tape. What recent writers have learned, and are true enough children of the Present Future to find exhilarating, is not only that the *Naïve* can be machine produced, but that dreams themselves can be manufactured, projected on TV or Laser beams with all the vividness of the visions of Saints. In the first wave of Romanticism, pre-electronic Romanticism, it took an act of faith on the part of Novalis to be able to say, 'Life is not a dream, but it can be and probably should be made one.' And echoing his German producer, in the pages of both *Lilith* and *Phantastes*, George Macdonald, maddest of the Victorian mad visionaries, echoes the tone of desperate hope. But to the young in America, who have learned to read Macdonald once more, along with his English successors, Charles Williams and C.S. Lewis and Tolkien, the declaration of faith has become a matter of fact.

The Dream, the Vision, *ekstasis*: these have again become the avowed goals of literature; for our latest poets realize in this time of Endings, what their remotest ancestors knew in the era of Beginnings, that merely 'to instruct and delight' is not enough. Like Longinus, the new novelists and critics believe that great art releases and liberates as well; but unlike him, they are convinced that wonder and fantasy, which deliver the mind from the body, the body from the mind, must be naturalized to a world of machines – subverted perhaps or even transformed, but certainly not destroyed or denied. The ending of Ken Kesey's *One Flew Over the Cuckoo's Next* expresses fictionally, metaphorically, that conviction, when the Indian who is his second hero breaks out of the Insane Asylum in which 'The System' has kept him impotent and trapped – and flees to join his fellows who are building a fishing weir on a giant hydro-electric power dam. The Dam and Weir both are essential to post-electronic Romanticism, which knows that the point is no longer to pursue some uncorrupted West over the next horizon, since there is no incorruption and all our horizons have been reached. It is rather to make a thousand little Wests in the interstices of a machine civilization, and, as it were, on its steel and concrete back; to live the tribal life among and with the support of machines; to shelter new communes under domes constructed according to the technology of Buckminster Fuller; and warm the nakedness of New Primitives with advanced techniques of solar heating.

All this is less a matter of choice than of necessity because, it has turned out, machine civilization tends inevitably to synthesize the primitive, and *ekstasis* is the unforeseen end of advanced technology, mysticism the by-product – no more nor no less accidental in penicillin – of scientific research. In the antiseptic laboratories of Switzerland, the psychedelic drug LSD was first developed, first tried by two white-coated experimenters; and even now Dow Chemical which manufactures napalm also produces the even more powerful psychedelic agent STP. It is, in large part, thanks to machines – the supermachines which, unlike their simpler prototypes, insist on tending us rather than demanding we tend them – that we live in the midst of a great religious revival, scarcely noticed by the official spokesmen of established Christian churches since it speaks quite another language. Yet many among us feel that they are able to live honestly only by what machines cannot do better than they – which is why certain poets and novelists, as well as pop singers and pornographic playwrights, are suggesting in print, on the air, everywhere, that not Work but Vision is the proper activity of men, and that, therefore, the contemplative life may, after all, be preferable to the active one. In such an age, *our* age, it is not surprising that the books which most move the young are essentially religious books, as, indeed, pop art is always religious.

In the immediate past, however, when an absolute distinction was made between High Art and Pop, works of the latter category tended to be the secret scriptures of a kind of shabby, store-front church – a religion as exclusive in its attempt to remain the humble possession of the unambitious and unlettered, as the canonical works of High Art in their claim to be an esoteric Gospel of art itself, available only to a cultivated elite. But in a time of Closing the Gap, literature becomes again prophetic and universal – a continuing revelation appropriate to a permanent religious revolution, whose function is precisely to transform the secular crowd into a sacred community: one with each other, and equally at home in the world of technology and the realm of wonder. Pledged like Isaiah to speaking the language of everyone, the prophets of the new dispensation can afford to be neither finicky nor genteel; and they echo, therefore, the desperate cry of the Hebrew prototype: 'I am a man of unclean lips in the midst of a people of unclean lips.'

Let those to whom religion means security beware, for it is no New

Established Church that is in the process of being founded; and its communicants are, therefore, less like the pillars of the Lutheran Church or Anglican gentlemen than they are like ranters, enthusiasts, Dionysiacs, Anabaptists: holy disturbers of the peace of the devout. Leonard Cohen, in a moment of vision which constitutes the climax of *Beautiful Losers*, aptly calls them 'New Jews'; for he sees them as a saved remnant moving across deserts of boredom, out of that exile from our authentic selves which we all share, toward a salvation none of us can quite imagine. Such New Jews, Cohen (himself a Jew as well as a Canadian) adds, do not have to be Jewish but probably do have to be Americans – by which he must surely mean 'Imaginary Americans,' since, as we have been observing all along, there were never any other kind.

---

5   Susan Sontag

From *Against Interpretation*

A Susan Sontag Reader, Harmondsworth, 1982, pp 95–104.

Content is a glimpse of something, an encounter like a flash. It's very tiny – very tiny, content.

Willem De Kooning,
in an interview

It is only shallow people who do not judge by appearances. The mystery of the world is the visible, not the invisible.

Oscar Wilde,
in a letter

The earliest experience of art must have been that it was incantatory, magical; art was an instrument of ritual. (cf. the paintings in the caves of Lascaux, Altamira, Niaux, La Pasiega, etc.) The earliest *theory* of art, that of the Greek philosophers, proposed that art was mimesis, imitation of reality.

It is at this point that the peculiar question of the value of art arose. For the mimetic theory, by its very terms, challenges art to justify itself.

Plato, who proposed the theory, seems to have done so in order to rule that the value of art is dubious. Since he considered ordinary material things as themselves mimetic objects, imitations of transcendent forms or structures, even the best painting of a bed would be only an 'imitation of an imitation.' For Plato, art is neither particularly useful (the painting of a bed is no good to sleep on) nor, in the strict sense, true. And Aristotle's arguments in defense of art do not really challenge Plato's view that all art is an elaborate *trompe l'oeil*, and therefore a lie. But he does dispute Plato's idea that art is useless. Lie or no, art has a certain value according to Aristotle because it is a form of therapy. Art is useful, after all, Aristotle counters, medicinally useful in that it arouses and purges dangerous emotions.

In Plato and Aristotle, the mimetic theory of art goes hand in hand with the assumption that art is always figurative. But advocates of the mimetic theory need not close their eyes to decorative and abstract art. The fallacy that art is necessarily a 'realism' can be modified or scrapped without ever moving outside the problems delimited by the mimetic theory.

The fact is, all Western consciousness of and reflection upon art have remained within the confines staked out by the Greek theory of art as mimesis or representation. It is through this theory that art as such – above and beyond given works of art – becomes problematic, in need of defense. And it is the defense of art which gives birth to the odd vision by which something we have learned to call 'form' is separated off from something we have learned to call 'content,' and to the well-intentioned move which makes content essential and form accessory.

Even in modern times, when most artists and critics have discarded the theory of art as representation of an outer reality in favor of the theory of art as subjective expression, the main feature of the mimetic theory persists. Whether we conceive of the work of art on the model of a picture (art as a picture of reality) or on the model of a statement (art as the statement of the artist), content still comes first. The content may have changed. It may now be less figurative, less lucidly realistic. But it is still assumed that a work of art *is* its content. Or, as it's usually put today, that a work of art by definition says something. ('What X is saying is . . .' 'What X is trying to say is . . .' 'What X said is . . .' etc., etc.)

None of us can ever retrieve that innocence before all theory when art knew no need to justify itself, when one did not ask of a work of art what it said because one knew (or thought one knew) what it did. From now to the end of consciousness, we are stuck with the task of defending art. We can only quarrel with one or another means of defense. Indeed, we have an obligation to overthrow any means of defending and justifying art which becomes particularly obtuse or onerous or insensitive to contemporary needs and practice.

This is the case, today, with the very idea of content itself. Whatever it may have been in the past, the idea of content is today mainly a hindrance, a nuisance, a subtle or not so subtle philistinism.

Though the actual developments in many arts may seem to be leading us away from the idea that a work of art is primarily its content, the idea still exerts an extraordinary hegemony. I want to suggest that this is because the idea is now perpetuated in the guise of a certain way of encountering works of art thoroughly ingrained among most people who take any of the arts seriously. What the overemphasis on the idea of content entails is the perennial, never consummated project of *interpretation*. And, conversely, it is the habit of approaching works of art in order to *interpret* them that sustains the fancy that there really is such a thing as the content of a work of art.

Of course, I don't mean interpretation in the broadest sense, the sense in which Nietzsche (rightly) says, 'There are no facts, only interpretations.' By interpretation, I mean here a conscious act of the mind which illustrates a certain code, certain 'rules' of interpretation.

Directed to art, interpretation means plucking a set of elements (the X, the Y, the Z, and so forth) from the whole work. The task of interpretation is virtually one of translation. The interpreter says, Look, don't you see that X is really – or, really means – A? That Y is really B? That Z is really C?

What situation could prompt this curious project for transforming a text? History gives us the materials for an answer. Interpretation first appears in the culture of late classical antiquity, when the power and credibility of myth had been broken by the 'realistic' view of the world introduced by scientific enlightenment. Once the question that haunts post-mythic consciousness – that of the *seemliness* of religious symbols – had been asked, the ancient texts were, in their pristine form, no longer acceptable. Then interpretation was summoned, to reconcile the ancient texts to 'modern' demands. Thus, the Stoics, to accord with their view that the gods had to be moral, allegorized away the rude features of Zeus and his boisterous clan in Homer's epics. What Homer really designated by the adultery of Zeus with Leto, they explained, was the union between power and wisdom. In the same vein, Philo of Alexandria interpreted the literal historical narratives of the Hebrew Bible as spiritual paradigms. The story of the exodus from Egypt, the wandering in the desert for forty years, and the entry into the promised land, said Philo, was really an allegory of the individual soul's emancipation, tribulations, and final deliverance. Interpretation thus presupposes a discrepancy between the clear meaning of the text and the demands of (later) readers. It seeks to resolve that discrepancy. The situation is that for some reason a text has become unacceptable; yet it cannot be discarded. Interpretation is a radical strategy for conserving an old text, which is thought too precious to repudiate, by revamping it. The interpreter, without actually erasing or rewriting the text, *is* altering it. But he can't admit to doing this. He claims to be only making it intelligible, by disclosing its true meaning. However far the interpreters alter the text (another notorious example is the rabbinic and Christian 'spiritual' interpretations of the clearly erotic Song of Songs), they must claim to be reading off a sense that is already there.

Interpretation in our own time, however, is even more complex. For the contemporary zeal for the project of interpretation is often prompted not by piety toward the troublesome text (which may conceal an aggression) but by an open aggressiveness, an overt contempt for appearances. The old style of interpretation was insistent, but respectful; it erected another meaning on top of the literal one. The modern style of interpretation excavates, and as it excavates, destroys; it digs 'behind' the text, to find a sub-text which is the true one. The most celebrated and influential modern doctrines, those of Marx and Freud, actually amount to elaborate systems of hermeneutics, aggressive and impious theories of interpretation. All observable phenomena are bracketed, in Freud's phrase, as *manifest content*. This manifest content must be probed and pushed aside to find the true meaning – the *latent content* – beneath. For Marx, social events like revolutions and wars; for Freud, the events of individual lives (like neurotic symptoms and slips of the tongue) as well as texts (like a dream or a work of art) – all are treated as occasions for interpretation. According to Marx and Freud, these events only *seem* to be intelligible. Actually, they have no meaning without interpretation. To understand *is* to interpret. And to interpret is to restate the phenomenon, in effect to find an equivalent for it.

Thus, interpretation is not (as most people assume) an absolute value, a gesture of mind situated in some timeless realm of capabilities. Interpretation must itself be evaluated, within a historical view of human consciousness. In some cultural contexts, interpretation is a liberating act. It is a means of revising, of transvaluing, of escaping the dead past. In other cultural contexts, it is reactionary, impertinent, cowardly, stifling.

Today is such a time, when the project of interpretation is largely reactionary, stifling. Like the fumes of the automobile and of heavy industry which befoul the urban atmosphere, the effusion of interpretations of art today poisons our sensibilities. In a culture whose already classical dilemma is the hypertrophy of the intellect at the expense of energy and sensual capability, interpretation is the revenge of the intellect upon art.

Even more. It is the revenge of the intellect upon the world. To interpret is to impoverish, to deplete the world – in order to set up a shadow world of 'meanings.' It is to turn *the* world into *this* world. ('This world'! As if there were any other.)

The world, our world, is depleted, impoverished enough. Away with all duplicates of it, until we again experience more immediately what we have.

In most modern instances, interpretation amounts to the philistine refusal to leave the work of art alone. Real art has the capacity to make us nervous. By reducing the work of art to its content and then interpreting *that*, one tames the work of art. Interpretation makes art manageable, comfortable.

This philistinism of interpretation is more rife in literature than in any other art. For decades now, literary critics have understood it to be their task to translate the elements of the poem or play or novel or story into something else. Sometimes a writer will be so uneasy before the naked power of his art that he will install within the work itself – albeit with a little shyness, a touch of the good taste of irony – the clear and explicit interpretation of it. Thomas Mann is an example of such an overcooperative author. In the case of more stubborn authors, the critic is only too happy to perform the job.

The work of Kafka, for example, has been subjected to a mass ravishment by no less than three armies of interpreters. Those who read Kafka as a social allegory see case studies of the frustrations and insanity of modern bureaucracy and its ultimate issuance in the totalitarian state. Those who read Kafka as a psychoanalytic allegory see desperate revelations of Kafka's fear of his father, his castration anxieties, his sense of his own impotence, his thralldom to his dreams. Those who read Kafka as a religious allegory explain that K. in *The Castle* is trying to gain access to heaven, that Joseph K. in *The Trial* is being judged by the inexorable and mysterious justice of God . . . Another body of work that has attracted interpreters like leeches is that of Samuel Beckett. Beckett's delicate dramas of the withdrawn consciousness – pared down to essentials, cut off, often represented as physically immobilized – are read as a statement about modern man's alienation from meaning or from God, or as an allegory of psychopathology.

Proust, Joyce, Faulkner, Rilke, Lawrence, Gide . . . one could go on citing author after author; the list is endless of those around whom thick encrustations of interpretation have taken hold. But it should be noted that interpretation is not simply the compliment that mediocrity pays to genius. It is, indeed, the modern way of understanding something, and is applied to works of every quality. Thus, in the notes that Elia Kazan published on his production of *A Streetcar Named Desire*, it becomes clear that, in order to direct the play, Kazan had to discover that Stanley Kowalski represented the sensual and vengeful barbarism that was engulfing our culture, while Blanche DuBois was Western civilization, poetry, delicate apparel, dim lighting, refined feelings and all, though a little the worse for wear, to be sure. Tennessee Williams's forceful psychological melodrama now became intelligible: it was about something, about the decline of Western civilization. Apparently, were it to go on being a play about a handsome brute named Stanley Kowalski and a faded mangy belle named Blanche DuBois, it would not be manageable.

It doesn't matter whether artists intend, or don't intend, for their works to be interpreted. Perhaps Tennessee Williams thinks *Streetcar* is about what Kazan thinks it to be about. It may be that Cocteau in *The Blood of a Poet* and in *Orpheus* wanted the elaborate readings which have been given these films, in terms of Freudian symbolism and social critique. But the merit of these works certainly lies elsewhere than in their 'meanings.' Indeed, it is precisely to the extent that Williams's plays and Cocteau's films do suggest these portentous meanings that they are defective, false, contrived, lacking in conviction.

From interviews, it appears that Resnais and Robbe-Grillet consciously designed *Last Year at Marienbad* to accommodate a multiplicity of equally plausible interpretations. But the temptation to interpret *Marienbad* should be resisted. What matters in *Marienbad* is the pure, untranslatable, sensuous immediacy of some of its images, and its rigorous if narrow solutions to certain problems of cinematic form.

Again, Ingmar Bergman may have meant the tank rumbling down the empty night street in *The Silence* as a phallic symbol. But if he did, it was a foolish thought. ('Never trust the teller, trust the tale,' said Lawrence.) Taken as a brute object, as an immediate sensory equivalent for the mysterious abrupt armored happenings going on inside the hotel, that sequence with the tank is the most striking moment in the film. Those who reach for a Freudian interpretation of the tank are only expressing their lack of response to what is there on the screen.

It is always the case that interpretation of this type indicates a dissatisfaction (conscious or unconscious) with the work, a wish to replace it by something else.

Interpretation, based on the highly dubious theory that a work of art is composed of items of content, violates art. It makes art into an article for use, for arrangement into a mental scheme of categories.

Interpretation does not, of course, always prevail. In fact, a great deal of today's art may be understood as motivated by a flight from interpretation. To avoid interpretation, art may become parody. Or it may become abstract. Or it may become ('merely') decorative. Or it may become non-art.

The flight from interpretation seems particularly a feature of modern painting. Abstract painting is the attempt to have, in the ordinary sense, no content; since there is no content, there can be no interpretation. Pop Art works by the opposite means to the same result; using a content so blatant, so 'what it is,' it, too, ends by being uninterpretable.

A great deal of modern poetry as well, starting from the great experiments of French poetry (including the movement that is misleadingly called Symbolism) to put silence into poems and to reinstate the *magic* of the word, has escaped from the rough grip of interpretation. The most recent revolution in contemporary taste in poetry – the revolution that has deposed Eliot and elevated Pound – represents a turning away from content in poetry in the old sense, an impatience with what made modern poetry prey to the zeal of interpreters.

I am speaking mainly of the situation in America, of course. Interpretation runs rampant here in those arts with a feeble and negligible avant-garde: fiction and the drama. Most American novelists and playwrights are really either journalists or gentlemen sociologists and psychologists. They are writing the literary equivalent of program music. And so rudimentary, uninspired, and stagnant has been the sense of what might be done with form in fiction and drama that even when the content isn't simply information, news, it is still peculiarly visible, handier, more exposed. To the extent that novels and plays (in America), unlike poetry and painting and music, don't reflect any interesting concern with changes in their form, these arts remain prone to assault by interpretation.

But programmatic avant-gardism – which has meant, mostly, experiments with form at the expense of content – is not the only defense against the infestation of art by interpretations. At least, I hope not. For this would be to commit art to being perpetually on the run. (It also perpetuates the very distinction between form and content which is, ultimately, an illusion.) Ideally, it is possible to elude the interpreters in another way, by making works of art whose surface is so unified and clean, whose momentum is so rapid, whose address is so direct that the work can be . . . just what it is. Is this possible now? It does happen in films, I believe. This is why cinema is the most alive, the most exciting, the most important of all art forms right now. Perhaps the way one tells how alive a particular art form is is by the latitude it gives for making mistakes in it and still being good. For example, a few of the films of Bergman – though crammed with lame messages about the modern spirit, thereby inviting interpretations – still triumph over the pretentious intentions of their director. (In *Winter Light* and *The Silence*, the beauty and visual sophistication of the images subvert before our eyes the callow pseudo-intellectuality of the story and some of the dialogue. (The most remarkable instance of this sort of discrepancy is the work of D.W. Griffith.) In good films, there is always a directness that entirely frees us from the itch to interpret. Many old Hollywood films, like those of Cukor, Walsh, Hawks, and countless other directors, have this liberating anti-symbolic quality, no less than the best work of the new European directors, like Truffaut's *Shoot the Piano Player* and *Jules and Jim*, Godard's *Breathless* and *Vivre sa Vie*, Antonioni's *L'Avventura*, and Olmi's *The Fiancés*.

The fact that films have not been overrun by interpreters is in part due simply to the newness of cinema as an art. It also owes to the happy accident that films for such a long time were just movies; in other words, that they were understood to be part of mass, as opposed to high, culture, and were left alone by most people with minds. Then, too, there is always something other than content in the cinema to grab hold of, for those who want to analyze. For the cinema, unlike the novel, possesses a vocabulary of forms – the explicit, complex, and discussable technology of camera movements, cutting, and composition of the frame that goes into the making of a film.

What kind of criticism, of commentary on the arts, is desirable today? For I am not saying that works of art are ineffable, that they cannot be described or paraphrased. They can be. The question is how. What would criticism look like that would serve the work of art, not usurp its place?

What is needed, first, is more attention to form in art. If excessive stress on *content* provokes the arrogance of interpretation, more extended and more thorough descriptions of *form* would silence. What is needed is a vocabulary –a descriptive, rather than prescriptive, vocabulary – for forms.[1] The best criticism, and it is uncommon, is of this sort that dissolves considerations of content into those of form. On film, drama, and painting respectively, I can think of Erwin Panofsky's essay 'Style and Medium in the Motion Pictures,' Northrop Frye's essay 'A Conspectus of Dramatic Genres,' Pierre Francastel's essay 'The Destruction of a Plastic Space.' Roland Barthes's book *On Racine* and his two essays on Robbe-Grillet are examples of formal analysis applied to the work of a single author. (The best essays in Erich Auerbach's *Mimesis*, like 'The Scar of Odysseus,' are also of this type.) An example of formal analysis applied simultaneously to genre and author is Walter Benjamin's essay 'The Storyteller: Reflections on the Works of Nicolai Leskov.'

Equally valuable would be acts of criticism which would supply a really accurate, sharp, loving description of the appearance of a work of art. This seems even harder to do than formal analysis. Some of Manny Farber's film criticism, Dorothy Van Ghent's essay 'The Dickens World: A View from

---

[1] One of the difficulties is that our idea of form is spatial (the Greek metaphors for form are all derived from notions of space). This is why we have a more ready vocabulary of forms for the spatial than for the temporal arts. The exception among the temporal arts, of course, is the drama; perhaps this is because the drama is a narrative (i.e. temporal) form that extends itself visually and pictorially, upon a stage. What we don't have yet is a poetics of the novel, any clear notion of the forms of narration. Perhaps film criticism will be the occasion of a breakthrough here, since films are primarily a visual form, yet they are also a subdivision of literature.

Todgers',' Randall Jarrell's essay on Walt Whitman are among the rare examples of what I mean. These are essays which reveal the sensuous surface of art without mucking about in it.

Transparence is the highest, most liberating value in art – and in criticism – today. Transparence means experiencing the luminousness of the thing in itself, of things being what they are. This is the greatness of, for example, the films of Bresson and Ozu and Renoir's *The Rules of the Game*.

Once upon a time (say, for Dante), it must have been a revolutionary and creative move to design works of art so that they might be experienced on several levels. Now it is not. It reinforces the principle of redundancy that is the principal affliction of modern life.

Once upon a time (a time when high art was scarce), it must have been a revolutionary and creative move to interpret works of art. Now it is not. What we decidedly do not need now is further to assimilate Art into Thought, or (worse yet) Art into Culture.

Interpretation takes the sensory experience of the work of art for granted, and proceeds from there. This cannot be taken for granted now. Think of the sheer multiplication of works of art available to every one of us, super-added to the conflicting tastes and odors and sights of the urban environment that bombard our senses. Ours is a culture based on excess, on overproduction; the result is a steady loss of sharpness in our sensory experience. All the conditions of modern life – its material plenitude, its sheer crowdedness – conjoin to dull our sensory faculties. And it is in the light of the condition of our senses, our capacities (rather than those of another age), that the task of the critic must be assessed.

What is important now is to recover our senses. We must learn to *see* more, to *hear* more, to *feel* more.

Our task is not to find the maximum amount of content in a work of art, much less to squeeze more content out of the work than is already there. Our task is to cut back content so that we can see the thing at all.

The aim of all commentary on art now should be to make works of art – and, by analogy, our own experience – more, rather than less, real to us. The function of criticism should be to show *how it is what it is*, even *that it is what it is*, rather than to show *what it means*.

In place of a hermeneutics we need an erotics of art.

6 Frank Kermode

From *Fictions*

A Sense of an Ending, Oxford University Press, 1967, pp 35–43.

What can be thought must certainly be fiction.

Nietzsche

. . . the nicer knowledge of
Belief, that what it believes in is not true.

Wallace Stevens

Who can deny that things to come are not yet?
Yet already there is in the mind an expectation
of things to come.

St. Augustine

C'est par l'effort et le désir que nous avons fait connaissance avec le temps; nous
guidons l'habitude d'estimer le temps selon désirs, nos efforts, notre volonté propre.
Guyau, *Le Genèse de l'idée de temps.*

One of my tasks in this second talk is to answer some of the questions which I
begged in the first. I wanted to concentrate on eschatological fictions, fictions of
the End, in relation to apocalypse itself; and though I did say something about
these as analogous to literary fictions, by means of which we impose other
patterns on historical time, I did little to justify the analogy. And when I spoke
of the degree to which fictions vary from the paradigmatic base, I again
confined myself largely to straight apocalypse – the way the type figures were
modified, made to refer not to a common End but to personal death or to crisis,
or to epoch. I mentioned that literary fictions changed in the same way –
perpetually recurring crises of the person, and the death of that person, took
over from myths which purport to relate one's experience to grand beginnings
and ends. And I suggested that there have been great changes, especially in
recent times when our attitudes to fiction in general have grown so sophistic-
ated; although it seems, at the same time, that in 'making sense' of the world we
still feel a need, harder than ever to satisfy because of an accumulated
scepticism, to experience that concordance of beginning, middle, and end
which is the essence of our explanatory fictions, and especially when they
belong to cultural traditions which treat historical time as primarily rectilinear
rather than cyclic.

Obviously I now need to say more about the way I have been using such
words as 'fiction' and 'concordance.' First, then, let us reflect that it is pretty
surprising, given the range and minuteness of modern literary theory, that
nobody, so far as I know, has ever tried to relate the theory of literary fictions to
the theory of fictions in general, though I think something of the sort may have
been in Ogden's mind when he assembled *Bentham's Theory of Fictions*; and
there are relevant implications, not developed in this direction, in Richards on
'speculative instruments' and what he calls 'experimental submission.'

Richards is certainly concerned with the nature and quality of one's assent to fictions as a means to personal freedom or perhaps simply to personal comfort.

But that there *is* a simple relation between literary and other fictions seems, if one attends to it, more obvious than has appeared. If we think first of modern fictions, it can hardly be an accident that ever since Nietzsche generalized and developed the Kantian insights, literature has increasingly asserted its right to an arbitrary and private choice of fictional norms, just as historiography has become a discipline more devious and dubious because of our recognition that its methods depend to an unsuspected degree on myths and fictions. After Nietzsche it was possible to say, as Stevens did, that 'the final belief must be in a fiction.' This poet, to whom the whole question was of perpetual interest, saw that to think in this way was to postpone the End – when the fiction might be said to coincide with reality – for ever; to make of it a fiction, an imaginary moment when 'at last' the world of fact and the *mundo* of fiction shall be one. Such a fiction – the last section of *Notes toward a Supreme Fiction* is, appropriately the place where *Stevens* gives it his fullest attention – such a fiction of the end is like infinity plus one and imaginary numbers in mathematics, something we know does not exist, but which helps us to make sense of and to move in the world. *Mundo* is itself such a fiction. I think Stevens, who certainly thought we have to make our sense out of whatever materials we find to hand, borrowed it from Ortega. His general doctrine of fictions he took from Vaihinger, from Nietzsche, perhaps also from American pragmatism.

First, an ethical problem. If literary fictions *are* related to all others, then it must be said that they have some dangerous relations. 'The falseness of an opinion is not . . . any objection to it,' says Nietzsche, adding that the only relevant question is 'how far the opinion is life-furthering, life-preserving, species-preserving.' A man who thinks this is in some danger of resembling the Cretan Liar, for his opinion can be no less fictive than the opinions to which it alludes. He may be in worse danger; he may be encouraging people who hold the fictive view that death on a large scale is life-furthering and species-preserving. On the one hand you have a relatively innocent theory, a way of coming to terms with the modern way of recognizing the gulf between being and knowing, the sense that nature can always be made to answer our questions, comply with our fictions. This is what Wordsworth curiously and touchingly predicted when he asserted that 'Nature never did betray / The heart that loved her.' In its purely operational form this is the basis of the theoretical physicist's life, since he assumes that there will always be experimental confirmation for positions arrived at by pure mathematics. Naturally, the answers, like the questions, are purely human. 'Nature is patient of interpretation in terms of laws that happen to interest us,' as Whitehead remarked. But on the other hand you have the gas-chambers. Alfred Rosenberg used the innocent speculations of William James, John Dewey, and F.C.S. Schiller to argue that knowledge was at the service of 'organic' truth, which he identified with the furthering of the life of what he called the 'German race.' If the value of an opinion is to be tested only by its success in the world, the propositions of dementia can become as valuable as any other fictions. The validity of one's opinion of the Jews can be proved by killing six million Jews.

Hannah Arendt, who has written with clarity and passion on this issue, argues that the philosophical or anti-philosophical assumptions of the Nazis were not generically different from those of the scientist, or indeed of any of us in an age 'where man, wherever he goes, encounters only himself.' How, in such a situation, can our paradigms of concord, our beginnings and ends, our humanly ordered picture of the world satisfy us, make sense? How can apocalypse or tragedy make sense, or more sense than any arbitrary nonsense can be made to make sense? If *King Lear* is an image of the promised end, so is Buchenwald; and both stand under the accusation of being horrible, rootless fantasies, the one no more true or more false than the other, so that the best you say is that *King Lear* does less harm.

I think we have to admit that the consciously false apocalypse of the Third Reich and the consciously false apocalypse of *King Lear* imply equally a recognition that it is ourselves we are encountering whenever we invent fictions. There may even be a real relation between certain kinds of effectiveness in literature and totalitarianism in politics. But although the fictions are alike ways of finding out about the human world, anti-Semitism is a fiction of escape which tells you nothing about death but projects it onto others; whereas *King Lear* is a fiction that inescapably involves an encounter with oneself, and the image of one's end. This is one difference; and there is another. We have to distinguish between myths and fictions. Fictions can degenerate into myths whenever they are not consciously held to be fictive. In this sense anti-Semitism is a degenerate fiction, a myth; and *Lear* is a fiction. Myth operates within the diagrams of ritual, which presupposes total and adequate explanations of things as they are and were; it is a sequence of radically unchangeable gestures. Fictions are for finding things out, and they change as the needs of sense-making change. Myths are the agents of stability, fictions the agents of change. Myths call for absolute, fictions for conditional assent. Myths make sense in terms of a lost order of time, *illud tempus* as Eliade calls it; fictions, if successful, make sense of the here and now, *hoc tempus*. It may be that treating literary fictions as myths sounds good just now, but as Marianne Moore so rightly said of poems, 'these things are important not because a / high-sounding interpretation can be put upon them but because they are / useful.'

On Vaihinger's view, the fictional *as if* is distinguished also from hypothesis because it is not in question that at the end of the finding-out process it will be dropped. In some ways this is obviously true of the literary fictions. We are never in danger of thinking that the death of King Lear, which explains so much, is *true*. To the statement that he died thus and thus – speaking these words over Cordelia's body, calling for a looking-glass, fumbling with a button – we make an experimental assent. If we make it well, the gain is that we shall never quite resume the posture towards life and death that we formerly held. Of course it may be said that in changing ourselves we have, in the best possible indirect way, changed the world.

So my suggestion is that literary fictions belong to Vaihinger's category of 'the consciously false.' They are not subject, like hypotheses, to proof or disconfirmation, only, if they come to lose their operational effectiveness, to neglect. They are then thrown, in Stevens's figure, on to the 'dump' – 'to sit among mattresses of the dead.' In this they resemble the fictions of science, mathematics, and law, and differ from those of theology only because religious fictions are harder to free from the mythical 'deposit.' I see no reason why we cannot apply to literary fictions what Vaihinger says of fictions in general, that they 'are mental structures. The psyche weaves this or that thought out of itself; for the mind is invention; under the compulsion of necessity, stimulated by the outer world, it discovers the store of contrivances hidden within itself. The organism finds itself in a world of contradictory sensations, it is exposed to the assaults of a hostile world, and in order to preserve itself is forced to seek every possible means of assistance.' He distinguishes many different types of fiction: the paradigmatic, for example, which includes Utopias, and we may add apocalypses; the legal, where the fiction has a function in equity (as when a court may deem that a wife who died at the same instant as, or even some time later than her husband, pre-deceased him, so as to obviate an inequitable double payment of estate duties; or as when, after a certain lapse of time, after receipt, one is presumed to have accepted delivery of a postal packet); the fictive zero-cases of mathematics; the fictions of the thing-in-itself, or of causality; and what Vaihinger calls, in words remembered by Stevens, 'the last and greatest fiction,' 'the fiction of an Absolute.' If we forget that fictions are fictive we regress to myth (as when the Neo-Platonists forgot the fictiveness of Plato's fictions and Professor Frye forgets the fictiveness of *all* fictions). This is as if we were to believe, because of the grace of the court, that by an immutable dispensation it always happens that when a husband and wife are involved in a car crash the wife dies first, though in ordinary life we may 'displace' or 'ironize' this basic truth. What Vaihinger calls 'reunion with reality' and I call 'making sense' or 'making human sense' is something that literature achieves only so long as we remember the status of fictions. They are not myths, and they are not hypotheses; you neither rearrange the world to suit them, nor test them by experiment, for instance in gas-chambers.

When Vaihinger had to deal with the situation that arises when men make fictions apparently too elaborate and ingenious to be explained simply in terms of survival in a hostile environment (more splendid than seems proper merely to the mitigation of 'poverty') he made up his Law of Preponderance of Means over End. We can do without this, but need to remember not only that we have what Bergson called a *fonction fabulatrice*, but that we do set ourselves problems of the kind that would presumably not arise as a matter of simple biological necessity. When Nietzsche asked, 'why might not the world *which concerns us* be a fiction?' he was imagining a very large degree of human curiosity.

> Meanwhile the mind, from pleasure less,
> Withdraws into its happiness –

but having reached the point it does not cease to produce fictions beyond necessity:

> it creates, transcending these,
> Far other worlds and other seas.

There are the green thoughts of fantasy, concerned not only with providing each kind with some convenient mental equivalent but projecting the desires of the mind on to reality. When the fictions change, therefore, the world changes in step with them. This is what the poet meant when he said that modern poetry was 'the act of finding / What will suffice.' He adds that this used to be easier than it is now, because 'the scene was set' – we had our paradigmatic fictions, which he calls 'Romantic tenements of rose and ice.' These no longer serve, and the fiction of the modern poet must 'speak words in the ear, / The delicatest ear of the mind, repeat, / Exactly, that which it wants to hear . . .' The satisfactions required are too subtle for the paradigms; but the poem needs to provide them. 'It must be the finding of a satisfaction, and may / Be of a man skating, a woman dancing, a woman / Combing.' It has moved, if you like, under the pressure of the Law of Preponderance of Means over End, away from the paradigm with its simpler biological function; it is a subtler matter now that utopia or apocalypse or tragedy. Those Noble Riders have come to look rigid, a bit absurd, as the same poet remarks.

Nor is it only in literary fictions that the satisfactions, especially the satisfactions of sceptical clerks, grow more devious and refined. The recognition, now commonplace, that the writing of history involves the use of regulative fictions, is part of the same process. World history, the imposition of a plot on time, is a substitute for myth, and the substitution of anti-historic criticism for it is another step in the direction of harder satisfactions, in the clerkly rejection of romantic tenements. There is no history, says Karl Popper, only histories; an insight in which he was anticipated by novelists, who wrote Histories (of, say, Tom Jones, or of the Life and Opinions of Tristram Shandy) in a period of paradigmatic historiography, as expounded by Carl Becker in his lectures called *The Heavenly City of the Eighteenth-Century Philosophers*. The decline of paradigmatic history, and our growing consciousness of historiography's irreducible element of fiction, are, like the sophistication of literary plotting, contributions to what Wilde called 'the decay of lying.' We fall into 'careless habits of accuracy.' We know that if we want to find out about ourselves, make sense, we must avoid the regress into myth which has deceived poet, historian, and critic. Our satisfactions will be hard to find.

And yet, it is clear, this is an exaggerated statement of the case. The paradigms do survive, somehow. If there was a time when, in Stevens's words, 'the scene was set,' it must be allowed that is has not yet been finally and totally struck. The survival of the paradigms is as much our business as their erosion. For that reason it is time to look more closely at them.

---

7 Ihab Hassan

From *The New Gnosticism: Speculations on an Aspect of the Postmodern Mind*

Paracriticisms, University of Illinois Press, 1975, pp 121–51.

Epigraphs[1]

Thine own consciousness, shining, void, and inseparable from the Great Body of Radiance, hath no birth, nor death, and is the Immutable Light.

[1] Epigraph references are on last page of this section.

The Gospel of Truth is *joy* for those who have received the *grace* of *knowing* from the Father of Truth. . . . He who knows is a being from above. If he is called, he hears, he replies, he turns to him who calls him, in order to come back to him. . . . He who thus possesses gnosis knows whence he has come and whither he goes.

The Circumference is Within, Without is formed the Selfish Center, / And the Circumference still expands going forward to Eternity. . . .

The sublime remark of Euler on his law of arches, 'This will be found contrary to all experience, yet is true,' had already transferred nature into the mind, and left matter to be an outcast corpse.

The origins of the process of mechanization are more mystical than we imagine.

The universe begins to look more like a great thought than like a great machine.

Spiritualized Energy is the flower of Cosmic Energy. To dominate and canalize the powers of the air and the sea is all very well. But what is this triumph, compared with the world-wide mastery of human thought and love?

Today computers hold out the promise of a means of instant translation of any code or language into any other code or language. The computer, in short, promises by technology a Pentecostal condition of universal understanding and unity. The next logical step would seem to be, not to translate, but to bypass languages in favor of a general cosmic consciousness. . . .

All scientific generalizations
Are pure metaphysics
All metaphysics are weightless
And physically unlimited.

Because of the millennial nature of the goal of extending consciousness, we can expect that, if we adopt it, it will exert a small but persistent influence on human activities over a very long period of time.

The real world . . . is the world where thoughts are omnipotent, where no distinction is drawn between wish and deed. As in the New Testament. . . .

We are actually born out of light, you might say. I believe light is the maker of all material. Material is spent light.

But what do twelve epigraphs prove? Surely they do not answer an appeal to authority since few of us now accept the same authorities. Do they evoke a mood, declare a theme, insinuate a conclusion? Possibly. Yet, coming at the start, they do nothing that the text itself will not confirm or deny. Thus epigraphs become a kind of preparation for failure. Or is the function of epigraphs to release metaphors and ideas from the bounds of a single time, place, and mind? Can quotation marks hold back a thought from seeking a larger identity in Thought? And of what are the walls within Language made? These are questions that the im-mediate mind sometimes asks.

The Convergence of Consciousness

The theme of this paracritical essay is the growing insistence of Mind to apprehend reality im-mediately; to gather more and more mind in itself: thus to become its own reality. Consciousness becomes all. And as in a gnostic dream, matter dissolves before the Light.

Certainly, consciousness has become one of our key terms, replacing honor, faith, reason, or sensibility as the token of intellectual passion, the instrument of our cultural will. Cold-eyed behaviorists may eschew the term; yet its nimbus still hangs over our rhetoric as we discourse on politics and pornography, language and literature, morality and metaphysics. Thus we 'raise,' 'expand,' 'alter,' 'criticize,' and 'bracket' consciousness, among so many other things we do to it nowadays.

This cultural chatter may not be wholly idle. A certain dematerialization of our world is taking place, from the 'etherealization' of culture (Arnold Toynbee) to the 'ephemeralization' of substance (Buckminster Fuller) to the 'de-definition' of art (Harold Rosenberg). The literary author 'dies' (Roland Barthes), and the literary text vanishes into a generic abstraction, *l'écriture*. How many forms, disciplines, institutions, have we seen dissolve, in the last few decades, into amorphous new shapes? How many objects, solidly mattered, have we seen dissolve into a process, an image, a mental frame? 'We are beyond space and time,' John Brockman says in *Afterwords*; 'we are beyond good and evil; there is only information; it is the control; the measure by which the operation of the brain changes. . . .' Dissolution again?

> The impact of the computer is felt in virtually every corner of American life, from the ghetto to the moon. And data-processing is the world's fastest growing major business; sometime during the next decade, it is expected to become the world's largest industry.
>
> *The New York Times*, Oct. 22, 1972

From hardware to software, from software to pure mind? Actually, the process may be one of convergence far more than of dissolution. The syntropic force of consciousness is remaking our world in every way. Thus Daniel Bell, like Buckminster Fuller, identifies the major source of transformation as 'the exponential growth and branching of science, the rise of a new intellectual technology, the creation of systematic research . . . and, as the calyx of all this, the codification of theoretical knowledge' (*The Coming of the Post-Industrial Society*). The codification of theoretical knowledge unifies consciousness even as it enlarges it. Curiously, we are not far from Teilhard de Chardin, who said: 'Everything that rises must converge.' That is a hypothesis that we need, at least, to entertain.

Teilhard's famous phrase, however, provides Flannery O'Connor with an ironic title to a collection of stories. Why ironic? Because the stories reveal isolation, terror, and waste, reveal life without Grace. Here is another hypothesis of the human condition that we can not entirely repudiate. The radical insufficiency of that condition – I do not wish to say: of man – still offers intractable resistance to the old gnostic dream. Whether we call it evil, Ananke, or (mawkishly) The System, this resistance must be acknowledged. *Without assent.*

Beyond Arcardians and Technophiles

The New Gnosticism is the result of various synergies. Myth and Technology, for instance, now easily blend in the mind. A great part of our culture, however, still abets opposition, division. Consider, for instance, the current distinction between Arcadians and Technophiles:

The Arcardians look for the unspoiled life in nature. They tend to be mythically minded and edenic. Hostile to technology, they like communes, ecology, health foods, folk music, occult and visonary literature. They are children of the Earth, mother-oriented, ruled by the great archetypes. See Charles Reich's *The Greening of America*, Theodore Roszak's *Where the Wasteland Ends*, or George B. Leonard's *The Transformation*.

The Technophiles favor the active life of cities. They tend to be technically minded and utopian. They like gadgets, science fiction, electronic music, space programs, futuristic designs of their environment. They are children of the Sky, father-oriented, struggling to create neo-types. See Zbigniew Brzezinsky's *Between Two Ages: America's Role in the Technetronic Era*, F.M. Esfandiary's *Optimism One: The Emerging Radicalism*, or Victor Ferkiss' *Technological Man*.

These, to be sure, are stereotypes. Yet their historic tensions inform such serious works as Leo Marx's *The Machine in the Garden*, Arthur Koestler's *The Ghost in the Machine*, and Lewis Mumford's *The Myth of the Machine* – note the titles – works that prefigure some of our post-modern perplexities.

Though the antipathy between Arcadians and Technophiles may derive from an ancient wound in the human psyche, there is nothing ineluctable about it. Earth and sky, myth and technology have joined before and their gap is narrowing. Eden and Utopia, the first and last perfection, are homologous, imaginative constructs, mirror images of the same primal desire. Furthermore, the laws of myth and of science have this in common: both are partial codifications of reality, ways in which the mind imitates itself. Their structures, their functions, their predictive logic may not be identical; yet both are part of the human creative process. This assumption has led an eminent savant, Karl Friedrich von Weizsäcker, to explore the relation of yoga to physics at his institute near Munich. Again, neither myth nor science escapes the influence of the imagination. Einstein notes in *Ideas and Opinions*: 'The axiomatic basis of theoretical physics cannot be extracted from experience, but must be freely invented.' And J. Bronowski: 'The step by which a new axiom is added cannot itself by mechanized. It is a free play of the mind, an invention outside the logical processes. This is the central act of imagination in science and it is in all respects like any similar act in literature' [*The American Scholar* (Spring, 1966)]. Why, then, should we wonder that Isaac Newton labored secretly in alchemical pursuits, seeking the universal signature of life in all matter? And who knows what hieratic converse Newton carried on with Paracelsus across the centuries? And Kepler? The origins of mechanization are indeed more mystical than we suppose.[2]

That is a crucial intuition Arcadians tend to ignore – enough of dialectics; multilectics abound – even as they belabor Technophiles for their 'single vision and Newton's sleep.' Roszak's *Where the Wasteland Ends*, for instance, a work that engages some of my deepest sympathies, resolutely denies the potential of

---

[2] Arthur Koestler's *The Roots of Coincidence* (1972) amplifies this point in interesting ways; regrettably, I read it after the completion of this essay.

spiritual transformation contained in modern science. In so doing, it banishes imagination from a large area of consciousness, and evades the metaphysical meaning of change, innovation, and human evolution. I think it more likely that 'mystics' and 'mechanists,' as William Irwin Thompson calls them, will move toward a new issue:

> Western civilization is drawing to a close in an age of apocalyptic turmoil in which the old species, collectivizing mankind with machines, and the new species, unifying it in consciousness, are in collusion, with one another to end what we know as human nature.

> *At the Edge of History*

But the convergence of which I speak manifests itself not only in broad cultural contexts; it finds a voice in private lives when least we expect it. Here is the late Jimi Hendrix:

> It's music. . . . It's electric-icity . . . that will take us all to that spiritual high I call the electric church. . . .
> Mind expansion . . . I expanded mine the first time I turned on and plugged into an electric amplifier . . . someday it's going to carry me all the way there, too: pure mind.

> (bibliographic reference lost)

The mythological bard becomes a technological mystic. Consider now a high-flier of a different kind, not a freaked-out black musician but a shy exemplar of WASP rectitude. Here is Charles Lindbergh:

> Gradually, I diverted hours from aviation into biological research. How mechanical, how mystical was man? Could longevity be extended? . . .
> Decades spent in contact with science and its vehicles have directed my mind and senses to areas beyond their reach. I now see scientific accomplishment as a path, not an end; a path leading to and disappearing in mystery.

> *Life*, July 4, 1969

Lindbergh, the romantic adventurer, evolves into a technocrat, and the technocrat soon becomes a nature mystic. Does his vision blend into that of Jimi Hendrix? And those astronauts who have returned from space to explore occult sciences, the inner matrix?

Admittedly, a few instances do not prove a trend. Yet the instances are scattered throughout our lives, as if each of us were compelled to discover his own Beulah, his own 'place where Contrarieties are equally True.' We have seen computer art aspire to Pythagorean mysteries. And even the dark avatars have disengaged themselves from our dreams to become, as in '2001: A Space Odyssey,' technological prophecies.

The New Gnosticism eludes distinctions of the old mind, seeking yet unknown synergies.

Entropies:

> Does the mind also create unknown entropies?
> Ivan Karamazov: 'It's not that I don't accept
> God, you understand, it's the world created by
> him that I don't accept.
> And still it seems the same: Death, Dearth, Deceit.
> Everywhere the fullness of decay.

A Digression on Prometheus

Myth, Technology, and Literature meet in the various figures and fables of Prometheus.

As a Titan, Prometheus reverts to the chthonic forces of the Earth, of nature and instinct. Yet this Titan is clever; he allies himself with the new Parnassian order of Zeus. He reaches for the sky, and his name means foresight.

This Titan may be too clever. A natural trickster, he represents the creative principle of intelligence, creative yet essentially flawed because it is ignorant of its limit, its purpose. Prometheus begins lacking in wisdom.

> This, then, is the true basis for the respect shown to flame: if the child brings his hand close to the fire his father raps him over the knuckles with a ruler. Fire, then, can strike without having to burn. Whether this fire be flame or heat, lamp or stove, the parents' vigilance is the same. Thus fire is initially the object of a *general prohibition*; hence this conclusion: the social interdiction is our first *general knowledge* of fire. . . . Consequently, since the prohibitions are primarily social interdictions, the problem of obtaining a personal knowledge of fire is the problem of *clever disobedience*. The child wishes to do what his father does, but far away from his father's presence, and so like a little Prometheus he steals some matches.
>
> Gaston Bachelard, *The Psychoanalysis of Fire*

At Mecone, where gods and men come to settle their dispute, Prometheus tricks the gods of their share of the feast's meat. Henceforth, gods and men will stand apart. Prometheus defies Zeus again by bestowing fire on man, and bestowing mind (alphabet, number, all the practical and occult arts).

Prometheus: Titan of nature, creative trickster, master of technics. His sufferings begin. Perhaps he acquires dignity only on the terrible rock, spiked, chained, liver torn. Some say his torment is redemptive (Aeschylus), some say it proves only the absurdity of gods (Goethe). It is certain only that Prometheus suffers on Tartarus, and of his suffering creates an ambiguous prophecy. Or is it simply another trick? Probably not: this creature haruspicates with his own organs.

The prophecy promises – if you can penetrate it – deliverance: Deliverance of Prometheus, deliverance really of man. Does it also promise the abolition of the gods? The matter is not yet clear.

Consider the Promethean fable in these texts:

a   Hesiod's *Theogony, Works and Days*
b   Aeschylus' *Prometheus Bound*
c   Goethe's *Prometheus: A Dramatic Fragment*
d   Percy Bysshe Shelley's *Prometheus Unbound*
e   Mary Shelley's *Frankenstein*: or, *The Modern Prometheus*
f   Gerald Feinberg's *The Prometheus Project*

At the origin there is an action: trickery, defiance, creation, hope, an alliance with man that defines the human condition in terms of limits and transgressions, lapses and transcendences. Fire is stolen, yes, and with it consciousness is wrested from its divine place. But like fire, consciousness is perverse; it seeks its solid opposite; and it devours its own pain. Released in the world, consciousness questions all, questions matter and every matter, vexing itself to the last. What, then, is the Promethean answer?

a Hesiod largely reports the myth. Here and there he speaks with some didactic relish; but the redemption of Prometheus scarcely troubles his mind.

b Aeschylus adheres to prophecy and patience. Let us wait for the advent of heroes (Herakles) who can mediate between men and gods, between death and eternity. But who are 'heroes'? For us they are past; for Prometheus they are future. Or does Prometheus know some other secret about the end of Zeus?

c Goethe thinks revolt. As C.K. Kerényi puts it: 'Goethe's Prometheus is no God, no Titan, no man, but the immortal prototype of man as the original rebel and affirmer of his fate: the original inhabitant of the earth, seen as an antigod, as Lord of the Earth. In this connection he seems more Gnostic than Greek . . .' (*Prometheus: Archetypal Image of Human Existence*). Above all, he seems romantic and therefore nearly modern.

d Percy Bysshe Shelley will not fully explain his Prometheus, a creature both of will and vision. Shelley sees him as kin to Milton's Satan, yet exempt from the 'pernicious casuistry' of the rebel archangel. Bound by his own hate, by his own divided faculties, Prometheus strives to liberate himself from himself. To become whole again, he must find renewal in the Imagination. This Imagination is also teleological. At the end, Demogorgon assures Prometheus: '. . . to hope till Hope creates/From its own wreck the thing it contemplates / . . . This is alone Life, Joy, Empire, and Victory.'

e Mary Shelley divines the point at which scientism and idealism, reason and revelation, meet. It is a point shrouded in terror. Frankenstein, the modern Prometheus, surrenders to Albertus Magnus and Paracelsus before he masters the exact sciences. 'I was required,' he says, 'to exchange chimeras of boundless grandeur for realities of little worth.' But his great error lies elsewhere. Self-absorbed and self-obsessed, he blights the powers of sympathy in himself. His solitary 'fiend' returns to haunt him and haunt us, a ghastly embodiment of Prometheanism without responsibility or love. 'Hateful day when I received life!' the fiend cries. Is that the curse of life born of pure mind? Frankenstein and his fiend are neither twain nor really one; but in this they are compact: both together adumbrate the perils of consciousness in its (heroic-demonic) labors of self-creation. This Promethean adventure ends in a world not of fire but of ice.

f Feinberg has fewer qualms about Prometheanism, about the increase of self-consciousness without bound. That increase is his project, and his Prometheus is ourselves. His premise is this: 'My own feeling is that the despair of the conscious mind at the recognition of its own finitude is such that man cannot achieve an abiding contentment in his present form or anything like it. Therefore, I believe that a transformation of man into something very different from what he is now is called for.' Calmly, lucidly, simplistically, Feinberg argues that mankind needs to set long-range ends for itself, and to devise corresponding means. The goal he proposes as the most likely human destiny is Promethean indeed: man will become a total consciousness. 'Because of the inner logic of the conflict between the unity of one consciousness and the diversity of phenomena in the external world, there is probably no level of consciousness in which the conscious being will rest content until the sway of consciousness is extended indefinitely.' We do not require the theology of Teilhard de Chardin to achieve this extension nor the science fiction of Olaf Stapledon. 'I firmly believe,' Feinberg notes, 'that in trying to predict the future of technology, reality is likely to outstrip one's most extreme vision.' The postmodern Prometheus reaches for the fire in distant stars.

The Promethean archetype (and I have left out many versions, including Gide's) is a focus of convergences that reappear in our midst. The archetype contains a gnostic dream or project:

the creation and continual re-creation of human consciousness until consciousness redeems itself in complete knowledge.
The Project implies will: Prometheus wills, and even wills to be wrong.
It implies also prophecy: Prometheus, that far-seer, falls forward into the fullness of time.
Above all, it implies imagination: Prometheus attempts a radical reconstitution of the given world, the fixed order of things.

Hence Prometheanism remains the arch human endeavor for that 'visionary company' of poets about whom Harold Bloom has written vividly. Yes, there are acute dangers: solipsism, willfulness, self-corruption. Yet only in a spirit of extreme piety can we conclude, as William F. Lynch does in *Christ and Prometheus*, that 'Prometheanism is the project of a will separated from the imagination and from reality, separated, therefore, from most of the human.' Prometheanism, I think, veers towards the demonic when it denies the female principle of creation. Therefore, Aeschylus includes in his fable both Themis and Io, and Percy Shelley includes Asia. (Significantly, Mary Shelley's Frankenstein never consummates his relation to Elizabeth, nor is his relation to any man or woman but perfunctory.) There is a dark, moon-like side to Promethean nature, Kerényi insists, a side shaped by maternal forces. That side Prometheus can never afford to ignore.

No more than the Sky can ignore the Earth, or Technology, Mythology.

Myth

I do not for a moment suggest that the New Gnosticism reverts directly to those ancient or medieval cults expounded, say, in Hans Jonas' excellent work, *The Gnostic Religion*. Still, new and old forms of gnosis may find a common source in certain myths, in certain persistencies of human dreams.

As in the beginning, so in the end; as above, so below. Such are the principles of mythical thought. Yet myth appears mainly retrograde, its focus on some event in the immemorial past, *in illo tempore*. Into that far, dim, and sacred time, a privileged state of existence is usually projected. Is that state one of universal consciousness?

We know the story of the Garden of Eden. There is also that other strange story in the Book of Genesis:

> And the whole earth was of one language and of one speech. . . .
> And they said, Go to, let us build us a city and a tower whose top may reach unto heaven. . . .
> And the Lord said, Behold, *the people is one, and they have all one language*; and this they begin to do: and now nothing will be restrained from them, which they have *imagined* to do.
> Go to, let us go down, and there confound their language, that they may not understand one another's speech (italics mine).

Just what was that unitary language of mankind before a jealous God struck it into a babel of tongues? Music? Mathematics? Telepathy? *Finnegans Wake?* Chomsky's deep structures of the mind or linquistic universals ringing each to each? Vico's primal language by mute religious acts?

Or was it the same language Orpheus spoke in distant Thrace, singing Orpheus, he who became himself bird and tree and rock and wolf and cloud? A poetry of silence? The silence of mind and nature when they perfectly meet? The silence that Norman O. Brown calls 'the mother tongue?'

According to Erich Neumann, the ancient pleromatic or uroboric condition of existence is less conscious than unconscious, a state ruled by the Great Mother, a state, therefore, of *participation mystique*. Gnosticism, however, insists of spiritualizing this condition. 'Consequently, in Gnosticism,' Neumann says, 'the way of salvation lies in heightening consciousness and returning to the transcendent spirit, with loss of the unconscious side; whereas uroboric salvation through the Great Mother demands the abandonment of the conscious principle and a homecoming to the unconscious' (*The Origins and History of Consciousness*).

The shift, then, seems to be from unconsciousness to consciousness. Teilhard agrees: 'Mythology and folklore . . . are, in fact, filled with symbols and fables expressing the deeply rooted resolve of Earth to find its way to Heaven' (*The Future of Man*).

> Now the earth has been elevated symbolically into the heavens, matter has been spiritualized . . . NASA has given us empirical proof that the only world we can experience is conditioned by the mathematics of space. So the old dichotomy between spirit and matter, God and man, is finished.
> Joseph Campbell, *Psychology Today*, July, 1971, (on the moonwalks)

Yet if beginnings and ends are cognate, they must express, on some concealed level at least, a point of contact, perhaps even of identity. In the Jewish *Midrash*, for instance, the unborn babe in its womb carries a prophetic light around its head in which it sees the end of the world. (Recall, again, the eschatological image of the luminous intergalactic foetus at the end of '2001.') Furthermore, the mystic trance and shamanistic journey are both ways of recovering the first and last moment into the present.

Can it be, then, that the shift from unconsciousness to consciousness is true only in a partial perspective of reality? Can it be that conscious and unconscious are both implicit in the larger state of mind that myth projects far back into the sacred past and far forward into the sacred future? The state of mind that dream, vision, and trance recover in the im-mediate present?

> In India a whole literature has been devoted to explanations of this paradoxical relationship between what is pre-eminently unconscious – Matter – and pure 'consciousness,' the Spirit, which by its own mode of being is atemporal, free, uninvolved in the becoming. And one of the most unexpected results of this philosophic labor has been its conclusion that the Unconscious (i.e. *pakriti*), moving by a kind of 'teleological instinct,' imitates the behaviour of the Spirit; that the Unconscious behaves in such a way that its activity seems to *prefigure* the mode of being of the Spirit.
>
> Mircea Eliade, *Myths, Dreams, and Mysteries*

I doubt that such questions can be answered at this time in any terms that would satisfy those who insist on an answer; yet they are the very questions that myth raises repeatedly before the skeptical mind. Behind these questions lurks a desire, an intuition, perhaps even a gnosis, of a universal consciousness that transcends time, and transcends the organization of our most complex language.

Technology

We all acknowledge that science and its extension in technology are the major agents of transformation in our world. Sometimes we acknowledge it fearfully, and like Jacques Ellul in *The Technological Society*, we see only dark portents of our future. 'Enclosed within his artificial creation,' Ellul writes, 'man finds that there is "no exit"; that he cannot pierce the shell of technology to find again the ancient milieu to which he was adapted for hundreds of thousands of years.' Certainly, anyone over thirty will remember that the earth was a cleaner place in the past, more surprising, and more sensuously various. Science and technology, however, also operate in other dimensions, silently, invisibly, making always a little more life available to us. Even a pessimist such as Ellul predicts: 'There will be no need of attention or effort. What is needed will pass directly from the machine to the brain without going through consciousness.'

> Query
> The communication explosion is a product not only of technology but also of the population explosion. There are, literally, more brains on earth, working all at the same time. How does this fact affect the degree of sentience on earth?
> End of Query

Consider that familiar rubric, 'the communication explosion.' Quite precisely, a layer of sentience or awareness now envelops the earth, much like Teilhard's 'noösphere' moving ever outwards. Furthermore, communication itself is becoming increasingly immediate, requiring less and less mediation. It is a far cry from a stone hieroglyph weighing fifty tons to a wireless set weighing less than a pound. Even now we casually use 'slow-motion telepathy,' as Barry Schwartz puts it, devices that require only microseconds to elapse between coded communication, decoded message, and feedback [*Arts in Society* (Summer-Fall, 1972)]. The process can be extended by radio or laser far into the universe. There are also other means.

Tonight, if all goes well, the United States will launch the longest space mission in history. . . . It is the first official effort of mankind to draw attention to itself. As the vehicle, Pioneer 10, passes Jupiter, the gravity of that planet will seize it and hurl it out of the solar system. It will sail indefinitely through the vast reaches of the Milky Way Galaxy, carrying a message. . . .

The New York Times, Feb. 27, 1972

The message is not composed of quotations from Shakespeare. It includes visual representations of the male and female figures, and mathematical symbols referring to the structure of the hydrogen molecule and the frequency of pulsars. Can the basic rhythms of the universe provide a Pythagorean alphabet of universal intelligence?

Matter is giving way. As Buckminster Fuller puts it in *Intuiton*:

In short, physics has discovered
That there are no solids,
No continuous surfaces,
No straight lines;
Only waves,
No things,
Only energy *event* complexes,
Only behaviors,
Only verbs,
Only relationships. . . .

This discovery bolsters the process of 'ephemeralization': doing constantly more with constantly less. As a result, matter intervenes less and less in the transactions of mankind. And mind is free to pursue its destiny: to become the antientropic, or syntropic, force in the universe, gathering knowledge, expanding consciousness, regenerating *metaphysically* a *physically* decaying universe. In this ambience of sentience, telepathy becomes a new possibility. Thus Fuller again: 'I think that possibly within ten years we'll discover scientifically that what has been telepathy and has been thought of as very mysterious is, in fact, ultra, ultra, high frequency electromagnetic wave propagation' (*House and Garden*, May, 1972).

Telepathy, the gnostic language, in technology?

a   In 1954, Norbert Wiener, father of cybernetics, said in his book, *The Human Use of Human Beings*:

Let us admit that the idea that one might conceivably travel by telegraph, in addition to traveling by train or airplane, is not intrinsically absurd, far as it may be from realization.

Within two decades, we hear that Japanese researchers are trying to develop 'Intersex' or 'Cybersex': long-distance sex between consenting partners. The idea is to record as fully as possible – oh, much more than Masters and Johnson ever dreamed – all sexual stimuli, visual, tactile, auditory, olfactory, and even kinetic, and to transmit these stimuli, through electronic devices and computers, to sexual partners. Furthermore: 'By the end of the century, Hikari expects to see commercial Cybersex tapes, recorded by prominent male and female celebrities, generally available, much as one buys a phonograph recording today' (*Architectural Design*, September, 1969).

b   In 1964, Marshall McLuhan stated in his book *Understanding Media*:

Electric technology does not need words any more than the digital computer needs numbers. Electricity points the way to an extension of the process of consciousness itself, on a world scale, and without any verbalization whatever.

Within less than a decade, we hear that Dr José Delgado at Yale has implanted electrodes in special brain areas of a fighting bull. By pushing a button, he was able to stop the bull in the middle of the fiercest charge. There is nothing to prevent Dr Delgado from 'wiring' his bull to a computer, and programming its existence. There is no theoretical difficulty to prevent us from doing the same thing with human beings, as the television program 'Search' weekly suggests to oblivious audiences. 'Soon,' Dr Delgado says, 'with the aid of the computer, we may have direct contact between two different brains – without the participation of the senses' (*The New York Times Magazine*, November 15, 1970). Soon, too, with the aid of 'Dream Machines' acting directly on the brain, we may simulate, we may *possess*, any sensuous experience while sitting at home: a three-star meal at Lasserre in Paris or free-fall from a plane over the Andes.

We can imagine the utopian and dystopian possibilities of these and other developments; indeed, many of them have been imagined already in science fiction. Yet a hysterical rejection of science and its applications will not do; for there is no way for us to repress what we already know, what we already are and can be, without grave consequences to our psychic health. We must find a way to restore the deep rhythms of life within us without forgoing the dream that may be leaving its imprint – a biological code? – on our evolution.

Already, our senses are becoming coextensive with the cosmos: we can 'touch' things on the moon and 'hear' quasars at the edge of the universe. Slowly, we are all entering a multi-dimensional, non-Euclidean, and still sensuous – for sense and mind are one – realm of existence. We can begin to 'speak' to one another, and to the animals at hand, as well as to invite, as we have done, voices farther out in space to speak to us.

> Within the next decade or two the human species will establish communication with another species: nonhuman, alien, possibly extra-terrestrial, more probably marine; but definitely highly intelligent, perhaps even intellectual. . . . Our own spot in the universe, our own view of ourselves, will be tremendously modified if such a communication is established. Any other species that could talk with us on our own level will give us a perspective of which we can only be dimly aware at the present time. Our own communication among ourselves will be enhanced and improved by such contact. Our own views of one another will change radically under the influence of interspecies communication. The very fact that we try to communicate with them is an important indication of our own stage of evolutionary maturity.
>
> John C. Lilly *Man and Dolphin*

We can further insist that technology become not only pollution-free but also invisible. There are those who believe that technology can imitate the inherent order of things. Here, for instance, is John Cage:

> Just as Fuller domes (dome within dome, translucent, plants between) will give impression of living in no home at all (outdoors), so all technology must move toward way things were before man began changing them: identification with nature in her manner of operation, complete mystery.
>
> *A Year from Monday*

In short, like myth, technology suggests that man is creating a universal consciousness which renders mediated action and speech gradually obsolete. A measure of radical American Innocence is required to hold this view. Cage has it. So has Charles Lindbergh, who may be even a greater technological gnostic:

> Will we discover that only *without* spaceships can we reach the galaxies; that only *without* cyclotrons can we know the interior of atoms?
>
> *Life*, July 4, 1969

Jonathan Livingston Seagull speaking?

Literature

Men of letters tend to believe that the word gives the mind its flesh; and critics are even more stringent than the authors they criticize in defense of that view. Literature is the keystone of the humanities; it stands, like Man, between Earth and Sky, severed from neither. We expect it, therefore, to show a certain recalcitrance toward the im-mediate mind.

Yet there are signal exceptions. Giordano Bruno, for instance: 'The actual and the possible are not different in eternity.' Or William Blake: 'Mental things are alone real; what is called corporeal, nobody knows of its dwelling place: it is in fallacy, & its existence an imposture . . .' ('A Vision of the Last Judgment'). Curiously enough, Blake's contemporary, Donatien Alphonse François de Sade, would have agreed entirely, for reasons demoniac of his own. One is tempted to argue – as I have in *The Dismemberment of Orpheus* – that Blake and Sade stand at the threshold of the modern experience, exemplars of two kinds of gnosticism. But there are, of course, other kinds, the gnostic impulse, restricted as it may be in literature, touches visionary, antinomian, or romantic writers of every age.

The unmediated will, however, asserts itself as a cultural phenomenon in the late eighteenth century. The artist begins his journey to the interior, there to end by discovering the languages of silence. Hegel provides Romanticism with a point of philosophical reference, and also of reaction.

> In both the early Romantics and Hegel, the human mind puts forward a total claim for itself, a claim in which revolution and eschatology are uneasily mingled. The world must become imagination and poetry, say the Romantics; and Hegel says, the world must become rational consciousness. But the poetry meant by the Romantics, and the rational consciousness meant by Hegel, have much in common: above all the ambition of the human mind to dominate the real world to the point of usurping its place.
>
> Erich Heller, *The Artist's Journey into the Interior*

The world becomes poetry even as the final unfolding of the World-Spirit makes all poetry redundant, all art obsolete. That is the paradoxical prophecy of the Romantic 'soul.'

The journey into the interior is a journey toward consciousness, toward mind claiming more and more for itself in terms less and less conditional. It is a gnostic journey only in the very broadest sense, and its shadowy paths may be discerned in various human endeavors. Philosophy, for instance, moving from Hegel to Heidegger, Husserl, Sartre, and Wittgenstein, finds itself in an immense new field of subjectivity which it hopelessly sets out to survey. Literary criticism follows a similar path in the different works of Poulet, Blanchot, Barthes, Foucault, Derrida, a path that leaves 'texts' behind, wanders brilliantly through language, and vanishes finally into consciousness.

As for literature itself, we have heard its story told many times, going as far back as Erich Kahler does in *The Inward Turn of Narrative*, or as far forward as Sharon Spencer in *Space, Time and Structure in the Modern Novel*. From the great modernists – Valéry, Proust, Rilke, Kafka, Joyce, Yeats, Pound, Eliot, Stevens, etc. – to the enigmatic postmodernists – Beckett, Borges, Genet, Butor, Cortazar, Barth, etc. – the tendency of literature has been to escape itself, to subvert or transcend its forms, to re-imagine imagination; and, as it were, to create a state of unmediated literary awareness. Yet a generalization of this kind cries for qualifications that I can scarcely begin to make here. We need a narrower focus: not gnostic tendencies in their shadowy outlines but the New Gnosticism in American literature particularly. This will bring us eventually to science fiction.

An Aside: Burroughs and Others

Ever since *Naked Lunch*, William Burroughs has declared himself, in words certainly, the enemy of language: 'To speak is to lie'; 'Rub out the Word Forever.' Or in *The Ticket That Exploded*: 'The word is now a virus. . . . The word may once have been a healthy neural cell. It is now a parasitic organism that invades and damages the central nervous system. Modern man has lost the option of silence.'

Burroughs' icy rage against language is partly self-parodic. But it is also directed against the Old Consciousness, all its deceptions, inhibitions, and controls, which he identifies with the Word. Above all, his aversion sustains a failed dream of pure consciousness. 'Words – at least the way we use them – can stand in the way of what I call non-body experience,' he says. 'It's time we thought about leaving the body behind' (*Writers at Work: The Paris Review Interviews, Third Series*). And leaving also the earth behind, Burroughs insists; for in doing so, we gain a new perspective on our conditioned existence, on the meaning of gravity. Burroughs, then, is a technological gnostic; quite explicitly, he hopes that science will help to remake man. Autonomic processes, hallucinogenic drugs, electric stimulation of the brain, telepathy and telekinesis – all these interest him because they exercise the powers of the mind to transform itself, to act directly upon itself without tiresome interventions of body or matter ('Interview,' *Penthouse*, March, 1972).

But is the case of Burroughs relevant to our general cultural condition, or is it simply a terminal case of literature? The answer, I suspect, depends on how we value other writers, mentalists all of different kinds. In the background stands Wallace Stevens: 'Modern reality is a reality of decreation, in which our revelations are not the revelations of belief, but the precious portents of our own powers. The greatest truth we could hope to discover . . . is that man's truth is the final resolution of everything.' Closer to us stand Nabokov, Beckett, Borges. And closer still, consider the playful 'ultimacy' of John Barth's *Chimera*; the entropic indeterminacy of Thomas Pynchon's *The Crying of Lot 49*; the pop or 'dreck' surrealism of Donald Barthelme's *City Life*; the oneiric death-denying abandon of Robert Coover's *The Universal Baseball Association*, the epistemological introversion of Rudolph Wurlitzer's *Flats*; the self-reflexive exuberance of Raymond Federman's *Double or Nothing* and its typographic laughter; and the regenerative narrative blanks of Ronald Sukenick's *Out*. Admittedly these fictions are distinct, and their postmodern authors even more so. But do not these authors share with Burroughs a complex desire to dissolve the world – or at least to recognize its dissolution – and to remake it as an absurd or decaying or parodic or private – *and still imaginative* – construct? Geomancers more than mystics, they still abolish the terror, dreariness, and hazards of given things by FANTASY. Is this FANTASY, then, a novel type of secular gnosis? Perhaps like that 'obscure man' in Borges' 'The Circular Ruins,' we all dream our successor into being. Perhaps we need a still narrower focus.

> The contemporary writer – the writer who is acutely in touch with the life of which he is part – is forced to start from scratch: Reality doesn't exist, time doesn't exist, personality doesn't exist. God was the omniscient author, but he died; now no one knows the plot, and since our reality lacks the sanction of a creator, there's no guarantee as to the authenticity of the received version.
>
> Ronald Sukenick, *The Death of the Novel and Other Stories*
> Also quoted in Jerome Klinkowitz & John Somer (eds),
> *Innovative Fiction: Stories for the Seventies.*

Science Fiction

A sharper view of the New Gnosticism in American literature would focus on science fiction. This may appear the easy way out of certain cultural and aesthetic complexities. Yet it is right for us to be curious about science fiction at this time. It is the imaginative form that creates new myths of our machines, new models of our social existence, new images of our destiny in the universe. As fable, as satire, as prophecy, then, the best science fiction deserves a quality of critical attention that we have tended to deny it. This attention may be forthcoming, particularly since so many 'serious' novelists – as different from one another as Burgess, Burroughs, and Vonnegut – are finding the genre congenial.

And here is the point: some of the finest science fiction concerns itself, like its two parents, Myth and Technology, with the question of a universal consciousness. Sometimes the assumption appears to be that wherever life obtains in heightened forms, intelligence also functions in im-mediate ways. At other times, the assumption is simply that human minds are good enough to imagine better minds with, but good for little more.

European science fiction has richly rendered its own versions of this theme (see Fred Hoyle's *The Black Cloud*, Olaf Stapledon's *Last and First Men*, and Stanislaw Lem's *Solaris*). My examples, however, will refer to four works that are part of the American scene.

a Robert Heinlein's *Stranger in a Strange Land*
b Alfred Bester's *The Demolished Man*
c Theodore Sturgeon's *More Than Human*
d Ursula LeGuin's *The Lathe of Heaven*

a   There are rumors that Heinlein's famous work, full of dull and jolly claptrap, has influenced the commune of Charles Manson. But the erotic and religious cults that fill the novel are less crucial than the 'grokking' powers of its presumably Martian hero. These cults reveal that Earthlings are still corporeal, that their imperfect grokking faculties must be mediated mystically through the flesh. Grokking itself means complete identification, total understanding, a momentary fusion of two beings into a larger awareness. The concept carries the mythic feeling of *participation mystique* and the technological idea of telepathy to their point of contact.

b   Bester's novel shows that in some distant future the fate of the human race depends on a nearly incorruptible society of mind readers, called 'Espers' or, colloquially, 'peepers.' Third-class peepers can penetrate the conscious mind of 'normals'; second-class, the pre-conscious mind; and first-class, the deep subconscious. But the whole society of mind readers constitutes a link with the future development of man, his evolution toward a larger consciousness. When a powerful, egotistic, and homicidal tycoon threatens this evolution, his 'normal' brain is flooded with the collective psychic energy of all the peepers. Thus he receives illumination, perceives the mystery of his own identity and of cosmic love. He is 'demolished' only as a willful and isolate self, caged in its obsolete needs.

c   But the most subtle of these science fictions may be Sturgeon's. The time is the present; somewhere in the woods of America a community accidentally takes shape. This community is composed of a grown telepathic idiot; twin little black girls who are teleports; a slightly older white telekineticist; and her charge, a mongoloid infant with the mind of a computer and extraterrestrial connections. Solitary and freakish apart, together they form a preternatural organism, a new kind of intelligent life, called *homo gestalt*, that also possesses the means to conquer gravity. 'Gravitics,' it seems, would add Psyche to the Unified Field that already includes Matter, Energy, Space, and Time. But as it turns out, *homo gestalt* must learn from *homo sapiens* something about a moral ethos before making its quantum spiritual jump.

d   Dreams create and literally re-create reality, which may itself be the final version of dream, in *The Lathe of Heaven*. The year is around 2002. Under the hypnotic influence of Dr Haber and his electric Augmentor, Orr is made to dream utopia. Orr's dreams 'solve' the problems of population, pollution, war, and race; these dreams expunge six billion people and convert an alien race of galactic invaders into wise allies. Yet somehow things always get a little worse after each of these effective and retroactive dreams. For the central argument of the book is between being and becoming, change and stillness. Orr's dreams, as the aliens teach him, are part of a cosmic, will-less, incommunicable force: 'Everything dreams. The play of form, of being, is the dreaming of substance. . . . But when the mind becomes conscious, when the rate of evolution speeds up, then you have to be careful.' The cautionary note is struck by Chuang Tse in an epigraph: 'To let understanding stop at what cannot be understood is a high attainment. Those who cannot do it will be destroyed on the lathe of heaven.' So much for the omnipotence of mind.

These four science fictions are by no means unique in presaging – and warning against! – the transformation of man into a vast noetic reality, a universal consciousness capable of im-mediate exchanges of knowledge. Can such anticipatory myths become slow, self-fulfilling prophecies? Or is the future simply our most widely shared, treasured, and revised fantasy?

Coda

Once again, I should stress that I am not concerned here with the old Gnostic religions, their theories of creation and apocalypse, their dualisms and demi-urges, their Elohims, Sophias, Abraxas, and Helens. I am concerned, however, with a new sense of the im-mediacy of Mind, of complete gnosis or knowledge. This sense implies a vast, new role of Consciousness in the universe. The role was vaguely prefigured by the ancient Gnostics, authors of a passionate subjectivity.

But the New Gnosticism does not rest only on mystical experiences of mythical archetypes; it insinuates itself into postmodern literature; and it appears as a condition of our science, of our technology. The New Gnosticism, in fact, presupposes convergences that are silently altering the definitions of culture.

> (Brown's mythical vision of polymorphous perversity and McLuhan's technological idea of electricity as a human nervous system both decenter the ego and diffuse the brain; and Marcuse's new Reality Principle assumes an order 'under which a new sensibility and a desublimated scientific intelligence would combine in the creation of an *aesthetic ethos*.')

Will such convergences end by changing the definitions of man?

I have spoken in a speculative voice. I have assumed, as some others have, that we are witnessing a radical transformation of man. But there are alterna-tives to this assumption. We may, for instance, obliterate ourselves as a race. Or we may develop apace, doing more or less what we do now, without any radical change in our destiny. Or again, we may indeed change radically in a way that entails no universal consciousness. Everything that rises must con-verge? Perhaps it is also everything that falls.

I have spoken in a speculative voice to raise questions, not to foreclose them; but speculations may also clear the way for theory, judgment, or belief. No doubt every reader will have his responses. The questions that remain concern us, more specifically, as readers and writers of literature. How shall we respond to these new realities? Should we sever ourselves from the sources of imagina-tion and change in our time? Can we enter the gnostic dream to give it a larger and richer shape? Or will we continue to sustain ourselves on our own traditions, with piety, skepticism, and complex hope?

An Exemplum: Norman Mailer

He has always strained to become exemplary in America. His home, we know, is the domain of the Self: power, instinct, vision. Closer to the older magic than to the new, he has been a deep and ambiguous critic of technology. Yet here, perhaps, is a failure: he conceals from himself what I think he senses, that magic and technology meet at a vital point in human evolution. Mailer, at any rate, sees that shamans and computers enjoy their intercourse in the surreal world of today and tomorrow:

Yet even this model of the future was too simple. For the society of the rational and the world of the irrational would be without boundaries. Computersville had no cure for skin disease but filth in the wound, and the guru had no remedy for insomnia but a trip to the moon, so people would be forever migrating between the societies. Sex would be a new form of currency in both worlds – on that you could count.

Of a Fire on the Moon

Sex – and also its primordial equivalents. Gravity and Light? Who knows what the sexual consciousness – body, seeking body, energy freed from itself – might become?

The example Mailer sets before the community of letters is that of its own endeavor, that of the literary act itself, in our time. His vaulting ambition, imagination, irony attempt to comprehend some final facts and fancies of the age. But the recalcitrance of our palpable life, the persistence of our prejudice and pain, contrast so sharply with the invisible possibilities of the human race that even the most extreme vision must hedge itself. In our quotidian existence, hunger and anger still rule the day far more than imagination prevails.

End of Exemplum

The New Gnosticism assumes that the more consciousness increases, the more fact and fancy will converge, the more is and can, sensation and thought, become one. The literary imagination can only hold the New Gnosticism in suspicion; the latter doubts that Imagination will still find its primary fulfillment in Literature.

Quite probably the great chain of being, extending from hell to heaven, running through all the intermediate forms of creation, is broken. Or more precisely: the great chain of being is reconstituting itself in one great link or loop of consciousness, not linear but multiform. Men and Women no longer stand between Earth and Sky; they are becoming both and either.

Yet how many within or without academies of mind of every kind can truly perceive where this metaphor of our friend (Blake) ends? (Not I).

. . . each grain of Sand,
Every stone on the land,
Each rock & each hill,
Each fountain & rill,
Each herb & each tree,
Mountain, hill, earth, & sea,
Cloud, Meteor, & Star,
Are Men Seen Afar.

[3] Epigraph references: *The Tibetan Book of the Dead*; *The Gospel of Truth*; William Blake, *Jerusalem*; Ralph Waldo Emerson, *Nature*; Henri Bergson, *The Two Sources of Morality and Religion*; Sir James Jeans, *The Mysterious Universe*; Teilhard de Chardin, *Building the Earth*; Marshall McLuhan, *Understanding Media*; R. Buckminster Fuller, *Intuition*; Gerald Feinberg, *The Prometheus Project*; Norman O. Brown, *Love's Body*; Louis Kahn, *Time*, January 15, 1973.

8   William Spanos

From *the Detective and the Boundary: Some Notes on the Postmodern Literary Imagination*

Boundary 2, volume 2; 1, 1972, pp 147–68.

As the profound influence of certain kinds of literature on existential philosophy suggests, the impulse of the Western writer to refuse to fulfill causal
expectations, to refuse to provide 'solutions' for the 'crime' of existence,
historically precedes the existential critique of Westernism. We discover it in,
say, Euripides' *Orestes*, Shakespeare's problem plays, the tragi-comedies of
the Jacobeans, Wycherley's *The Plain Dealer*, Dickens's *Edwin Drood*, and
more recently in Tolstoy's *The Death of Ivan Ilych*, Dostoevsky's *Notes from
Underground*, Alfred Jarry's *Ubu Roi*, Kafka's *The Trial*, Pirandello's *Six
Characters in Search of an Author*, and even in T.S. Eliot's *Sweeney Agonistes*.
(These are works, it is worth observing, the radical temporality of which does
not yield readily to the spatial methodology of the New Criticism, which has its
source in the iconic art of Symbolist modernism.) In *Notes from Underground*,
for example, Dostoevsky as editor 'concludes' this anti-novel:

> The 'notes' of this paradoxalist do not end here. However, he could not resist and
> continued them. But it also seems to be that we may stop here.

Fully conscious of the psychological need of the 'straightforward' Gentleman
of the hyper-Westernized St Petersburg – the 'most intentional city in the whole
world' – Dostoevsky refuses to transform the discordant experience of this
terrible voice into a 'sublime and beautiful,' that is, 'straightforward' and
distancing *story*. So also in *Six Characters in Search of an Author*. Seeking relief
from the agony of their ambiguous relationships, the characters express their
need to give artistic shape to the 'infinite absurdities' of their lives. But when
the Director (I want to emphasize the coercive implications of the word) – who
hates their authorless, i.e., inconclusive drama ('it seems to me you are trying
to imitate the manner of a certain author whom I heartily detest') – tries to
make a well-made play, a melodrama in the manner of Eugène Scribe or
Alexander Dumas *fils* of their dreadful experience ('What we've got to do is to
combine and group up all the facts in one simultaneous close-knit action'), they
refuse to be coerced into that comforting but fraudulent 'arrangement.'
Similarly in *Sweeney Agonistes*, just as Sweeney will not allow his anxious
listeners to package the terrible 'anti-Aristotelian' murder story he tells them
('Well here again that don't apply / But I've gotta use words when I talk to
you'), so Eliot in his great anti-detective play will not allow his audience of
middle class fugitives to fulfill their positivistically conditioned need to experience the explanatory and cathartic conclusion. Rather, like Dostoevsky, he
ends the play inconclusively with the dreadful knocking at the door.

But in each of these earlier works, one has the feeling that the writer has only
reluctantly resisted the conventional ending. It is actually the unconscious

pressure of the powerfully felt content – the recognition and acknowledgment of contingency, or what I prefer to call the ontological invasion – that has driven him into undermining the traditional Aristotelian dramatic or fictional form. The existential diagnosis and critique of the humanistic tradition had not yet emerged to suggest the formal implications of metaphysical disintegration. Only after the existentialist philosophers revealed that the perception of the universe as a well-made fiction, obsessive to the Western consciousness, is in reality a self-deceptive effort to evade the anxiety of contingent existence by objectifying and taking hold of 'it,' did it become clear to the modern writer that the ending-as-solution is the literary agency of this evasive objectification. And it is the discovery of the 'anti-formal' imperatives of absurd time for fiction and drama and poetry (though poetry, which in our time means lyric poetry, as Sartre has said in *What is Literature?*, tends by its natural amenability to spatialization to be non-historical) that constitutes the most dynamic thrust of the contemporary Western literary imagination and differentiates the new from Symbolist modernism.

Taking their lead from the existentialists, the postmodern absurdists – writers like the Sartre of *Nausea* and *No Exit*, the Beckett of *Watt* and the Molloy trilogy as well as *Waiting for Godot*, *Endgame*, and *Krapp's Last Tape* (the titles should not be overlooked), Ionesco, Genet, Pinter, Frisch, Sarraute, Pynchon, etc. – thus view the well-made play or novel (*la pièce bien faite*), the post-Shakespearian allotrope of the Aristotelian form, as the inevitable analogue of the well-made positivistic universe delineated by the post-Renaissance humanistic structure of consciousness. More specifically, they view the rigid deterministic plot of the well-made fiction, like that of its metaphysical counterpart, as having its source in bad faith. I mean (to appropriate the metaphor Heidegger uses to remind us of the archetypal flight of the Apollonian Orestes from the *Erinyes*) the self-deceptive effort of the 'fallen "they"' (*das verfalene 'Man'*) 'to flee in the face of death' and the ominous absurd by finding objects for the dread of Nothing, that is, *by imposing coercively a distancing and tranquillizing ending or* telos *from the beginning on the invading contingencies of existence.* What Roquentin says in Sartre's *Nausea* about *l'aventure* (which is the aesthetic equivalent of the Bouville merchants' arrogant positivism – their certain 'right to exist') in distinguishing it from *la vie* is precisely what the postmodern absurdists seem to imply in their 'de-composed' drama and fiction about the modern humanistic structure of consciousness and its metaphysical and aesthetic paradigms:

> . . . everything changes when you tell about life [*raconte la vie:* Sartre seems to be pointing here to the relationship between the mathematical associations of the etymology and the concept of story or well-made plot and, ultimately, the re-counting of existence from the vantage point of the end]; it's a change no one notices: . . . Things happen one way and we tell about them in the opposite sense. You seem to start at the beginning: 'It was a fine autumn evening in 1922. I was a notary clerk in Marommes.' And in reality you have started at the end. It was there, invisible and present, it is the one which gives to words the pomp and value of a beginning. 'I was out walking, I had left the town without realizing it, I was thinking about my money troubles.' This sentence, taken simply for what it is, means that the man was absorbed, morose, a hundred leagues from adventure, exactly in the mood to let things happen without noticing them. But the end is there, transforming everything.

For us, the man is already the hero of the story. His moroseness, his money troubles are much more precious than ours, they are all gilded by the light of future passions. And the story goes on in the reverse: instants have stopped piling themselves in a lighthearted way one on top of the other [as in life], they are snapped up by the end of the story which draws them and each one of them in turn, draws out the preceding instant: 'It was night, the street was deserted.' *The phrase is cast out negligently, it seems superfluous [superflue:* an equivalent of *de trop,* Sartre's term for the condition of man in the primordial realm of existence which is prior to essence]; *but we do not let ourselves be caught and put it aside: this is a piece of information whose value we shall subsequently appreciate.* And we feel that the hero has lived all the details of this night like annunciations, promises, or even that he lives only those that were promises, blind and deaf to all that did not herald adventure. . . .

I wanted the moments of my life to follow and order themselves like those of a life remembered. You might as well try and catch time by the tail. (My emphasis.)

In short, the postmodern absurdists interpret this obsession for what Roland Barthes, perhaps with Sartre in mind, calls the fiction of 'the preterite mode,' for the rigidly causal plot of the well-made work of the humanistic tradition, as catering to and thus further hardening the expectation of – and aggravating the need for – the rational solution generated by the scientific analysis of man-in-the-world. As the reference to the technique of the detective story in the passage from *Nausea* suggests, these expectations demand the kind of fiction and drama that achieves its absolute fulfillment in the utterly formularized clock-work certainties of plot in the innumerable detective drama series – *Perry Mason, The FBI, Hawaii 5-0, Mannix, Mission Impossible,* etc. – which use up, or rather, 'kill,' prime television time. Ultimately they also demand the kind of social and political organization that finds its fulfillment in the imposed certainties of the well-made world of the totalitarian state, where investigation or inquisition in behalf of the achievement of a total, that is, pre-ordained or teleologically determined structure – a 'final solution' – is the defining activity. It is, therefore, no accident that the paradigmatic archetype of the postmodern literary imagination is the anti-detective story (and its anti-psychoanalytical analogue), the formal purpose of which is to evoke the impulse to 'detect' and/ or to psychoanalyze in order to violently frustrate it by refusing to solve the crime (or find the cause of the neurosis). I am referring, for example, to works like Kafka's *The Trial,* T.S. Eliot's *Sweeney Agonistes* (subtitled significantly *Fragments of an Aristophanic Melodrama*), Graham Greene's *Brighton Rock,* Arthur Koestler's *Arrival and Departure,* Beckett's *Watt* and *Molloy* (especially the Moran section), Ionesco's *Victims of Duty,* Robbe-Grillet's *The Erasers,* and Nathalie Sarraute's *Portrait of a Man Unknown* (which Sartre, in his characteristically seminal way, refers to as an 'anti-novel that reads like a detective story' and goes on to characterize as 'a parody on the novel of "quest" into which the author has introduced a sort of impassioned amateur detective' who 'doesn't find anything . . . and gives up the investigation as a result of a metamorphosis; just as though Agatha Christie's detective, on the verge of unmasking the villain, had himself suddenly turned criminal').

In *Victims of Duty,* for example, the Detective, like Sherlock Holmes, is certain in the beginning that 'everything hangs together, everything can be comprehended in time' and thus 'keeps moving forward . . . one step at a time, tracking down the extraordinary': 'Mallot, with a "t" at the end, or Mallod with a "d".' Holmes, of course, eventually gets his man (though the foregone certainty, especially of the monstrous evilness of the criminal, should not obscure the grimness of the metaphor that characterizes Conan Doyle's fictional and real universe): 'This chance of the picture has supplied us with one of our most obvious missing links. We have him, Watson, we have him, and I dare swear that before tomorrow he will be fluttering in our net as helpless as one of his own butterflies. A pin, a cork, and a card, and we add him to the Baker Street collection!' But the Detective in the process of Ionesco's play cannot make Choubert 'catch hold of' the elusive Mallot. Despite his brutal efforts to 'plug the gaps [of his wayward memory]' by stuffing food down his throat, what he 'finds' is only the bottomless hole of Choubert's being: that is, Nothing. And so, instead of ending with 'A Retrospective' that ties everything together (clarifies the mystery) as in *The Hound of the Baskervilles*, *Victims of Duty* 'ends' in verbal, formal and, analogously, ontological disintegration. The disturbing mystery still survives the brutal coercion.

What I am suggesting is that it was the recognition of the ultimately 'totalitarian' implications of the Western structure of consciousness – of the expanding analogy that encompasses art, politics, and metaphysics in the name of the security of rational order – that compelled the postmodern imagination to undertake the deliberate and systematic subversion of plot – the beginning, middle, and end structure – which has enjoyed virtually unchallenged supremacy in the Western literary imagination ever since Aristotle or, at any rate, since the Renaissance interpreters of Aristotle claimed it to be the most important of the constitutive elements of literature. In the familiar language of Aristotle's *Poetics*, then, the postmodern strategy of de-composition exists to generate rather than to purge pity and terror; to disintegrate, to atomize rather than to create a community. In the more immediate language of existentialism, it exists to generate anxiety or dread: to dislodge the tranquillized individual from the 'at-home of publicness,' from the domesticated, the scientifically charted and organized familiarity of the totalized world, to make him experience what Roquentin sees from the top of a hill overlooking the not so 'solid, bourgeois city,' Bouville:

> They come out of their offices after their day of work, they look at the houses and the squares with satisfaction, they think it is *their* city, a good, solid, bourgeois city. They aren't afraid, they feel at home. . . . They have proof, a hundred times a day, that everything happens mechanically, that the world obeys fixed, unchangeable laws. In a vacuum all bodies fall at the same rate of speed, the public park is closed at 4 p.m. in winter, at 6 p.m. in summer, lead melts at 335 degrees centigrade. . . . And all this time, great, vague nature has slipped into their city, it has infiltrated everywhere, in their house, in their office, in themselves. It doesn't move, it stays quietly and they are full of it inside, they breathe it, and they don't see it, they imagine it to be outside, twenty miles from the city. I *see* it, I *see* this nature. . . . I know that its obedience is idleness, I know it has no laws: what they take for constancy is only habit and it can change tomorrow.
>
> What if something were to happen? What if something suddenly started throbbing? Then they would notice it was there and they'd think their hearts were going to burst. Then what good would their dykes, bulwarks, power houses, furnaces and pile drivers be to them?

This aesthetic of de-composition is not, as is too often protested, a purely negative one. For the *depaysment* – the ejection from one's 'homeland' – as Ionesco calls it after Heidegger, which is effected by the carefully articulated discontinuities of absurdist literary form, reveals the *Urgrund*, the primordial not-at-home, where dread, as Kierkegaard and Heidegger and Sartre and Tillich tell us, becomes not just the agency of despair but also and simultaneously of hope, that is, of freedom and infinite possibility:

> [If] a man were a beast or an angel [Kierkegaard, echoing Pascal, writes in *The Concept of Dread*], he would not be able to be in dread. Since he is a synthesis he can be in dread, and the greater the dread, the greater the man. And no Grand Inquisitor has in readiness such terrible tortures as has dread, and no spy knows how to attack more artfully the man he suspects, choosing the instant when he is weakest, nor knows how to lay traps where he will be caught and ensnared as dread knows how, and no sharpwitted judge knows how to interrogate, to examine the accused, as dread does, which never lets him escape, neither by diversion nor by noise, neither at work nor at play, neither by day nor by night.
>
> Dread is the possibility of freedom. Only this dread is by the aid of faith absolutely educative, *laying bare as it does all finite aims and discovering all their deceptions.* . . .
>
> He who is educated by dread is educated by possibility, and only the man who is educated by possibility is educated in accordance with his infinity. (My emphasis.)

Thus on the psychological level too this dislodgement not only undermines the confident positivistic structure of consciousness that really demands answers it already has (i.e., the expectation of *catharsis*). It also compels the new self to ask, like Orestes or Job – the Job who, against the certain advice of his comforters, the advocates of the Law, 'spoke of God that which is right' – the ultimate, the authentically humanizing questions: *die Seinfragen*, as Heidegger puts it. To evoke the buried metaphor I have hinted at in the passage from *The Concept of Dread*, the postmodern anti-literature of the absurd exists to strip its audience of positivized fugitives of their protective garments of rational explanation and leave them standing naked and unaccommodated – poor, bare, forked animals – before the encroaching Nothingness. Here, to add another dimension to the metaphor, in the precincts of their last evasions, in the realm of silence, where the language that objectifies (clothes), whether the syntax of plot or of sentence, as Sweeney says, 'don't apply' (is seen to be mere noise), they must choose authentically (*eigentlich*: in the context of the naked my-ownness of death and Nothingness) whether to capitulate to Nothingness, to endure it (this is what Tillich calls the courage to be in the face of despair), to affirm the Somethingness of Nothingness 'by virtue of the absurd,' or to risk letting Being be. It is this metaphor of divestment and silence, which finds its most forceful pre-modern expression in such works as *King Lear*, *Fear and Trembling*, *Crime and Punishment*, and *The Death of Ivan Ilych*, that gives postmodern anti-novels and anti-plays like Sartre's *Nausea* and *No Exit*, Ionesco's *Victims of Duty*; Tardieu's *The Keyhole (La Serrure)*; Beckett's *Watt* and *Molloy*; Genet's *The Maids*; Pinter's *The Homecoming* and Sarraute's *Tropisms* their special ambience.

We have seen during the twentieth century the gradual emergence of an articulate minority point of view – especially in the arts – that interprets

Western technological civilization as a progress not towards the Utopian *polis* idealized by the Greeks, but towards a rationally mass produced City which, like the St Petersburg of Dostoevsky's and Tolstoy's novels, is a microcosm of universal madness. This point of view involves a growing recognition of one of the most significant paradoxes of modern life: that in the pursuit of order the positivistic structure of consciousness, having gone beyond the point of equilibrium, generates radical imbalances in nature which are inversely proportional to the intensity with which it is coerced. However, it has not been able to call the arrogant anthropomorphic Western mind and its well-made universe into serious question.

As I have suggested, this is largely because the affirmative formal strategy of Symbolist modernism was one of religio-aesthetic withdrawal from existential time into the eternal simultaneity of essential art. The Symbolist movement, that is, tried to deconstruct language, to drive it out of its traditional temporal orbit – established by the humanistic commitment to *kinesis* and utility and given its overwhelming socio-literary authority, as Marshall McLuhan has shown, by the invention of the printing press – in order to achieve iconic or, more inclusively, spatial values. Its purpose was to undermine its utilitarian function in order to disintegrate the reader's linear-temporal orientation and to make him *see* synchronically – as one sees a painting or a circular mythological paradigm – what the temporal words express. In other words, its purpose was to *reveal* (in the etymological sense of 'unveil') the whole and by so doing raise the reader above the messiness or, as Yeats calls the realm of existence in 'Phases of the Moon,' 'that raving tide,' into a higher and more permanent reality.

This impulse to transcend the historicity of the human condition in the 'allatonceness' (the term is McLuhan's) of the spatialized work of Symbolist literary art is brought into remarkably sharp focus when one perceives the similarity between the poetic implicit in W.B. Yeats's 'Sailing to Byzantium' with Stephen Dedalus's aesthetic of *stasis* in *Portrait of the Artist as a Young Man*, which has often been taken, especially by the New Critics, as a theoretical definition of modern Symbolist literary form:

> You see I use the word *arrest*. I mean that the tragic emotion is static. Or rather the dramatic emotion is. The feelings excited by improper art are kinetic, desire and loathing. Desire urges us to possess, to go to something; loathing urges us to abandon, to go from something. These are kinetic emotions. The arts which excite them, pornographical or didactic, are therefore improper arts. The esthetic emotion (I use the general term) is therefore static. The mind is arrested and raised above desire and loathing.

> O sages standing in God's holy fire
> As in the gold mosaic of a wall,
> Come from the holy fire, perne in a gyre,
> And be the singing-masters of my soul.
> Consume my heart away; sick with desire
> And fastened to a dying animal
> It knows not what it is; and gather me
> Into the artifice of eternity.

> Once out of nature I shall never take
> My bodily form from any natural thing,

> But such a form as Grecian goldsmiths make
> Of hammered gold and gold enamelling
> To keep a drowsy Emperor awake;
> Or set upon a golden bough to sing
> To lords and ladies of Byzantium
> Of what is past, or passing, or to come.

For Stephen, growing up has been a terrible process of discovering the paradox that the City – for Plato, for Virgil, for Augustine, for Justinian, for Dante, for Plethon, for Campanella, the image of beauty, of order, of repose – has become in the modern world the space of radical ugliness and disorder. To put it in Heidegger's terms, it has been a process of discovering that the at-home of the modern world has in fact become the realm of the not-at-home. This process, that is, has been one of *dislocation*. Thus for Stephen the ugliness and disorder, the 'squalor' and 'sordidness,' that assault has sensitive consciousness after his 'Ptolemaic' universe (which he diagrams on the fly-leaf of his geography book) has been utterly shattered during the catastrophic and traumatic Christmas dinner, is primarily or, at any rate, ontologically, a matter of random motion:

> He sat near them [his numerous brothers and sisters] at the table and asked where his father and mother were. One answered:
> – Goneboro toboro lookboro atboro aboro houseboro.
> Still another removal! A boy named Fallon in Belvedere had often asked him with a silly laugh why they moved so often. . . .
> He asked:
> – Why are we on the move again, if it's a fair question?
> The sister answered:
> – Becauseboro theboro landboro lordbobo willboro putbobo usboro outboro. . . .
> He waited for some moments, listening [to the children sing 'Oft in the Stilly Night'], before he too took up the air with them. He was listening with pain of spirit to the overtones of weariness behind their frail fresh innocent voices. Even before they set out on life's journey they seemed weary already of the way.
> . . . All seemed weary of life even before entering upon it. And he remembered that Newman had heard this note also in the broken line of Virgil *giving utterance, like the voice of Nature herself, to that pain and weariness yet hope of better things which has been the experience of her children in every time.*

(Walter Pater too had heard this sad Virgilian note and in quoting the passage in *Marius the Epicurean*, another novel having its setting in a disintegrating world, established the nostalgia for rest as the essential motive of the aesthetic movement in England.)

Seen in the light of his discovery that random motion is the radical category of modern urban life – that existence is prior to essence, which the postmodern writer will later present as the Un-Naming in the Garden-City – Stephen's well-known aesthetic or rather (to clarify what persistent critical reference to Stephen's 'aesthetic' has obscured) his iconic poetics of stasis, both its volitional ground and its formal character, becomes clear. He wants, like T.E. Hulme, like Proust, like Virginia Woolf and like most other Symbolists, a poetry the iconic – and autotelic – nature of which *arrests* the mind – neutralizes the anguish, the schism in the spirit – and *raises* it above desire and loathing, which is to say, the realm of radical motion, of contingency, of historicity, in the distancing moment when the whole is seen simultaneously.

The 'epiphanic' – one is tempted to say 'Oriental' – nature of this iconic poetic is further clarified in Stephen's amplification of the principle of *stasis* in terms of Saint Thomas's '*ad pulcritudinem tria requiuntur, integritas, consonantia, claritas*,' especially the first and, above all, the most important third categories. *Integritas* or 'wholeness,' Stephen observes, is the apprehension of 'a bounding line drawn about the object' no matter whether it is in space or in time: '. . . temporal or spatial, the esthetic image is first luminously apprehended as selfbounded and selfcontained upon the immeasurable background of space or time which is not it. You apprehend it as *one* thing. You see it as one whole.' *Consonantia* or 'harmony' is the apprehension of the 'rhythm of its structure'; the feeling that 'it is a *thing*,' 'complex, multiple, divisible, separable, made up of parts, the result of its parts and their sum, harmonious.' Finally, and most important for Stephen, *claritas* or 'radiance' (the etymology of his translation – 'radiance' is the light emitted in rays from a center or *logos* – and his analysis of the term clearly suggest its relation with revelation) is the apprehension of 'that thing which it is and no other thing. The radiance of which [Saint Thomas] speaks is the scholastic *quidditas*, the *whatness* of a thing. This supreme quality is felt by the artist when the esthetic image is first conceived in his imagination. . . . The instant wherein that supreme quality of beauty, the clear radiance of the esthetic image, is apprehended *luminously by the mind which has been arrested by its wholeness* and fascinated by its harmony in the *luminous silent stasis of esthetic pleasure*. . . .' (My emphasis)

So also in 'Sailing to Byzantium' – though the metaphysical context is more ontological than social in orientation – Yeats's speaker, like Stephen, is articulating, both in the content and form of the poem, an iconic poetic that has its source in an impulse for epiphanic transcendence – what Wilhelm Worringer (the proponent of primitive and oriental, including Byzantine, artistic models who influenced T.E. Hulme) in *Abstraction and Empathy* calls the 'urge to abstraction.' As fully, if more implicitly, conscious of the paradoxical horror of the modern Western City as Stephen, the poet has come to the City of the iconic imagination – the City of Phase 15 – to pray his mosaic models to teach him *an art of poetry* that will 'consume my heart away' – a heart like Stephen's which, 'sick with desire / And fastened to a dying animal / . . . knows not what it is.' Such a heart is ignorant because, as Yeats says here and reiterates in innumerable ways throughout his early and middle poetry, its *immediate* relationship to history makes everything appear to be random motion, that is, absurd. Clearly, to continue with the phenomenological language of existentialism, this heart is a synecdoche for the dislodged and thus anguish-ridden man-in-the-world, the alienated man in the dreadful realm of *das Unheimliche*. And, as in Stephen's iconic poetic, Yeats's moment of consummation (the parallel with 'radiance' should not be overlooked) which negates the human heart and neutralizes (arrests) desire – the Western, the empathetic urge 'to possess, to go to something' – is the consummation of the creative act, the metamorphosis of kinesis into stasis, becoming into being, the uncertain temporal life into assured iconic artifact, 'selfbounded and selfcontained upon the immeasurable background of space or time which is not it.' (Similarly, the image of a Byzantine mosaic Panaghia or Saint is sharply articulated upon a depthless and vast gold space that suggests the absolute purity of eternity.) Like Stephen's 'instant' of 'luminous silent stasis,' Yeats's moment of consummation is thus the distancing moment when all time can be seen simultaneously. Whereas the real birds of the first stanza – 'those dying generations' – know not what they are because they are 'caught' *in* time, the poet in this moment of consummation, having assumed the form 'as Grecian goldsmiths make / Of hammered gold and gold enamelling,' can sing in *full knowledge* from a perspective beyond or 'out of nature' of the world below, which is to say, of history seen all at once, i.e., spatially:

Of what is past, or passing, or to come.

In the words that Yeats's myth or rather his 'sacred book' insists on, this burning moment, like that of Joyce's 'priest of the eternal imagination,' and of so many other Symbolist poets and novelists, is, in Ortega's term, the 'dehumanizing' epiphanic moment of transcendence.

SECTION THREE

The Critique of Enlightened Modernity: Philosophical Precursors

For many commentators, Postmodernism is a term synonymous with that current of contemporary theoretical debate whose main focus is the representation and analysis of a perceived breakdown in the universalising and rationalist metanarratives of the Enlightenment: those grand theories which have grounded modern Western politics, knowledge, art and ethics, for the last two hundred and fifty years. The first piece in this section is a central, short but definitive, statement of the ideals of Enlightenment which postmodernists now claim to be exhausted, dangerous, redundant or in need of revision. Kant wrote his essay 'What is Enlightenment' in 1784 and its essential argument is that Enlightenment is release from 'self-incurred' tutelage. He assumes the existence of a stable entity called self which has access to its inner states and the world outside and through the application of its rational faculties can arrive at knowledge of both and thus rise above their 'tutelage'. The essay castigates lazy people who will not think for themselves, for Enlightenment must be initially self-willed but, once established, exerts a centrifugal force to become a social dynamic. Enlightenment is not simply a method of thought, but the existence of the conditions for freedom of thought. Only if human thought can be spontaneously self-determining, freeing itself from emotional determinants within and institutional pressures without, can it be truly critical and therefore truly enlightened.

Kant's thought is 'foundationalist' because it is dependent upon the acceptance of certain priori grounds, the categories, which determine the nature of truth, justice and freedom. Accordingly, the mind can discover correspondences between priori forms of thought and the structures of world. As long as we can think or reason in the right kind of way, then we can know world and self and achieve inner harmony through transcendence of the irrational forces within and prejudices without. In order to discover the categorical imperative, the one true principle, however, we must transcend local situation, emotional distraction and personal prejudice, otherwise reason cannot be consistent and no universal system of truth or ethics can be established. Through the application to our situation of this universal rational faculty, we can achieve that moral and intellectual self-realisation which is emancipation. Obviously, this pure form of Enlightenment has been challenged and weakened in a variety of ways since 1784, not least by that upholder and subverter of it,

Sigmund Freud. In a post-Freudian age, few of us, perhaps, believe that we can be free of emotional impingements on rational consciousness, above prejudice, unswayed by the contingencies of everyday life. However, we are not necessarily, therefore, postmodernists. To be postmodern may be to assume that one can neither talk about truth nor truth-effects and, even more dismissive of Enlightenment, to claim that we do not need and should not want to do so. We should give up Enlightenment as an ideal informing our ethical, political, and aesthetic practices.

Why should this be the case? The Foucault essay is one response to this, and a strong one. The weaker argument is that Enlightenment is redundant to the needs of late modernity. In an age of 'disorganised capital', global economics, information technology and media images, enlightened notions of self, nation and representation are inappropriate foundations for our systems of law, politics and aesthetics. The stronger argument is that it is enlightened reason which has placed us in the iron grip of forms of oppression, external and internalised, which though more invisible, are more insidiously powerful than pre-modern forms of control. Enlightenment is seen to be the ideological arm of the rationalising and dehumanising logic of industrial capital's drive towards an efficiency which is its own (ultimately irrational) end. This has consistently been Foucault's position (see introductory discussion) and his work sets out to expose reason as the clarification of a world set up in its own terms through the insidious exclusion of everything it identifies as non-rational. In this later essay, however, he somewhat modifies his earlier position and commends Enlightenment's critical perspective, its sense of history and emphasis on autonomy. He argues that it is naïve simply to reject Enlightenment, but he shifts the emphasis from the idea of knowledge as discovery to that of modernity as the necessity to 'invent' rather than discover oneself. The hero of modern life, for Foucault as for Baudelaire before him, is the Dandy who has perceived the fundamental role of the aesthetic in the formulation of existence.

This brings us to the third excerpt in this section, for Foucault derives this concept of an aesthetics of existence from the work of Friedrich Nietzsche. For Nietzsche, in the text represented here and in late works such as *Ecce Homo*, self is always a fiction, a willed unity masking a chaos of conflicting and contradictory desires. Definitions of self and world are always struggles for conceptual mastery. The most persuasive have been those Platonic forms of thought which seduce us into believing that mental and conceptual representations can reflect the structure of an ultimately fixed and unchanging reality of essences. One can respond to these passively and, in herd-like fashion, allow others to impose their definitions upon one. Alternatively, in recognising that existence is entirely an aesthetic act, one can become the author of one's own life, become what one is as one's own supreme fiction. Nietzsche has been read in a variety of ways and even within Postmodernism he is sometimes seized upon as a philosopher of 'intensities' (a proponent of Dionysian excess constantly reminding us of what Reason excludes and out of which it arises) and sometimes as an advocate of life as art (existence as aesthetic shaping). Both these emphases have influenced Foucault, but, increasingly, it was the latter interpretation of Nietzsche which interested him. Although they appear to contradict each other, the first ostensibly about loss of control and the second about the need for careful self-control, they are, in fact, quite compatible. For Nietzsche's self cannot be arrived at simply through the imposition of a pre-existing idea. As he says in *Ecce Homo* (written in 1888): to become what one is, one must have no idea of what one is. Authentic creation is not simply consciously directed and formulated will for it arises out of body: out of instinct and desire. For both Foucault and Nietzsche then, human nature is not a hidden essence waiting to be discovered through self-analysis, but an artefact, a sedimented aggregate of those available forms we must choose to shape into coherent identity with no prototype to guide our activity. Otherwise, if we shun the responsibility of authentic self-creation, we are entirely a fabrication of others. For both, there is no originary moment establishing pure identity which can be rationally excavated, but only a flux of experiences ever being shaped into new wholes, reproduced through new vocabularies and new stories. We cannot simply, wilfully, fashion a new self, but we can use aesthetic strategies to reformulate available materials. Again, therefore, one sees the rootedness of postmodern thought in the aesthetic, but an aesthetic extended into the demesne of the existential. The next section will examine the controversies about the desirability or otherwise of collapsing the aesthetic into the realms of knowledge and ethics, for these questions are at the heart of the postmodern debate.

---

9 Immanuel Kant

From *An Answer to the Question: What is Enlightenment?*
[Beantwortung der Frage: Was ist Aufklärung? (1784)]

German Aesthetic and Literary Criticism, D. Simpson (ed.), Cambridge: Cambridge University Press, 1984, pp 29–34.

The following translation is a modified reprint of that by Lewis White Beck, in his *Kant on History* (1963), pp. 3–10.

The German text may be found in *Kants gesammelte Schriften*, published by the Königlich Preussische Akademie der Wissenschaften, 22 vols. (Berlin, 1900–42), VIII, 33–42.

Introductory note

I have explained in the general Introduction the reasons behind the apparent perversity of including in this anthology essays or extracts which do not comment directly on art or aesthetics. The ramifications of this essay of Kant's are not always traceable in the letter – as they certainly are, for example, in Fichte's lectures *On the Nature of Scholar* or in his analysis of his own generation in the *Characteristics of the Present Age* – but in the spirit they are all-pervasive. In as much as what follows is an exemplary summary of what one of the greatest of thinkers understood by the term 'enlightenment', and stands also as a statement of the principal insights of the philosophers who constituted *the* Enlightenment, the importance of this piece seems self-evident. Readers familiar with the British Romantic writers will perceive many points of comparison and contrast in terms of the implications and responsibilities of a writer's relation to his public: one thinks of Blake's assertive declarations of independence from the systems of other men; of Coleridge's meditations on the paradoxes of authority – how he can persuade or *guide* his reader to the exercise of *independent* judgement; and of Wordsworth's plea to his ideal reader as one who would 'decide by his own feelings genuinely, and not by reflection upon what will probably be the judgement of others'.

Much of what Kant has to say here marks him out as a man of the Enlightenment rather than as a Romantic, though any extreme version of this historian's dichotomy must inhibit our understanding of the period. Here, the emphasis on the possibility of clear and rational thinking and its salutary effects on society at large is presented with only hints of the darker forces working to complicate the establishment or dissemination of truth. Or perhaps we should say, as we would have to say of William Godwin, that the negative forces are recognized in the argument at the same time as a faith in the possibility of their disappearance is preserved. But for the most part in what follows, superstition and prejudice are external enemies rather than inward ones who may sometimes masquerade as friends.

Enlightenment is man's release from his self-incurred tutelage. Tutelage [Unmundigkeit] is man's inability to make use of his understanding [Verstand] without direction from another. It is self-incurred when its cause lies not in lack of understanding but in lack of resolution and courage to use it without direction from another. *Sapere aude!* 'Have courage to exercise your own understanding!' – that is the motto of enlightenment.[1]

Laziness and cowardice are the reasons why so great a portion of mankind, after nature has long since discharged them from external direction (*naturaliter maiorennes*), nevertheless remain under lifelong tutelage, and why it is so easy

---

[Beck's notes are indicated by the initial B.]

[1] More literally, 'dare to be wise' (Horace, *Epistles*, I, 2, 40). B. notes that this was the motto adopted in 1736 by the Society of the Friends of Truth, an important circle in the German *Aufklärung*. For further information, see the introduction to *AE* by Wilkinson and Willoughby, pp. lxxiv-lxxv. Schiller borrows Kant's phrase and some of his thoughts in letter VIII. In the *Anthropology* of 1797, Kant has this to say of the Germans (1974, p. 180):

The German's negative side is his tendency to imitate others and his diffidence about his ability to be original (which is diametrically opposed to the Englishman's defiance). Still worse, he has a certain mania for method which leads him to renounce the principle that, e.g., fellow citizens should approach equality, in favour of classifying them punctiliously according to degrees of precedence and hierarchy.

for others to set themselves up as their guardians. It is so easy not to be of age. If I have a book which understands for me, a pastor who has a conscience for me, a physician who decides my diet, and so forth, I need not trouble myself. I need not think, if I can only pay – others will readily undertake the irksome work for me.

That the initiative towards independence and majority [Mündigkeit] is held to be very dangerous by the far greater portion of mankind (and by the entire fair sex) – quite apart from its being arduous – is seen to by those guardians who have so kindly assumed superintendence over them. After the guardians have first made their domestic cattle dumb and have made sure that these placid creatures will not dare take a single step without the harness of the cart to which they are tethered, the guardians then show them the danger which threatens if they try to go alone. Actually, however, this danger is not so great, for by failing a few times they would finally learn to walk alone. But an example of this failure makes them timid and ordinarily frightens them away from all further trials.

For any single individual to work himself out of the life under tutelage which has become almost his nature is very difficult. He has come to be fond of this state, and he is for the present really incapable of making use of his understanding, for no one has ever let him try it out. Statues and formulas, those mechanical tools of the rational employment or rather mis-employment of his natural gifts, are the fetters of an everlasting tutelage. Whoever throws them off makes only an uncertain leap over the narrowest ditch because he is not accustomed to that kind of free motion. Therefore, there are few who have succeeded by their own exercise of mind and spirit [Geist] both in freeing themselves from tutelage and in achieving a steady pace.

But that the public should enlighten itself is more possible; indeed, if only freedom is granted, enlightenment is almost sure to follow. For there will always be some independent thinkers, even among the established guardians of the great masses, who, after throwing off the yoke of tutelage from their own shoulders, will disseminate the spirit of the rational appreciation of both their own worth and every man's vocation for thinking for himself. But be it noted that the public, which has first been brought under this yoke by their guardians, forces the guardians themselves to remain bound when it is later incited to do so by those among these guardians who are themselves incapable of all enlightenment[2] – so harmful is it to implant prejudices, for in the end they take vengeance on their cultivators or on their descendants. Thus the public can only slowly attain enlightenment. Perhaps a decrease in personal despotism and of avaricious or tyrannical oppression may be accomplished by revolution, but never a true reform in ways of thinking. Rather, new prejudices will serve as old ones to harness the great thoughtless masses.[3]

---

[2] I have substantially altered the translation here, which seems to depend upon a misreading.

[3] After the experience of the Terror in post-revolutionary France, many thinkers of the 1790s echoed this belief in the patient publication of truth unassisted by any revolutionary activity, Schiller and Godwin among them. That this is Kant's view even before the outbreak of the French Revolution should remind us that the argument was already available. In fact, Kant himself never completely lost faith in the evidence offered by the French experience for an intrinsic 'moral disposition within the human race', and he could say this even in 1798 (cited by E. Cassirer (1981), p. 407; *Ak.* VII, 85).

For this enlightenment, however, nothing is required but freedom, and freedom of the most harmless sort among its various definitions: freedom to make public use of one's reason [Vernunft][4] at every point. But I hear on all sides, 'Do not argue!' The officer says: 'Do not argue but drill!' The tax collector: 'Do not argue but pay!' The cleric: 'Do not argue but believe!' Only one prince in the world says, 'Argue as much as you will, and about what you will, but obey!' Everywhere there is restriction on freedom.[5]

Which restriction is an obstacle to enlightenment, and which is not an obstacle but a promoter of it? I answer: The public use of one's reason must always be free, and it alone can bring about enlightenment among men. The private use of reason, on the other hand, may often be very narrowly restricted without particularly hindering the progress of enlightenment. By the public use of one's reason I understand the use which a person makes of it as a scholar before the reading public. Private use I call that which one may make of it in a particular civil post or office which is entrusted to him. Many affairs which are conducted in the interest of the community require a certain mechanism through which some members of the community must passively conduct themselves with an artificial unanimity, so that the government may direct them to public ends, or at least prevent them from destroying those ends. Here argument is certainly not allowed – one must obey. But so far as a part of the mechanism regards himself at the same time as a member of the whole community or of a society of world citizens, and thus in the role of a scholar who addresses the public (in the proper sense of the word) through his writings, he certainly can argue without hurting the affairs for which he is in part responsible as a passive member. Thus it would be ruinous for an officer in service to debate about the suitability or utility of a command given to him by his superior; he must obey. But the right to make remarks on errors in the military service and to lay them before the public for judgement cannot equitably be refused him as a scholar. The citizen cannot refuse to pay the taxes imposed on him; indeed, an impudent complaint at those levied on him can be punished as a scandal (as it could occasion general refractoriness). But the same person nevertheless does not act contrary to his duty as a citizen when, as a scholar, he publicly expresses his thoughts on the inappropriateness or even the injustice of these levies. Similarly a clergyman is obligated to make his sermon to his pupils in catechism and his congregation conform to the symbol of the church which he serves, for he has been accepted on this condition. But as a scholar he has complete freedom, even the calling, to communicate to the public all his carefully tested and well-meaning thoughts on that which is erroneous in the symbol and to make suggestions for the better organization of the religious body and church. In doing this there is nothing that could be laid as a burden on his conscience. For what he teaches as a consequence of his office as a

---

[4] Although Kant's technical distinction between *Verstand* and *Vernunft* had already been formulated by 1784, they appear to have their 'precritical' senses in this essay, as roughly synonymous. However, I have translated them as 'understanding' and 'reason' in order that the synonymity may *appear* as such.

[5] The princely exception is Frederick the Great, King of Prussia from 1740 to 1786, whose own career went through a period of anti-authoritarianism followed by a cultivation of the military virtues. Whilst the size of Prussia doubled during his reign, he remains famous for his interest in philosophy and the arts and sciences – he played host to many of the *philosophes* – and is usually cited as the ideal of enlightened despotism.

representative of the church, this he considers something about which he has no freedom to teach according to his own lights; it is something which he is appointed to propound at the dictation of and in the name of another. He will say, 'Our church teaches this or that; those are the proofs which it adduces.' He thus extracts all practical uses for his congregation from statutes to which he himself would not subscribe with full conviction but to the enunciation of which he can very well pledge himself because it is not impossible that truth lies hidden in them, and, in any case, there is at least nothing in them contradictory to inner religion. For if he believed he had found such in them, he could not conscientiously discharge the duties of his office; he would have to give it up. The use, therefore, which an appointed teacher makes of his reason before his congregation is merely private, because this congregation is only a domestic one (even if it be a large gathering); with respect to it, as a priest, he is not free, nor can he be free, because he carries out the orders of another. But as a scholar, whose writings speak to his true public, the world, the clergyman in the public use of his reason enjoys an unlimited freedom to use his own reason and to speak in his own person. That the guardians of the people (in spiritual things) should themselves be incompetent is an absurdity which amounts to the eternalization of absurdities.[6]

But would not a society of clergymen, perhaps a church conference or a venerable classis (as they call themselves among the Dutch), be justified in obligating itself by oath to a certain unchangeable symbol in order to enjoy an unceasing guardianship over each of its members and thereby over the people [das Volk] as a whole, and even to make it eternal? I answer that this is altogether impossible. Such a contract, made to shut off all further enlightenment from the human race, is absolutely null and void even if confirmed by the supreme power, by parliaments, and by the most ceremonious of peace treaties. An age cannot bind itself and ordain to put the succeeding one into such a condition that it cannot extend its (at best very occasional) knowledge, purify itself of errors, and progress in general enlightenment. That would be a crime against human nature, the proper destination of which lies precisely in this progress; and the descendants would be fully justified in rejecting those decrees as having been made in an unwarranted and malicious manner.

The touchstone of everything that can be concluded as a law for a people lies in the question whether the people could have imposed such a law on itself. Now such a religious compact might be possible for a short and definitely limited time, as it were, in expectation of a better. One might let every citizen, and especially the clergyman, in the role of scholar, make his comments freely and publicly, i.e., through writing, on the erroneous aspects of the present institution. The newly introduced order might last until insight into the nature of these things had become so general and widely approved that through uniting their voices (even if not unanimously) they could bring a proposal to the throne to take those congregations under protection which had united into a

---

[6] In this distinction between 'public' and 'private' Kant seems to have in mind that between the published and the spoken word. We may infer from this that the written word is viewed as calling forth the most seriously meditated powers of its author and, reciprocally, the most authentic and rational faculties of its readers. It is thus a more proper medium for free speculation than say, oratory, which may become improperly persuasive. Cf. Fichte, *On the Nature of the Scholar*, and note 9, below.

changed religious organization according to their better ideas, without, however, hindering others who wish to remain in the old order. But to unite in a permanent religious institution which is not to be subject to doubt before the public even in the lifetime of one man, and thereby to make a period of time fruitless in the progress of mankind toward improvement, thus working to the disadvantage of posterity – that is absolutely forbidden. For himself (and only for a short time) a man may postpone enlightenment in what he ought to know, but to renounce it for himself and even more to renounce it for posterity is to injure and trample on the rights of mankind.

And what a people may not decree for itself can even less be decreed for them by a monarch, for his law-giving authority rests on his uniting the general public will in his own. If he only sees to it that all true or alleged improvement stands together with civil order, he can leave it to his subjects to do what they find necessary for their spiritual welfare. This is not his concern, though it is incumbent on him to prevent one of them from violently hindering another in determining and promoting this welfare to the best of his ability. To meddle in these matters lowers his own majesty, since by the writings in which his subjects seek to present their views he may evaluate his own governance. He can do this when, with deepest understanding, he lays upon himself the reproach, *Caesar non est supra grammaticos*.[7] Far more does he injure his own majesty when he degrades his supreme power by supporting the ecclesiastical despotism of some tyrants in his state over his other subjects.

If we are asked, 'Do we now live in an *enlightened* age?' the answer is, 'No', but we do live in an age of *enlightenment*.[8] As things now stand, much is lacking which prevents men from being, or easily becoming, capable of correctly using their own understandings in religious matters with assurance and free from outside direction. But, on the other hand, we have clear indications that the field has now been opened wherein men may freely deal with these things and that the obstacles to general enlightenment or the release from self-imposed tutelage are gradually being reduced. In this respect, this is the age of enlightenment, or the century of Frederick.

A prince who does not find it unworthy of himself to say that he holds it to be his duty to prescribe nothing to men in religious matters but to give them complete freedom while renouncing the haughty name of *tolerance*, is himself enlightened and deserves to be esteemed by the grateful world and posterity as the first, at least from the side of government, who divested the human race of its tutelage and left each man free to make use of his reason in matters of conscience. Under him venerable ecclesiastics are allowed, in the role of scholars, and without infringing on their official duties, freely to submit for public testing their judgements and views which here and there diverge from the established symbol. And an even greater freedom is enjoyed by those who are restricted by no official duties. This spirit of freedom spreads beyond this

---

[7] 'The emperor is not above the grammarians.' Perhaps an allusion to a response to Voltaire said to have been made by Frederick the Great: 'Caesar est supra grammaticam.' But the sentiment was not original with Frederick, and has been attributed to the Emperor Sigismund at the Council of Constance (1414): 'Ego sum rex Romanus et supra grammaticam' [B].

[8] Cf. The preface to the first *Critique*: 'Our age is, in especial degree, the age of criticism, and to criticism everything must submit' (Kant, 1933, p. 9) [B].

land, even to those in which it must struggle with external obstacles erected by a government which misunderstands its own interest. For an example gives evidence to such a government that in freedom there is not the least cause for concern about public peace and the stability of the community. Men work themselves gradually out of barbarity if only intentional artifices are not made to hold them in it.

I have placed the main point of enlightenment – the escape of men from their self-incurred tutelage – chiefly in matters of religion because our rulers have no interest in playing the guardian with respect to the arts and sciences and also because religious incompetence is not only the most harmful but also the most degrading of all. But the manner of thinking of the head of a state who favours religious enlightenment goes further, and he sees that there is no danger in his law-giving in allowing his subjects to make public use of their reason and to publish their thoughts on a better formulation of his legislation and even their open-minded criticisms of the laws already made. Of this we have a shining example wherein no monarch is superior to him whom we honour.[9]

But only one who is himself enlightened, is not afraid of shadows, and who has a numerous and well-disciplined army to assure public peace, can say: 'Argue as much as you will, and about what you will, only obey!' A republic could not dare say such a thing. Here is shown a strange and unexpected trend in human affairs in which almost everything, looked at in the large, is paradoxical. A greater degree of civil freedom appears advantageous to the freedom of mind of the people, and yet it places inescapable limitations upon it; a lower degree of civil freedom, on the contrary, provides the mind with room for each man to extend himself to his full capacity. As nature has uncovered from under this hard shell the seed for which she most tenderly cares – the propensity and vocation to free thinking – this gradually works back upon the character of the people, who thereby gradually become capable of managing freedom; finally, it affects the principles of government, which finds it to its advantage to treat men, who are now more than machines, in accordance with their dignity.[10]

[9] In fact, during the reign of his successor Frederick William II (1786–97) freedom of thought and publication was to be threatened again, and Kant himself would be forbidden to publish any further religious publications after *Religion Within the Limits of Reason Alone* (1793–4).

[10] 'Today I read in the *Büschingsche Wöchentliche Nachrichten* for 13 September an announcement of the *Berlinische Monatsschrift* for this month, which cites the answer to the same question by Mr Mendelssohn. But this issue has not yet come to me; if it had, I would have held back the present essay, which is now put forth only in order to see how much agreement in thought can be brought about by chance.' [Kant's own note.] Mendelssohn's answer was that enlightenment lay in intellectual cultivation, which he distinguished from the practical. Kant, quite in line with his latter essay on theory and practice, refuses to make this distinction fundamental [B].

10   Michael Foucault

From *What is Enlightenment*

The Foucault Reader, P. Rabinow (ed.), trans C. Porter,
Harmondsworth, 1984, pp 32–50.

Today when a periodical asks its readers a question, it does so in order to collect opinions on some subject about which everyone has an opinion already; there is not much likelihood of learning anything new. In the eighteenth century, editors preferred to question the public on problems that did not yet have solutions. I don't know whether or not that practice was more effective; it was unquestionably more entertaining.

In any event, in line with this custom, in November 1784 a German periodical, *Berlinische Monatschrift*, published a response to the question: *Was ist Aufklärung?* And the respondent was Kant.

A minor text, perhaps. But it seems to me that it marks the discreet entrance into the history of thought of a question that modern philosophy has not been capable of answering, but that it has never managed to get rid of, either. And one that has been repeated in various forms for two centuries now. From Hegel through Nietzsche or Max Weber to Horkheimer or Habermas, hardly any philosophy has failed to confront this same question, directly or indirectly. What, then, is this event that is called the *Aufklärung* and that has determined, at least in part, what we are, what we think, and what we do today? Let us imagine that the *Berlinische Monatschrift* still exists and that it is asking its readers the question: What is modern philosophy? Perhaps we could respond with an echo: modern philosophy is the philosophy that is attempting to answer the question raised so imprudently two centuries ago: *Was ist Aufklärung?*

Let us linger a few moments over Kant's text. It merits attention for several reasons.

1   To this same question, Moses Mendelssohn had also replied in the same journal, just two months earlier. But Kant had not seen Mendelssohn's text when he wrote his. To be sure, the encounter of the German philosophical movement with the new development of Jewish culture does not date from this precise moment. Mendelssohn had been at that crossroads for thirty years or so, in company with Lessing. But up to this point it had been a matter of making a place for Jewish culture within German thought – which Lessing had tried to do in *Die Juden* or else of identifying problems common to Jewish thought and to German philosophy; this is what Mendelssohn had done in his *Phädon; oder, Über die Unsterblichkeit der Seele*. With the two texts published in the *Berlinische Monatschrift*, the German *Aufklärung* and the Jewish *Haskala* recognize that they belong to the same history; they are seeking to identify the

common processes from which they stem. And it is perhaps a way of announc- ing the acceptance of a common destiny – we now know to what drama that was to lead.

2   But there is more. In itself and within the Christian tradition, Kant's text poses a new problem.

It was certainly not the first time that philosophical thought had sought to reflect on its own present. But, speaking schematically, we may say that this reflection had until then taken three main forms.

a   The present may be represented as belonging to a certain era of the world, distinct from the others through some inherent characteristics, or separated from the others by some dramatic event. Thus, in Plato's *The Statesman* the interlocutors recognize that they belong to one of those revolu- tions of the world in which the world is turning backwards, with all the negative consequences that may ensure.

b   The present may be interrogated in an attempt to decipher in it the heralding signs of a forthcoming event. Here we have the principle of a kind of historical hermeneutics of which Augustine might provide an example.

c   The present may also be analyzed as a point of transition toward the dawning of a new world. That is what Vico describes in the last chapter of *La Scienza Nuova*; what he sees 'today' is 'a complete humanity . . . spread abroad through all nations, for a few great monarchs rule over this world of peoples'; it is also 'Europe . . . radiant with such humanity that it abounds in all the good things that make for the happiness of human life.'[1]

Now the way Kant poses the question of *Aufklärung* is entirely different: it is neither a world era to which one belongs, nor an event whose signs are perceived, nor the dawning of an accomplishment. Kant defines *Aufklärung* in an almost entirely negative way, as an *Ausgang*, an 'exit,' a 'way out'. In his other texts on history, Kant occasionally raises questions of origin or defines the internal teleology of a historical process. In the text on *Aufklärung*, he deals with the question of contemporary reality alone. He is not seeking to understand the present on the basis of a totality or of a future achievement. He is looking for a difference: What difference does today introduce with respect to yesterday?

3   I shall not go into detail here concerning this text, which is not always very clear despite its brevity. I should simply like to point out three or four features that seem to me important if we are to understand how Kant raised the philosophical question of the present day.

Kant indicates right away that the 'way out' that characterizes Enlighten- ment is a process that releases us from the status of 'immaturity.' And by 'immaturity,' he means a certain state of our will that makes us accept someone else's authority to lead us in areas where the use of reason is called for. Kant gives three examples: we are in a state of 'immaturity' when a book takes the place of our understanding, when a spiritual director takes the place of our conscience, when a doctor decides for us what our diet is to be. (Let us note in

---

[1] Giambattista Vico, *The New Science of Giambattista Vico*, 3rd ed., (1744), abridged trans. T.G. Bergin and M.H. Fisch (Ithaca/London: Cornell University Press, 1970), pp. 370, 372.

passing that the register of these three critiques is easy to recognize, even though the text does not make it explicit.) In any case, Enlightenment is defined by a modification of the preexisting relation linking will, authority, and the use of reason.

We must also note that this way out is presented by Kant in a rather ambiguous manner. He characterizes it as a phenomenon, an ongoing process; but he also presents it as a task and an obligation. From the very first paragraph, he notes that man himself is responsible for his immature status. Thus it has to be supported that he will be able to escape from it only by a change that he himself will bring about in himself. Significantly, Kant says that this Enlightenment has a *Wahlspruch*: now a *Wahlspruch* is a heraldic device, that is, a distinctive feature by which one can be recognized, and it is also a motto, an instruction that one gives oneself and proposes to others. What, then, is this instruction? *Aude sapere*: 'dare to know,' 'have the courage, the audacity, to know.' Thus Enlightenment must be considered both as a process in which men participate collectively and as an act of courage to be accomplished personally. Men are at once elements and agents of a single process. They may be actors in the process to the extent that they participate in it; and the process occurs to the extent that men decide to be its voluntary actors.

A third difficulty appears here in Kant's text, in his use of the word 'mankind,' *Menschheit*. The importance of this word in the Kantian conception of history is well known. Are we to understand that the entire human race is caught up in the process of Enlightenment? In that case, we must imagine Enlightenment as a historical change that affects the political and social existence of all people on the face of the earth. Or are we to understand that it involves a change affecting what constitutes the humanity of human beings? But the question then arises of knowing what this change is. Here again, Kant's answer is not without a certain ambiguity. In any case, beneath its appearance of simplicity, it is rather complex.

Kant defines two essential conditions under which mankind can escape from its immaturity. And these two conditions are at once spiritual and institutional, ethical and political.

The first of these conditions is that the realm of obedience and the realm of the use of reason be clearly distinguished. Briefly characterizing the immature status, Kant invokes the familiar expression: 'Don't think, just follow orders'; such is, according to him, the form in which military discipline, political power, and religious authority are usually exercised. Humanity will reach maturity when it is no longer required to obey, but when men are told: 'Obey, and you will be able to reason as much as you like.' We must note that the German word used here is *räsonieren*; this word, which is also used in the *Critiques*, does not refer to just any use of reason, but to a use of reason in which reason has no other end but itself: *räsonieren* is to reason for reasoning's sake. And Kant gives examples, these too being perfectly trivial in appearance: paying one's taxes, while being able to argue as much as one likes about the system of taxation, would be characteristic of the mature state; or again, taking responsibility for parish service, if one is a pastor, while reasoning freely about religious dogmas.

We might think that there is nothing very different here from what has been meant, since the sixteenth century, by freedom of conscience: the right to think as one pleases so long as one obeys as one must. Yet it is here that Kant brings into play another distinction, and in a rather surprising way. The distinction he introduces is between the private and public uses of reason. But he adds at once that reason must be free in its public use, and must be submissive in its private use. Which is, term for term, the opposite of what is ordinarily called freedom of conscience.

But we must be somewhat more precise. What constitutes, for Kant, this private use of reason? In what area is it exercised? Man, Kant says, makes a private use of reason when he is 'a cog in a machine'; that is, when he has a role to play in society and jobs to do: to be a soldier, to have taxes to pay, to be in charge of a parish, to be a civil servant, all this makes the human being a particular segment of society; he finds himself thereby placed in a circumscribed position, where he has to apply particular rules and pursue particular ends. Kant does not ask that people practice a blind and foolish obedience, but that they adapt the use they make of their reason to these determined circumstances; and reason must then be subjected to the particular ends in view. Thus there cannot be, here, any free use of reason.

On the other hand, when one is reasoning only in order to use one's reason, when one is reasoning as a reasonable being (and not as a cog in a machine), when one is reasoning as a member of reasonable humanity, then the use of reason must be free and public. Enlightenment is thus not merely the process by which individuals would see their own personal freedom of thought guaranteed. There is Enlightenment when the universal, the free, and the public uses of reason are superimposed on one another.

Now this leads us to a fourth question that must be put to Kant's text. We can readily see how the universal use of reason (apart from any private end) is the business of the subject himself as an individual; we can readily see, too, how the freedom of this use may be assured in a purely negative manner through the absence of any challenge to it; but how is a public use of that reason to be assured? Enlightenment, as we see, must not be conceived simply as a general process affecting all humanity; it must not be conceived only as an obligation prescribed to individuals: it now appears as a political problem. The question, in any event, is that of knowing how the use of reason can take the public form that it requires, how the audacity to know can be exercised in broad daylight, while individuals are obeying as scrupulously as possible. And Kant, in conclusion, proposes to Frederick II, in scarcely veiled terms, a sort of contract – what might be called the contract of rational despotism with free reason: the public and free use of autonomous reason will be the best guarantee of obedience, on condition, however, that the political principle that must be obeyed itself be in conformity with universal reason.

Let us leave Kant's text here. I do not by any means propose to consider it as capable of constituting an adequate description of Enlightenment; and no historian, I think, could be satisfied with it for an analysis of the social, political, and cultural transformations that occurred at the end of the eighteenth century.

Nevertheless, notwithstanding its circumstantial nature, and without intending to give it an exaggerated place in Kant's work, I believe that it is necessary to stress the connection that exists between this brief article and the three

Critiques. Kant in fact describes Enlightenment as the moment when humanity is going to put its own reason to use, without subjecting itself to any authority; now it is precisely at this moment that the critique is necessary, since its role is that of defining the conditions under which the use of reason is legitimate in order to determine what can be known, what must be done, and what may be hoped. Illegitimate uses of reason are what give rise to dogmatism and heteronomy, along with illusion; on the other hand, it is when the legitimate use of reason has been clearly defined in its principles that its autonomy can be assured. The critique is, in a sense, the handbook of reason that has grown up in Enlightenment; and, conversely, the Enlightenment is the age of the critique.

It is also necessary I think, to underline the relation between this text of Kant's and the other texts he devoted to history. These latter, for the most part, seek to define the internal teleology of time and the point toward which the history of humanity is moving. Now the analysis of Enlightenment, defining this history as humanity's passage to its adult status, situates contemporary reality with respect to the overall movement and its basic directions. But at the same time, it shows how, at this very moment, each individual is responsible in a certain way for that overall process.

The hypothesis I should like to propose is that this little text is located in a sense at the crossroads of critical reflection and reflection on history. It is a reflection by Kant on the contemporary status of his own enterprise. No doubt it is not the first time that a philosopher has given his reasons for undertaking his work at a particular moment. But it seems to me that it is the first time that a philosopher has connected in this way, closely and from the inside, the significance of his work with respect to knowledge, a reflection on history and a particular analysis of the specific moment at which he is writing and because of which he is writing. It is in the reflection on 'today' as difference in history and as motive for a particular philosophical task that the novelty of this text appears to me to lie.

And, by looking at it in this way, it seems to me we may recognize a point of departure: the outline of what one might call the attitude of modernity.

I know that modernity is often spoken of as an epoch, or at least as a set of features characteristic of an epoch; situated on a calendar, it would be preceded by a more or less naïve or archaic premodernity, and followed by an enigmatic and troubling 'postmodernity.' And then we find ourselves asking whether modernity constitutes the sequel to the Enlightenment and its development, or whether we are to see it as a rupture or a deviation with respect to the basic principles of the eighteenth century.

Thinking back on Kant's text, I wonder whether we may not envisage modernity rather as an attitude than as a period of history. And by 'attitude,' I mean a mode of relating to contemporary reality; a voluntary choice made by certain people; in the end, a way of thinking and feeling; a way, too, of acting and behaving that at one and the same time marks a relation of belonging and presents itself as a task. A bit, no doubt, like what the Greeks called an *ethos*. And consequently, rather than seeking to distinguish the 'modern era' from the 'premodern' or 'postmodern,' I think it would be more useful to try to find out how the attitude of modernity, ever since its formation, has found itself struggling with attitudes of 'countermodernity.'

To characterize briefly this attitude of modernity, I shall take an almost indispensable example, namely, Baudelaire; for his consciousness of modernity is widely recognized as one of the most acute in the nineteenth century.

1   Modernity is often characterized in terms of consciousness of the discontinuity of time: a break with tradition, a feeling of novelty, of vertigo in the face of the passing moment. And this is indeed what Baudelaire seems to be saying when he defines modernity as 'the ephemeral, the fleeting, the contingent.'[2] But, for him, being modern does not lie in recognizing and accepting this perpetual movement; on the contrary, it lies in adopting a certain attitude with respect to this movement; and this deliberate, difficult attitude consists in recapturing something eternal that is not beyond the present instant, nor behind it, but within it. Modernity is distinct from fashion, which does no more than call into question the course of time; modernity is the attitude that makes it possible to grasp the 'heroic' aspect of the present moment. Modernity is not a phenomenon of sensitivity to the fleeting present; it is the will to 'heroize' the present.

I shall restrict myself to what Baudelaire says about the painting of his contemporaries. Baudelaire makes fun of those painters, who, finding nineteenth-century dress excessively ugly, want to depict nothing but ancient togas. But modernity in painting does not consist, for Baudelaire, in introducing black clothing onto the canvas. The modern painter is the one who can show the dark frock-coat as 'the necessary costume of our time,' the one who knows how to make manifest, in the fashion of the day, the essential, permanent, obsessive relation that our age entertains with death. 'The dress-coat and frock-coat not only possess their political beauty, which is an expression of universal equality, but also their poetic beauty, which is an expression of the public soul – an immense cortège of undertaker's mutes (mutes in love, political mutes, bourgeois mutes . . .). We are each of us celebrating some funeral.'[3] To designate this attitude of modernity, Baudelaire sometimes employs a litotes that is highly significant because it is presented in the form of a precept: 'You have no right to despise the present.'

2   This heroization is ironical, needless to say. The attitude of modernity does not treat the passing moment as sacred in order to try to maintain or perpetuate it. It certainly does not involve harvesting it as a fleeting and interesting curiosity. That would be what Baudelaire would call the spectator's posture. The *flâneur*, the idle, strolling spectator, is satisfied to keep his eyes open, to pay attention and build up a storehouse of memories. In opposition to the *flâneur*, Baudelaire describes the man of modernity: 'Away he goes, hurrying, searching. . . . Be very sure that this man . . . – this solitary, gifted with an active imagination, ceaselessly journeying across the great human desert – has

---

²   Charles Baudelaire, *The Painter of Modern Life and Other Essays*, trans. Jonathan Mayne (London: Phaidon, 1964), p. 13.

³   Charles Baudelaire, 'On the Heroism of Modern Life,' in *The Mirror of Art: Critical Studies by Charles Baudelaire*, trans. Jonathan Mayne (London: Phaidon, 1955), p. 127.

an aim loftier than that of a mere *flâneur*, an aim more general, something other than the fugitive pleasure of circumstance. He is looking for that quality which you must allow me to call 'modernity.' . . . He makes it his business to extract from fashion whatever element it may contain of poetry within history.' As an example of modernity, Baudelaire cites the artist Constantin Guys. In appearance a spectator, a collector of curiosities, he remains 'the last to linger wherever there can be a glow of light, an echo of poetry, a quiver of life or a chord of music; wherever a passion can *pose* before him, wherever natural man and conventional man display themselves in a strange beauty, wherever the sun lights up the swift joys of the *depraved animal*.'[4]

But let us make no mistake. Constantin Guys is not a *flâneur*; what makes him the modern painter *par excellence* in Baudelaire's eyes is that, just when the whole world is falling asleep, he begins to work, and he transfigures that world. His transfiguration does not entail an annulling of reality, but a difficult interplay between the truth of what is real and the exercise of freedom; 'natural' things become 'more than natural,' 'beautiful' things become 'more than beautiful,' and individual objects appear 'endowed with an impulsive life like the soul of [their] creator.'[5] For the attitude of modernity, the high value of the present is indissociable from a desperate eagerness to imagine it, to imagine it otherwise than it is, and to transform it not by destroying it but by grasping it in what it is. Baudelairean modernity is an exercise in which extreme attention to what is real is confronted with the practice of a liberty that simultaneously respects this reality and violates it.

3   However, modernity for Baudelaire is not simply a form of relationship to the present; it is also a mode of relationship that has to be established with oneself. The deliberate attitude of modernity is tied to an indispensable asceticism. To be modern is not to accept oneself as one is in the flux of the passing moments; it is to take oneself as object of a complex and difficult elaboration: what Baudelaire, in the vocabulary of his day, calls *dandysme*. Here I shall not recall in detail the well-known passages on 'vulgar, earthy, vile nature'; on man's indispensable revolt against himself; on the 'doctrine of elegance' which imposes 'upon its ambitious and humble disciples' a discipline more despotic than the most terrible religions; the pages, finally, on the asceticism of the dandy who makes of his body, his behavior, his feelings and passions, his very existence, a work of art. Modern man, for Baudelaire, is not the man who goes off to discover himself, his secrets and his hidden truth; he is the man who tries to invent himself. This modernity does not 'liberate man in his own being'; it compels him to face the task of producing himself.

4   Let me add just one final word. This ironic heroization of the present, this transfiguring play of freedom with reality, this ascetic elaboration of the self – Baudelaire does not imagine that these have any place in society itself, or in the body politic. They can only be produced in another, a different place, which Baudelaire calls art.

---

4 Baudelaire, *Painter*, pp. 12, 11.
5 Ibid., p. 12.

I do not pretend to be summarizing in these few lines either the complex historical event that was the Enlightenment, at the end of the eighteenth century, or the attitude of modernity in the various guises it may have taken on during the last two centuries.

I have been seeking, on the one hand, to emphasize the extent to which a type of philosophical interrogation – one that simultaneously problematizes man's relation to the present, man's historical mode of being, and the constitution of the self as an autonomous subject – is rooted in the Enlightenment. On the other hand, I have been seeking to stress that the thread that may connect us with the Enlightenment is not faithfulness to doctrinal elements, but rather the permanent reactivation of an attitude – that is, of a philosophical ethos that could be described as a permanent critique of our historical era. I should like to characterize this ethos very briefly.

Negatively

1   This ethos implies, first, the refusal of what I like to call the 'blackmail' of the Enlightenment. I think that the Enlightenment, as a set of political, economic, social, institutional, and cultural events on which we still depend in large part, constitutes a privileged domain for analysis. I also think that as an enterprise for linking the progress of truth and the history of liberty in a bond of direct relation, it formulated a philosophical question that remains for us to consider. I think, finally, as I have tried to show with reference to Kant's text, that it defined a certain manner of philosophizing.

But that does not mean that one has to be 'for' or 'against' the Enlightenment. It even means precisely that one has to refuse everything that might present itself in the form of a simplistic and authoritarian alternative: you either accept the Enlightenment and remain within the tradition of its rationalism (this is considered a positive term by some and used by others, on the contrary, as a reproach); or else you criticize the Enlightenment and then try to escape from its principles of rationality (which may be seen once again as good or bad). And we do not break free of this blackmail by introducing 'dialectical' nuances while seeking to determine what good and bad elements there may have been in the Enlightenment.

We must try to proceed with the analysis of ourselves as beings who are historically determined, to a certain extent, by the Enlightenment. Such an analysis implies a series of historical inquiries that are as precise as possible; and these inquiries will not be oriented retrospectively toward the 'essential kernel of rationality' that can be found in the Enlightenment and that would have to be preserved in any event; they will be oriented toward the 'contemporary limits of the necessary,' that is, toward what is not or is no longer indispensable for the constitution of ourselves as autonomous subjects.

2   This permanent critique of ourselves has to avoid the always too facile confusions between humanism and Enlightenment.

We must never forget that the Enlightenment is an event, or a set of events and complex historical processes, that is located at a certain point in the development of European societies. As such, it includes elements of social transformation, types of political institution, forms of knowledge, projects of rationalization of knowledge and practices, technological mutations that are very difficult to sum up in a word, even if many of these phenomena remain important today. The one I have pointed out and that seems to me to have been at the basis of an entire form of philosophical reflection concerns only the mode of reflective relation to the present.

Humanism is something entirely different. It is a theme or, rather, a set of themes that have reappeared on several occasions, over time, in European societies; these themes, always tied to value judgements, have obviously varied greatly in their content, as well as in the values they have preserved. Furthermore, they have served as a critical principle of differentiation. In the seventeenth century, there was a humanism that presented itself as a critique of Christianity or of religion in general; there was a Christian humanism opposed to an ascetic and much more theocentric humanism. In the nineteenth century, there was a suspicious humanism, hostile and critical toward science, and another that, to the contrary, placed its hope in that same science. Marxism has been a humanism; so have existentialism and personalism; there was a time when people supported the humanistic values represented by National Socialism, and when the Stalinists themselves said they were humanists.

From this, we must not conclude that everything that has ever been linked with humanism is to be rejected, but that the humanistic thematic is in itself too supple, too diverse, too inconsistent to serve as an axis for reflection. And it is a fact that, at least since the seventeenth century, what is called humanism has always been obliged to lean on certain conceptions of man borrowed from religion, science, or politics. Humanism serves to color and to justify the conceptions of man to which it is, after all, obliged to take recourse.

Now, in this connection, I believe that this thematic, which so often recurs and which always depends on humanism, can be opposed by the principle of a critique and a permanent creation of ourselves in our autonomy: that is, a principle that is at the heart of the historical consciousness that the Enlightenment has of itself. From this standpoint, I am inclined to see Enlightenment and humanism in a state of tension rather than identity.

In any case, it seems to me dangerous to confuse them; and further, it seems historically inaccurate. If the question of man, of the human species, of the humanist, was important throughout the eighteenth century, this is very rarely, I believe, because the Enlightenment considered itself a humanism. It is worthwhile, too, to note that throughout the nineteenth century, the historiography of sixteenth-century humanism, which was so important for people like Saint-Beuve or Burckhardt, was always distinct from and sometimes explicitly opposed to the Enlightenment and the eighteenth century. The nineteenth century had a tendency to oppose the two, at least as much as to confuse them.

In any case, I think that, just as we must free ourselves from the intellectual blackmail of 'being for or against the Enlightenment,' we must escape from the historical and moral confusionism that mixes the theme of humanism with the question of the Enlightenment. An analysis of their complex relations in the course of the last two centuries would be a worthwhile project, an important one if we are to bring some measure of clarity to the consciousness that we have of ourselves and of our past.

Positively

Yet while taking these precautions into account, we must obviously give a more positive content to what may be a philosophical ethos consisting in a critique of what we are saying, thinking, and doing, through a historical ontology of ourselves.

1   This philosophical ethos may be characterized as a *limit-attitude*. We are not talking about a gesture of rejection. We have to move beyond the outside-inside alternative; we have to be at the frontiers. Criticism indeed consists of analyzing and reflecting upon limits. But if the Kantian question was that of knowing what limits knowledge has to renounce transgressing, it seems to me that the critical question today has to be turned back into a positive one: in what is given to us as universal, necessary, obligatory, what place is occupied by whatever is singular, contingent, and the product of arbitrary constraints? The point, in brief, is to transform the critique conducted in the form of necessary limitation into a practical critique that takes the form of a possible transgression.
   This entails an obvious consequence: that criticism is no longer going to be practiced in the search for formal structures with universal value, but rather as a historical investigation into the events that have led us to constitute ourselves and to recognize ourselves as subjects of what we are doing, thinking, saying. In that sense, this criticism is not transcendental, and its goal is not that of making a metaphysics possible: it is genealogical in its design and archaelogical in its method. Archaeological – and not transcendental – in the sense that it will not seek to identify the universal structures of all knowledge or of all possible moral action, but will seek to treat the instances of discourse that articulate what we think, say, and do as so many historical events. And this critique will be genealogical in the sense that it will not deduce from the form of what we are what it is impossible for us to do and to know; but it will separate out, from the contingency that has made us what we are, the possibility of no longer being, doing, or thinking what we are, do, or think. It is not seeking to make possible a metaphysics that has finally become a science; it is seeking to give new impetus, as far and wide as possible, to the undefined work of freedom.

2   But if we are not to settle for the affirmation or the empty dream of freedom, it seems to me that this historico-critical attitude must also be an experimental one. I mean that this work done at the limits of ourselves must, on the one hand, open up a realm of historical inquiry and, on the other, put itself to the test of reality, of contemporary reality, both to grasp the points where change is possible and desirable, and to determine the precise form this change should take. This means that the historical ontology of ourselves must turn away from all projects that claim to be global or radical. In fact we know from experience that the claim to escape from the system of contemporary reality so as to produce the overall programs of another society, of another way of thinking, another culture, another vision of the world, has led only to the return of the most dangerous traditions.
   I prefer the very specific transformations that have proved to be possible in the last twenty years in a certain number of areas that concern our ways of being

and thinking, relations to authority, relations between the sexes, the way in which we perceive insanity or illness; I prefer even these partial transformations that have been made in the correlation of historical analysis and the practical attitude, to the programs for a new man that the worst political systems have repeated throughout the twentieth century.

I shall thus characterize the philosophical ethos appropriate to the critical ontology of ourselves as a historico-practical test of the limits that we may go beyond, and thus as work carried out by ourselves upon ourselves as free beings.

3   Still, the following objection would no doubt be entirely legitimate: if we limit ourselves to this type of always partial and local inquiry or test, do we not run the risk of letting ourselves be determined by more general structures of which we may well not be conscious, and over which we may have no control?

To this, two responses. It is true that we have to give up hope of ever acceding to a point of view that could give us access to any complete and definitive knowledge of what may constitute our historical limits. And from this point of view the theoretical and practical experience that we have of our limits and of the possibility of moving beyond them is always limited and determined; thus we are always in the position of beginning again.

But that does not mean that no work can be done except in disorder and contingency. The work in question has its generality, its systematicity, its homogeneity, and its stakes.

a) Its Stakes   These are indicated by what might be called 'the paradox of the relations of capacity and power.' We know that the great promise or the great hope of the eighteenth century, or a part of the eighteenth century, lay in the simultaneous and proportional growth of individuals with respect to one another. And, moreover, we can see that throughout the entire history of Western societies (it is perhaps here that the root of their singular historical destiny is located – such a peculiar destiny, so different from the others in its trajectory and so universalizing, so dominant with respect to the others), the acquisition of capabilities and the struggle for freedom have constituted permanent elements. Now the relations between the growth of capabilities and the growth of autonomy are not as simple as the eighteenth century may have believed. And we have been able to see what forms of power relation were conveyed by various technologies (whether we are speaking of productions with economic aims, or institutions whose goal is social regulation, or of techniques of communication): disciplines, both collective and individual, procedures of normalization exercised in the name of the power of the state, demands of society or of population zones, are examples. What is at stake, then, is this: How can the growth of capabilities be disconnected from the intensification of power relations?

b) Homogeneity   This leads to the study of what could be called 'practical systems'. Here we are taking as a homogeneous domain of reference not the representations that men give of themselves, not the conditions that determine them without their knowledge, but rather what they do and the way they do it. That is, the forms of rationality that organize their ways of doing things (this might be called the technological aspect) and the freedom with which they act within these practical systems, reacting to what others do, modifying the rules of the game, up to a certain point (this might be called the strategic side of these practices). The homogeneity of these historico-critical analyses is thus ensured by this realm of practices, with their technological side and their strategic side.

c) Systematicity These practical systems stem from three broad areas: relations of control over things, relations of action upon others, relations with oneself. This does not mean that each of these three areas is completely foreign to the others. It is well known that control over things is mediated by relations with others; and relations with others in turn always entail relations with oneself, and vice versa. But we have three axes whose specificity and whose interconnections have to be analyzed: the axis of knowledge, the axis of power, the axis of ethics. In other terms, the historical ontology of ourselves has to answer an open series of questions; it has to make an indefinite number of inquiries which may be multiplied and specified as much as we like, but which will all address the questions systematized as follows: How are we constituted as subjects of our own knowledge? How are we constituted as subjects who exercise or submit to power relations? How are we constituted as moral subjects of our own actions?

d) Generality Finally, these historico-critical investigations are quite specific in the sense that they always bear upon a material, an epoch, a body of determined practices and discourses. And yet, at least at the level of the Western societies from which we derive, they have their generality, in the sense that they have continued to recur up to our time: for example, the problem of the relationship between sanity and insanity, or sickness and health, or crime and the law; the problem of the role of sexual relations; and so on.

But by evoking this generality, I do not mean to suggest that it has to be retraced in its metahistorical continuity over time, nor that its variations have to be pursued. What must be grasped is the extent to which what we know of it, the forms of power that are exercised in it, and the experience that we have in it of ourselves constitute nothing but determined historical figures, through a certain form of problematization that defines objects, rules of action, modes of relation to oneself. The study of [modes of] problematization (that is, of what is neither an anthropological constant nor a chronological variation) is thus the way to analyze questions of general import in their historically unique form.

A brief summary, to conclude and to come back to Kant.

I do not know whether we will ever reach mature adulthood. Many things in our experience convince us that the historical event of the Enlightenment did not make us mature adults, and we have not reached that stage yet. However, it seems to me that a meaning can be attributed to that critical interrogation on the present and on ourselves which Kant formulated by reflecting on the Enlightenment. It seems to me that Kant's reflection is even a way of philosophizing that has not been without its importance or effectiveness during the last two centuries. The critical ontology of ourselves has to be considered not, certainly, as a theory, a doctrine, nor even as a permanent body of knowledge that is accumulating; it has to be conceived as an attitude, an ethos, a philosophical life in which the critique of what we are is at one and the same time the historical analysis of the limits that are imposed on us and an experiment with the possibility of going beyond them.

This philosophical attitude has to be translated into the labor of diverse inquiries. These inquiries have their methodological coherence in the at once archaeological and genealogical study of practices envisaged simultaneously as a technological type of rationality and as strategic games of liberties; they have their theoretical coherence in the definition of the historically unique forms in which the generalities of our relations to things, to others, to ourselves, have been problematized. They have their practical coherence in the care brought to the process of putting historico-critical reflection to the test of concrete practices. I do not know whether it must be said today that the critical task still entails faith in Enlightenment; I continue to think that this task requires work on our limits, that is, a patient labor giving form to our impatience for liberty.

---

11 Friedrich Nietzsche

From *Twilight of the Idols*

trans. R. J. Hollingdale, Harmondsworth, 1990, pp 45–51.

You ask me about the idiosyncrasies of philosophers? . . . There is their lack of historical sense, their hatred of even the idea of becoming, their Egyptianism. They think they are doing a thing *honour* when they dehistoricize it, *sub specie aeterni* [1] – when they make a mummy of it. All that philosophers have handled for millennia has been conceptual mummies; nothing actual has escaped from their hands alive. They kill, they stuff, when they worship, these conceptual idolaters – they become a mortal danger to everything when they worship. Death, change, age, as well as procreation and growth, are for them objections – refutations even. What is, does not *become*; what becomes, *is* not. . . . Now they all believe, even to the point of despair, in that which is. But since they cannot get hold of it, they look for reasons why it is being withheld from them. 'It must be an illusion, a deception which prevents us from perceiving that which is: where is the deceiver to be found?' - 'We've got it,' they cry in delight,

---

[1] from the viewpoint of eternity.

'it is the senses! These senses, *which are so immoral as well*, it is they which deceive us about the *real* world. Moral: escape from sense-deception, from becoming, from history, from falsehood – history is nothing but belief in the senses, belief in falsehood. Moral: denial of all that believes in the senses, of all the rest of mankind: all of that is mere 'people'. Be a philosopher, be a mummy, represent monotono-theism by a gravedigger-mimicry! – And away, above all, with the *body*, that pitiable *idée fixe* of the senses! infected with every error of logic there is, refuted, impossible even, notwithstanding it is impudent enough to behave as if it actually existed!' . . .

I set apart with high reverence the name of *Heraclitus*. When the rest of the philosopher crowd rejected the evidence of the senses because these showed plurality and change, he rejected their evidence because they showed things as if they possessed duration and unity. Heraclitus too was unjust to the senses, which lie neither in the way the Eleatics[2] believe nor as he believed – they do not lie at all. It is what we *make* of their evidence that first introduces a lie into it, for example the lie of unity, the lie of materiality, of substance, of duration. . . . 'Reason' is the cause of our falsification of the evidence of the senses. In so far as the senses show becoming, passing away, change, they do not lie. . . . But Heraclitus will always be right in this, that being is an empty fiction. The 'apparent' world is the only one: the 'real' world has only been *lyingly added* . . .

And what subtle instruments for observation we possess in our senses! This nose, for example, of which no philosopher has hitherto spoken with respect and gratitude, is nonetheless the most delicate tool we have at our command: it can detect minimal differences in movement which even the spectroscope cannot detect. We possess scientific knowledge today to precisely the extent that we have decided to *accept* the evidence of the senses – to the extent that we have learned to sharpen and arm them and to think them through to their conclusions. The rest is abortion and not-yet-science: which is to say meta-physics, theology, psychology, epistemology. *Or* science of formulae, sign-systems: such as logic and that applied logic, mathematics. In these reality does not appear at all, not even as a problem; just as little as does the question what value a system of conventional signs such as constitutes logic can possibly possess.

The *other* idiosyncrasy of philosophers is no less perilous: it consists in mistaking the last for the first. They put that which comes at the end – unfortunately! for it ought not to come at all! – the 'highest concepts', that is to

---

[2] The school of Parmenides of Elea (fifth century BC), who denied the logical possibility of change and motion and argued that the only logical possibility was unchanging being.

say the most general, the emptiest concepts, the last fumes of evaporating reality, at the beginning *as* the beginning. It is again only the expression of their way of doing reverence: the high must not be *allowed* to grow out of the lower, must not be *allowed* to have grown at all. . . . Moral: everything of the first rank must be *causa sui*.[3] Origin in something else counts as an objection, as casting a doubt on value. All supreme values are of the first rank, all the supreme concepts – that which is, the unconditioned, the good, the true, the perfect – all that cannot have become, *must* therefore be *causa sui*. But neither can these supreme concepts be incommensurate with one another, be incompatible with one another. . . . Thus they acquired their stupendous concept 'God'. . . . The last, thinnest, emptiest is placed as the first, as cause in itself, as *ens realissimum*.[4] . . . That mankind should have taken seriously the brainsick fancies of morbid cobweb-spinners! – And it has paid dearly for doing so! . . .

Let us, in conclusion, set against this the very different way in which *we* (I say 'we' out of politeness . . .) view the problem of error and appearance. Change, mutation, becoming in general were formerly taken as proof of appearance, as a sign of the presence of something which led us astray. Today, on the contrary, we see ourselves as it were entangled in error, *necessitated* to error, to precisely the extent that our prejudice in favour of reason compels us to posit unity, identity, duration, substance, cause, materiality, being; however sure we may be, on the basis of a strict reckoning, *that* error is to be found here. The situation is the same as with the motions of the sun: in that case error has our eyes, in the present case our *language* as a perpetual advocate. Language belongs in its origin to the age of the most rudimentary form of psychology: we find ourselves in the midst of a rude fetishism when we call to mind the basic presuppositions of the metaphysics of language – which is to say, of *reason*. It is *this* which sees everywhere deed and doer; this which believes in will as cause in general; this which believes in the 'ego', in the ego as being, in the ego as substance, and which *projects* its belief in the ego-substance on to all things – only thus does it *create* the concept 'thing'. . . . Being is everywhere thought in, *foisted on*, as cause; it is only from the conception 'ego' that there follows, derivatively, the concept 'being'. . . . At the beginning stands the great fateful error that the will is something which *produces an effect* – that will is a *faculty*. . . . Today we know it is merely a word. . . . Very much later, in a world a thousand times more enlightened, the *security*, the subjective *certainty* with which the categories of reason[5] could be employed came all of a sudden into philosophers' heads: they concluded that these could not have originated in the empirical world – indeed, the entire empirical world was incompatible with them. *Where then do they originate?* – And in India as in Greece they committed the same blunder: 'We must once have dwelt in a higher world' – instead of *in a very much lower one*, which would have been the truth! – 'we

---

[3] the cause of itself.

[4] the most real being.

[5] The context makes it clear that this Kantian-sounding term is not being employed in the sense of Kant's twelve *a priori* 'categories,' but simply to mean the faculty of reasoning.

must have been divine, *for* we possess reason!' . . . Nothing, in fact, has hitherto had a more direct power of persuasion than the error of being as it was formulated by, for example, the Eleatics: for every word, every sentence we utter speaks in its favour! – Even the opponents of the Eleatics were still subject to the seductive influence of their concept of being: Democritus, among others, when he invented his *atom*. . . . 'Reason' in language: oh what a deceitful old woman! I fear we are not getting rid of God because we still believe in grammar . . .

It will be a matter for gratitude if I now compress so fundamental and new an insight into four theses: I shall thereby make it easier to understand, I shall thereby challenge contradiction.

First proposition. The grounds upon which 'this' world has been designated as apparent establish rather its reality – *another* kind of reality is absolutely undemonstrable.

Second proposition. The characteristics which have been assigned to the 'real being' of things are the characteristics of non-being, of *nothingness* – the 'real world' has been constructed out of the contradiction to the actual world: an apparent world indeed, in so far as it is no more than a *moral-optical* illusion.

Third proposition. To talk about 'another' world than this is quite pointless, provided that an instinct for slandering, disparaging and accusing life is not strong within us: in the latter case we *revenge* ourselves on life by means of the phantasmagoria of 'another', a 'better' life.

Fourth proposition. To divide the world into a 'real' and an 'apparent' world, whether in the manner of Christianity or in the manner of Kant (which is, after all, that of a *cunning* Christian –) is only a suggestion of *décadence* – a symptom of *declining* life. . . . That the artist places a higher value on appearance than on reality constitutes no objection to this proposition. For 'appearance' here signifies reality *once more*, only selected, strengthened, corrected. . . . The tragic artist is *not* a pessimist – it is precisely he who *affirms* all that is questionable and terrible in existence, he is *Dionysian* . . .

How the 'Real World' at last Became a Myth

History of an Error

1   The real world, attainable to the wise, the pious, the virtuous man – he dwells in it, *he is it*. (Oldest form of the idea, relatively sensible, simple, convincing. Transcription of the proposition 'I, Plato, *am* the truth.')[6]
2   The real world, unattainable for the moment, but promised to the wise, the pious, the virtuous man ('to the sinner who repents'). (Progress of the idea: it grows more refined, more enticing, more incomprehensible – *it becomes a woman*, it becomes Christian . . .)
3   The real world, unattainable, undemonstrable, cannot be promised, but

---

[6] the truth = *Wahrbeit*, corresponding to *wahre Welt* = real world.

even when merely thought of a consolation, a duty, an imperative. (Fundamentally the same old sun, but shining through mist and scepticism; the idea grown sublime, pale, northerly, Königsbergian.)[7]

4   The real world – unattainable? Unattained, at any rate. And if unattained also *unknown*. Consequently also no consolation, no redemption, no duty: how could we have a duty towards something unknown? (The grey of dawn. First yawnings of reason. Cock-crow of positivism.)[8]

5   The 'real world' – an idea no longer of any use, not even a duty any longer – an idea grown useless, superfluous, *consequently* a refuted idea: let us abolish it! (Broad daylight; breakfast; return of cheerfulness and *bon sens*; Plato blushes for shame; all free spirits run riot.)

6   We have abolished the real world: what world is left? the apparent world perhaps? . . . But no! *with the real world we have also abolished the apparent world!* (Mid-day; moment of the shortest shadow; end of the longest error: zenith of mankind; INCIPIT ZARATHUSTRA.)[9]

[7] i.e. Kantian, from the northerly German city in which Kant was born and in which he lived and died.
[8] Here meaning empiricism, philosophy founded on observation and experiment.
[9] Zarathustra begins.

SECTION FOUR

Postmodern Theory: The Current Debate

The essays collected in this section offer a range of different positions on Postmodernism and examples of postmodern theory. By way of introduction, I will discuss those which constitute commentaries on Postmodernism viewed as a mood or term for a cultural epoch (Eagleton, Jameson, Baudrillard) and those which can be seen to be postmodern theories as opposed to theories of the postmodern (Lyotard, Rorty and, though he is a defender of modernity, Habermas). Let us begin by considering the first group in relation to the way in which Postmodernism has been understood as a period concept. A central issue in this area is whether 'Postmodernism' exists: has there been a break with modernity or Modernism, or are we still in a condition of Late rather than Post- modernity? Postmodernism as a period concept tends to be constructed through the selection of a particular dominant for modernity which is then seen to be exhausted or to have been surpassed. There have been a flood of 'Posts' over the last twenty years: Post- Christian, -Capitalism, -liberal, -Fordism, -Marxism, -feminism, -industrial. In each case the present is constructed through a hermeneutic relation with a past conceived in one of the above terms. A major difficulty, as so often with Postmodernism, is whether such conceptualisations seem to reflect, as far as one can ever know, the facts that we have about the past, or to what extent they are 'totalisations' based on a primary desire to establish the present as distinctively different. The very proliferation of 'Posts', however, in itself, suggests that we are living in a period where the multiplication of value systems has produced a major crisis of legitimation (which, of course, is part of Lyotard's definition of the postmodern condition).

Eagleton's essay criticises Lyotard for dehistoricising Postmodernism by defining it in aesthetic terms. For Eagleton, Lyotard's Postmodernism is one aspect of a naïve post-structuralist embrace of 'desire' as that which can explode out of history in order to deny its own historicity: it simply co-extensive with the commodification of all life in consumer capitalism. In a commercially aestheticised world, art is simply an aesthetic reflection of already aestheticised images. Postmodern art is simply another depthless surface mirroring the unreality of the images which construct similar depthless surfaces of a consumer society where all commodities are packaged fetishes. Postmodernism is a debasement of the avant-garde desire to take art out of a sphere of autonomous withdrawal from mass culture and to reintegrate it into life as an oppositional praxis. Postmodern integration is simply complicity. Eagleton does not offer detailed analysis of postmodern cultural artefacts and he accepts the construction of Modernism in terms of aesthetic autonomy. However, he does draw attention to the possibility that Postmodernism may, in effect, simply be the cultural logic of late capitalism and his commentary is valuable in pointing out its contradictions and in exposing the naïvete of some versions of its politics or poetics of desire. The position is developed in Jameson's work in the early eighties. However, Jameson's argument is that we cannot simply put forward a position for or against Postmodernism for, as the logic of Late Capitalism, it has invaded everything and there is no longer a pure outside from which to offer critique or opposition. Jameson's earlier work had accepted the Hegelian assumption that there are spaces outside the logic of capitalism even in its consumerist forms: deep structures to be explained and metanarrative positions from which to explain them. In his more recent work, however, all theories, including Marxism, become problematic because they can only conduct their critique from the very metaposition which Postmodernism, as the cultural logic of Late Capitalism, has abolished. With this in mind, commentators like Callinicos (1990) and Anderson (1983), have argued that Marxist intellectuals like Jameson have simply arrived at a quietist position as a consequence of disillusionment after the failure of 1968: Postmodernism can only function as a weakened, necessarily internal critique of Western instrumentalism. In fact, as early as 1971, Jameson had begun to develop the idea that what characterises the contemporary period is loss of depth: the belief there is nothing to uncover, only surfaces to inhabit. The essay reprinted here basically explores Postmodernism as a configuration of effects arising from this: the loss of historical depth, of affective depth and of symbolic meaning expressive of a latent core structure. Jameson here surveys historical trends characteristic of Postmodernism and offers an economic analysis of them in terms of Ernst Mandel's categories in his book *Late Capitalism* (1978). Paradoxically, of course, in seeing this as the logic of Late Capitalism, he draws on an economic model still located in an enlightened theory of political economy. However, if Late Capitalism is a totality, it is one which cannot be thought: in its fragmentariness and depthless surfaces it can only be grasped within the logic of its own terms. Reason will not save us from it. Like everything else, it has been appropriated to the postmodern in its erasure of the distinction between the critical and the functional. There are echoes of Baudrillard here (see below), of the concept of the universe of simulacra, but Jameson does not share his technological determinism nor his purely reproductive economy of the sign. He does, however, view Postmodernism as a crisis in the belief in the possibility of authentic self-expression or objective representation. Strictly speaking, his own arguments about the invasion of late capitalism contradict the attempt to offer a depth or 'total' economic analysis. Although the essay begins with a Foucauldian view of the manifestation of Postmodernism in the sixties, seeing power as a multiplicity of contradictory relations immanent in all cultural forms, defying total resistance and given no clear foundation in economics, he then proceeds to give his analysis a foundation in a total economic theory. There are a number of other problems in the essay. Mandel dated the rise of late capitalism around 1945 and Jameson shifts it to 1960. Moreover, he tends to overlook the continuation of both pre-modern and modern political and cultural forms, not only in the post-colonial world, but also in the West. Certainly, he overlooks the multiac-centual nature of signs and cultural symbols which suggests that no economic mode can ever entirely colonise meaning and value. Others, such as Charles Jencks (1977), have seen Postmodernism as genuinely offering the possibility of critique and disruption from within, refusing to submerge difference into universalism and therefore preserving multiplicity and local cultures. For Jencks (see Hutcheon below for a literary critical version of this position), the values of mass-society have not colonised the lifeworld, but neither do the values of High Art define the universal good. If, for Eagleton and Jameson, Postmodernism is complicity with commodification, for Jencks and Hutcheon, it represents a genuine democratisation of art and a realistic political strategy of internal disruption.

Baudrillard's postmodern scenario is perhaps the bleakest of them all. In his account, technology rather than Capitalism, becomes the focus of his critique. To live in the postmodern condition is not so much to inhabit a world saturated with consumer logic as with media reproduction. We have moved out of an economy of production not simply through surpassing Fordism or entering a new economy where knowledge is the key commodity, but because we have entered the culture of the 'simulacrum'. Since the seventies, Baudrillard's work has moved entirely away from analysis of political economy to a concern with the culture of 'hyperreality': models replace the real and determine the real: Disneyland becomes America, hyperreality is everyday reality. Media messages saturate the cultural field so entirely that the 'masses' are reduced, through an overload of information, to an inert and silent majority and all meaning implodes into the black hole of simulacra. The post-structuralist critique of reference is taken to a nihilistic limit.

Turning now to the second group of postmodern theorists represented here, I will confine my introductory remarks largely to the debate between Habermas and Lyotard, for the more general issues have already been discussed in the introduction to this Reader. Lyotard's essay was added as a post-script to the English translation of *The Postmodern Condition*. It is included here because its emphasis on the sublime makes explicit the aestheticist assumptions of Lyotard's thought and because it represents the crux of his disagreement with Habermas, for whom modernity is not exhausted but incomplete. Central to Lyotard's definition of the postmodern is the Kantian notion of the sublime as confirming the incommensurability of reality as pure Idea to concept as tool of human understanding. This is in contradistinction to the beautiful which has the effect of seeming to affirm a realisable correspondence between internal and external orders. Sublimity, for Kant, is that experience of an object which invokes an idea of pure reason, but one which is radically indeterminate and cannot be formulated or known. Kant suggests that the imagination, in this mode, can excite in us ideas which cannot be realised in sensory form, though the experience in itself liberates us into a sense of the magnitude of the human mind. Lyotard's sublime is a self-consciously postmodern mode in which all striving for correspondence between Real and concept is abandoned: the aesthetic is to be preserved in the form of a non-utilitarian autonomy.

If this seems to contradict what most readers have assumed to be central to all Postmodernisms (the aestheticisation of politics, knowledge and ethics), attention to Habermas's essay may help to unravel the confusions. Lyotard's essay is an implicit dialogue with Habermas's piece (which was originally delivered as a lecture on receipt of the Adorno prize in 1980). The two should be read as a dialogue. Habermas defends Enlightenment but argues that it is unfinished because distorted by an inadequate and instrumental definition of reason. Subject-centred philosophies of consciousness have facilitated the development of 'expert cultures' which have fragmented and instrumentalised knowledge, divorcing it from context and reproducing it in impoverished terms of abstraction. We need a new balance of the cognitive, practical and aesthetic (Kant's three categories), though they must retain their distinctiveness. Art can enhance life by allowing us to connect with pre-reflective and bodily aspects of experience but only as one aspect of the expansion of our concept of reason. He is opposed to the collapse of knowledge and ethics into the aesthetic and he continues to believe that the discourses which shape these former categories must partake of public forms of rationality, though facilitated by aesthetic awareness. The latter though must itself be released from appropriation by 'expert cultures' (professionalised literary critics) if it is fully to participate in the lifeworld.

Although Postmodernism is normally seen to involve the aestheticisation of the entire lifeworld, positions in the debate are always liable to shift. Lyotard speaks for Postmodernism, yet he sees as highly dangerous any ideal of social integration which draws on the aesthetic as a facilitating vehicle. The sublime must exceed all that can be presented. All attempts to graft the ideal onto the real have produced Terror and must be resisted. The beautiful may induce consensus, conformism and integration by seeming to embody the correspondence of idea to concept through the imaginatively produced image: Lyotard implies that Habermas's aesthetic is one of the beautiful. Lyotard's, an aesthetic of the sublime, asserts dissensus, radical incommensurability. It will not provide comfort and consolatory order or unity and exists as a mode of resistance to the banal and automatising effects of modern life. To attempt to realise it, however, as a blueprint for political intervention in the historical world, would be dangerously to conflate language games which can only function within their own discrete regulatory orders. Existence may be aestheticised, but the aesthetic must not be used to underpin political ideologies which set out to produce new cultures through ideal frameworks. The sublime as the most authentic form of the aesthetic must remain ever in a beyond, always in a 'Post' condition.

The final essay in this section is my own exploration of relations between feminism and Postmodernism: I will not attempt in this introduction to write a metacommentary on my own views. If nothing else, Postmodernism has taught me the futility of such an exercise.

12   Jean-François Lyotard

From *Answering the Question: What is Postmodernism?*

The Postmodern Condition, trans. R. Durand, Manchester University Press, 1986, pp 71–82.

A Demand

This is a period of slackening – I refer to the color of the times. From every direction we are being urged to put an end to experimentation, in the arts and elsewhere. I have read an art historian who extols realism and is militant for the advent of a new subjectivity. I have read an art critic who packages and sells 'Transavantgardism' in the marketplace of painting. I have read that under the name of postmodernism, architects are getting rid of the Bauhaus project, throwing out the baby of experimentation with the bathwater of functionalism. I have read that a new philosopher is discovering what he drolly calls Judaeo-Christianism, and intends by it to put an end to the impiety which we are supposed to have spread. I have read in a French weekly that some are displeased with *Mille Plateaux* [by Deleuze and Guattari] because they expect, especially when reading a work of philosophy, to be gratified with a little sense. I have read from the pen of a reputable historian that writers and thinkers of the 1960 and 1970 avant-gardes spread a reign of terror in the use of language, and that the conditions for a fruitful exchange must be restored by imposing on the intellectuals a common way of speaking, that of the historians. I have been reading a young philosopher of language who complains that Continental thinking, under the challenge of speaking machines, has surrendered to the machines the concern for reality, that it has substituted for the referential paradigm that of 'adlinguisticity' (one speaks about speech, writes about writing, intertextuality), and who thinks that the time has now come to restore a solid anchorage of language in the referent. I have read a talented theatrologist for whom postmodernism, with its games and fantasies, carries very little weight in front of political authority, especially when a worried public opinion encourages authority to a politics of totalitarian surveillance in the face of nuclear warfare threats.

I have read a thinker of repute who defends modernity against those he calls the neoconservatives. Under the banner of postmodernism, the latter would like, he believes, to get rid of the uncompleted project of modernism, that of the Enlightenment. Even the last advocates of *Aufklärung*, such as Popper or Adorno, were only able, according to him, to defend the project in a few particular spheres of life – that of politics for the author of *The Open Society*, and that of art for the author of *Ästhetische Theorie*. Jürgen Habermas (everyone had recognized him) thinks that if modernity has failed, it is in allowing the totality of life to be splintered into independent specialties which are left to the narrow competence of experts, while the concrete individual experiences 'desublimated meaning' and 'destructured form,' not as a liberation but in the mode of that immense *ennui* which Baudelaire described over a century ago.

Following a prescription of Albrecht Wellmer, Habermas considers that the remedy for this splintering of culture and its separation from life can only come from 'changing the status of aesthetic experience when it is no longer primarily expressed in judgments of taste,' but when it is 'used to explore a living historical situation,' that is, when 'it is put in relation with problems of existence.' For this experience then 'becomes a part of a language game which is no longer that of aesthetic criticism'; it takes part 'in cognitive processes and normative expectations'; 'it alters the manner in which those different moments *refer* to one another.' What Habermas requires from the arts and the experiences they provide is, in short, to bridge the gap between cognitive, ethical, and political discourses, thus opening the way to a unity of experience.

My question is to determine what sort of unity Habermas has in mind. Is the aim of the project of modernity the constitution of sociocultural unity within which all the elements of daily life and of thought would take their places as in an organic whole? Or does the passage that has to be charted between heterogeneous language games – those of cognition, of ethics, of politics – belong to a different order from that? And if so, would it be capable of effecting a real synthesis between them?

The first hypothesis, of a Hegelian inspiration, does not challenge the notion of a dialectically totalizing *experience*; the second is closer to the spirit of Kant's *Critique of Judgment*; but must be submitted, like the *Critique*, to that severe reexamination which postmodernity imposes on the thought of the Enlightenment, on the idea of a unitary end of history and of a subject. It is this critique which not only Wittgenstein and Adorno have initiated, but also a few other thinkers (French or other) who do not have the honor to be read by Professor Habermas – which at least saves them from getting a poor grade for their neoconservatism.

Realism

The demands I began by citing are not all equivalent. They can even be contradictory. Some are made in the name of postmodernism, others in order to combat it. It is not necessarily the same thing to formulate a demand for some referent (and objective reality), for some sense (and credible transcendence), for an addressee (and audience), or an addressor (and subjective expressiveness) or for some communicational consensus (and a general code of exchanges, such as the genre of historical discourse). But in the diverse invitations to suspend artistic experimentation, there is an identical call for order, a desire for unity, for identity, for security, or popularity (in the sense of *Öffentlichkeit*, of 'finding a public'). Artists and writers must be brought back into the bosom of the community, or at least, if the latter is considered to be ill, they must be assigned the task of healing it.

There is an irrefutable sign of this common disposition: it is that for all those writers nothing is more urgent than to liquidate the heritage of the avant-gardes. Such is the case, in particular, of the so-called transavantgardism. The answers given by Achille Bonito Oliva to the questions asked by Bernard Lamarche-Vadel and Michel Enric leave no room for doubt about this. By putting the avant-gardes through a mixing process, the artist and critic feel more confident that they can suppress them than by launching a frontal attack. For they can pass off the most cynical eclecticism as a way of going beyond the fragmentary character of the preceding experiments; whereas if they openly turned their backs on them, they would run the risk of appearing ridiculously neoacademic. The *Salons* and the *Académies*, at the time when the bourgeoisie was establishing itself in history, were able to function as purgation and to grant awards for good plastic and literary conduct under the cover of realism. But capitalism inherently possesses the power to derealize familiar objects, social roles, and institutions to such a degree that the so-called realistic representations can no longer evoke reality except as nostalgia or mockery, as an occasion for suffering rather than for satisfaction. Classicism seems to be ruled out in a world in which reality is so destabilized that it offers no occasion for experience but one for ratings and experimentation.

This theme is familiar to all readers of Walter Benjamin. But it is necessary to assess its exact reach. Photography did not appear as a challenge to painting from the outside, any more than industrial cinema did to narrative literature. The former was only putting the final touch to the program of ordering the visible elaborated by the quattrocento; while the latter was the last step in rounding off diachronies as organic wholes, which had been the ideal of the great novels of education since the eighteenth century. That the mechanical and the industrial should appear as substitutes for hand or craft was not in itself a disaster – except if one believes that art is in its essence the expression of an individuality of genius assisted by an elite craftsmanship.

The challenge lay essentially in that photographic and cinematographic processes can accomplish better, faster, and with a circulation a hundred thousand times larger than narrative or pictorial realism, the task which academicism had assigned to realism: to preserve various consciousnesses from doubt. Industrial photography and cinema will be superior to painting and the novel whenever the objective is to stabilize the referent, to arrange it according to a point of view which endows it with a recognizable meaning, to reproduce the syntax and vocabulary which enable the addressee to decipher images and sequences quickly, and so to arrive easily at the consciousness of his own identity as well as the approval which he thereby receives from others – since such structures of images and sequences constitute a communication code among all of them. This is the way the effects of reality, or if one prefers, the fantasies of realism, multiply.

If they too do not wish to become supporters (of minor importance at that) of what exists, the painter and novelist must refuse to lend themselves to such therapeutic uses. They must question the rules of the art of painting or of narrative as they have learned and received them from their predecessors. Soon those rules must appear to them as a means to deceive, to seduce, and to reassure, which makes it impossible for them to be 'true.' Under the common name of painting and literature, an unprecedented split is taking place. Those who refuse to reexamine the rules of art pursue successful careers in mass conformism by communicating, by means of the 'correct rules,' the endemic desire for reality with objects and situations capable of gratifying it. Pornography is the use of photography and film to such an end. It is becoming a general model for the visual or narrative arts which have not met the challenge of the mass media.

As for the artists and writers who question the rules of plastic and narrative arts and possibly share their suspicions by circulating their work, they are destined to have little credibility in the eyes of those concerned with 'reality' and 'identity'; they have no guarantee of an audience. Thus it is possible to ascribe the dialectics of the avant-gardes to the challenge posed by the realisms of industry and mass communication to painting and the narrative arts. Duchamp's 'ready made' does nothing but actively and parodistically signify this constant process of dispossession of the craft of painting or even of being an artist. As Thierry de Duve penetratingly observes, the modern aesthetic question is not 'What is beautiful?' but 'What can be said to be art (and literature)?'

Realism, whose only definition is that it intends to avoid the question of reality implicated in that of art, always stands somewhere between academicism and kitsch. When power assumes the name of a party, realism and its neoclassical complement triumph over the experimental avant-garde by slandering and banning it – that is, provided the 'correct' images, the 'correct' narratives, the 'correct' forms which the party requests, selects, and propagates can find a public to desire them as the appropriate remedy for the anxiety and depression that public experiences. The demand for reality – that is, for unity, simplicity, communicability, etc. – did not have the same intensity nor the same continuity in German society between the two world wars and in Russian society after the Revolution: this provides a basis for a distinction between Nazi and Stalinist realism.

What is clear, however, is that when it is launched by the political apparatus, the attack on artistic experimentation is specifically reactionary: aesthetic judgment would only be required to decide whether such or such work is in conformity with the established rules of the beautiful. Instead of the work of art having to investigate what makes it an art object and whether it will be able to find an audience, political academicism possesses and imposes a priori criteria of the beautiful, which designate some works and a public at a stroke and forever. The use of categories in aesthetic judgment would thus be of the same nature as in cognitive judgment. To speak like Kant, both would be determining judgments: the expression is 'well formed' first in the understanding, then the only cases retained in experience are those which can be subsumed under this expression.

When power is that of capital and not that of a party, the 'transavantgardist' or 'postmodern' (in Jencks's sense) solution proves to be better adapted than the antimodern solution. Eclecticism is the degree zero of contemporary general culture: one listens to reggae, watches a western, eats McDonald's food for lunch and local cuisine for dinner, wears Paris perfume in Tokyo and 'retro' clothes in Hong Kong; knowledge is a matter for TV games. It is easy to find a public for eclectic works. By becoming kitsch, art panders to the confusion which reigns in the 'taste' of the patrons. Artists, gallery owners, critics, and public wallow together in the 'anything goes,' and the epoch is one of slackening. But this realism of the 'anything goes' is in fact that of money; in the absence of aesthetic criteria, it remains possible and useful to assess the value of works of art according to the profits they yield. Such realism accommodates all tendencies, just as capital accommodates all 'needs,' providing that the tendencies and needs have purchasing power. As for taste, there is no need to be delicate when one speculates or entertains oneself.

Artistic and literary research is doubly threatened, once by the 'cultural policy' and once by the art and book market. What is advised, sometimes through one channel, sometimes through the other, is to offer works which, first, are relative to subjects which exist in the eyes of the public they address, and second, works so made ('well made') that the public will recognize what they are about, will understand what is signified, will be able to give or refuse its approval knowingly, and if possible, even to derive from such work a certain amount of comfort.

The interpretation which has just been given of the contact between the industrial and mechanical arts, and literature and the fine arts is correct in its outline, but it remains narrowly sociologizing and historicizing – in other words, one-sided. Stepping over Benjamin's and Adorno's reticences, it must be recalled that science and industry are no more free of the suspicion which concerns reality than are art and writing. To believe otherwise would be to entertain an excessively humanistic notion of the mephistophelian functionalism of sciences and technologies. There is no denying the dominant existence today of techno-science, that is, the massive subordination of cognitive statements to the finality of the best possible performance, which is the technological criterion. But the mechanical and the industrial, especially when they enter fields traditionally reserved for artists, are carrying with them much more than power effects. The objects and the thoughts which originate in scientific knowledge and the capitalist economy convey with them one of the rules which supports their possibility: the rule that there is no reality unless testified by a consensus between partners over a certain knowledge and certain commitments.

This rule is of no little consequence. It is the imprint left on the politics of the scientist and the trustee of capital by a kind of flight of reality out of the metaphysical, religious, and political certainties that the mind believed it held. This withdrawal is absolutely necessary to the emergence of science and capitalism. No industry is possible without a suspicion of the Aristotelian theory of motion, no industry without a refutation of corporatism, of mercantilism, and of physiocracy. Modernity, in whatever age it appears, cannot exist without a shattering of belief and without discovery of the 'lack of reality' of reality, together with the invention of other realities.

What does this 'lack of reality' signify if one tries to free it from a narrowly historicized interpretation? The phrase is of course akin to what Nietzsche calls nihilism. But I see a much earlier modulation of Nietzschean perspectivism in the Kantian theme of the sublime. I think in particular that it is in the aesthetic of the sublime that modern art (including literature) finds its impetus and the logic of avant-gardes finds its axioms.

The sublime sentiment, which is also the sentiment of the sublime, is, according to Kant, a strong and equivocal emotion: it carries with it both pleasure and pain. Better still, in it pleasure derives from pain. Within the tradition of the subject, which comes from Augustine and Descartes and which Kant does not radically challenge, this contradiction, which some would call neurosis or masochism, develops as a conflict between the faculties of a subject, the faculty to conceive of something and the faculty to 'present' something. Knowledge exists if, first, the statement is intelligible, and second, if 'cases' can be derived from the experience which 'corresponds' to it. Beauty exists if a certain 'case' (the work of art), given first by the sensibility without any conceptual determination, the sentiment of pleasure independent of any interest the work may elicit, appeals to the principle of a universal consensus (which may never be attained).

Taste, therefore, testifies that between the capacity to conceive and the capacity to present an object corresponding to the concept, an undetermined agreement, without rules, giving rise to a judgment which Kant calls reflective, may be experienced as pleasure. The sublime is a different sentiment. It takes place, on the contrary, when the imagination fails to present an object which might, if only in principle, come to match a concept. We have the idea of the world (the totality of what is), but we do not have the capacity to show an example of it. We have the idea of the simple (that which cannot be broken down, decomposed), but we cannot illustrate it with a sensible object which would be a 'case' of it. We can conceive the infinitely great, the infinitely powerful, but every presentation of an object destined to 'make visible' this absolute greatness or power appears to us painfully inadequate. Those are ideas of which no presentation is possible. Therefore, they impart no knowledge about reality (experience); they also prevent the free union of the faculties which gives rise to the sentiment of the beautiful; and they prevent the formation and the stabilization of taste. They can be said to be unpresentable.

I shall call modern the art which devotes its 'little technical expertise' (*son 'petit technique'*), as Diderot used to say, to present the fact that the unpresentable exists. To make visible that there is something which can be conceived and which can neither be seen nor made visible: this is what is at stake in modern painting. But how to make visible that there is something which cannot be seen? Kant himself shows the way when he names 'formlessness, the absence of form,' as a possible index to the unpresentable. He also says of the empty 'abstraction' which the imagination experiences when in search for a presentation of the infinite (another unpresentable): this abstraction itself is like a presentation of the infinite, its 'negative presentation.' He cites the commandment, 'Thou shalt not make graven images' (*Exodus*), as the most sublime passage in the Bible in that it forbids all presentation of the Absolute. Little needs to be added to those observations to outline an aesthetic of sublime paintings. As painting, it will of course 'present' something though negatively; it will therefore avoid figuration or representation. It will be 'white' like one of Malevitch's squares; it will enable us to see only by making it impossible to see; it will please only by causing pain. One recognizes in those instructions the axioms of avant-gardes in painting, inasmuch as they devote themselves to making an allusion to the unpresentable by means of visible presentations. The systems in the name of which, or with which, this task has been able to support or to justify itself deserve the greatest attention; but they can originate only in the vocation of the sublime in order to legitimize it, that is, to conceal it. They remain inexplicable without the incommensurability of reality to concept which is implied in the Kantian philosophy of the sublime.

It is not my intention to analyze here in detail the manner in which the various avant-gardes have, so to speak, humbled and disqualified reality by examining the pictorial techniques which are so many devices to make us believe in it. Local tone, drawing, the mixing of colors, linear perspective, the nature of the support and that of the instrument, the treatment, the display, the museum: the avant-gardes are perpetually flushing out artifices of presentation which make it possible to subordinate thought to the gaze and to turn it away from the unpresentable. If Habermas, like Marcuse, understands the task of derealization as an aspect of the (repressive) 'desublimation' which character-izes the avant-garde, it is because he confuses the Kantian sublime with Freudian sublimation, and because aesthetics has remained for him that of the beautiful.

The Postmodern

What, then, is the postmodern? What place does it or does it not occupy in the vertiginous work of the questions hurled at the rules of image and narration? It is undoubtedly a part of the modern. All that has been received, if only yesterday (*modo, modo*, Petronius used to say), must be suspected. What space does Cézanne challenge? The Impressionists'. What objects do Picasso and Braque attack? Cézanne's. What presupposition does Duchamp break with in 1912? That which says one must make a painting, be it cubist. And Buren questions that other presupposition which he believes had survived untouched by the work of Duchamp: the place of presentation of the work. In an amazing acceleration, the generations precipitate themselves. A work can become modern only if it is first postmodern. Postmodernism thus understood is not modernism at its end but in the nascent state, and this state is constant.

Yet I would like not to remain with this slightly mechanistic meaning of the word. If it is true that modernity takes place in the withdrawal of the real and according to the sublime relation between the presentable and the conceivable, it is possible, within this relation, to distinguish two modes (to use the musician's language). The emphasis can be placed on the powerlessness of the faculty of presentation, on the nostalgia for presence felt by the human subject, on the obscure and futile will which inhabits him in spite of everything. The emphasis can be placed, rather, on the power of the faculty to conceive, on its 'inhumanity' so to speak (it was the quality Apollinaire demanded of modern artists), since it is not the business of our understanding whether or not human sensibility or imagination can match what it conceives. The emphasis can also be placed on the increase of being and the jubilation which result from the invention of new rules of the game, be it pictorial, artistic, or any other. What I have in mind will become clear if we dispose very schematically a few names on the chessboard of the history of avant-gardes: on the side of melancholia, the German Expressionists, and on the side of *novatio*, Braque and Picasso, on the former Malevitch and on the latter Lissitsky, on the one Chirico and on the other Duchamp. The nuance which distinguishes these two modes may be infinitesimal; they often coexist in the same piece, are almost indistinguishable; and yet they testify to a difference (*un différend*) on which the fate of thought depends and will depend for a long time, between regret and assay.

The work of Proust and that of Joyce both allude to something which does not allow itself to be made present. Allusion, to which Paolo Fabbri recently called my attention, is perhaps a form of expression indispensable to the works which belong to an aesthetic of the sublime. In Proust, what is being eluded as the price to pay for this allusion is the identity of consciousness, a victim to the excess of time (*au trop de temps*). But in Joyce, it is the identity of writing which is the victim of an excess of the book (*au trop de livre*) or of literature.

Proust calls forth the unpresentable by means of a language unaltered in its syntax and vocabulary and of a writing which in many of its operators still belongs to the genre of novelistic narration. The literary institution, as Proust inherits it from Balzac and Flaubert, is admittedly subverted in that the hero is no longer a character but the inner consciousness of time, and in that the diegetic diachrony, already damaged by Flaubert, is here put in question because of the narrative voice. Nevertheless, the unity of the book, the odyssey of that consciousness, even if it is deferred from chapter to chapter, is not seriously challenged: the identity of the writing with itself throughout the labyrinth of the interminable narration is enough to connote such unity, which has been compared to that of *The Phenomenology of Mind*.

Joyce allows the unpresentable to become perceptible in his writing itself, in the signifier. The whole range of available narrative and even stylistic operators is put into play without concern for the unity of the whole, and new operators are tried. The grammar and vocabulary of literary language are no longer accepted as given; rather they appear as academic forms, as rituals originating in piety (as Nietzsche said) which prevent the unpresentable from being put forward.

Here, then, lies the difference: modern aesthetics is an aesthetic of the sublime, though a nostalgic one. It allows the unpresentable to be put forward only as the missing contents; but the form, because of its recognizable consistency, continues to offer to the reader or viewer matter for solace and pleasure. Yet these sentiments do not constitute the real sublime sentiment, which is in an intrinsic combination of pleasure and pain: the pleasure that reason should exceed all presentation, the pain that imagination or sensibility should not be equal to the concept.

The postmodern would be that which, in the moderns puts forward the unpresentable in presentation itself; that which denies itself the solace of good forms, the consensus of a taste which would make it possible to share collectively the nostalgia for the unattainable; that which searches for new presentations, not in order to enjoy them but in order to impart a stronger sense of the unpresentable. A postmodern artist or writer is in the position of a philosopher: the text he writes, the work he produces are not in principle governed by preestablished rules, and they cannot be judged according to a determining judgment, by applying familiar categories to the text or to the work. Those rules and categories are what the work of art itself is looking for. The artist and the writer, then, are working without rules in order to formulate the rules of what *will have been done*. Hence the fact that work and text have the characters of an *event*; hence also, they always come too late for their author, or, what amounts to the same thing, their being put into work, their realization (*mise en oeuvre*) always begin too soon. *Post modern* would have to be understood according to the paradox of the future (*post*) anterior (*modo*).

It seems to me that the essay (Montaigne) is postmodern, while the fragment (*The Athaeneum*) is modern.

Finally, it must be clear that it is our business not to supply reality but to invent allusions to the conceivable which cannot be presented. And it is not to be expected that this task will effect the last reconciliation between language games (which, under the name of faculties, Kant knew to be separated by a chasm), and that only the transcendental illusion (that of Hegel) can hope to totalize them into a real unity. But Kant also knew that the price to pay for such an illusion is terror. The nineteenth and twentieth centuries have given us as much terror as we can take. We have paid a high enough price for the nostalgia of the whole and the one, for the reconciliation of the concept and the sensible, of the transparent and the communicable experience. Under the general demand for slackening and for appeasement, we can hear the mutterings of the desire for a return of terror, for the realization of the fantasy to seize reality. The answer is: Let us wage a war on totality; let us be witnesses to the unpresentable; let us activate the differences and save the honor of the name.

---

13   Fredric Jameson

From *Periodising the Sixties*

The Ideologies of Theory (Essays 1971–86), pp 53–92.

Nostalgic commemoration of the glories of the 60s and abject public confession of the decade's many failures and missed opportunities are two errors that cannot be avoided by some middle path that threads its way in between. The following sketch starts from the position that History is Necessity, that the 60s had to happen the way it did, and that its opportunities and failures were inextricably intertwined, marked by the objective constraints and openings of a determinate historical situation, of which I thus wish to offer a tentative and provisional model.

To speak of the 'situation' of the 60s, however, is necessarily to think in terms of historical periods and to work with models of historical periodization, which are at the present moment theoretically unfashionable, to say the least. Leave aside the existential fact that the veterans of the decade, who have seen so many things change dramatically from year to year think more historically than their predecessors; the classification by generations has become as meaningful for us as it was for the Russians of the late nineteenth century, who sorted character types out with reference to specific decades. And intellectuals of a certain age now find it normal to justify their current positions by way of a historical narrative ('then the limits of Althusserianism began to be evident,' etc.). Now, this is not the place for a theoretical justification of periodization in the writing of history, but to those who think that cultural periodization implies some massive kinship and homogeneity or identity within a given period, it may quickly be replied that it is surely only against a certain conception of what is historically dominant or hegemonic that the full value of the exceptional – what Raymond Williams calls the 'residual' or 'emergent' – can be assessed. Here, in any case, the 'period' in question is understood not as some omnipresent and uniform shared style or way of thinking and acting, but rather as the sharing of an objective situation, to which a whole range of varied responses and creative innovations is then possible, but always within that situation's structural limits.

Yet a whole range of rather different theoretical objections will also bear on the selectiveness of such a historical narrative: if the critique of periodization questions the possibilities of diachrony, these involve the problems of synchrony and in particular of the relationship to be established between the various 'levels' of historical change singled out for attention. Indeed, the present narrative will claim to say something meaningful about the 60s by way of brief sketches of but four of those levels: the history of philosophy, revolutionary political theory and practice, cultural production, and economic cycles (and this in a context limited essentially to the United States, France, and the Third World). Such selectiveness seems not merely to give equal historical weight to base and superstructure indifferently, but also to raise the specter of a practice of homologies – the kind of analogical parallelism in which the poetic production of Wallace Stevens is somehow 'the same' as the political practice of Che Guevara – which have been thought abusive at least as far back as Spengler.

There is of course no reason why specialized and elite phenomena, such as the writing of poetry, cannot reveal historical trends and tendencies as vividly as 'real life' – or perhaps even more visibly, in their isolation and semi-autonomy which approximates a laboratory situation. In any case, there is a fundamental difference between the present narrative and those of an older organic history that sought 'expressive' unification through analogies and homologies between widely distinct levels of social life. Where the latter proposed identities between the forms on such various levels, what will be argued here is a series of significant homologies between the *breaks* in those forms and their development. What is at stake, then, is not some proposition about the organic unity of the 60s on all its levels, but rather a hypothesis about the rhythm and dynamics of the fundamental situation in which those very different levels develop according to their own internal laws.

At that point, what looked like a weakness in this historical or narrative procedure turns out to be an unexpected strength, particularly in allowing for some sort of 'verification' of the separate strands of the narrative. One sometimes believes – especially in the area of culture and cultural histories and critiques – that an infinite number of narrative interpretations of history are possible, limited only by the ingenuity of the practitioners whose claim to originality depends on the novelty of the new theory of history they bring to market. It is more reassuring, then, to find the regularities hypothetically proposed for one field of activity (e.g., the cognitive, or the aesthetic, or the revolutionary) dramatically and surprisingly 'confirmed' by the reappearance of just such regularities in a widely different and seemingly unrelated field, as will be the case with the economic in the present context.

At any rate, it will already have become clear that nothing like a history of the 60s in the traditional, narrative sense will be offered here. But historical representation is just as surely in crisis as its distant cousin, the linear novel, and for much the same reasons. The most intelligent 'solution' to such a crisis does not consist in abandoning historiography altogether, as an impossible aim and an ideological category all at once, but rather – as in the modernist aesthetic itself – in reorganizing its traditional procedures on a different level. Althusser's proposal seems the wisest in this situation: as old-fashioned narrative or 'realistic' historiography became problematical, the historian should reformulate her vocation – not any longer to produce some vivid representation of History 'as it really happened,' but rather to produce the *concept* of history. Such will at least be the gamble of the following pages.

1   Third World Beginnings

It does not seem particularly controversial to mark the beginnings of what will come to be called the 60s in the Third World with the great movement of decolonization in British and French Africa. It can be argued that the most characteristic expressions of a properly First World 60s are all later than this, whether they are understood in countercultural terms – drugs and rock – or in the political terms of a student New Left and a mass antiwar movement. Indeed, politically, a First World 60s owed much to Third-Worldism in terms of politicocultural models, as in a symbolic Maoism, and, moreover, found its mission to resistance to wars aimed precisely at stemming the new revolutionary forces in the Third World. Belden Fields has indeed suggested that the two First World nations in which the most powerful student mass movements emerged – the United States and France – became privileged political spaces precisely *because* these were two countries involved in colonial wars, although the French New Left appears after the resolution of the Algerian conflict. The one significant exception to all this is in many ways the most important First World political movement of all – the new black politics and the civil rights movement, which must be dated, not from the Supreme Court decision of 1954, but rather from the first sit-ins in Greensboro, North Carolina, in February of 1960. Yet it might be argued that this was also a movement of decolonization, and in any case the constant exchange and mutual influences between the American black movements and the various African and Caribbean ones are continuous and incalculable throughout this period.

The independence of Ghana (1957), the agony of the Congo (Lumumba was murdered in January 1961), the independence of France's sub-Saharan colonies following the Gaullist referendum of 1959, finally the Algerian Revolution (which might plausibly mark our schema here with its internal high point, the Battle of Algiers, in January–March 1957, as with its diplomatic resolution in 1962) – all of these signal the convulsive birth of what will come in time to be known as the 60s:

> Not so very long ago, the earth numbered two thousand million inhabitants: five hundred million *men* and one thousand five hundred million *natives*. The former had the Word; the others merely had use of it.[1]

[1] J.P. Sartre, 'Preface' to Frantz Fanon, *The Wretched of the Earth*, trans. Constance Farrington (New York, 1965).

The 60s was, then, the period when all these 'natives' became human beings, and this internally as well as externally: those inner colonized of the First World – 'minorities,' marginals, and women – fully as much as its external subjects and official 'natives.' The process can and has been described in a number of ways, each one of which implies a certain 'vision of History' and a certain uniquely thematized reading of the 60s proper: it can be seen as a decisive and global chapter in Croce's conception of history as the history of human freedom; as a more classically Hegelian process of the coming to self-consciousness of subject peoples; as some post-Lukácsean or more Marcusean, New Left conception of the emergence of new 'subjects of history' of a nonclass type (blacks, students, Third World peoples); or as some poststructuralist, Foucaultean notion (significantly anticipated by Sartre in the passage just quoted) of the conquest of the right to speak in a new collective voice, never before heard on the world stage – and of the concomitant dismissal of the intermediaries (liberals, First World intellectuals) who had hitherto claimed to talk in your name; not forgetting the more properly political rhetoric of self-determination or independence or the more psychological and cultural rhetoric of new collective 'identities.'

It is, however, important to situate the emergence of these new collective 'identities' or 'subjects of history' in the historical situation which made that emergence possible, and in particular to relate the emergence of these new social and political categories (the colonized, race, marginality, gender, and the like) to something like a crisis in the more universal category that had hitherto seemed to subsume all the varieties of social resistance, namely the classical conception of social class. This is to be understood, however, not in some intellectual but rather in an institutional sense; it would be idealistic to suppose the deficiencies in the abstract idea of social class, and in particular in the Marxian conception of class struggle, can have been responsible for the emergence of what seem to be new nonclass forces. What can be noted, rather, is a crisis in the institutions through which a real class politics had however imperfectly been able to express itself. In this respect, the merge of the AFL and the CIO in 1955 can be seen as a fundamental 'condition of possibility' for the unleashing of the new social and political dynamics of the 60s: that merger, a triumph of McCarthyism, secured the expulsion of the Communists from the American labor movement, consolidated the new antipolitical 'social contract' between American business and the American labor unions, and created a situation in which the privileges of a white male labor force take precedence over the demands of black and women workers and other minorities. These last have therefore no place in the classical institutions of an older working-class politics. They will thus be 'liberated' from social class, in the charged and ambivalent sense that Marxism gives to that word (in the context of enclosure, for instance): they are separated from the older institutions and thus 'released' to find new modes of social and political expression.

The virtual disappearance of the American Communist Party as a small but significant political force in American society in 1956 suggests another dimension to this general situation: the crisis of the American party is 'overdetermined' by its repression under McCarthyism and by the 'revolution' in the Soviet bloc unleashed by Khrushchev's de-Stalinization campaign, which will have analogous but distinct and specific equivalents for the European Communist parties. In France, in particular, after the brief moment of a Communist 'humanism,' developed essentially by philosophers in the eastern countries, and with the fall of Khrushchev himself and the definitive failure of his various experiments in 1964, an unparalleled situation emerges in which, virtually for the first time since the Congress of Tours in 1919, it becomes possible for radical intellectuals to conceive of revolutionary work outside and independent of the French Communist Party. (The older attitudes – 'we know all about it, we don't like it much, but nothing is to be done politically without the CP' – are classically expressed in Sartre's own political journalism, in particular in *Les Communists et la paix*.) Now Trotskyism gets a new lease on life, and the new Maoist forms, followed by a whole explosion of extraparliamentary formations of all ideological complexions, the so-called groupuscules, offer the promise of a new kind of politics equally 'liberated' from the traditional class categories.

Two further key events need to be noted here before we go on. For many of us, indeed, the crucial detonator – a new Year I, the palpable demonstration that revolution was not merely a historical concept and a museum piece but real and achievable – was furnished by a people whose imperialist subjugation had developed among North Americans a sympathy and a sense of fraternity we could never have for other Third World peoples in their struggle, except in an abstract and intellectual way. Yet by January 1, 1959, the Cuban Revolution remained symbolically ambiguous. It could be read as a Third World revolution of a type different from either the classical Leninist one or the Maoist experience, for it had a revolutionary strategy entirely its own, the *foco* theory, which we will discuss later. This great event also announces the impending 60s as a period of unexpected political innovation rather than as the confirmation of older social and conceptual schemes.

Meanwhile, personal testimony seems to make it clear that for many white American students – in particular for many of those later active in the New Left – the assassination of President Kennedy played a significant role in delegitimizing the state itself and in discrediting the parliamentary process, seeming to mark the decisive end of the well-known passing of the torch to a younger generation of leadership, as well as the dramatic defeat of some new spirit of public or civic idealism. As for the reality of the appearance, it does not much matter that, in hindsight, such a view of the Kennedy presidency may be wholly erroneous, considering his conservatism and anticommunism, the gruesome gamble of the 'missile crisis,' and his responsibility for the American engagement in Vietnam itself. More significant, the legacy of the Kennedy regime to the development of a 60s politics may well have been the rhetoric of youth and of the 'generation gap' which he exploited, but which outlived him and dialectically offered itself as an expressive form through which the political discontent of American students and young people could articulate itself.

Such were some of the preconditions or 'conditions of possibility' – both in traditional working-class political institutions and in the arena of the legitimation of state power – for the 'new' social forces of the 60s to develop as they did. Returning to these new forces, there is a way in which their ultimate fate marks the close of the 60s as well: the end of 'Third-Worldism' in the US and Europe largely predates the Chinese Thermidor, and coincides with the awareness of increasing institutional corruption in many of the newly independent states of Africa and the almost complete militarization of the Latin American regimes after the Chilean coup of 1973 (the later revolutionary triumphs in the former Portuguese colonies are henceforth felt to be 'Marxist' rather than 'Third-Worldist,' whereas Vietnam vanishes from American consciousness as completely after the ultimate American withdrawal as did Algeria from French consciousness after the Evian accords of 1963). In the First World of the late 60s, there is certainly a return to a more internal politics, as the antiwar movement in the United States and May 68 in France testify. Yet the American movement remains organically linked to its Third World 'occasion' in the Vietnam War itself, as well as to the Maoist inspiration of the Progressive Labor-type groups which emerge from SDS, such that the movement as a whole will lose its momentum as the war winds down and the draft ceases. In France, the 'common program' of the left (1972) – in which the current Socialist government finds its origins – marks a new turn toward Gramscian models and a new kind of 'Eurocommunist' spirit which owes very little to Third World antecedents of any kind. Finally, the black movement in the US enters into a crisis at much the same time, as its dominant ideology – cultural nationalism, an ideology profoundly linked to Third World models – is exhausted. The women's movement also owed something to this kind of Third World inspiration, but it too, in the period 1972–74, will know an increasing articulation into relatively distinct ideological positions ('Bourgeois' feminism, lesbian separatism, socialist feminism).

For reasons enumerated above, and others, it seems plausible to mark the end of the 60s around 1972–74; the problem of this general 'break' will be returned to at the end of this sketch. For the moment we must complete our characterization of the overall dynamic of Third World history during this period, particularly if it is granted that this dynamic or 'narrative line' entertains some privileged relationship of influence on the unfolding of a First World 60s (through direct intervention – wars of national liberation – or through the prestige of exotic political models – most obviously, the Maoist one – or finally, owing to some global dynamic which both worlds share and respond to in relatively distinct ways).

This is, of course, the moment to observe that the 'liberation' of new forces in the Third World is as ambiguous as this term frequently tends to be (freedom as separation from older systems); to put it more sharply, it is the moment to recall the obvious, that decolonization historically went hand in hand with neocolonialism, and that the graceful, grudging, or violent end of an old-fashioned imperialism certainly meant the end of one kind of domination but evidently also the invention and construction of a new kind – symbolically, something like the replacement of the British Empire by the International Monetary Fund. This is, incidentally, why the currently fashionable rhetoric of power and domination (Foucault is the most influential of these rhetoricians, but the basic displacement from the economic to the political is already made by Max Weber) is ultimately unsatisfactory; it is of course politically important to 'contest' the various forms of power and domination, but the latter cannot be understood unless their functional relationships to economic exploitation are articulated – that is, until the political is once again subsumed beneath the economic. (On the other hand – particularly in the historicizing perspective of the present essay – it will obviously be a significant historical and social *symptom* that, in the mid-60s, people felt it necessary to express their sense of the situation and their projected praxis in a reified political language of power, domination, authority and antiauthoritarianism, and so forth: here, Second and Third World developments – with their conceptions of a 'primacy of the political' under socialism – offer an interesting and curious cross-lighting.) Meanwhile, something similar can be said of the conceptions of collective identity and in particular of the poststructuralist slogan of the conquest of speech, of the right to speak in your own voice, for yourself; but to articulate new demands, in your own voice, is not necessarily to satisfy them, and to speak is not necessarily to achieve a Hegelian recognition from the Other (or at least then only in the more somber and baleful sense that the Other now has to take you into consideration in a new way and to invent new methods for dealing with that new presence you have achieved). In hindsight, the 'materialist kernel' of this characteristic rhetoric or ideological vision of the 60s may be found in a more fundamental reflection on the nature of cultural revolution itself (now independent of its local and now historical Chinese manifestation).

The paradoxical, or dialectical, combination of decolonization and neo-colonialism can perhaps best be grasped in economic terms by a reflection on the nature of another process whose beginning coincides with the general beginnings we have suggested for this period as a whole. This is a process generally described in the neutral but obviously ideological language of a technological 'revolution' in agriculture: the so-called Green Revolution, with its new applications of chemical procedures to fertilization, its intensified strategies of mechanization, and its predictable celebration of progress and wonder-working technology, supposedly destined to free the world from hunger (the Green Revolution, incidentally, finds its Second World equivalent in Khrushchev's disastrous 'virgin lands' experiment). But these are far from neutral achievements; nor is their export – essentially pioneered by the Kennedys – a benevolent and altruistic activity. In the nineteenth and early twentieth centuries, capitalist penetration of the Third World did not necessarily mean a capitalist transformation of the latter's traditional modes of production. Rather, they were for the most part left intact, 'merely' exploited by a more political and military structure. The very enclave nature of these older agricultural modes – in combination with the violence of the occupier and that other violence, the introduction of money – established a sort of tributary relation that was beneficial to the imperialist metropolis for a considerable period. The Green Revolution carries this penetration and expansion of the 'logic of capital' into a new stage.

The older village structure and precapitalist forms of agriculture are now systematically destroyed, to be replaced by an industrial agriculture whose effects are fully as disastrous as, and analogous to, the moment of enclosure in the emergence of capital in what was to become the First World. The 'organic' social relations of village societies are now shattered, an enormous landless preproletariat 'produced,' which migrates to the urban areas (as the tremendous growth of Mexico City can testify), while new, more proletarian, wage-working forms of agricultural labor replaced the older collective or traditional kinds. Such ambiguous 'liberation' needs to be described with all the dialectical ambivalence with which Marx and Engels celebrate the dynamism of capital itself in the *Manifesto* or the historical progress achieved by the British occupation of India.

The conception of the Third World 60s as a moment when all over the world chains and shackles of a classical imperialist kind were thrown off in a stirring wave of 'wars of national liberation' is an altogether mythical simplification. Such resistance is generated as much by the new penetration of the Green Revolution as it is by the ultimate impatience with the older imperialist structures, the latter itself overdetermined by the historical spectacle of the supremacy of another former Third World entity, namely Japan, in its sweeping initial victories over the old imperial powers in World War II. Eric Wolf's indispensable *Peasant Wars of the Twentieth Century* (1969) underscores the relationship between possibilities of resistance, the development of a revolutionary ethos, and a certain constitutive distance from the more absolutely demoralizing social and economic logic of capital.

The final ambiguity with which we leave this topic is the following: the 60s, often imagined as a period when capital and First World power are in retreat all over the globe, can just as easily be conceptualized as a period when capital is in full dynamic and innovative expansion, equipped with a whole armature of fresh production techniques and new 'means of production.' It now remains to be seen whether this ambiguity, and the far greater specificity of the agricultural developments in the Third World, have any equivalent in the dynamics with which the 60s unfold in the advanced countries themselves.

2   The Politics of Otherness

If the history of philosophy is understood not as some sequence of timeless yet somehow finite positions in the eternal, but rather as the history of attempts to conceptualize a historical and social substance itself in constant dialectical transformation, whose aporias and contradictions mark all of those successive philosophies as determinate failures, yet failures from which we can read off something of the nature of the object on which they themselves came to grief – then it does not seem quite so farfetched to scan the more limited trajectory of that now highly specialized discipline for symptoms of the deeper rhythms of the 'real' or 'concrete' 60s itself.

As far as the history of philosophy during that period is concerned, one of the more influential versions of its story is told as follows: the gradual supersession of a hegemonic Sartrean existentialism (with its essentially phenomenological perspectives) by what is often loosely called 'structuralism,' namely, by a variety of new theoretical attempts which share at least a single fundamental 'experience' – the discovery of the primacy of Language or the Symbolic (an area in which phenomenology and Sartrean existentialism remain relatively conventional or traditional). The moment of high structuralism – whose most influential monuments are seemingly not philosophical at all, but can be characterized, alongside the new linguistics itself, as linguistic transformations of anthropology and psychoanalysis by Claude Lévi-Strauss and Jacques Lacan respectively – is, however, inherently unstable and has the vocation of becoming a new type of universal mathesis, under pain of vanishing as one more intellectual fad. The breakdown products of that moment of high structuralism can then be seen, on the one hand, as the reduction to a kind of scientism, to sheer method and analytical technique (in *semiotics*); and, on the other hand, as the transformation of structuralist approaches into active ideologies in which ethical, political, and historical consequences are drawn from the hitherto more epistemological 'structuralist' positions; this last is of course the moment of what is now generally known as *poststructuralism*, associated with familiar names like those of Foucault, Deleuze, Derrida, and so forth. That the paradigm, although obviously French in its references, is not merely local can be judged from an analogous mutation of the classical Frankfurt School via problems of communication, in the work of Habermas; or by the current revival of pragmatism in the work of Richard Rorty, which has a home-grown American 'poststructuralist' feeling to it (Pierce after all having largely preceded and outclassed Saussure).

The crisis of the philosophical institution and the gradual extinction of the philosopher's classic political vocation, of which Sartre was for our time the supreme embodiment, can in some ways be said to be about the so-called death of the subject: the individual ego or personality, but also the supreme philosophical Subject, the cogito but also the *auteur* of the great philosophical *system*. It is certainly possible to see Sartre as one of the last great system builders of traditional philosophy (but then at least one dimension of classical existentialism must also be seen as an ideology or a metaphysic: that of the heroic pathos of existential choice and freedom in the void, and that of the 'absurd,' more particularly in Camus). Some of us also came to *Marxism* through dialectical elements in the early Sartre (he himself then turning to follow up this avenue in his own later, more Marxian work, such as the *Critique of Dialectical Reason* [1960]). But on balance the component of his work that underwent the richest practical elaboration at other people's hands as well as his own was his theory of interpersonal relations, his stunning rewrite of Hegel's Master/Slave chapter, his conception of the Look as the most concrete mode in which I relate to other subjects and struggle with them, the dimension of my alienation in my 'being-for-other-people,' in which each of us vainly attempts, by looking at the other, to turn the tables and transform the baleful alienating gaze of the Other into an object for my equally alienating gaze. Sartre will go on, in the *Critique*, to try to erect a more positive and political theory of group dynamics on this seemingly sterile territory; the struggle between two people now becoming dialectically transformed into the struggle between groups themselves. The *Critique* was an anticipatory work, however, whose import and significance would not finally be recognized until May 68 and beyond, whose rich consequences indeed have not even fully been drawn to this day. Suffice it to say, in the present context, that the *Critique* fails to reach its appointed terminus, and to complete the projected highway that was to have led from the individual subject of existential experience all the way to fully constituted social classes. It breaks down at the point of the constitution of small groups and is ultimately usable principally for ideologies of small guerilla bands (in a latter moment of the 60s) and of microgroups (at the period's end). The significance of this trajectory will soon be clear.

However, at the dawn of the 60s, the Sartrean paradigm of the Look and the struggle for recognition between individual subjects will also be appropriated dramatically for a very different model of political struggle, in Frantz Fanon's enormously influential vision (*The Wretched of the Earth* [1961]) of the struggle between Colonizer and Colonized, where the objectifying reversal of the Look is apocalyptically rewritten as the act of redemptive violence of Slave against Master, the moment when, in fear and the anxiety of death, the hierarchical positions of Self and Other, Center and Margin, are forcibly reversed, and when the subservient consciousness of the Colonized achieves collective identity and self-affirmation in the face of coloniziers in abject fight.

What is at once significant is the way in which what had been a technical philosophical subject (the 'problem' of solipsism, the nature of relationships between individual subjects or 'cogitos') has fallen into the world and become an explosive and scandalous political ideology: a piece of the old-fashioned technical philosophical system of high existentialism breaking off and migrating outside philosophy departments altogether, into a more frightening landscape of praxis and terror. Fanon's great myth could be read at the time, by those it appalled equally well as by those it energized, as an irresponsible call to mindless violence. In retrospect, and in the light of Fanon's other, clinical work (he was a psychiatrist working with victims of colonization and of the torture and terror of the Algerian war), it can more appropriately be read as a significant contribution to a whole theory of cultural revolution as the collective reeducation (or even collective psychoanalysis) of oppressed peoples or unrevolutionary working classes. Cultural revolution as a strategy for breaking the immemorial habits of subalternity and obedience which have become internalized as a kind of second nature in all the laborious and exploited classes in human history – such is the vaster problematic to which, today, Gramsci and Wilhelm Reich, Fanon and Rudolf Bahro, can be seen as contributing as richly as the more official practices of Maoism.

3   Digression on Maoism

But with this new and fateful reference, an awkward but unavoidable parenthetical digression is in order: Maoism, richest of all the great new ideologies of the 60s, will be a shadowy but central presence throughout this essay, yet owing to its very polyvalence it cannot be neatly inserted at any point or exhaustively confronted on its own. One understands, of course, why Left militants here and abroad, fatigued by Maoist dogmatisms, must have heaved a collective sigh of relief when the Chinese turn consigned 'Maoism' itself to the ashcan of history. Theories, however, are often liberated on their own terms when they are thus radically disjoined from the practical interests of state power. Meanwhile, as I have suggested above, the symbolic terrain of the present debate is fully as much chosen and dictated by the Right as by Left survivors; and the current propaganda campaign, everywhere in the world, to Stalinize and discredit Maoism and the experience of the Chinese cultural revolution – now rewritten as yet another Gulag to the East – all of this, make no mistake about it, is part and parcel of the larger attempt to trash the 60s generally. It would not be prudent to abandon rapidly and without thoughtful reconsideration any of this terrain to the 'other side.'

As for the more ludicrous features of Western Third-Worldism generally – a kind of modern exotic or orientalist version of Marx's revolutionaries of 1848, who 'anxiously conjure up the spirits of (the Great Revolution of 1789) to their service and borrow from them names, battle cries and costumes'[2] – these are now widely understood in a more cynical light, as in Régis Debray's remark: 'In France, the Columbuses of political modernity thought that following Godards's *La Chinoise* they were discovering China in Paris, when in fact they were landing in California.'[3]

Most paradoxical and fascinating of all, however, is the unexpected and unpredictable sequel to the Sino-Soviet split itself: the new Chinese rhetoric, intent on castigating the Soviet bureaucracy as revisionistic and 'bourgeois,' will have the curious effect of evacuating the class content of these slogans. There is then an inevitable terminological slippage and displacement: the new binary opposite to the term 'bourgeois' will no longer be 'proletarian' but rather 'revolutionary,' and the new qualifications for political judgments of this kind are no longer made in terms of class or party affiliation but rather in terms of personal life – your relationship to special privileges, to middle-class luxuries and dachas and managerial incomes and other perks – Mao Zedong's own monthly 'salary,' we are told, was something in the neighborhood of a hundred American dollars. As with all forms of anticommunism, this rhetoric can of course be appropriated by the anti-Marxist thematics of 'bureaucracy,' of the end of ideology and social class, and so forth. But it is important to understand how for Western militants what began to emerge from this at first merely tactical and rhetorical shift was a whole new political space, a space which will come to be articulated by the slogan 'the personal is the political,' and into which – in one of the most stunning and unforeseeable of historical turns – the women's movement will triumphantly move at the end of the decade, building a Yenan of a new and unpredictable kind which is still impregnable at the present moment.

4　The Withering Away of Philosophy

The limit as well as the strength of the stark Fanonian model of struggle was set by the relative simplicity of the colonial situation; this can be shown in two ways, first of all in the sequel to the 'war of national independence.' For with the Slave's symbolic and literal victory over the (now former) Master, the 'politics of otherness' touches its limits as well; the rhetoric of a conquest of collective identity has then nowhere else to go but into a kind of secessionary logic of which black cultural nationalism and (later on) lesbian separatism are the most dramatic examples (the dialectic of cultural and linguistic independence in Quebec province would be yet another instructive one). But this result is also contradictory, insofar as the newly constituted group (we here pick up Sartre's account in the *Critique*) *needs* outside enemies to survive as a group, to produce and perpetuate a sense of collective cohesion and identity. Ultimately, in the absence of the clear-cut Manichean situation of the older imperialist period, this hard-won collective self-definition of a first moment of resistance will break up into the smaller and more comfortable unities of face-to-face microgroups (of which the official political sects are only one example).

[2] Karl Marx, *The Eighteenth Brumaire of Louis Bonaparte* (New York, 1969), p. 15.
[3] Régis Debray, 'A Modest Contribution,' *New Literary Review*, 115 (May–June 1979), p. 58

The gradual waning of the Fanonian model can also be described from the perspective of what will shortly become its 'structuralist' critique. On this view, it is still a model based on a conception of individual subjects, albeit mythical and collective ones. It is thereby both anthropomorphic and transparent, in the sense in which nothing intervenes between the great collective adversaries, between the Master and the Slave, between the Colonizer and the Colonized. Yet even in Hegel, there was always a third term, namely matter itself, the raw materials on which the Slave is made to labor and to work out a long and anonymous salvation through the rest of history. The 'third term' of the 60s is, however, rather different from this. It was as though the protracted experiences of the earlier part of the decade gradually burned into the minds of the participants of specific lesson. In the United States, it was the experience of the interminable Vietnam War itself; in France, it was the astonishing and apparently invincible technocratic dynamism, and the seemingly unshakable inertia and resistance to de-Stalinization of the French Communist party; and everywhere, it was the tremendous expansion of the media apparatus and the culture of consumerism. This lesson might well be described as the discovery, within a hitherto antagonistic and 'transparent' political praxis, of the opacity of the Institution itself as the radically transindividual, with its own inner dynamic and laws, which are not those of individual human action or intention, something which Sartre theorized in the *Critique* as the 'practico-inert,' and which will take the definitive form, in competing 'structuralism,' of 'structure' or 'synchronic system,' a realm of impersonal logic in terms of which human consciousness is itself little more than an 'effect of structure.'

On this reading, then, the new philosophical turn will be interpreted less in the idealistic perspective of some discovery of a new scientific truth (the Symbolic) than as the symptom of an essentially protopolitical and social experience, the shock of some new, hard, unconceptualized, resistant object which the older conceptuality cannot process and which thus gradually generates a whole new problematic. The conceptualization of this new problematic in the coding of linguistics or information theory may then be attributed to the unexpected explosions of information and messages of all kinds in the media revolution, which will be discussed in more detail in the following section. Suffice it to remark at this point that there is some historical irony in the way in which this moment, essentially the Third Technological Revolution in the West (electronics, nuclear energy) – in other words, a whole new step in the conquest of nature by human praxis – is philosophically greeted and conceptually expressed in a kind of thought officially designated as 'antihumanist' and concerned to think what transcends or escapes human consciousness and intention. Similarly, the Second Technological Revolution of the late nineteenth century – an unparalleled quantum leap in human power over nature – was the moment of expression of a whole range of nihilisms associated with 'modernity' or with high modernism in culture.

In the present context, the Althusserian experiment of the mid- to late 60s is the most revealing and suggestive of the various 'structuralisms,' since it was the only one to be explicitly political and indeed to have very wide-ranging political effects in Europe and Latin America. The story of Althusserianism can be told only schematically here: its initial thrust is twofold, against the unliquidated Stalinist tradition (strategically designated by the code words

'Hegel' and 'expressive causality' in Althusser's own texts), and against the 'transparence' of the Eastern attempts to reinvent a Marxist humanism on the basis of the theory of alienation in Marx's early manuscripts. That Althusserianism is essentially a meditation on the 'institutional' and on the opacity of the 'practico-inert' may be judged by the three successive formulations of this object by Althusser himself in the course of the 60s: that of a 'structure in dominance' or *structure à dominante* (in *For Marx*), that of 'structural causality' (in *Reading Capital*), and that of 'ideological state apparatuses' (in the essay of that name). What is less often remembered, but what should be perfectly obvious from any rereading of *For Marx*, is the origin of this new problematic in Maoism itself, and particularly in Mao Zedong's essay 'On Contradiction,' in which the notion of the complex, already-given *overdetermined* conjuncture of various kinds of antagonistic and nonantagonistic contradictions is mapped out.

The modification that will emerge from Althusser's 'process of theoretical production' as it works over its Maoist 'raw materials' can be conveyed by the problem and slogan of the 'semi-autonomy' of the levels of social life (a problem already invoked in our opening pages). This formula will involve a struggle on two fronts: on the one hand, against the monism or 'expressive causality' of Stalinism, in which the 'levels' are identified, conflated, and brutally collapsed into one another (changes in economic production will be 'the same' as political and cultural changes), and, on the other, against bourgeois avant-garde philosophy, which finds just such a denunciation of organic concepts of totality most congenial, but draws from it the consequence of a post- or anti-Marxist celebration of Nietzschean heterogeneity. The notion of a semi-autonomy of the various levels or instances, most notably of the political instance and of the dynamics of state power, will have enormous resonance (outstandingly in the work of Nicos Poulantzas), since it seems to reflect, and to offer a way of theorizing, the enormous growth of the state bureaucracy since the war, the 'relative autonomy' of the state apparatus from any classical and reductive functionality in the service of big business, as well as the very active new terrain of political struggle presented by government or public sector workers. The theory could also be appealed to justify a semi-autonomy in the cultural sphere, as well, and especially a semi-autonomous cultural politics, of a variety that ranges from Godard's films and *situationnisme* to the 'festival' of May 68 and the Yippie movement here (not excluding, perhaps, even those forms of so-called terrorism that aimed, not at any classical seizure of state power, but rather at essentially pedagogical or informational demonstrations, e.g., 'forcing the state to reveal its fundamentally fascist nature').

Nonetheless, the attempt to open up a semi-autonomy of the levels in one hand, while holding them altogether in the ultimate unity of some 'structural totality' (with its still classical Marxian ultimately determining instance of the economic), tends under its own momentum, in the centrifugal force of the critique of totality it had itself elaborated, to self-destruct (most dramatically so in the trajectory of Hindess and Hirst). What will emerge is not merely a heterogeneity of *levels* – henceforth, semi-autonomy will relax into autonomy *tout court*, and it will be conceivable that in the decentered and 'schizophrenic' world of late capitalism the various instances may really have no organic relationship to one another at all – but, more important, the idea will emerge that the struggles appropriate to each of these levels (purely political struggles, purely economic struggles, purely cultural struggles, purely 'theoretical' struggles) may have no necessary relationship to one another either. With his ultimate 'meltdown' of the Althusserian apparatus, we are in the (still contemporary) world of microgroups and micropolitics – variously theorized as local or molecular politics, but clearly characterized, however different the various conceptions are, as a repudiation of old-fashioned class and party politics of a 'totalizing' kind, and most obviously epitomized by the challenge of the women's movement, whose unique new strategies and concerns cut across (or in some cases undermine and discredit altogether) many classical inherited forms of 'public' or 'official' political action, including the electoral kind. The repudiation of 'theory' itself is an essentially masculine enterprise of 'power through knowledge' in French feminism (see in particular the work of Luce Irigaray) may be taken as the final moment in this particular 'withering away of philosophy.'

Yet there is another way to read the density of Althusserianism, a way that will form the transition to our subsequent discussion of the transformation of the cultural sphere in the 60s; and this involves the significance of the slogan of 'theory' itself as it comes to replace the older term 'philosophy' throughout this period. The 'discovery' of the Symbolic, the development of its linguistic-related thematics (as, e.g., in the notion of understanding as an essentially synchronic process, which influences the construction of relatively ahistorical 'structures,' such as the Althusserian one describe above), is now to be correlated with a modification of the practice of the symbolic, of language itself in the 'structuralist' tests, henceforth characterized as 'theory,' rather than work in a particular traditional discipline. Two features of this evolution, or mutation, must be stressed. The first is a consequence of the crisis in, or the disappearance of, classical *canon* of philosophical writings which necessarily results from the contestation of philosophy as a discipline and an institution. Henceforth, the new 'philosophical' text will no longer draw its significance from an insertion into the issues and debates of the philosophical tradition, which means that its basic 'intertextual' references become random, an *ad hoc* constellation that forms and dissolves on the occasion of each new text. The new text must necessarily be a commentary on other texts (indeed, that dependence on a body of texts to be glossed, rewritten, interconnected in fresh ways will now intensify if anything), yet those texts, drawn from the most wildly distant disciplines (anthropology, psychiatry, literature, history of science), will be selected in a seemingly arbitrary fashion: Mumford side by side with Antonin Artaud, Kant with Sade, pre-Socratic philosophy, President Schreber, a novel of Maurice Blanchot, Owen Lattimore on Mongolia, and a host of obscure Latin medical treatises from the eighteenth century. The vocation of what was formerly 'philosophy' is thereby restructured and displaced: since there is no longer a tradition of philosophical problems in terms of which new positions and new statements can meaningfully be proposed, such works now tend toward what can be called metaphilosophy – the very different work of coordinating a series of pregiven, already constituted codes or systems of signifiers, of producing a discourse fashioned out of the already fashioned discourse of the constellation of *ad hoc* reference works. 'Philosophy' thereby becomes radically occasional; one would want to call it disposable theory, the production of a *metabook*, to be replaced by a different one next season, rather than the ambition to express a proposition, a position, or a system with greater 'truth' value. (The obvious analogy with the evolution of literary and cultural studies today, with the crisis and disappearance of the latter's own canon of great books – the last one having been augmented to include the once recalcitrant 'masterpieces' of high modernism – will be taken for granted in our next section.)

All of this can perhaps be grasped in a different way by tracing the effects of another significant feature of contemporary theory, namely its privileged theme in the so-called critique of representation. Traditional philosophy will now be grasped in those terms, as a practice of representation in which philosophical text or system (misguidedly) attempts to express something other than itself, namely truth or meaning (which now stands as the 'signified' to the 'signifier' of the system). If, however, the whole aesthetic of representation is metaphysical and ideological, philosophical discourse can no longer entertain this vocation, and it must stand as the mere addition of another text to what is now conceived as an infinite chain of texts (not necessarily all verbal – daily life is a text, clothing is a text, state power is a text, that whole external world, about which 'meaning' or 'truth' were once asserted and which is now contemptuously characterized as the illusion of reference or the 'referent,' is an indeterminate superposition of texts of all kinds). Whence the significance of the currently fashionable slogan of 'materialism' when sounded in the area of philosophy and theory: materialism here means the dissolution of any belief in 'meaning' or in the 'signified' conceived as ideas or concepts that are distinct from their linguistic expressions. However paradoxical a 'materialist' philosophy may be in this respect, a 'materialist theory of language' will clearly transform the very function and operation of 'theory,' since it opens up a dynamic in which it is no longer ideas, but rather texts, material texts, which struggle with one another. Theory so defined (and it will have become clear that the term now greatly transcends what used to be called philosophy and its specialized content) conceives of its vocation, not as the discovery of truth and the repudiation of error, but rather as a struggle about purely linguistic formulations, as the attempt to formulate verbal propositions (material language) in such a way that they are unable to imply unwanted or ideological consequences. Since this aim is evidently impossible to achieve, what emerges from the practice of theory – and this was most dramatic and visible during the high point of Althusserianism itself in 1967–68 – is a violent and obsessive return to ideological critique in the new form of a perpetual guerrilla war among the material signifiers of textual formulations. With the transformation of philosophy into a material practice, however, we touch on a development that cannot fully be appreciated until it is replaced in the context of a general mutation of culture throughout this period, a context in which 'theory' will come to be grasped as a specific (or semi-autonomous) form of what must be called postmodernism generally.

5   The Adventures of the Sign

Postmodernism is one significant framework in which to describe what happened to culture in the 60s, but a full discussion of this hotly contested concept is not possible here. Such a discussion would want to cover, among other things, the following features: that well-known poststructuralist theme, the 'death' of the subject (including the creative subject, the *auteur* or the 'genius'); the nature and function of a *culture of the simulacrum* (an idea developed out of Plato by Deleuze and Baudrillard to convey some specificity of a reproducible object world, not of copies or reproductions marked as such, but of a proliferation of trompe-l'oeil copies *without originals*); the relation of this last to media culture of the 'society of the spectacle' (Debord), under two heads: 1) the peculiar new status of the image, the 'material' or what might better be called the 'literal,' signifier: a materiality or literality from which the older sensory richness of the medium has been abstracted (just as on the other side of the dialectical relationship, the old individuality of the subject and his/her 'brushstrokes' have equally been effaced); and 2) the emergence, in the work's temporality, of an aesthetic of *textuality* or what is often described as schizophrenic time; the eclipse, finally, of all depth, especially *historicity* itself, with the subsequent appearance of pastiche and nostalgia art (what the French call *la mode rétro*), and including the supersession of the accompanying models of depth-interpretation in philosophy (the various forms of hermeneutics, as well as the Freudian conception of 'repression,' of manifest and latent levels).

What is generally objected to in characterizations of this kind is the empirical observation that all these features can be abundantly located in this or that variety of high modernism; indeed, one of the difficulties in specifying postmodernism lies in its symbiotic or parasitical relationship to the latter. In effect, with the canonization of a hitherto scandalous, ugly, disonant, amoral, antisocial, bohemian high modernism offensive to the middle classes, its promotion to the very figure of high culture generally, and perhaps most important, its enshrinement in the academic institution, postmodernism emerges as a way of making creative space for artists now oppressed by those henceforth hegemonic modernist categories of irony, complexity, ambiguity, dense temporality, and particularly, aesthetic and utopian monumentality. In some analogous way, it will be said, high modernism itself won its autonomy from the preceding hegemonic realism (the symbolic language or mode of representation of classical or market capitalism). But there is a difference in that realism itself underwent a significant mutation: it became *naturalism* and at once generated the representation forms of mass culture (the narrative apparatus of the contemporary best seller is an invention of naturalism and one of the most stunningly successful of French cultural exports). High modernism and mass culture then develop in dialectical opposition and interrelationship with one another. It is precisely the waning of their opposition, and some new conflation of the forms of high and mass culture, that characterizes postmodernism itself.

The historical specificity of postmodernism must therefore finally be argued in terms of the social functionality of culture itself. As stated above, high modernism, whatever its overt political content, was oppositional and marginal within a middle-class Victorian or philistine or gilded age culture. Although postmodernism is equally offensive in all the respects enumerated (think of punk rock or pornography), it is no longer at all 'oppositional' in that sense; indeed, it constitutes the very dominant or hegemonic aesthetic of consumer society itself and significantly serves the latter's commodity production as a virtual laboratory of new forms and fashions. The argument for a conception of postmodernism as a periodizing category is thus based on the presupposition that, even if *all* the formal features enumerated above were already present in the older high modernism, the very significance of those features changes when they become a cultural *dominant*, with a precise socio-economic functionality.

At this point it may be well to shift the terms (or the 'code') of our description to the seemingly more traditional one of a cultural 'sphere,' a conception developed by Herbert Marcuse in what is to my mind his single most important text, the great essay 'The Affirmative Character of Culture' (1937). (It should be added that the conception of a 'public sphere' generally is a very contemporary one in Germany in the works of Habermas and Hegt and Kluge, where such a system of categories stands in interesting contrast to the code of 'levels' or 'instances' in French poststructuralism.) Marcuse there rehearses the paradoxical dialectic of the classical (German) aesthetic, which projects as play and 'purposefulness without purpose' a Utopian realm of beauty and culture beyond the fallen empirical world of money and business activity, thereby winning a powerful critical and negative value through its capacity to condemn, by its own very existence, the totality of *what* is, at the same time forfeiting all ability to social or political intervention in what is, by virtue of its constitutive disjunction or autonomy from society and history.

The account therefore begins to coincide in a suggestive way with the problematic of autonomous or semi-autonomous levels developed in the preceding section. To historicize Marcuse's dialectic, however, would demand that we take into account the possibility that in our time this very autonomy of the cultural sphere (or level or instance) may be in the process of modification; and that we develop the means to furnish a description of the process whereby such modification might take place, as well as of the prior process whereby culture became 'autonomous' or 'semi-autonomous' in the first place.

This requires recourse to yet another (unrelated) analytic code, one more generally familiar to us today, since it involves the now classical structural concept of the *sign*, with its two components, the signifier (the material vehicle or image – sound or printed word) and the signified (the mental image, meaning, or 'conceptual' content), and a third component – the external object of the sign, its reference or 'referent' – henceforth expelled from the unity and yet haunting it as a ghostly residual aftereffect (illusion or ideology). The scientific value of this conception of the sign will be bracketed here since we are concerned, on the one hand, to historicize it, to interpret it as a conceptual symptom of developments in the period, and, on the other, to 'set in motion,' to see whether changes in its inner structure can offer some adequate small-scale emblem or electrocardiogram of changes and permutation in the cultural sphere generally throughout this period.

Such changes are already suggested by the fate of the 'referent' in the 'conditions of possibility' of the new structural concept of the sign (a significant ambiguity must be noted, however: theorists of the sign notoriously glide from a conception of reference as designating a 'real' object outside the unity of signifier and signified to a position in which the signified itself – or meaning, or the idea or the concept of a thing – becomes somehow identified with the referent and stigmatized along with it; we will return to this below). Saussure, at the dawn of the semiotic revolution, liked to describe the relationship of signifier to signified as that of the two sides, the recto and verso, of a sheet of paper. In what is then a logical sequel, and a text that naturally enough becomes equally canonical, Borges will push 'representation' to the point of imagining a map so rigorous and referential that it becomes coterminous with its object. The stage is then set for the structuralist emblem par excellence, the Moebius Strip, which succeeds in peeling itself off its referent altogether and thus achieves a free-floating closure in the void, a kind of absolute self-referentiality and autocirculatory from which all remaining traces of reference, or of any externality, have triumphantly been effaced.

To be even more eclectic about it, I will suggest that this process, seemingly internal to the sign itself, requires a supplementary explanatory code, that of the more universal process of reification and fragmentation at one with the logic of capital itself. Nonetheless, taken on its own terms, the inner convulsions of the sign is a useful initial figure of the process of transformation of culture generally, which must in some first moment (that described by Marcuse) separate itself from the 'referent', the existing social and historical world itself, only in a subsequent stage of the 60s, in what is here termed 'postmodernism,' to develop further into some new and heightened, free-floating, self-referential 'autonomy.'

The problem now turns around this very term, 'autonomy,' with its paradoxical Althusserian modification, the concept of 'semi-autonomy.' The paradox is that the sign, as an 'autonomous' unity in its own right as a realm divorced from the referent, can preserve that initial autonomy, and the unity and coherence demanded by it, only at the price of keeping a phantom of reference alive, as the ghostly reminder of its own outside or exterior, since this allows it closure, self-definition, and an essential boundary line. Marcuse's own tormented dialectic expresses this dramatically in the curious oscillation whereby his autonomous realm of beauty and culture returns upon some 'real world' to judge and negate it, at the same time separating itself so radically from that real world as to become a place of mere illusion and impotent 'ideals,' the 'infinite,' and so on.

The first moment in the adventures of the sign is perplexing enough as to demand more concrete, if schematic, illustration in the most characteristic cultural productions themselves. It might well be demonstrated in the classical French *nouveau roman* (in particular the novels of Robbe-Grillet himself), which established its new language in the early 1960s, using systematic variations of narrative segments to 'undermine' representation, yet in some sense confirming this last by teasing and stimulating an appetite for it.

Because an American illustration seems more appropriate, however, something similar may be seen in connection with the final and canonical form of high modernism in American poetry, namely the work of Wallace Stevens, which becomes, in the years following the poet's death in 1956, institutionalized in the university as a purer and more quintessential fulfillment of poetic language than the still impure (read: ideological and political) works of an Eliot or a Pound, and can therefore be numbered among the literary 'events' of the early 60s. As Frank Lentricchia has shown, in *After the New Criticism,*[4] the serviceability of Stevens' poetic production for this normative and hegemonic role depends in large measure on the increasing conflation, in that work, of poetic practice and poetic theory:

This endlessly elaborating poem
Displays the theory of poetry
As the life of poetry . . .

'Stevens' is therefore a locus and fulfillment of aesthetics and aesthetic theory fully as much as the latter's exemplar and privileged exegetical object; the theory or aesthetic ideology in question is very much an affirmation of the 'autonomy' of the cultural sphere in the sense developed above, a valorization of the supreme power of the poetic imagination over the 'reality' it produces. Stevens' work, therefore, offers an extraordinary laboratory situation in which to observe the autonomization of culture as a process: a detailed examination of his development (something for which we have no space here) would show how some initial 'set toward' or 'attention to' a kind of poetic *pensée sauvage*, the operation of great preconscious *stereotypes*, opens up a vast inner world in which little by little the images of things and their 'ideas' begin to be substituted for the things themselves. Yet what distinguishes this experience in Stevens is the sense of a vast systematicity in all this, the operation of a whole set of cosmic oppositions far too complex to be reduced to the schemata of 'structuralist' binary oppositions, yet akin to those in spirit, and somehow pregiven in the Symbolic Order of the mind, discoverable to the passive exploration of the 'poetic imagination,' that is, of some heightened and impersonal power of free association in the realm of 'objective spirit' or 'objective culture.' The examination would further show the strategic limitation of this process to landscape, the reduction of the ideas and images of things to the names for things, and finally to those irreducibles that are place names, among which the exotic has a privileged function (Key West, Oklahoma, Yucatan, Java). Here the poetic 'totality' begins to trace a ghostly mimesis or *analogon* of the totality of the imperialist world system itself, with Third World materials in a similar strategic, marginal, yet essential place (much as Adorno showed how Schoenberg's twelve-tone system unconsciously produced a formal imitation of the 'total system' of capital). This very unconscious replication of the 'real' totality of the world system in the mind is then what allows culture to separate itself as a closed and self-sufficient 'system' in its own right: reduplication, and at the same time, floating above the real. It is an impulse shared by most of the great high modernisms, as has been shown most dramatically in the recent critiques of architectural modernism, in particular of the international style, whose great monumental objects constitute themselves, by protecting a protopolitical and utopian spirit of transformation *against* a fallen city fabric all around them and, as Venturi has demonstrated, end up necessarily displaying and speaking of themselves alone. Now, this also accounts for what must puzzle any serious reader of Stevens' verse, namely the extraordinary combination of verbal richness and experimental hollowness or impoverishment in it (the latter being attributable as well to the impersonality of the poetic imagination in Stevens,

---

[4] Frank Lentricchia, *After the New Criticism* (Chicago, 1980), esp. pp. 31–35.

and to the essentially contemplative and epistemological stance of the subject in it, over and against the static world of his landscapes).

The essential point here, however, is that this characteristic movement of the high modernist impulse needs to justify itself by way of an ideology, an ideological supplement which can generally be described as that of 'existentialism' (the supreme fiction, the meaninglessness of a contingent object world unredeemed by the imagination, etc.). This is the most uninteresting and banal dimension of Stevens' work, yet it betrays along with other existentialisms (e.g. Sartre's tree root in *Nausea*) that fatal seam or link that must be retained in order for the contingent, the 'outside world,' the meaningless referent, to be just present enough dramatically to be overcome within the language. Nowhere in this ultimate point so clearly deduced, over and over again, as in Stevens, in the eye of the blackbird, the angels, or the Sun itself – that last residual vanishing point of reference as distant as a dwarf star upon the horizon, yet which cannot disappear altogether without the whole vocation of poetry and the poetic imagination being called back into question. Stevens thus exemplifies for us the fundamental paradox of the 'autonomy' of the cultural sphere: the sign can become autonomous only by remaining semi-autonomous, and the realm of culture can absolutize itself over against the real world only at the price of retaining a final tenuous sense of that exterior or external world of which it is the replication and the imaginary double.

All of this can also be demonstrated by showing what happens when, in a second moment, the perfectly logical conclusion is drawn that the referent is itself a myth and does not exist, a second moment hitherto described as postmodernism. Its trajectory can be seen as a movement from the older *Nouveau roman* to that of Sollers or of properly 'schizophrenic' writing, or from the primacy of Stevens to that of John Ashbery. This new moment is a radical break (which can be localized around 1967 for reasons to be given later), but it is important to grasp it as dialectical, that is, as a passage from quantity to quality in which the *same* force, reaching a certain threshold of excess, in its prolongation now produces qualitatively distinct effects and seems to generate a whole new system.

That force has been described as reification, but we can now also begin to make some connection with another figural language used earlier: in a first moment, reification 'liberated' the sign from its referent, but this is not a force to be released with impunity. Now, in a second moment, it continues its work of dissolution, penetrating the interior of the sign itself and liberating the signifier from the signified, or from meaning proper. This play, no longer of a realm of signs, but of pure or literal signifiers freed from the ballast of their signifieds, their former meanings, now generates a new kind of textuality in all the arts (and in philosophy as well, as we have seen above) and begins to project the mirage of some ultimate language of pure signifiers which is also frequently associated with schizophrenic discourse. (Indeed, the Lacanian theory of schizophrenia – a language disorder in which syntactical time breaks down and leaves a succession of empty signifiers, absolute moments of a perpetual present, behind itself – has offered one of the most influential explanations and ideological justifications for postmodernist textual practice.)

Such an account would have to be demonstrated in some detail by way of a concrete analysis of the postmodernist experience in all the arts today; but the present argument can be concluded by drawing the consequences of this second moment – the aculture of the signifier or of the simulacrum – for the whole problematic of some 'autonomy' of the cultural sphere which has concerned us here. For that autonomous realm is not itself spared by the intensified process by which the classical sign is dissolved; if its autonomy depended paradoxically on its possibility of remaining 'semi-autonomous' (in an Althusserian sense) and of preserving the last tenuous link with some ultimate referent (or, in Althusserian language, of preserving the ultimate unity of a properly 'structural totality'), then evidently in the new cultural moment culture will have ceased to be autonomous, and the realm of an autonomous play of signs becomes impossible, when that ultimate final referent to which the balloon of the mind was moored is now definitively cut. The break-up of the sign in mid-air determines a fall back into a now absolutely fragmented and anarchic social reality; the broken pieces of language (the pure signifiers) now fall again into the world, as so many more pieces of material junk among all the other rusting and superannuated apparatuses and buildings that litter the commodity landscape and that strew the 'collage city,' the 'delirious New York' of a postmodernist late capitalism in full crisis.

But, returning to a Marcusean terminology, all of this can also be said in a different way: with the eclipse of culture as an autonomous space or sphere, culture itself falls into the world, and the result is not its disappearance but its prodigious expansion, to the point where culture becomes coterminous with social life in general; now all the levels become 'acculturated,' and in the society of the spectacle, the image, or the simulacrum, everything has at length become cultural, from the superstructures down into the mechanisms of the infrastructure itself. If this development then places acutely on the agenda the neo-Gramscian problem of a new cultural politics today – in a social system in which the very status of both culture and politics have been profoundly, functionally, and structurally modified – it also renders problematic any further discussion of what used to be called 'culture' proper, whose artifacts have become the random experiences of daily life itself.

6   In the Sierra Maestra

The preceding section will, however, have been little more than a lengthy excursion into a very specialized (or 'elite') area, unless it can be shown that the dynamic therein visible, with something of the artificial simplification of the laboratory situation, finds striking analogies or homologies in very different and distant areas of social practice. It is precisely this replication of a common diachronic rhythm or 'genetic code' which we will not observe in the very different realities of revolutionary practice and theory in the course of the 60s in the Third World.

From the beginning, the Cuban experience affirmed itself as an original one, as a new revolutionary model, to be radically distinguished from more traditional forms of revolutionary practice. *Foco* theory, indeed, as it was associated with Che Guevara and theorized in Regis Debray's influential handbook, *Revolution in the Revolution?* (1967), asserted itself (as the title of the book suggests) both against a more traditional Leninist conception of party practice and against the experience of the Chinese revolution in its first essential stage of the conquest of power (what will later come to be designated as 'Maoism,' China's own very different 'revolution in the revolution,' or Great Proletarian Cultural Revolution, will not become visible to the outside world until the moment when the fate of the Cuban strategy has been sealed).

A reading of Debray's text shows that *foco* strategy, the strategy of the mobile guerrilla base or revolutionary *foyer*, is conceived as yet a third term, as something distinct from *either* the traditional model of class struggle (an essentially *urban* proletariat rising against a bourgeoisie or ruling class) *or* the Chinese experience of a mass peasant movement in the countryside (and also has little in common with a Fanonian struggle for recognition between Colonizer and Colonized). The *foco*, or guerrilla operation, is conceptualized as being neither 'in' nor 'of' either country or city; geographically, of course, it is positioned in the countryside, yet that location is not the permanently 'liberated territory' of the Yenan region, well beyond the reach of the enemy forces of Chiang Kai-shek or of the Japanese occupier. It is not indeed located in the cultivated area of the peasant fields at all, but rather in that third or nonplace which is the wilderness of the Sierra Maestra, neither country nor city, but rather a whole new element in which the guerrilla band moves in perpetual displacement.

This peculiarity of the way in which the spatial coordinates of the Cuban strategy is conceived has, then, immediate consequences for the way in which the class elements of the revolutionary movement are theorized. Neither city nor country; by the same token, paradoxically, the guerrillas themselves are grasped as being neither workers nor peasants (still less, intellectuals), but rather something entirely new, for which the prerevolutionary class society has no categories: new revolutionary subjects, forged in the guerrilla struggle indifferently out of the social material of peasants, city workers, or intellectuals, yet now largely transcending those class categories (just as this moment of Cuban theory will claim largely to transcend the older revolutionary ideologies predicted on class categories, whether those of Trotskyist workerism, Maoist populism and peasant consciousness, or of Leninist vanguard intellectualism).

What becomes clear in a text like Debray's is that the guerrilla *foco* – so mobile as to be beyond geography in the static sense – is in and of itself a *figure* for the transformed, revolutionary society to come. Its revolutionary militants are not simply 'soldiers' to whose specialized role and function one would then have to 'add' supplementary roles in the revolutionary division of labor, such as political commissars and the political vanguard party itself, both explicitly rejected here. Rather, in them is abolished all such prerevolutionary divisions and categories. This conception of a newly emergent revolutionary 'space' – situated outside the 'real' political, social, and geographical world of country and city, and of the historical social classes, yet at one and the same time a figure or small-scale image and prefiguration of the revolutionary transformation of that real world – may be designated as a properly Utopian space, an Hegelian 'inverted world,' an autonomous revolutionary sphere, in which the fallen real world over against it is itself set right and transformed into a new socialist society.

For all practical purposes, this powerful model is exhausted, even before

Che's own tragic death in Bolivia in 1967, with the failure of the guerrilla movements in Peru and Venezuela in 1966; not uncoincidentally, that failure will be accompanied by something like a disinvestment of revolutionary libido and fascination on the part of a First World Left, the return (with some leavening of the new Maoism) to its own current situation, in the American antiwar movement and May 68. In Latin America, however, the radical strategy that effectively replaces *foco* theory is that of the so-called urban guerrilla movement, pioneered in Uruguay by the Tupamaros; it will have become clear that this break-up of the utopian space of the older guerrilla *foco*, the fall of politics back into the world in the form of a very different style of political practice indeed – one that seeks to dramatize features of state power, rather than, as in traditional revolutionary movements, to build toward some ultimate encounter with it – will be interpreted here as something of a structural equivalent to the final stage of the sign as characterized above.

Several qualifications must be made, however. For one thing, it is clear that this new form of political activity will be endowed, by association, with something of the tragic prestige of the Palestinian liberation movement, which comes into being in its contemporary form as a result of the Israeli seizure of the West Bank and the Gaza Strip in 1967, and which will thereafter become one of the dominant worldwide symbols of revolutionary praxis in the late 60s. Equally clearly, however, the struggle of this desperate and victimized people cannot be made to bear responsibility for the excesses of this kind of strategy elsewhere in the world, whose universal results (whether in Latin America, or with Cointelpro in the United States, or, belatedly, in West Germany and Italy) have been to legitimize an intensification of the repressive apparatus of state power.

This objective coincidence between a misguided assessment of the social and political situation on the part of Left militants (for the most part students and intellectuals eager to force a revolutionary conjuncture by voluntaristic acts) and a willing exploitation by the state of precisely those provocations suggests that what is often loosely called 'terrorism' must be the object of complex and properly dialectical analysis. However rightly a responsible Left chooses to dissociate itself from such strategy (and the Marxian opposition to terrorism is an old and established tradition that goes back to the nineteenth century), it is important to remember that 'terrorism,' as a 'concept,' is also an ideologeme of the Right and must therefore be refused in that form. Along with the disaster films of the late 60s and early 70s, mass culture itself makes clear that 'terrorism' – the image of the 'terrorist' – is one of the privileged forms in which an ahistorical society images radical social change; meanwhile, an inspection of the content of the modern thriller or adventure story also makes it clear that the 'otherness' of so-called terrorism has begun to replace older images of criminal 'insanity' as an unexamined and seemingly 'natural' motivation in the construction of plots – yet another sign of the ideological nature of this particular pseudoconcept. Understood in this way, 'terrorism' is a collective obsession, a symptomatic fantasy of the American political unconscious, which demands a decoding and analysis in its own right.

As for the thing itself, for all practical purposes it comes to an end with the Chilean coup in 1973 and the fall of virtually all the Latin American countries to various forms of military dictatorship. The belated reemergence of this kind of political activity in West Germany and in Italy must surely at least in part be attributed to the fascist past of these two countries, to their failure to liquidate that past after the war, and to a violent moral revulsion against it on the part of a segment of the youth and intellectuals who grew up in the 60s.

7 Return of the 'Ultimately Determining Instance'

The two 'breaks' that have emerged in the preceding section – one in the general area around 1967, the other in the immediate neighborhood of 1973 – will not serve as the framework for a more general hypothesis about the periodization of the 60s in general. Beginning with the second of these, a whole series of other, seemingly unrelated events in the general area of 1972–74 suggests that this moment is not merely a decisive one on the relatively specialized level of Third World or Latin American radical politics, but signals the definitive end of what is called the 60s in a far more global way. In the First World, for example, the end of the draft and the withdrawal of American forces from Vietnam (in 1973) spell the end of the mass politics of the antiwar movement (the crisis of the New Left itself – which can be largely dated from the break-up of SDS in 1969 – would seem related to the other break mentioned, to which we will return below), while the signing of the Common Program between the Communist party and the new Socialist party in France (as well as the wider currency of slogans associated with 'Eurocommunism' at this time) would seem to mark a strategic turn away from the kinds of political activities associated with May 68 and its sequels. This is also the movement when as a result of the Yom Kippur war, the oil weapon emerges and administers a different kind of shock to the economies, the political strategies, and the daily life habits of the advanced countries. Concomitantly, on the more general cultural and ideological level, the intellectuals associated with the establishment itself (particularly in the United States) begin to recover from the fright and defensive posture that was theirs during the decade now ending, and again find their voices in a series of attacks on 60s culture and 60s politics, which, as was noted at the beginning, are not even yet at an end. One of the more influential documents was Lionel Trilling's *Sincerity and Authenticity* (1972), an Arnoldian call to reverse the tide of 60s' countercultural 'barbarism.' (This will, of course, be followed by the equally influential diagnosis of some 60s concept of 'authenticity' in terms of a 'culture of narcissism.') Meanwhile, in July 1973, some rather different 'intellectuals,' representing various concrete forms of political and economic power, will begin to rethink the failure in Vietnam in terms of a new global strategy for American and First World interests; their establishment of the Trilateral Commission will at least symbolically be a significant marker in the recovery of momentum by what must be called 'the ruling classes.' The emergence of a widely accepted new popular concept and term at this same time, the notion of the 'multinational corporation,' is also another symptom, signifying, as the authors of *Global Reach* have suggested, the moment when private business finds itself obliged to emerge in public as a visible 'subject of history' and a visible actor on the world stage – think of the role of ITT in Chile – when the American government, having been badly burned by the failure of the Vietnam intervention, is generally reluctant to undertake further ventures of this kind.

For all these reasons it seems appropriate to mark the definitive end of the '60s' in the general area of 1972–74. But we have omitted until now the decisive element in any argument for a periodization or 'punctuation' of this kind, and this new kind of material will direct our attention to a 'level' or 'instance' which has hitherto significantly been absent from the present discussion, namely the economic itself. For 1973–74 is the moment of the onset of a worldwide economic crisis, whose dynamic is still with us today, and which put a decisive full stop to the economic expansion and prosperity characteristic of the postwar period generally and of the 60s in particular. When we add to this another key economic marker – the recession in West Germany in 1966 and that in the other advanced countries, in particular in the United States a year or so later – we may well thereby find ourselves in a better position more formally to conceptualize the sense of a secondary break around 1967–68 which has begun to surface on the philosophical, cultural, and political levels as they were analyzed or 'narrated' above.

Such confirmation by the economic 'level' itself of periodizing reading derived from other, sample levels or instances of social life during the 60s will now perhaps put us in a better position to answer the two theoretical issues raised at the beginning of this essay. The first had to do with the validity of Marxist analysis for a period whose active political categories no longer seemed to be those of social class, and in which in a more general way traditional forms of Marxist theory and practice seemed to have entered a 'crisis.' The second involved the problem of some 'unified field theory' in terms of which such seemingly distant realities as Third World peasant movements and First World mass culture (or indeed, more abstractly, intellectual or superstructural levels like philosophy and culture generally, and those of mass resistance and political practice) might conceptually be related in some coherent way.

A pathbreaking synthesis of Ernest Mandel, in his book *Late Capitalism*,[5] will suggest a hypothetical answer to both these questions at once. The book presents, among other things, an elaborate system of business cycles under capitalism, whose most familiar unit, the seven-to-ten-year alternation of boom, overproduction, recession, and economic recovery, adequately enough accounts for the midpoint break in the 60s suggested above.

Mandel's account of the worldwide crisis of 1974, however, draws on a far more controversial conception of vaster cycles of some thirty- to fifty-year periods each – cycles which are then obviously much more difficult to perceive experientially or 'phenomenologically' insofar as they transcend the rhythms and limits of the biological life of individuals. These 'Kondratiev waves' (named after the Soviet economist who hypothesized them) have, according to Mandel, been renewed four times since the eighteenth century, and are characterized by quantum leaps in the technology of production, which enable decisive increases in the rate of profit generally, until at length the advantages of the new production processes have been explored and exhausted and the cycle therewith comes to an end. The latest of these Kondratiev cycles is that marked by computer technology, nuclear energy, and the mechanization of

[5] Ernest Mandel, *Late Capitalism* (London, 1978).

agriculture (particularly in foodstuffs and also primary materials), which Mandel dates from 1940 in North America and the postwar period in the other imperialist countries; what is decisive in the present context is his notion that, with the worldwide recession of 1973–74, the dynamics of this latest 'long wave' are spent.

The hypothesis is attractive, however, not only because of its abstract usefulness in confirming our periodization schemes, but also because of the actual analysis of this latest wave of capitalist expansion, and of the properly Marxian version he gives of a whole range of developments that have generally been thought to demonstrate the end of the 'classical' capitalism theorized by Marx and to require this or that post-Marxist theory of social mutation (as in theories of consumer society, postindustrial society, and the like).

We have already described the way in which neocolonialism is characterized by the radically new technology (the so-called Green Revolution in agriculture: new machinery, new farming methods, and new types of chemical fertilizer and genetic experiments with hybrid plants and the like), with which capitalism transforms its relationship to its colonies from an old-fashioned imperialist control to market penetration, destroying the older village communities and creating a whole new wage-labor pool and lumpenproletariat. The militancy of the new social forces is at one and the same time a result of the 'liberation' of peasants from the older self-sustaining village communities, and a movement of self-defense, generally originating in the stabler yet more isolated areas of a given Third World country, against what is rightly perceived as a far more thoroughgoing form of penetration and colonization than the older colonial armies.

It is now in terms of this process of 'mechanization' that Mandel will make the link between the neocolonialist transformation of the Third World during the 60s and the emergence of that seemingly very different thing in the First World, variously termed consumer society, postindustrial society, media society, and the like:

> Far from representing a postindustrial society, late capitalism . . . constitutes *generalized universal industrialization* for the first time in history. Mechanization, standardization, overspecialization and parcellization of labor, which in the past determined only the realm of commodity production in actual industry, now penetrate into all sectors of social life. It is characteristic of late capitalism that agriculture is step by step becoming just as industrialized as industry, the sphere of circulation [e.g., credit cards and the like] just as much as the sphere of production, and recreation just as much as the organization of work. (p. 387).

With this last, Mandel touches on what he elsewhere calls the mechanization of the superstructure, or, in other words, the penetration of culture itself by what the Frankfurt School called the culture industry, and of which the growth of the media is only a part. We may thus generalize his description as follows: late capitalism in general (and the 60s in particular) constitute a process in which the last surviving internal and external zones of precapitalism – the last vestiges of noncommodified or traditional space within and outside the advanced world – are now ultimately penetrated and colonized in their turn. Late capitalism can therefore be described as the moment when the last vestiges of Nature which survived on into classical capitalism are at length eliminated:

namely the Third World and the unconscious. The 60s will then have been the momentous transformational period when this systemic restructuring takes place on a global scale.

With such an account, our 'unified field theory' of the 60s is given: the discovery of a single process at work in First and Third Worlds, in global economy, and in consciousness and culture, a properly *dialectical* process, in which 'liberation' and domination are inextricably combined. We may now therefore proceed to a final characterization of the period as a whole.

The simplest yet most universal formulation surely remains the widely shared feeling that in the 60s, for a time, everything was possible; that this period, in other words, was a moment of a universal liberation, a global unbinding of energies. Mao Zedong's figure for this process is in this respect most revealing: 'Our nation,' he cried, 'is like an atom. . . . When this atom's nucleus is smashed, the thermal energy released will have really tremendous power!'[6] The image evokes the emergence of a genuine mass democracy from the breakup of the older feudal and village structures, and from the therapeutic dissolution of the habits of those structures in cultural revolutions. Yet the effects of fission, the release of molecular energies, the unbinding of 'material signifiers,' can be a properly terrifying spectacle; and we now know that Mao Zedong himself drew back from the ultimate consequences of the process he had set in motion, when, at the supreme moment of the Cultural Revolution, that of the founding of the Shanghai Commune, he called a halt to the dissolution of the party apparatus and effectively reversed the direction of this collective experiment as a whole (with consequences only too obvious at the present time). In the West, also, the great explosions of the 60s have led, in the worldwide economic crisis, to powerful restorations of the social order and a renewal of the repressive power of the various state apparatuses.

Yet the forces these must now confront, contain, and control are new ones, on which the older methods do not necessarily work. We have described the 60s as a moment when the enlargement of capitalism on a global scale simultaneously produced an immense freeing or unbinding of social energies, a prodigious release of untheorized new forces: the ethnic forces of black and 'minority,' or Third World, movements everywhere, regionalisms, the development of new and militant bearers of 'surplus consciousness' in the student and women's movements, as well as in a host of struggles of other kinds. Such newly released forces do not only not seem to compute in the dichotomous class model of traditional Marxism; they also seem to offer a realm of freedom and voluntarist possibility beyond the classical constraints of the economic infrastructure. Yet this sense of freedom and possibility – which is for the course of the 60s a momentarily objective reality, as well as (from the hindsight of the 80s) a historical illusion – can perhaps best be explained in terms of the superstructural movement and play enabled by the transition from one infrastructural or systemic stage of capitalism to another. The 60s were in that sense an immense and inflationary issuing of superstructural credit; a universal abandonment of the referential gold standard; an extraordinary printing up of ever more devalued signifiers. With the end of the 60s, with the world economic crisis, all the old infrastructural bills then slowly come due once more; and the

[6] Mao Zedong, *Chairman Mao Talks to the People*, ed. S. Schram (New York, 1974), pp. 92–93.

80s will be characterized by an effort, on a world scale, to proletarianize all those unbound social forces that gave the 60s their energy, by an extension of class struggle, in other words, into the farthest reaches of the globe as well as the most minute configurations of local institutions (such as the university system). The unifying force here is the new vocation of a henceforth global capitalism, which may also be expected to unify the unequal, fragmented, or local resistances to the process. And this is finally also the solution to the so-called crisis of Marxism and to the widely noted inapplicability of its forms of class analysis to the new social realities with which the 60s confronted us: 'traditional' Marxism, if 'untrue' during this period of a proliferation of new subjects of history, must necessarily become true again when the dreary realities of exploitation, extraction of surplus value, proletarianization, and the resistance to it in the form of class struggle, all slowly reassert themselves on a new and expanded world scale, as they seem currently in the process of doing.

14　Terry Eagleton

From *Capitalism, Modernism and Postmodernism*

New Left Review, volume 152, 1985, pp 60–73.

The Aesthetics of Postmodernism

The productivist aesthetics of the early twentieth-century avant garde spurned the notion of artistic 'representation' for an art which would be less 'reflection' than material intervention and organizing forces. The aesthetics of postmodernism is a dark parody of such anti-representationalism: if art no longer reflects it is not because it seeks to change the world rather than mimic it, but because there is in truth nothing there to be reflected, no reality which is not itself already image, spectacle, simulacrum, gratuitous fiction. To say that social reality is pervasively commodified is to say that it is always already 'aesthetic' – textured, packaged, fetishized, libidinalized; and for art to reflect reality is then for it to do no more than mirror itself, in a cryptic self-referentiality which is indeed one of the inmost structures of the commodity fetish. The commodity is less an image in the sense of a 'reflection' than an image of itself, its entire material being devoted to its own self-presentation; and in such a condition the most authentically representational art becomes, paradoxically, the anti-representational artefact whose contingency and facticity figures the fate of all late-capitalist objects. If the unreality of the artistic image mirrors the unreality of its society as a whole, then this is to say that it mirrors nothing real and so does not really mirror at all. Beneath this paradox lies the historical truth that the very autonomy and brute self-identity of the postmodernist artefact is the

effect of its thorough *integration* into an economic system where such autonomy, in the form of the commodity fetish, is the order of the day.

To see art in the manner of the revolutionary avant garde, not as institutionalized object but as practice, strategy, performance, production: all of this,
once again, is grotesquely caricatured by late capitalism, for which, as Jean-
François Lyotard has pointed out, the 'performativity principle' is really all that
counts. In his *The Postmodern Condition*, Lyotard calls attention to capitalism's 'massive subordination of cognitive statements to the finality of the best
possible performance'. 'The games of scientific language', he writes, 'become
the games of the rich, in which whoever is wealthiest has the best chance of
being right.'[1] It is not difficult, then, to see a relation between the philosophy of
J.L. Austin and IBM, or between the various neo-Nietzscheanisms of a post-
structuralist epoch and Standard Oil. It is not surprising that classical models of
truth and cognition are increasingly out of favour in a society where what
matters is whether you deliver the commercial or rhetorical goods. Whether
among discourse theorists or the Institute of Directors, the goal is no longer
truth but performativity, not reason but power. The CBI are in this sense
spontaneous post-structuralists to a man, utterly disenchanted (did they but
know it) with epistemological realism and the correspondence theory of truth.
That this is so is no reason for pretending that we can relievedly return to John
Locke or Georg Luckács; it is simply to recognize that it is not always easy to
distinguish politically radical assaults on classical epistemology (among which
the early Lukács must himself be numbered, alongside the Soviet avant garde)
from flagrantly reactionary ones. Indeed it is a sign of this difficulty that
Lyotard himself, having grimly outlined the most oppressive aspects of the
capitalist performativity principle, has really nothing to offer in its place but
what amounts in effect to an anarchist version of that very same epistemology,
namely to guerrilla skirmishes of a 'paralogism' which might from time to time
induce ruptures, instabilities, paradoxes and micro-catastrophic discontinuities into this terroristic techno-scientific system. A 'good' pragmatics, in
short, is turned against a 'bad' one; but it will always be a loser from the outset,
since it has long since abandoned the Enlightenment's grand narrative of
human emancipation, which we all now know to be disreputably metaphysical.
Lyotard is in no doubt that '(socialist) struggles and their instruments have
been transformed into regulators of the system' in all the advanced societies, an
Olympian certitude which, as I write, Mrs Thatcher might at once envy and
query. (Lyotard is wisely silent on the class-struggle outside the advanced
capitalist nations.) It is not easy to see how, if the capitalist system has been
effective enough to negate all class-struggle entirely, the odd unorthodox
scientific experiment is going to give it much trouble. 'Postmodernist science',
as Fredric Jameson suggests in his introduction to Lyotard's book, is here
playing the role once assumed by high modernist art, which was similarly an
experimental disruption of the given system; and Lyotard's desire to see
modernism and postmodernism as continuous with one another is in part a
refusal to confront the disturbing fact that modernism proved prey to institu-
tionalization. Both cultural phases are for Lyotard manifestations of that which

---

[1] Jean-François Lyotard, *The Postmodern Condition: A Report on Knowledge*, Manchester
University Press, 1984, p. 45.

escapes and confounds history with the explosive force of the Now, the 'paralogic' as some barely possible, mind-boggling leap into free air which gives the slip to the nightmare of temporality and global narrative from which some of us are trying to awaken. Paralogism, like the poor, is always with us, but just because the system is always with us too. The 'modern' is less a particular cultural practice or historical period, which may then suffer defeat or incorporation, than a kind of permanent ontological possibility of disrupting all such historical periodization, an essential timeless gesture which cannot be recited or reckoned up within historical narrative because it is no more than an atemporal force which gives the lie to all such linear categorization.

History and Modernity

As with all such anarchistic or Camusian revolt, modernism can thus never really die – it has resurfaced in our own time as paralogical science. But the reason why it can never be worsted – the fact that it does not occupy the same temporal terrain or logical space as its antagonists – is exactly the reason why it can never defeat the system either. The characteristic post-structuralist blend of pessimism and euphoria springs precisely from this paradox. History and modernity play a ceaseless cat-and-mouse game in and out of time, neither able to slay the other because they occupy different ontological sites. 'Game' in the positive sense – the ludic disportings of disruption and desire – plays itself out in the crevices of 'game' in the negative sense – game theory, the techno-scientific system – in an endless conflict and collusion. Modernity here really means a Nietzschean 'active forgetting' of history: the healthy spontaneous amnesia of the animal who has wilfully repressed its own sordid determinations and so is free. It is thus the exact opposite of Walter Benjamin's 'revolutionary nostalgia': the power of active remembrance as a ritual summoning and invocation of the traditions of the oppressed in violent constellation with the political present. It is no wonder that Lyotard is deeply opposed to any such historical consciousness, with his reactionary celebrations of narrative as an eternal present rather than a revolutionary recollection of the unjustly quelled. If he could remember in this Benjaminesque mode, he might be less confident that the class struggle could be merely extirpated. Nor, if he had adequately engaged Benjamin's work, could he polarize in such simplistic binary opposition – one typical of much post-structuralist thought – the grand totalizing narratives of the Enlightenment on the one hand and the micropolitical or paralogistic on the other (postmodernism as the death of metanarrative). For Benjamin's unfathomably subtle meditations on history throw any such binary poststructuralist scheme into instant disarray. Benjamin's 'tradition' is certainly a totality of a kind, but at the same time a ceaseless detotalization of a triumphalist ruling-class history; it is in some sense a given, yet is always constructed from the vantage-point of the present; it operates as a deconstructive force within hegemonic ideologies of history, yet can be seen too as a totalizing movement within which sudden affinities, correspondences and constellations may be fashioned between disparate struggles.

A Nietzschean sense of the 'modern' also informs the work of the most influential of American deconstructionists, Paul de Man, though with an added twist of irony. For 'active forgetting', de Man argues, can never be entirely successful: the distinctively modernist act, which seeks to erase or arrest history, finds itself surrendered in that very moment to the lineage it seeks to repress, perpetuating rather than abolishing it. Indeed literature for de Man is nothing less than this constantly doomed, ironically self-undoing attempt to make it new, this ceaseless incapacity ever quite to awaken from the nightmare of history: 'The continuous appeal of modernity, the desire to break out of literature toward the reality of the moment, prevails and, in its turn, folding back upon itself, engenders the repetition and the continuation of literature.'[2] Since action and temporality are indissociable, modernism's dream of self-origination, its hunger for some historically unmediated encounter with the real, is internally fissured and self-thwarting: to write is to disrupt a tradition which depends on such disruption for its very self-reproduction. We are all, simultaneously and inextricably, modernists and traditionalists, terms which for de Man designate neither cultural movements nor aesthetic ideologies but the very structure of that duplicitous phenomenon, always in and out of time simultaneously, named literature, where this common dilemma figures itself with rhetorical self-consciousness. Literary history here, de Man contends, 'could in fact be paradigmatic for history in general'; and what this means, translated from deManese, is that though we will never abandon our radical political illusions (the fond fantasy of emancipating ourselves from tradition and confronting the real eyeball-to-eyeball being, as it were, a permanent pathological state of human affairs), such actions will always prove self-defeating, will always be incorporated by a history which has foreseen them and seized upon them as ruses for its own self-perpetuation. The daringly 'radical' recourse to Nietzsche, that is to say, turns out to land one in a maturely liberal Democrat position, wryly sceptical but genially tolerant of the radical antics of the young.

What is at stake here, under the guise of a debate about history and modernity, is nothing less than the dialectical relation of theory and practice. For if practice is defined in neo-Nietzschean style as spontaneous error, productive blindness or historical amnesia, then theory can of course be no more than a jaded reflection upon its ultimate impossibility. Literature, that aporetic spot in which truth and error indissolubly entwine, is at once practice and the deconstruction of practice, spontaneous act and theoretical fact, a gesture which in pursuing an unmediated encounter with reality in the same instant interprets that very impulse as metaphysical fiction. Writing is both action and a reflection upon that action, but the two are ontologically disjunct; and literature is the privileged place where practice comes to know and name its eternal difference from theory. It is not surprising, then, that the last sentence of de Man's essay makes a sudden swerve to the political: 'If we extend this notion beyond literature, it merely confirms that the bases for historical knowledge are not empirical facts but written texts, even if these texts masquerade in the guise of wars and revolutions.' A text which starts out with a problem in literary history ends up as an assault on Marxism. For it is of course Marxism above all which has insisted that actions may be theoretically in-

---

[2] Paul de Man, 'Literary History and Literary Modernity', in *Blindness and Insight*, University of Minnesota Press, Minneapolis 1983, p. 162.

formed and histories emancipatory, notions capable of scuppering de Man's entire case. It is only by virtue of an initial Nietzschean dogmatism – practice is necessarily self-blinded, tradition necessarily impeding – that de Man is able to arrive at his politically quietistic aporias.[3] Given these initial definitions, a certain judicious deconstruction of their binary opposition is politically essential, if the Nietzschean belief in affirmative action is to transform the metaphysical trust that there is indeed a single dominant structure of action (blindness, error), and a single form of tradition (obfuscating rather than enabling an encounter with the 'real'). The Marxism of Louis Althusser comes close to this Nietzscheanism: practice is an 'imaginary' affair which thrives upon the repression of truly theoretical understanding, theory a reflection upon the necessary fictionality of such action. The two, as with Nietzsche and de Man, are ontologically disjunct, necessarily non-synchronous.

. . . .

'A Desiring Machine'

In some postmodernist theory, the injunction to glimpse the good in the bad has been pursued with a vengeance. Capitalist technology can be viewed as an immense desiring machine, an enormous circuit of messages and exchanges in which pluralistic idioms proliferate and random objects, bodies, surfaces come to glow with libidinal intensity. 'The interesting thing', writes Lyotard in his *Economic libidinale*, 'would be to stay where we are – but to grab without noise all opportunities to function as bodies and good conductors of intensities. No need of declarations, manifestos, organizations; not even for exemplary actions. To let dissimulation play in favour of intensities.'[4] It is all rather closer to Walter Pater than to Walter Benjamin. Of course capitalism is not uncritically endorsed by such theory, for its libidinal flows are subject to a tyrannical ethical, semiotic and juridical order; what is wrong with late capitalism is not this or that desire but the fact that desire does not circulate freely enough. But if only we could kick our metaphysical nostalgia for truth, meaning and history, of which Marxism is perhaps the prototype, we might come to recognize that desire is here and now, fragments and surfaces all we ever have, kitsch quite as good as the real thing because there is in fact no real thing. What is amiss with old-fashioned modernism, from this perspective, is just the fact that it obstinately refuses to abandon the struggle for meaning. It is still agonizingly caught up in metaphysical depth and wretchedness, still able to experience psychic fragmentation and social alienation as spiritually wounding, and so embarrassingly enmortgaged to the very bourgeois humanism it otherwise seeks to subvert. Postmodernism, confidently post-metaphysical, has outlived all that fantasy of interiority, that pathological itch to scratch surfaces for concealed depths, it embraces instead the mystical positivism of the early Wittgenstein, for which the world – would you believe it – just is the way it is and not some other way. As with the early Wittgenstein, there cannot be a

---

[3] For a vigorous critique of the political implications of de Man's arguments, see Frank Lentricchia, *Criticism and Social Change*, University of Chicago Press, Chicago and London 1983, pp. 43–52.

[4] Jean-François Lyotard, *Economic libidinale*, Paris 1974, p. 311.

rational discourse of ethical or political value, for values are not the kind of thing which can be *in* the world in the first place, any more than the eye can be part of the field of vision. The dispersed, schizoid subject is nothing to be alarmed about after all: nothing could be more normative in late-capitalist experience. Modernism appears in this light as a deviation still enthralled to a norm, parasitic on what it sets out to deconstruct. But if we are now posterior to such metaphysical humanism there is really nothing left to struggle against, other than those inherited illusions (law, ethics, class-struggle, the Oedipus complex) which prevent us from seeing things as they are.

But the fact that modernism continues to struggle for meaning is exactly what makes it so interesting. For this struggle continually drives it towards classical styles of sense-making which are at once unacceptable and inescapable, traditional matrices of meaning which have become progressively empty but which nevertheless continue to exert their implacable force. It is in just this way that Walter Benjamin reads Franz Kafka, whose fiction inherits the form of a traditional storytelling without its truth contents. A whole traditional ideology of representation is in crisis, yet this does not mean that the search for truth is abandoned. Postmodernism, by contrast, commits the apocalyptic error of believing that the discrediting of this particular representational epistemology is the death of truth itself, just as it sometimes mistakes the disintegration of certain traditional ideologies of the subject for the subject's final disappearance. In both cases, the obituary notices are greatly exaggerated. Postmodernism persuades us to relinquish our epistemological paranoia and embrace the brute objectivity of random subjectivity; modernism, more productively, is torn by the contradictions between a still ineluctable bourgeois humanism and the pressures of a quite different rationality, which, still newly emergent, is not even able to name itself. If modernism's underminings of a traditional human-ism are at once anguished and exhilarated, it is in part because there are few more intractable problems in the modern epoch than of distinguishing between those critiques of classical rationality which are potentially progressive, and those which are irrationalist in the worst sense. It is the choice, so to speak, between feminism and fascism; and in any particular conjuncture the question of what counts as a revolutionary rather than barbarous break with the dominant Western ideologies of reason and humanity is sometimes undecid-able. There is a difference, for example, between the 'meaninglessness' fostered by some postmodernism, and the 'meaninglessness' deliberately injected by some trends of avant-garde culture into bourgeois normality.

The Bourgeois–Humanist Subject

The contradiction of modernism in this respect is that in order valuably to deconstruct the unified subject of bourgeois humanism, it draws upon key negative aspects of the actual experience of such subjects in late bourgeois society, which often enough does not at all correspond to the official ideological version. It thus pits what is increasingly felt to be the phenomenological reality of capitalism against its formal ideologies, and in doing so finds that it can fully embrace neither. The phenomenological reality of the subject throws formal humanist ideology into question, while the persistence of that ideology is precisely what enables the phenomenological reality to be characterized as negative. Modernism thus dramatizes in its very internal structures a crucial contradiction in the ideology of the subject, the force of which we can appreciate if we ask ourselves in what sense the bourgeois humanist conception of the subject as free, active, autonomous and self-identical is a workable or appropriate ideology for late capitalist society. The answer would seem to be that in one sense such an ideology is highly appropriate to such social conditions, and in another sense hardly at all. This ambiguity is overlooked by those post-structuralist theorists who appear to stake all on the assumption that the 'unified subject' is indeed an integral part of contemporary bourgeois ideology, and is thus ripe for urgent deconstruction. Against such a view, it is surely arguable that late capitalism has deconstructed such a subject much more efficiently than meditations on *écriture*. As postmodernist culture attests, the contemporary subject may be less the strenuous monadic agent of an earlier phase of capitalist ideology than a dispersed, decentred network of libidinal attachments, emptied of ethical substance and psychical interiority, the ephemeral function of this or that act of consumption, media experience, sexual relationship, trend or fashion. The 'unified subject' looms up in this light as more and more of a shibboleth or straw target, a hangover from an older liberal epoch of capitalism, before technology and consumerism scattered our bodies to the winds as so many bits and pieces of reified technique, appetite, mechanical operation or reflex of desire.

If this were wholly true, of course, postmodernist culture would be tri-umphantly vindicated: the unthinkable or the utopian, depending upon one's perspective, would already have happened. But the bourgeois humanist sub-ject is not in fact simply part of a clapped-out history we can all agreeably or reluctantly leave behind: if it is an increasingly inappropriate model at certain levels of subjecthood, it remains a potently relevant one at others. Consider, for example, the condition of being a father and a consumer simultaneously. The former role is governed by ideological imperatives of agency, duty, autonomy, authority, responsibility: the latter, while not wholly free of such strictures, puts them into significant question. The two roles are not of course merely disjunct; but though relations between them are practically negotiable, capitalism's current ideal consumer is strictly incompatible with its current ideal parent. The subject of late capitalism, in other words, is neither simply the self-regulating synthetic agent posited by classical humanist ideology, nor merely a decentred network of desire, but a contradictory amalgam of the two. The constitution of such a subject at the ethical, juridical and political levels is not wholly continuous with its constitution as a consuming or 'mass cultural' unit. 'Eclecticism,' writes Lyotard, 'is the degree zero of contemporary general culture: one listens to reggae, watches a western, eats McDonald's food for lunch and local cuisine for dinner, wears Paris perfume in Tokyo and 'retro' clothes in Hong Kong; knowledge is a matter of TV games.'[5] It is not just that there are millions of other human subjects, less exotic than Lyotard's jet-setters, who educate their children, vote as responsible citizens, withdraw their labour and clock in for work; it is also that many subjects live more and more at the points of contradictory intersection between these two definitions.

[5] *The Postmodern Condition*, p. 76.

This was also, in some sense, the site which modernism occupied, trusting as it still did to an experience of interiority which could however be less and less articulated in traditional ideological terms. It could expose the limits of such terms with styles of subjective experience they could not encompass; but it also remembered that language sufficiently to submit the definitively 'modern' condition to implicitly *critical* treatment. Whatever the blandishments of postmodernism, this is in my view the site of contradiction we still inhabit; and the most valuable forms of post-structuralism are therefore those which, as with much of Jacques Derrida's writing, refuse to credit the absurdity that we could ever simply have jettisoned the 'metaphysical' like a cast-off overcoat. The new post-metaphysical subject proposed by Bertolt Brecht and Walter Benjamin, the *Unmensch* emptied of all bourgeois interiority to become the faceless mobile functionary of revolutionary struggle, is at once a valuable metaphor for thinking ourselves beyond Proust, and too uncomfortably close to the faceless functionaries of advanced capitalism to be uncritically endorsed. In a similar way, the aesthetics of the revolutionary avant-garde break with the contemplative monad of bourgeois culture with their clarion call of 'production', only to rejoin in some respects the labouring or manufacturing subject of bourgeois utilitarianism. We are still, perhaps, poised as precariously as Benjamin's Baudelairian *flâneur* between the rapidly fading aura of the old humanist subject, and the ambivalently energizing and repellent shapes of a city landscape.

Postmodernism takes something from modernism and the avant-garde, and in a sense plays one off against the other. From modernism proper, postmodernism inherits the fragmentary or schizoid self, but eradicates all critical distance from it, countering this with a pokerfaced presentation of 'bizarre' experiences which resembles certain avant-garde gestures. From the avant-garde, postmodernism takes the dissolution of art into social life, the rejection of tradition, an opposition to 'high' culture as such, but crosses this with the unpolitical impulses of modernism. It thus unwittingly exposes the residual formalism of any radical art-form which identifies the de-institutionalization of art, and its reintegration with other social practices, as an intrinsically revolutionary move. For the question, rather, is under what conditions and with what likely effects such a reintegration may be attempted. An authentically political art in our own time might similarly draw upon both modernism and the avant-garde, but in a different combination from post-modernism.

The contradictions of the modernist work are, as I have tried to show, implicitly political in character; but since the 'political' seemed to such modernism to belong precisely to the traditional rationality it was trying to escape, this fact remained for the most part submerged beneath the mythological and metaphysical. Moreover, the typical self-reflexiveness of modernist culture was at once a form in which it could explore some of the key ideological issues I have outlined, and by the same stroke rendered its products opaque and unavailable to a wide public. An art today which, having learnt from the openly committed character of avant-garde culture, might cast the contradictions of modernism in a more explicitly political light, could do so effectively only if it had also learnt its lesson from modernism too – learnt, that is to say, that the 'political' itself is a question of the emergence of a transformed rationality, and if it is not presented as such will still seem part of the very tradition from which the adventurously modern is striving to free itself.

15 Jürgen Habermas

From *Modernity – An Incomplete Project*

Postmodern Culture, ed. Hal Foster, trans. S. Ben-Habib, Pluto Press: London and Sydney, 1985, pp 3–15.

In 1980, architects were admitted to the Biennial in Venice, following painters and filmmakers. The note sounded at this first Architecture Biennial was one of disappointment. I would describe it by saying that those who exhibited in Venice formed an avant-garde of reversed fronts. I mean that they sacrificed the tradition of modernity in order to make room for a new historicism. Upon this occasion, a critic of the German newspaper, *Frankfurter Allgemeine Zeitung*, advanced a thesis whose significance reaches beyond this particular event; it is a diagnosis of our times: 'Postmodernity definitely presents itself as Antimodernity.' This statement describes an emotional current of our times which has penetrated all spheres of intellectual life. It has placed on the agenda theories of postenlightenment, postmodernity, even of posthistory.

From history we know the phrase, 'The Ancients and the Moderns.' Let me begin by defining these concepts. The term 'modern' has a long history, one which has been investigated by Hans Robert Jauss.[1] The word 'modern' in its Latin form 'modernus' was used for the first time in the late 5th century in order to distinguish the present, which had become officially Christian, from the Roman and pagan past. With varying content, the term 'modern' again and again expresses the consciousness of an epoch that relates itself to the past of antiquity, in order to view itself as the result of a transition from the old to the new.

Some writers restrict this concept of 'modernity' to the Renaissance, but this is historically too narrow. People considered themselves modern during the period of Charles the Great in the 12th century, as well as in France of the late 17th century at the time of the famous 'Querelle des Anciens et des Modernes.' That is to say, the term 'modern' appeared and reappeared exactly during those periods in Europe when the consciousness of a new epoch formed itself through a renewed relationship to the ancients – whenever, moreover, antiquity was considered a model to be recovered through some kind of imitation.

This essay was originally delivered as a talk in September 1980 when Habermas was awarded the Theodor W. Adorno prize by the city of Frankfurt. It was subsequently delivered as a James Lecture of the New York Institute for the Humanities at New York University in March 1981 and published under the title 'Modernity Versus Postmodernity' in *New German Critique* 22 (Winter, 1981). It is reprinted here by permission of the author and the publisher.

[1] Jauss is a prominent German literary historian and critic involved in 'the aesthetics of reception,' a type of criticism related to reader-response criticism in this country. For a discussion of 'modern' see Jauss, *Asthetische Normen und Geschichtliche Reflexion in der Querelle des Anciens et des Modernes* (Munich, 1964). For a reference in English see Jauss, 'History of Art and Pragmatic History,' *Toward an Aesthetic of Reception*, trans. Timothy Bahti (Minneapolis: University of Minnesota Press, 1982), pp. 46–8. [ed.]

The spell which the classics of the ancient world cast upon the spirit of later times was first dissolved with the ideals of the French Enlightenment. Specifically, the idea of being 'modern' by looking back to the ancients changed with the belief, inspired by modern science, in the infinite progress of knowledge and in the infinite advance towards social and moral betterment. Another form of modernist consciousness was formed in the wake of this change. The romantic modernist sought to oppose the antique ideals of the classicists; he looked for a new historical epoch and found it in the idealized Middle Ages. However, this new ideal age, established early in the 19th century, did not remain a fixed ideal. In the course of the 19th century, there emerged out of this romantic spirit that radicalized consciousness of modernity which freed itself from all specific historical ties. This most recent modernism simply makes an abstract opposition between tradition and the present; and we are, in a way, still the contemporaries of that kind of aesthetic modernity which first appeared in the midst of the 19th century. Since then, the distinguishing mark of works which count as modern is 'the new' which will be overcome and made obsolete through the novelty of the next style. But, while that which is merely 'stylish' will soon become outmoded, that which is modern preserves a secret tie to the classical. Of course, whatever can survive time has always been considered to be a classic. But the emphatically modern document no longer borrows this power of being a classic from the authority of a past epoch; instead, a modern work becomes a classic because it has once been authentically modern. Our sense of modernity creates its own self-enclosed canons of being classic. In this sense we speak, e.g., in view of the history of modern art, of classical modernity. The relation between 'modern' and 'classical' has definitely lost a fixed historical reference.

The Discipline of Aesthetic Modernity

The spirit and discipline of aesthetic modernity assumed clear contours in the work of Baudelaire. Modernity then unfolded in various avant-garde movements and finally reached its climax in the Café Voltaire of the dadaists and in surrealism. Aesthetic modernity is characterized by attitudes which find a common focus in a changed consciousness of time. This time consciousness expresses itself through metaphors of the vanguard and the avant-garde. The avant-garde understands itself as invading unknown territory, exposing itself to the dangers of sudden, shocking encounters, conquering an as yet unoccupied future. The avant-garde must find a direction in a landscape into which no one seems to have yet ventured.

But these forward gropings, this anticipation of an undefined future and the cult of the new mean in fact the exaltation of the present. The new time consciousness, which enters philosophy in the writings of Bergson, does more than express the experience of mobility in society, of acceleration in history, of discontinuity in everyday life. The new value placed on the transitory, the elusive and the ephemeral, the very celebration of dynamism, discloses a longing for an undefiled, immaculate and stable present.

This explains the rather abstract language in which the modernist temper has spoken of the 'past.' Individual epochs lose their distinct forces. Historical memory is replaced by the heroic affinity of the present with the extremes of history – a sense of time wherein decadence immediately recognizes itself in the barbaric, the wild and the primitive. We observe the anarchistic intention of blowing up the continuum of history, and we can account for it in terms of the subversive force of this new aesthetic consciousness. Modernity revolts against the normalizing functions of tradition; modernity lives on the experience of rebelling against all that is normative. This revolt is one way to neutralize the standards of both morality and utility. This aesthetic consciousness continuously stages a dialectical play between secrecy and public scandal; it is addicted to a fascination with that horror which accompanies the act of profaning, and yet is always in flight from the trivial results of profanation.

On the other hand, the time consciousness articulated in avant-garde art is not simply ahistorical; it is directed against what might be called a false normativity in history. The modern, avant-garde spirit has sought to use the past in a different way; it disposes those pasts which have been made available by the objectifying scholarship of historicism, but it opposes at the same time a neutralized history which is locked up in the museum of historicism.

Drawing upon the spirit of surrealism, Walter Benjamin constructs the relationship of modernity to history in what I would call a posthistoricist attitude. He reminds us of the self-understanding of the French Revolution: 'The Revolution cited ancient Rome, just as fashion cites an antiquated dress. Fashion has a scent for what is current, whenever this moves within the thicket of what was once.' This is Benjamin's concept of the *Jetztzeit*, of the present as a moment of revelation; a time in which splinters of a messianic presence are enmeshed. In this sense, for Robespierre, the antique Rome was a past laden with momentary revelations.[2]

Now, this spirit of aesthetic modernity has recently begun to age. It has been recited once more in the 1960s: after the 1970s, however, we must admit to ourselves that this modernism arouses a much fainter response today than it did fifteen years ago. Octavio Paz, a fellow-traveller of modernity, noted already in the middle of the 1960s that 'the avant-garde of 1967 repeats the deeds and gestures of those of 1917. We are experiencing the end of the idea of modern art.' The work of Peter Bürger has since taught us to speak of 'post-avant-garde' art; this term is chosen to indicate the failure of the surrealist rebellion.[3] But what is the meaning of this failure? Does it signal a farewell to modernity? Thinking more generally, does the existence of a post-avant-garde mean there is a transition to that broader phenomenon called Postmodernity?

This is in fact how Daniel Bell, the most brilliant of the American neoconservatives, interprets matters. In his book, *The Cultural Contradictions of Capitalism*, Bell argues that the crises of the developed societies of the West are to be traced back to a split between culture and society. Modernist culture has come to penetrate the values of everyday life; the life-world is infected by modernism. Because of the forces of modernism, the principle of unlimited self-

---

[2] See Benjamin, 'Theses on the Philosophy of History,' *Illuminations*, trans. Harry Zohn (New York: Schocken, 1969), p. 261. [ed.]

[3] For Paz on the avant-garde see in particular *Children of the Mire: Modern Poetry from Romanticism to the Avant-Garde* (Cambridge: Harvard University Press, 1974), pp. 148–64. For Bürger see *Theory of the Avant-Garde* (Minneapolis: University of Minnesota Press, Fall 1983). [ed.]

realization, the demand for authentic self-experience and the subjectivism of a hyperstimulated sensitivity have come to be dominant. This temperament unleashes hedonistic motives irreconcilable with the discipline of professional life in society, Bell says. Moreover, modernist culture is altogether incompatible with the moral basis of a purposive, rational conduct of life. In this manner, Bell places the burden of responsibility for the dissolution of the Protestant ethic (a phenomenon which had already disturbed Max Weber) on the 'adversary culture.' Culture in its modern form stirs up hatred against the conventions and virtues of everyday life, which has become rationalized under the pressures of economic and administrative imperatives.

I would call your attention to a complex wrinkle in this view. The impulse of modernity, we are told on the other hand, is exhausted; anyone who considers himself avant-garde can read his own death warrant. Although the avant-garde is still considered to be expanding, it is supposedly no longer creative. Modernism is dominant but dead. For the neoconservative the question then arises: how can norms arise in society which will limit libertinism, reestablish the ethic of discipline and work? What new norms will put a brake on the levelling caused by the social welfare state so that the virtues of individual competition for achievement can again dominate? Bell sees a religious revival to be the only solution. Religious faith tied to a faith in tradition will provide individuals with clearly defined identities and existential security.

Cultural Modernity and Societal Modernization

One can certainly not conjure up by magic the compelling beliefs which command authority. Analyses like Bell's, therefore, only result in an attitude which is spread in Germany no less than in the States: an intellectual and political confrontation with the carriers of cultural modernity. I cite Peter Steinfels, an observer of the new style which the neoconservatives have imposed upon the intellectual scene in the 1970s:

> The struggle takes the form of exposing every manifestation of what could be considered an oppositionist mentality and tracing its 'logic' so as to link it to various forms of extremism: drawing the connection between modernism and nihilism . . . between government regulation and totalitarianism, between criticism of arms expenditures and subservience to communism, between Women's liberation or homosexual rights and the destruction of the family . . . between the Left generally and terrorism, anti-semitism, and fascism . . .[4]

The *ad hominem* approach and the bitterness of these intellectual accusations have also been trumpeted loudly in Germany. They should not be explained so much in terms of the psychology of neoconservative writers; rather, they are rooted in the analytical weaknesses of neoconservative doctrine itself.

Neoconservatism shifts onto cultural modernism the uncomfortable burdens of a more or less successful capitalist modernization of the economy and society. The neoconservative doctrine blurs the relationship between the welcomed process of societal modernization on the one hand, and the lamented cultural development on the other. The neoconservative does not

---

[4] Peter Steinfels, *The Neoconservatives* (New York: Simon and Schuster, 1979), p. 65.

uncover the economic and social causes for the altered attitudes towards work, consumption, achievement and leisure. Consequently, he attributes all of the following – hedonism, the lack of social identification, the lack of obedience, narcissism, the withdrawal from status and achievement competition – to the domain of 'culture.' In fact, however, culture is intervening in the creation of all these problems in only a very indirect and mediated fashion.

In the neoconservative view, those intellectuals who still feel themselves committed to the project of modernity are then presented as taking the place of those unanalyzed causes. The mood which feeds neoconservatism today in no way originates from discontent about the antinomian consequences of a culture breaking from the museums into the stream of ordinary life. This discontent has not been called into life by modernist intellectuals. It is rooted in deep-seated reactions against the process of *societal* modernization. Under the pressures of the dynamics of economic growth and the organizational accomplishments of the state, this social modernization penetrates deeper and deeper into previous forms of human existence. I would describe this subordination of the life-worlds under the system's imperatives as a matter of disturbing the communicative infrastructure of everyday life.

Thus, for example, neopopulist protests only express in pointed fashion a widespread fear regarding the destruction of the urban and natural environment and of forms of human sociability. There is a certain irony about these protests in terms of neoconservatism. The tasks of passing on a cultural tradition, of social integration and of socialization require adherence to what I call communicative rationality. But the occasions for protest and discontent originate precisely when spheres of communicative action, centred on the reproduction and transmission of values and norms, are penetrated by a form of modernization guided by standards of economic and administrative rationality – in other words, by standards of rationalization quite different from those of communicative rationality on which those spheres depend. But neoconservative doctrines turn our attention precisely away from such societal processes: they project the causes, which they do not bring to light, onto the plane of a subversive culture and its advocates.

To be sure, cultural modernity generates its own aporias as well. Independently from the consequences of *societal* modernization and within the perspective of *cultural* development itself, there originate motives for doubting the project of modernity. Having dealt with a feeble kind of criticism of modernity – that of neoconservatism – let me now move our discussion of modernity and its discontents into a different domain that touches on these aporias of cultural modernity – issues that often serve only as a pretense for those positions which either call for a postmodernity, recommend a return to some form of pre-modernity, or throw modernity radically overboard.

The Project of Enlightenment

The idea of modernity is intimately tied to the development of European art, but what I call 'the project of modernity' comes only into focus when we dispense with the usual concentration upon art. Let me start a different analysis by recalling an idea from Max Weber. He characterized cultural modernity as the separation of the substantive reason expressed in religion and metaphysics into three autonomous spheres. They are: science, morality and art. These came to be differentiated because the unified world-views of religion and metaphysics fell apart. Since the 18th century, the problems inherited from these older world-views could be arranged so as to fall under specific aspects of validity: truth, normative rightness, authenticity and beauty. They could then be handled as questions of knowledge, or of justice and morality, or of taste. Scientific discourse, theories of morality, jurisprudence, and the production and criticism of art could in turn be institutionalized. Each domain of culture could be made to correspond to cultural professions in which problems could be dealt with as the concern of special experts. This professionalized treatment of the cultural tradition brings to the fore the intrinsic structures of each of the three dimensions of culture. There appear the structures of cognitive-instrumental, of moral-practical and of aesthetic-expressive rationality, each of these under the control of specialists who seem more adept at being logical in these particular ways than other people are. As a result, the distance grows between the culture of the experts and that of the larger public. What accrues to culture through specialized treatment and reflection does not immediately and necessarily become the property of everyday praxis. With cultural rationalization of this sort, the threat increases that the life-world, whose traditional substance has already been devalued, will become more and more impoverished.

The project of modernity formulated in the 18th century by the philosophers of the Enlightenment consisted in their efforts to develop objective science, universal morality and law, and autonomous art according to their inner logic. At the same time, this project intended to release the cognitive potentials of each of these domains from their esoteric forms. The Enlightenment philosophers wanted to utilize this accumulation of specialized culture for the enrichment of everyday life – that is to say, for the rational organization of everyday social life.

Enlightenment thinkers of the cast of mind of Condorcet still had the extravagant expectation that the arts and sciences would promote not only the control of natural forces but also understanding of the world and of the self, moral progress, the justice of institutions and even the happiness of human beings. The 20th century has shattered this optimism. The differentiation of science, morality and art has come to mean the autonomy of the segments treated by the specialist and their separation from the hermeneutics of everyday communication. This splitting off is the problem that has given rise to efforts to 'negate' the culture of expertise. But the problem won't go away: should we try to hold on to the *intentions* of the Enlightenment, feeble as they may be, or should we declare the entire project of modernity a lost cause? I now want to return to the problem of artistic culture, having explained why, historically, aesthetic modernity is only a part of cultural modernity in general.

The False Programs of the Negation of Culture

Greatly oversimplifying, I would say that in the history of modern art one can detect a trend towards ever greater autonomy in the definition and practice of art. The category of 'beauty' and the domain of beautiful objects were first constituted in the Renaissance. In the course of the 18th century, literature, the fine arts and music were institutionalized as activities independent from sacred and courtly life. Finally, around the middle of the 19th century an aestheticist conception of art emerged, which encouraged the artist to produce his work according to the distinct consciousness of art for art's sake. The autonomy of the aesthetic sphere could then become a deliberate project: the talented artist could lend authentic expression to those experiences he had in encountering his own de-centered subjectivity, detached from the constraints of routinized cognition and everyday action.

In the mid-19th century, in painting and literature, a movement began which Ocatvio Paz finds epitomized already in the art criticism of Baudelaire. Color, lines, sounds and movement ceased to serve primarily the cause of representation; the media of expression and the techniques of production themselves became the aesthetic object. Theodor W. Adorno could therefore begin his *Aesthetic Theory* with the following sentence: 'It is now taken for granted that nothing which concerns art can be taken for granted any more: neither art itself, nor art in its relationship to the whole, nor even the right of art to exist.' And this is what surrealism then denied: *das Existenzrecht der Kunst als Kunst.* To be sure, surrealism would not have challenged the right of art to exist, if modern art no longer had advanced a promise of happiness concerning its own relationship 'to the whole' of life. For Schiller, such a promise was delivered by aesthetic intuition, but not fulfilled by it. Schiller's *Letters on the Aesthetic Education of Man* speaks to us of a utopia reaching beyond art itself. But by the time of Baudelaire, who repeated this *promesse de bonheur* via art, the utopia of reconciliation with society had gone sour. A relation of opposites had come into being; art had become a critical mirror, showing the irreconcilable nature of the aesthetic and the social worlds. This modernist transformation was all the more painfully realized, the more art alienated itself from life and withdrew into the untouchableness of complete autonomy. Out of such emotional currents finally gathered those explosive energies which unloaded in the surrealist attempt to blow up the autarkical sphere of art and to force a reconciliation of art and life.

But all those attempts to level art and life, fiction and praxis, appearance and reality to one plane; the attempts to remove the distinction between artifact and object of use, between conscious staging and spontaneous excitement; the attempts to declare everything to be art and everyone to be an artist, to retract all criteria and to equate aesthetic judgment with the expression of subjective experiences – all these undertakings have proved themselves to be sort of nonsense experiments. These experiments have served to bring back to life, and to illuminate all the more glaringly, exactly those structures of art which they were meant to dissolve. They gave a new legitimacy, as ends in themselves, to appearance as the medium of fiction, to the transcendence of the artwork over society, to the concentrated and planned character of artistic production as well as to the special cognitive status of judgments of taste. The radical attempt to negate art has ended up ironically by giving due exactly to these categories through which Enlightenment aesthetics had circumscribed its object domain. The surrealists waged the most extreme warfare, but two mistakes in particular destroyed their revolt. First, when the containers of an autonomously developed cultural sphere are shattered, the contents get dispersed. Nothing remains from a desublimated meaning or a destructured form; an emancipatory effect does not follow.

Their second mistake has more important consequences. In everyday communication, cognitive meanings, moral expectations, subjective expressions and evaluations must relate to one another. Communication processes need a cultural tradition covering all spheres – cognitive, moral-practical and expressive. A rationalized everyday life, therefore, could hardly be saved from cultural impoverishment through breaking open a single cultural sphere – art – and so providing access to just one of the specialized knowledge complexes. The surrealist revolt would have replaced only one abstraction.

In the spheres of theoretical knowledge and morality, there are parallels to this failed attempt of what we might call the false negation of culture. Only they are less pronounced. Since the days of the Young Hegelians, there has been talk about the negation of philosophy. Since Marx, the question of the relationship of theory and practice has been posed. However, Marxist intellectuals joined a social movement; and only at its peripheries were there sectarian attempts to carry out a program of the negation of philosophy similar to the surrealist program to negate art. A parallel to the surrealist mistakes becomes visible in these programs when one observes the consequences of dogmatism and of moral rigorism.

A reified everyday praxis can be cured only by creating unconstrained interaction of the cognitive with the moral-practical and the aesthetic-expressive elements. Reification cannot be overcome by forcing just one of those highly stylized cultural spheres to open up and become more accessible. Instead, we see under certain circumstances a relationship emerge between terroristic activities and the over-extension of any one of these spheres into other domains: examples would be tendencies to aestheticize politics, or to replace politics by moral rigorism or to submit it to the dogmatism of a doctrine. These phenomena should not lead us, however, into denouncing the intentions of the surviving Enlightenment tradition as intentions rooted in a 'terroristic reason.'[5] Those who lump together the very project of modernity with the state of consciousness and the spectacular action of the individual terrorist are no less short-sighted than those would claim that the incomparably more persistent and extensive bureaucratic terror practiced in the dark, in the cellars of the military and secret police, and in camps and institutions, is the *raison d'être* of the modern state, only because this kind of administrative terror makes use of the coercive means of modern bureaucracies.

Alternatives

I think that instead of giving up modernity and its project as a lost cause, we should learn from the mistakes of those extravagant programs which have tried

[5] The phrase 'to aestheticize politics' echoes Benjamin's famous formulation of the false social program of the fascists in 'The Work of Art in the Age of Mechanical Reproduction.' Habermas's criticism here of Enlightenment critics seems directed less at Adorno and Max Horkheimer than at the contemporary *nouveaux philosophes* (Bernard-Henri Lèvy, etc.) and their German and American counterparts. [ed.]

to negate modernity. Perhaps the types of reception of art may offer an example which at least indicates the direction of a way out.

Bourgeois art had two expectations at once from its audience. On the one hand, the layman who enjoyed art should educate himself to become an expert. On the other hand, he should also behave as a competent consumer who uses art and relates aesthetic experiences to his own life problems. This second, and seemingly harmless, manner of experiencing art has lost its radical implications exactly because it had a confused relation to the attitude of being expert and professional.

To be sure, artistic production would dry up, if it were not carried out in the form of a specialized treatment of autonomous problems and if it were to cease to be the concern of experts who do not pay so much attention to exoteric questions. Both artists and critics accept thereby the fact that such problems fall under the spell of what I earlier called the 'inner logic' of a cultural domain. But this sharp delineation, this exclusive concentration on one aspect of validity alone and the exclusion of aspects of truth and justice, break down as soon as aesthetic experience is drawn into an individual life history and is absorbed into ordinary life. The reception of art by the layman, or by the 'everyday expert,' goes in a rather different direction than the reception of art by the professional critic.

Albrecht Wellmer has drawn my attention to one way that an aesthetic experience which is not framed around the experts' critical judgments of taste can have its significance altered: as soon as such an experience is used to illuminate a life-historical situation and is related to life problems, it enters into a language game which is no longer that of the aesthetic critic. The aesthetic experience then not only renews the interpretation of our needs in whose light we perceive the world. It permeates as well our cognitive significations and our normative expectations and changes the manner in which all these moments refer to one another. Let me give an example of this process.

This manner of receiving and relating to art is suggested in the first volume of the work *The Aesthetics of Resistance* by the German-Swedish writer Peter Weiss. Weiss describes the process of reappropriating art by presenting a group of politically motivated, knowledge-hungry workers in 1937 in Berlin.[6] These were young people who, through an evening high-school education, acquired the intellectual means to fathom the general and social history of European art. Out of the resilient edifice of this objective mind, embodied in works of art which they saw again and again in the museums in Berlin, they started removing their own chips of stone, which they gathered together and reassembled in the context of their own milieu. This milieu was far removed from that of traditional education as well as from the then existing regime. These young workers went back and forth between the edifice of European art and their own milieu until they were able to illuminate both.

In examples like this which illustrate the reappropriation of the expert's culture from the standpoint of the life-world, we can discern an element which does justice to the intentions of the hopeless surrealist revolts, perhaps even more to Brecht's and Benjamin's interests in how art works, which having lost

---

[6] The reference is to the novel *Die Asthetik des Widerstands* (1975–8) by the author perhaps best known here for his 1965 play *Marat/Sade*. The work of art 'reappropriated' by the workers is the Pergamon altar, emblem of power, classicism and rationality. [ed.]

their aura, could yet be received in illuminating ways. In sum, the project of modernity has not yet been fulfilled. And the reception of art is only one of at least three of its aspects. The project aims at a differentiated relinking of modern culture with an everyday praxis that still depends on vital heritages, but would be impoverished through mere traditionalism. This new connection, however, can only be established under the condition that societal moderniza- tion will also be steered in a different direction. The life-world has to become able to develop institutions out of itself which set limits to the internal dynamics and imperatives of an almost autonomous economic system and its administra- tive complements.

If I am not mistaken, the chances for this today are not very good. More or less in the entire Western world a climate has developed that furthers capitalist modernization processes as well as trends critical of cultural modernism. The disillusionment with the very failures of those programs that called for the negation of art and philosophy has come to serve as a pretense for conservative positions. Let me briefly distinguish the anti-modernism of the 'young conser- vatives' from the premodernism of the 'old conservatives' and from the postmodernism of the neoconservatives.

The 'young conservatives' recapitulate the basic experience of aesthetic modernity. They claim as their own the revelations of a decentered subjec- tivity, emancipated from the imperatives of work and usefulness, and with this experience they step outside the modern world. On the basis of modernistic attitudes they justify an irreconcilable antimodernism. They remove into the sphere of the far-away and the archaic the spontaneous powers of imagination, self-experience and emotion. To instrumental reason they juxtapose in Mani- chean fashion a principle only accessible through evocation, be it the will to power or sovereignty, Being or the Dionysiac force of the poetical. In France this line leads from Georges Bataille via Michel Foucault to Jacques Derrida.

The 'old conservatives' do not allow themselves to be contaminated by cultural modernism. They observe the decline of substantive reason, the differentiation of science, morality and art, the modern world view and its merely procedural rationality, with sadness and recommend a withdrawal to a position *anterior* to modernity. Neo-Aristotelianism, in particular, enjoys a certain success today. In view of the problematic of ecology, it allows itself to call for a cosmological ethic. (As belonging to this school, which originates with Leo Strauss, one can count the interesting works of Hans Jonas and Robert Spaemann.)

Finally, the neoconservatives welcome the development of modern science, as long as this only goes beyond its sphere to carry forward technical progress, capitalist growth and rational administration. Moreover, they recommend a politics of defusing the explosive content of cultural modernity. According to one thesis, science, when properly understood, has become irrevocably mean- ingless for the orientation of the life-world. A further thesis is that politics must be kept as far aloof as possible from the demands of moral-practical justifica- tion. And a third thesis asserts the pure immanence of art, disputes that it has a utopian content, and points to its illusory character in order to limit the aesthetic experience to privacy. (One could name here the early Wittgenstein, Carl Schmitt of the middle period, and Gottfried Benn of the late period.) But with the decisive confinement of science, morality and art to autonomous spheres separated from the life-world and administered by experts, what remains from the project of cultural modernity is only what we would have if we were to give up the project of modernity altogether. As a replacement one points to traditions which, however, are held to be immune to demands of (normative) justification and validation.

This typology is like any other, of course, a simplification, but it may not prove totally useless for the analysis of contemporary intellectual and political confrontations. I fear that the ideas of antimodernity, together with an additional touch of premodernity, are becoming popular in the circles of alternative culture. When one observes the transformations of consciousness within political parties in Germany, a new ideological shift (*Tendenzwende*) becomes visible. And this is the alliance of postmodernists with premodernists. It seems to be that there is no party in particular that monopolizes the abuse of intellectuals and the position of neoconservatism. I therefore have good reason to be thankful for the liberal spirit in which the city of Frankfurt offers me a prize bearing the name of Theodor Adorno, a most significant son of this city, who as philosopher and writer has stamped the image of the intellectual in our country incomparable fashion, who, even more, has become the very image of emulation for the intellectual.

---

16 Richard Rorty

From *The Contingency of Language*

Contingency, Irony and Solidarity, Cambridge University Press, 1989, pp 3–22.

About two hundred years ago, the idea that truth was made rather than found began to take hold of the imagination of Europe. The French Revolution had shown that the whole vocabulary of social relations, and the whole spectrum of social institutions, could be replaced almost overnight. This precedent made utopian politics the rule rather than the exception among intellectuals. Utopian politics sets aside questions about both the will of God and the nature of man and dreams of creating a hitherto unknown form of society.

At about the same time, the Romantic poets were showing what happens when art is thought of no longer as imitation but, rather, as the artist's self-creation. The poets claimed for art the place in culture traditionally held by religion and philosophy, the place which the Enlightenment had claimed for science. The precedent the Romantics set lent initial plausibility to their claim. The actual role of novels, poems, plays, paintings, statues, and buildings in the social movements of the last century and a half has given it still greater plausibility.

By now these two tendencies have joined forces and have achieved cultural hegemony. For most contemporary intellectuals, questions of ends as opposed to means – questions about how to give a sense to one's own life or that of one's community – are questions for art or politics, or both, rather than for religion, philosophy, or science. This development has led to a split within philosophy. Some philosophers have remained faithful to the Enlightenment and have continued to identify themselves with the cause of science. They see the old struggle between science and religion, reason and unreason, as still going on, having now taken the form of a struggle between reason and all those forces within culture which think of truth as made rather than found. These philosophers take science as the paradigmatic human activity, and they insist that natural science discovers truth rather than makes it. They regard 'making truth' as a merely metaphorical, and thoroughly misleading, phrase. They think of politics and art as spheres in which the notion of 'truth' is out of place. Other philosophers, realizing that the world as it is described by the physical sciences teaches no moral lesson, offers no spiritual comfort, have concluded that science is no more than the handmaiden of technology. These philosophers have ranged themselves alongside the political utopian and the innovative artist.

Whereas the first kind of philosopher contrasts 'hard scientific fact' with the 'subjective' or with 'metaphor,' the second kind sees science as one more human activity, rather as the place at which human beings encounter a 'hard,' nonhuman reality. On this view, great scientists invent descriptions of the world which are useful for purposes of predicting and controlling what happens, just as poets and political thinkers invent other descriptions of it for other purposes. But there is no sense in which *any* of these descriptions is an accurate representation of the way the world is in itself. These philosophers regard the very idea of such a representation as pointless.

Had the first sort of philosopher, the sort whose hero is the natural scientist, always been the only sort, we should probably never have had an autonomous discipline called 'philosophy' – a discipline as distinct from the sciences as it is from theology or from the arts. As such a discipline, philosophy is no more than two hundred years old. It owes its existence to attempts by the German idealists to put the sciences in their place and to give a clear sense to the vague idea that human beings make truth rather than find it. Kant wanted to consign science to the realm of second-rate truth – truth about a phenomenal world. Hegel wanted to think of natural science as a description of spirit not yet fully conscious of its own spiritual nature, and thereby to elevate the sort of truth offered by the poet and the political revolutionary to first-rate status.

German idealism, however, was a short-lived and unsatisfactory compromise. For Kant and Hegel went only halfway in their repudiation of the idea that truth is 'out there.' They were willing to view the world of empirical science as a made world – to see matter as constructed by mind, or as consisting in mind insufficiently conscious of its own mental character. But they persisted in seeing mind, spirit, the depths of the human self, as having an intrinsic nature – one which could be known by a kind of nonempirical super science called philosophy. This meant that only half of truth – the bottom, scientific half – was made. Higher truth, the truth about mind, the province of philosophy, was still a matter of discovery rather than creation.

What was needed, and what the idealists were unable to envisage, was a repudiation of the very idea of anything – mind or matter, self or world – having an intrinsic nature to be expressed or represented. For the idealists confused the idea that nothing has such a nature with the idea that space and time are unreal, that human beings cause the spatiotemporal world to exist.

We need to make a distinction between the claim that the world is out there and the claim that truth is out there. To say that the world is out there, that it is not our creation, is to say, with common sense, that most things in space and time are the effects of causes which do not include human mental states. To say that truth is not out there is simply to say that where there are no sentences there is no truth, that sentences are elements of human languages, and that human languages are human creations.

Truth cannot be out there – cannot exist independently of the human mind – because sentences cannot so exist, or be out there. The world is out there, but descriptions of the world are not. Only descriptions of the world can be true or false. The world on its own – unaided by the describing activities of human beings – cannot.

The suggestion that truth, as well as the world, is out there is a legacy of an age in which the world was seen as the creation of a being who had a language of his own. If we cease to attempt to make sense of the idea of such a nonhuman language, we shall not be tempted to confuse the platitude that the world may cause us to be justified in believing a sentence true with the claim that the world splits itself up, on its own initiative, into sentence-shaped chunks called 'facts.' But if one clings to the notion of self-subsistent facts, it is easy to start capitalizing the word 'truth' and treating it as something identical either with God or with the world as God's project. Then one will say, for example, that Truth is great, and will prevail.

This conflation is facilitated by confining attention to single sentences as opposed to vocabularies. For we often let the world decide the competition between alternative sentences (e.g., between 'Red wins' and 'Black wins' or between 'The butler did it' and 'The doctor did it'). In such cases, it is easy to run together the fact that the world contains the causes of our being justified in holding a belief with the claim that some nonlinguistic state of the world is itself an example of truth, or that some such state 'makes a belief true' by 'corresponding' to it. But it is not so easy when we turn from individual sentences to vocabularies as wholes. When we consider examples of alternative language games – the vocabulary of ancient Athenian politics versus Jefferson's, the moral vocabulary of Saint Paul versus Freud's, the jargon of Newton versus that of Aristotle, the idiom of Blake versus that of Dryden – it is difficult to think of the world as making one of these better than another, of the world as deciding between them. When the notion of 'description of the world' is moved from the level of criterion-governed sentences within language games to language games as wholes, games which we do not choose between by reference to criteria, the idea that the world decides which descriptions are true can no longer be given a clear sense. It becomes hard to think that the vocabulary is somehow already out there in the world, waiting for us to discover it. Attention (of the sort fostered by intellectual historians like Thomas Kuhn and Quentin Skinner) to the vocabularies in which sentences are formulated, rather than to individual sentences, makes us realize, for example, that the fact that Newton's vocabulary lets us predict the world more easily than Aristotle's does not mean that the world speaks Newtonian.

The world does not speak. Only we do. The world can, once we have programmed ourselves with a language, cause us to hold beliefs. But it cannot propose a language for us to speak. Only other human beings can do that. The realization that the world does not tell us what language games to play should not, however, lead us to say that a decision about which to play is arbitrary, nor to say that it is the expression of something deep within us. The moral is not that objective criteria for choice of vocabulary are to be replaced with subjective criteria, reason with will or feeling. It is rather that the notions of criteria and choice (including that of 'arbitrary' choice) are no longer in point when it comes to changes from one language game to another. Europe did not *decide* to accept the idiom of Romantic poetry, or of socialist politics, or of Galilean mechanics. That sort of shift was no more an act of will than it was a result of argument. Rather, Europe gradually lost the habit of using certain words and gradually acquired the habit of using others.

As Kuhn argues in *The Copernican Revolution*, we did not decide on the basis of some telescopic observations, or on the basis of anything else, that the earth was not the center of the universe, that macroscopic behavior could be explained on the basis of microstructural motion, and that prediction and control should be the principal aim of scientific theorizing. Rather, after a hundred years of inconclusive muddle, the Europeans found themselves speaking in a way which took these interlocked theses for granted. Cultural change of this magnitude does not result from applying criteria (or from 'arbitrary decision') any more than individuals become theists or atheists, or shift from one spouse or circle of friends to another, as a result either of applying criteria or of *actes gratuits*. We should not look within ourselves for criteria of decision in such matters any more than we should look to the world.

The temptation to look for criteria is a species of the more general temptation to think of the world, or the human self, as possessing an intrinsic nature, an essence. That is, it is the result of the temptation to privilege some one among the many languages in which we habitually describe the world or ourselves. As long as we think that there is some relation called 'fitting the world' or 'expressing the real nature of the self' which can be possessed or lacked by vocabularies-as-wholes, we shall continue the traditional philosophical search for a criterion to tell us which vocabularies have this desirable feature. But if we could ever become reconciled to the idea that most of reality is indifferent to our descriptions of it, and that the human self is created by the use of a vocabulary rather than being adequately or inadequately expressed in a vocabulary, then we should at last have assimilated what was true in the Romantic idea that truth is made rather than found. What is true about this claim is just that *languages* are made rather than found, and that truth is a property of linguistic entities, of sentences.[1]

---

[1] I have no criterion of individuation for distinct languages or vocabularies to offer, but I am not sure that we need one. Philosophers have used phrases like 'in the language *L*' for a long time without worrying too much about how one can tell where one natural language ends and another begins, nor about when 'the scientific vocabulary of the sixteenth century" ends and 'the vocabulary of the New Science' begins. Roughly, a break of this sort occurs when we start using 'translation' rather than 'explanation' in talking about geographical or chronological differences. This will happen whenever we find it handy to start mentioning words rather than using them – to highlight the difference between two sets of human practices by putting quotation marks around elements of those practices.

I can sum up by redescribing what, in my view, the revolutionaries and poets of two centuries ago were getting at. What was glimpsed at the end of the eighteenth century was that anything could be made to look good or bad, important or unimportant, useful or useless, by being redescribed. What Hegel describes as the process of spirit gradually becoming self-conscious of its intrinsic nature is better described as the process of European linguistic practices changing at a faster and faster rate. The phenomenon Hegel describes is that of more people offering more radical redescriptions of more things than ever before, of young people going through half a dozen spiritual gestalt-switches before reaching adulthood. What the Romantics expressed as the claim that imagination, rather than reason, is the central human faculty was the realization that a talent for speaking differently, rather than for arguing well, is the chief instrument of cultural change. What political utopians since the French Revolution have sensed is not that an enduring, substratal human nature has been suppressed or repressed by 'unnatural' or 'irrational' social institutions but rather that changing languages and other social practices may produce human beings of a sort that had never before existed. The German idealists, the French revolutionaries, and the Romantic poets had in common a dim sense that human beings whose language changed so that they no longer spoke of themselves as responsible to nonhuman powers would thereby become of a new kind of human beings.

The difficulty faced by a philosopher who, like myself, is sympathetic to this suggestion – one thinks of himself as auxiliary to the poet rather than to the physicist – is to avoid hinting that this suggestion gets something right, that my sort of philosophy corresponds to the way things really are. For this talk of correspondence brings back just the idea my sort of philosopher wants to get rid of, the idea that the world or the self has an intrinsic nature. From our point of view, explaining the success of science, or the desirability of political liberalism, by talk of 'fitting the world' or 'expressing human nature' is like explaining why opium makes you sleepy by talking about its dormitive power. To say that Freud's vocabulary gets at the truth about human nature, or Newton's at the truth about the heavens, is not an explanation of anything. It is just an empty compliment – one traditionally paid to writers whose novel jargon we have found useful. To say that there is no such thing as intrinsic nature is not to say that the intrinsic nature of reality has turned out, suprisingly enough, to be extrinsic. It is to say that the term 'intrinsic nature' is one which it would pay us not to use, an expression which has caused more trouble than it has been worth. To say that we should drop the idea of truth as out there waiting to be discovered is not to say that we have discovered that, out there, there is no truth.[2] It is to say that our purposes would be served best by ceasing to see truth as a deep matter, as a topic of philosophical interest, or 'true' as a term which repays 'analysis.' 'The nature of truth' is an unprofitable topic,

---

[2] Nietzsche has caused a lot of confusion by inferring from 'truth is not a matter of correspondence to reality' to 'what we call "truths" are just useful lies.' The same confusion is occasionally found in Derrida, in the inference from 'there is no such reality as the metaphysicians have hoped to find' to 'what we call "real" is not really real.' Such confusions make Nietzsche and Derrida liable to charges of self-referential inconsistency – to claiming to know what they themselves claim cannot be known.

resembling in this respect 'the nature of man' and 'the nature of God,' and differing from 'the nature of the positron,' and 'the nature of Oedipal fixation.' But this claim about relative profitability, in turn, is just the recommendation that we in fact *say* little about these topics, and see how we get on.

On the view of philosophy which I am offering, philosophers should not be asked for arguments against, for example, the correspondence theory of truth or the idea of the 'intrinsic nature of reality.' The trouble with arguments against the use of a familiar and time-honored vocabulary is that they are expected to be phrased in that very vocabulary. They are expected to show that central elements in that vocabulary are 'inconsistent in their own terms' or that they 'deconstruct themselves.' But that can *never* be shown. Any argument to the effect that our familiar use of a familiar term is incoherent, or empty, or confused, or vague, or 'merely metaphorical' is bound to be inconclusive and question-begging. For such use is, after all, the paradigm of coherent, meaningful, literal, speech. Such arguments are always parasitic upon, and abbreviations for, claims that a better vocabulary is available. Interesting philosophy is rarely an examination of the pros and cons of a thesis. Usually it is, implicitly or explicitly, a contest between an entrenched vocabulary which has become a nuisance and a half-formed new vocabulary which vaguely promises great things.

The latter 'method' of philosophy is the same as the 'method' of utopian politics or revolutionary science (as opposed to parliamentary politics, or normal science). The method is to redescribe lots and lots of things in new ways, until you have created a pattern of linguistic behavior which will tempt the rising generation to adopt it, thereby causing them to look for appropriate new forms of nonlinguistic behavior, for example, the adoption of new scientific equipment or new social institutions. This sort of philosophy does not work piece by piece, analyzing concept after concept, or testing thesis after thesis. Rather, it works holistically and pragmatically. It says things like 'try thinking of it this way' – or more specifically, 'try to ignore the apparently futile traditional questions by substituting the following new and possibly interesting questions.' It does not pretend to have a better candidate for doing the same old things which we did when we spoke in the old way. Rather, it suggests that we might want to stop doing those things and do something else. But it does not argue for this suggestion on the basis of antecedent criteria common to the old and the new language games. For just insofar as the new language really is new, there will be no such criteria.

Conforming to my own precepts, I am not going to offer arguments against the vocabulary I want to replace. Instead, I am going to try to make the vocabulary I favor look attractive by showing how it may be used to describe a variety of topics. More specifically, in this chapter I shall be describing the work of Donald Davidson in philosophy of language as a manifestation of a willingness to drop the idea of 'intrinsic nature,' a willingness to face up to the *contingency* of the language we use. In subsequent chapters, I shall try to show how a recognition of that contingency leads to a recognition of the contingency of conscience, and how both recognitions lead to a picture of intellectual and moral progress as a history of increasingly useful metaphors rather than of increasing understandings of how things really are.

I begin, in this first chapter, with the philosophy of language because I want to spell out the consequence of my claims that only sentences can be true, and that human beings make truths by making languages in which to phrase sentences. I shall concentrate on the work of Davidson because he is the philosopher who has done most to explore these consequences.[3] Davidson's treatment of truth ties in with his treatment of language which breaks *completely* with the notion of language as something which can be adequate or inadequate to the world or to the self. For Davidson breaks with the notion that language is a *medium* – a medium either of representation or of expression.

I can explain what I mean by a medium by noting that the traditional picture of the human situation has been one in which human beings are not simply networks of beliefs and desires but rather beings which *have* those beliefs and desires. The traditional view is that there is a core self which can look at, decide among, use, and express itself by means of, such beliefs and desires. Further, these beliefs and desires are criticizable not simply by reference to their ability to cohere with one another, but by reference to something exterior to the network within which they are strands. Beliefs are, on this account, critizable because they fail to correspond to reality. Desires are criticizable because they fail to correspond to the essential nature of the human self – because they are 'irrational' or 'unnatural.' So we have a picture of the essential core of the self on one side of this network of beliefs and desires, and reality on the other side. In this picture, the network is the product of an interaction between the two, alternately expressing the one and representing the other. This is the traditional subject-object picture which idealism tried and failed to replace, and which Nietzsche, Heidegger, Derrida, James, Dewey, Goodman, Sellars, Putnam, Davidson and others have tried to replace without entangling themselves in the idealists' paradoxes.

One phase of this effort of replacement consisted in an attempt to substitute 'language' for 'mind' or 'consciousness' as the medium out of which beliefs and desires are constructed, the third, mediating, element between self and world. This turn toward language was thought of as a progressive, naturalizing move. It seemed so because it seemed easier to give a causal account of the evolutionary emergence of language-using organisms than of the metaphysical emergence of consciousness out of nonconsciousness. But in itself this substitution is ineffective. For if we stick to the picture of language as a medium, something standing between the self and the nonhuman reality with which the self seeks to be in touch, we have made no progress. We are still using a subject-object picture, and we are still stuck with issues about skepticism, idealism, and realism. For we are still able to ask questions about language of the same sort we asked about consciousness.

These are such questions as 'Does the medium between the self and reality get them together or keep them apart?' 'Should we see the medium primarily as a medium of expression – or articulating what lies deep within the self? Or should we see it as primarily a medium of representation – showing the self

---

[3] I should remark that Davidson cannot be held responsible for the interpretation I am putting on his views, nor for the further views I extrapolate from his. For an extended statement of that interpretation, see my 'Pragmatism, Davidson and Truth,' in Ernest Lepore, ed., *Truth and Interpretation: Perspectives on the Philosophy of Donald Davidson* (Oxford: Blackwell, 1984). For Davidson's reaction to this interpretation, see his 'After-thoughts' to 'A Coherence Theory of Truth and Knowledge,' in Alan Malachowski, *Reading Rorty* (Oxford: Blackwell, in press).

what lies outside it?' Idealist theories of knowledge and Romantic notions of the imagination can, also, easily be transposed from the jargon of 'consciousness' into that of 'language.' Realistic and moralistic reactions to such theories can be transposed equally easily. So the seesaw battles between romanticism and moralism, and between idealism and realism, will continue as long as one thinks there is a hope of making sense of the question of whether a given language is 'adequate' to a task – either the task of properly expressing the nature of the human species, or the task of properly representing the structure of nonhuman reality.

We need to get off this seesaw. Davidson helps us do so. For he does not view language as a medium for either expression or representation. So he is able to set aside the idea that both the self and reality have intrinsic natures, natures which are out there waiting to be known. Davidson's view of language is neither reductionist nor expansionist. It does not, as analytical philosophers sometimes have, purport to give reductive definitions of semantical notions like 'truth' or 'intentionality' or 'reference.' Nor does it resemble Heidegger's attempt to make language into a kind of divinity, something of which human beings are mere emanations. As Derrida has warned us, such an apotheosis of language is merely a transposed version of the idealists' apotheosis of consciousness.

In avoiding both reductionism and expansionism. Davidson resembles Wittgenstein. Both philosophers treat alternative vocabularies as more like alternative tools than like bits of a jigsaw puzzle. To treat them as pieces of a puzzle is to assume that all vocabularies are dispensable, or reducible to other vocabularies, or capable of being united with all other vocabularies in one grand unified super vocabulary. If we avoid this assumption, we shall not be inclined to ask questions like 'What is the place of consciousness in a world of molecules?' 'Are colors more mind-dependent than weights?' 'What is the place of value in a world of fact?' 'What is the place of intentionality in a world of causation?' 'What is the relation between the solid table of common sense and the unsolid table of microphysics?' or 'What is the relation of language to thought?' We should not try to answer such questions, for doing so leads either to the evident failures of reductionism or to the short-lived successes of expansionism. We should restrict ourselves to questions like 'Does our use of these words get in the way of our use of those other words?' This is a question about whether our use of tools is inefficient, not a question about whether our beliefs are contradictory.

'Merely philosophical' questions, like Eddington's question about the two tables, are attempts to stir up a factitious theoretical quarrel between vocabularies which have proved capable of peaceful coexistence. The questions I have recited above are all cases in which philosophers have given their subject a bad name by seeing difficulties nobody else sees. But this is not to say that vocabularies never do get in the way of each other. On the contrary, revolutionary achievements in the arts, in the sciences, and in moral and political thought typically occur when somebody realizes that two or more of our vocabularies are interfering with each other, and proceeds to invent a new vocabulary to replace both. For example, the traditional Aristotelian vocabulary got in the way of the mathematized vocabulary that was being developed in the sixteenth century by students of mechanics. Again, young German theology students of the late eighteenth century – like Hegel and Hölderlin – found that the vocabulary in which they worshiped Jesus was getting in the way of the vocabulary in which they worshiped the Greeks. Yet again, the use of Rossetti-like tropes got in the way of the early Yeats's use of Blakean tropes.

The gradual trial-and-error creation of a new, third, vocabulary – the sort of vocabulary developed by people like Galileo, Hegel, or the later Yeats – is not a discovery about how old vocabularies fit together. That is why it cannot be reached by an inferential process – by starting with premises formulated in the old vocabularies. Such creations are not the result of successfully fitting together pieces of a puzzle. They are not discoveries of a reality behind the appearances, of an undistorted view of the whole picture with which to replace myopic views of its parts. The proper analogy is with the invention of new tools to take the place of old tools. To come up with such a vocabulary is more like discarding the lever and the chock because one has envisaged the pully, or like discarding gesso and tempera because one has now figured out how to size canvas properly.

This Wittgensteinian analogy between vocabularies and tools has one obvious drawback. The craftsman typically knows what job he needs to do before picking or inventing tools with which to do it. By contrast, someone like Galileo, Yeats, or Hegel (a 'poet' in my wide sense of the term – the sense of 'one who makes things new') is typically unable to make clear exactly what it is that he wants to do before developing the language in which he succeeds in doing it. His new vocabulary makes possible, for the first time, a formulation of its own purpose. It is a tool for doing something which could not have been envisaged prior to the development of a particular set of descriptions, those which it itself helps to provide. But I shall, for the moment, ignore this disanalogy. I want simply to remark that the contrast between the jigsaw-puzzle and the 'tool' models of alternative vocabularies reflects the contrast between – in Nietzsche's slightly misleading terms – the will to truth and the will to self-overcoming. Both are expressions of the contrast between the attempt to represent or express something that was already there and the attempt to make something that never had been dreamed of before.

Davidson spells out the implications of Wittgenstein's treatment of vocabularies as tools by raising explicit doubts about the assumptions underlying traditional pre-Wittgensteinian accounts of language. These accounts have taken for granted that questions like 'Is the language we are presently using the "right" language – is it adequate to its task as a medium of expression or representation?' 'Is our language a transparent or an opaque medium?' make sense. Such questions assume there are relations such as 'fitting the world' or 'being faithful to the true nature of the self' in which language might stand to nonlanguage. This assumption goes along with the assumption that 'our language' – the language we speak now, the vocabulary at the disposal of educated inhabitants of the twentieth century – is somehow a unity, a third thing which stands in some determinate relation with two other unities – the self and reality. Both assumptions are natural enough, once we accept the idea that there are nonlinguistic things called 'meanings' which it is the task of language to express, as well as the idea that there are nonlinguistic things called 'facts' which it is the task of language to represent. Both ideas enshrine the notion of language as medium.

Davidson's polemics against the traditional philosophical uses of the terms 'fact' and 'meaning,' and against what he calls 'the scheme-content model' of thought and inquiry, are parts of a larger polemic against the idea that there is a fixed task for language to perform, and an entity called 'language' or 'the language' or 'our language' which may or may not be performing this task efficiently. Davidson's doubt that there is any such entity parallels Gilbert Ryle's and Daniel Dennett's doubts about whether there is anything called 'the mind' or 'consciousness.'[4] Both sets of doubts are doubts about the utility of the notion of a medium between the self and reality – the sort of medium which realists see as transparent and skeptics as opaque.

In a recent paper, nicely entitled 'A Nice Derangement of Epitaphs,'[5] Davidson tries to undermine the notion of languages as entities by developing the notion of what he calls 'a passing theory' about the noises and inscriptions presently being produced by a fellow human. Think of such a theory as part of a larger 'passing theory' about this person's total behavior – a set of guesses about what she will do under what conditions. Such a theory is 'passing' because it must constantly be corrected to allow for mumbles, stumbles, malapropisms, metaphors, tics, seizures, psychotic symptoms, egregious stupidity, strokes of genius, and the like. To make things easier, imagine that I am forming such a theory about the current behavior of a native of an exotic culture into which I have unexpectedly parachuted. This strange person, who presumably finds me equally strange, will simultaneously be busy forming a theory about my behavior. If we ever succeed in communicating easily and happily, it will be because her guesses about what I am going to do next, including what noises I am going to make next, and my own expectations about what I shall do or say under certain circumstances, come more or less to coincide, and because the converse is also true. She and I are coping with each other as we might cope with mangoes or boa constrictors – we are trying not to be taken by surprise. To say that we come to speak the same language is to say, as Davidson puts it, that 'we tend to converge on passing theories.' Davidson's point is that all 'two people need, if they are to understand one another through speech, is the ability to converge on passing theories from utterance to utterance.'

Davidson's account of linguistic communication dispenses with the picture of language as a third thing intervening between self and reality, and of different languages as barriers between persons or cultures. To say that one's previous language was inappropriate for dealing with some segment of the world (for example, the starry heavens above, or the raging passions within) is just to say that one is now, having learned a new language, able to handle that segment more easily. To say that two communities have trouble getting along because the words they use are so hard to translate into each other is just to say that the linguistic behavior of inhabitants of one community may, like the rest of their behavior, be hard for inhabitants of the other community to predict. As Davidson puts it,

---

[4] For an elaboration of these doubts, see my 'Contemporary Philosophy of Mind,' *Synthese* 53 (1982): 332–348. For Dennett's doubts about my interpretations of his views, see his 'Comments on Rorty,' pp. 348–354.

[5] This essay can be found in Lepore, ed., *Truth and Interpretation*.

We should realize that we have abandoned not only the ordinary notion of a language, but we have erased the boundary between knowing a language and knowing our way around the world generally. For there are no rules for arriving at passing theories that work. . . . There is no more chance of regularizing, or teaching, this process than there is of regularizing or teaching the process of creating new theories to cope with new data – for that is what this process involves. . . .

There is no such thing as a language, not if a language is anything like what philosophers, at least, have supposed. There is therefore no such thing to be learned or mastered. We must give up the idea of a clearly defined shared structure which language users master and then apply to cases . . . We should give up the attempt to illuminate how we communicate by appeal to conventions.[6]

This line of thought about language is analogous to the Ryle-Dennett view that when we use a mentalistic terminology we are simply using an efficient vocabulary – the vocabulary characteristic of what Dennett calls the 'intentional stance' – to predict what an organism is likely to do or say under various sets of circumstances. Davidson is a nonreductive behaviorist about language in the same way that Ryle was a nonreductive behaviorist about mind. Neither has any desire to give equivalents in Behaviorese for talk about beliefs or about reference. But both are saying: Think of the term 'mind' or 'language' not as the name of a medium between self and reality but simply as a flag which signals the desirability of using a certain vocabulary when trying to cope with certain kinds of organisms. To say that a given organism – or, for that matter, a given machine – has a mind is just to say that, for some purposes, it will pay to think of it as having beliefs and desires. To say that it is a language user is just to say that pairing off the marks and noises it makes with those we make will prove a useful tactic in predicting and controlling its future behavior.

This Wittgensteinian attitude, developed by Ryle and Dennett for minds and by Davidson for languages, naturalizes mind and language by making all questions about the relation of either to the rest of universe *causal* questions, as opposed to questions about adequacy of representation or expression. It makes perfectly good sense to ask how we got from the relative mindlessness of the monkey to the full-fledged mindedness of the human, or from speaking Neanderthal to speaking postmodern, if these are construed as straightforward causal questions. In the former case the answer takes us off into neurology and thence into evolutionary biology. But in the latter case it takes us into intellectual history viewed as the history of metaphor. For my purposes in this book, it is the latter which is important. So I shall spend the rest of this chapter sketching an account of intellectual and moral progress which squares with Davidson's account of language.

To see the history of language, and thus of the arts, the sciences, and the moral sense, as the history of metaphor is to drop the picture of the human mind, or human languages, becoming better and better suited to the purposes for which God or Nature designed them, for example, able to express more and more

---

[6] 'A Nice Derangement of Epitaphs,' in Lepore, ed., *Truth and Interpretation*, p. 446. Italics added.

meanings or to represent more and more facts. The idea that language has a purpose goes once the idea of language as medium goes. A culture which renounced both ideas would be the triumph of those tendencies in modern thought which began two hundred years ago, the tendencies common to German idealism, Romantic poetry, and utopian politics.

A nonteleological view of intellectual history, including the history of science, does for the theory of culture what the Mendelian, mechanistic, account of natural selection did for evolutionary theory. Mendel let us see mind as something which just happened rather than as something which was the point of the whole process. Davidson lets us think of the history of language, and thus of culture, as Darwin taught us to think of the history of a coral reef. Old metaphors are constantly dying off into literalness, and then serving as a platform and foil for new metaphors. This analogy lets us think of 'our language' – that is, of the science and culture of twentieth-century Europe – as something that took shape as a result of a great number of sheer contingencies. Our language and our culture are as much a contingency, as much a result of thousands of small mutations finding niches (and millions of others finding no niches), as are the orchids and the anthropoids.

To accept this analogy, we must follow Mary Hesse in thinking of scientific revolutions as 'metaphoric redescriptions' of nature rather than insights into the intrinsic nature of nature.[7] Further, we must resist the temptation to think that the redescriptions of reality offered by contemporary physical or biological science are somehow closer to 'the things themselves,' less 'mind-dependent,' than the redescriptions of history offered by contemporary culture criticism. We need to see the constellations of causal forces which produced talk of DNA or of the Big Bang as of a piece with the causal forces which produced talk of 'secularization' or of 'late capitalism.'[8] These various constellations are the random factors which have made some things of conversation for us and others not, have made some projects and not others possible and important.

I can develop the contrast between the idea that the history of culture has a *telos* – such as the discovery of truth, or the emancipation of humanity – and the Nietzschean and Davidsonian picture which I am sketching by noting that the latter picture is compatible with a bleakly mechanical description of the relation between human beings and the rest of the universe. For genuine novelty can, after all, occur in a world of blind, contingent, mechanical forces. Think of novelty as the sort of thing which happens when, for example, a cosmic ray scrambles the atoms in a DNA molecule, thus sending things off in the direction of the orchids or the anthropoids. The orchids, when their time came, were no less novel or marvelous for the sheer contingency of this necessary condition of their existence. Analogously, for all we know, or should care, Aristotle's metaphorical use of *ousia*, Saint Paul's metaphorical use of *agapē*, and Newton's metaphorical use of *gravitas*, were the results of cosmic

---

[7] See 'The Explanatory Function of Metaphor,' in Hesse, *Revolutions and Reconstructions in the Philosophy of Science* (Bloomington: Indiana University Press, 1980).

[8] This coalescence is resisted in Bernard Williams's discussion of Davidson's and my views in chap. 6 of his *Ethics and the Limits of Philosophy* (Cambridge, Mass.: Harvard University Press, 1985). For a partial reply to Williams, see my 'Is Natural Science a Natural Kind?' in Ernan McMullin, ed., *Construction and Constraint: The Shaping of Scientific Rationality* (Notre Dame, Ind.: University of Notre Dame Press, 1988).

rays scrambling the fine structure of some crucial neurons in their respective brains. Or, more plausibly, they were the result of some odd episodes in infancy – some obsessional kinks left in these brains by idiosyncratic traumata. It hardly matters how the trick was done. The results were marvelous. There had never been such things before.

This account of intellectual history chimes with Nietzsche's definition of 'truth' as 'a mobile army of metaphors.' It also chimes with the description I offered earlier of people like Galileo and Hegel and Yeats, people in whose minds new vocabularies developed, thereby equipping them with tools for doing things which could not even have been envisaged before these tools were available. But in order to accept this picture, we need to see the distinction between the literal and the metaphorical in the way Davidson sees it: not as a distinction between two sorts of meaning, nor as a distinction between two sorts of interpretation, but as a distinction between familiar and unfamiliar uses of noises and marks. The literal uses of noises and marks are the uses we can handle by our old theories about what people will say under various conditions. Their metaphorical use is the sort which makes us get busy developing a new theory.

Davidson puts this point by saying that one should not think of metaphorical expressions as having meanings distinct from their literal ones. To have a meaning is to have a place in a language game. Metaphors, by definition, do not. Davidson denies, in his words, 'the thesis that associated with a metaphor is a cognitive content that its author wishes to convey and that the interpreter must grasp if he is to get the message.'[9] In his view, tossing a metaphor into a conversation is like suddenly breaking off the conversation long enough to make a face, or pulling a photograph out of your pocket and displaying it, or pointing at a feature of the surroundings, or slapping your interlocutor's face, or kissing him. Tossing a metaphor into a text is like using italics, or illustrations, or odd punctuation or formats.

All these are ways of producing effects on your interlocutor or your reader, but not ways of conveying a message. To none of these is it appropriate to respond with 'What exactly are you trying to say?' If one had wanted to say something – if one had wanted to utter a sentence with a meaning – one would presumably have done so. But instead one thought that one's aim could be better carried out by other means. That one uses familiar words in unfamiliar ways – rather than slaps, kisses, pictures, gestures, or grimaces – does not show that what one said must have a meaning. An attempt to state that meaning would be an attempt to find some familiar (that is, literal) use of words – some sentence which already had a place in the language game – and, to claim that one might just as well have *that*. But the unparaphrasability of metaphor is just the unsuitability of any such familiar sentence for one's purpose.

Uttering a sentence without a fixed place in a language game is, as the positivists rightly have said, to utter something which is neither true nor false – something which is not, in Ian Hacking's terms, a 'truth-value candidate.' This is because it is a sentence which one cannot confirm or disconfirm, argue for or against. One can only savor it or spit it out. But this is not to say that it may not,

---

[9] Davidson, 'What Metaphors Mean,' in his *Inquiries into Truth and Interpretation* (Oxford University Press, 1984), p. 262.

in time, *become* a truth-value candidate. If it *is* savored rather than spat out, the sentence may be repeated, caught up, bandied about. Then it will gradually require a habitual use, a familiar place in the language game. It will thereby have ceased to be a metaphor – or, if you like, it will have become what most sentences of our language are, a dead metaphor. It will be just one more, literally true or literally false, sentence of the language. That is to say, our theories about the linguistic behavior of our fellows will suffice to let us cope with its utterance in the same unthinking way in which we cope with most of their other utterances.

The Davidsonian claim that metaphors do not have meanings may seem like a typical philosopher's quibble, but it is not.[10] It is part of an attempt to get us to stop thinking of language as a medium. This, in turn, is part of a larger attempt to get rid of the traditional philosophical picture of what it is to be human. The importance of Davidson's point can perhaps best be seen by contrasting his treatment of metaphor with those of the Platonist and the positivist on the one hand and the Romantic on the other. The Platonist and the positivist share a reductionist view of metaphor: They think metaphors are either paraphrasable or useless for the one serious purpose which language has, namely, representing reality. By contrast, the Romantic has an expansionist view: He thinks metaphor is strange, mystic, wonderful. Romantics attribute metaphor to a mysterious faculty called the 'imagination,' a faculty they suppose to be at the very center of the self, the deep heart's core. Whereas the metaphorical looks irrelevant to Platonists and positivists, the literal looks irrelevant to Romantics. For the former think that the point of language is to represent a hidden reality which lies outside us, and the latter thinks its purpose is to express a hidden reality which lies within us.

Positivist history of culture thus sees language as gradually shaping itself around the contours of the physical world. Romantic history of culture sees language as gradually bringing Spirit to self-consciousness. Nietzschean history of culture, and Davidsonian philosophy of language, see language as we now see evolution, as new forms of life constantly killing off old forms – not to accomplish a higher purpose, but blindly. Whereas the positivist sees Galileo as making a discovery – finally coming up with the words which were needed to fit the world properly, words Aristotle missed – the Davidsonian sees him as having hit upon a tool which happened to work better for certain purposes than any previous tool. Once we found out what could be done with a Galilean vocabulary, nobody was much interested in doing the things which used to be done (and which Thomists thought should still be done) with an Aristotelian vocabulary.

Similarly, whereas the Romantic sees Yeats as having gotten at something which nobody had previously gotten at, expressed, something which had long been yearning for expression, the Davidsonian sees him as having hit upon some tools which enabled him to write poems which were not just variations on the poems of his precursors. Once we had Yeats's later poems in hand, we were less interested in reading Rossetti's. What goes for revolutionary, strong

---

[10] For a further defense of Davidson against the charge of quibbling, and various other charges, see my 'Unfamiliar Noises: Hesse and Davidson on Metaphorm' *Proceedings of the Aristotelian Society*, supplementary vol. 61 (1987): 283–296.

scientists and poets goes also for strong philosophers – people like Hegel and Davidson, the sort of philosophers who are interested in dissolving inherited problems rather than in solving them. In this view, substituting dialectic for demonstration as the method of philosophy, or getting rid of the correspondence theory of truth, is not a discovery about the nature of a preexistent entity called 'philosophy' or 'truth.' It is changing the way we talk, and thereby changing what we want to do and what we think we are.

But in a Nietzschean view, one which drops the reality-appearance distinction, to change how we talk is to change what, for our own purposes, we are. To say, with Nietzsche, that God is dead, is to say that we serve no higher purposes. The Nietzschean substitution of self-creation for discovery substitutes a picture of the hungry generations treading each other down for a picture of humanity approaching closer and closer to the light. A culture in which Nietzschean metaphors were literalized would be one which took for granted that philosophical problems are as temporary as poetic problems, that there are no problems which bind the generations together into a single natural kind called 'humanity.' A sense of human history as the history of successive metaphors would let us see the poet, in the generic sense of the maker of new words, the shaper of new languages, as the vanguard of the species.

I shall try to develop this last point in Chapters 2 and 3 in terms of Harold Bloom's notion of the 'strong poet.' But I shall end this first chapter by going back to the claim, which has been central to what I have been saying, that the world does not provide us with any criterion of choice between alternative metaphors, that we can only compare languages or metaphors with one another, not with something beyond language called 'fact.'

The only way to argue for this claim is to do what philosophers like Goodman, Putnam, and Davidson have done: exhibit the sterility of attempts to give a sense to phrases like 'the way the world is' or 'fitting the facts.' Such efforts can be supplemented by the work of philosophers of science such as Kuhn and Hesse. These philosophers explain why there is no way to explain the fact that a Galilean vocabulary enables us to make better predictions than an Aristotelian vocabulary by the claim that the book of nature is written in the language of mathematics.

These sorts of arguments by philosophers of language and of science should be seen against the background of the work of intellectual historians: historians who, like Hans Blumenberg, have tried to trace the similarities and dissimilarities between the Age of Faith and the Age of Reason.[11] These historians have made the point I mentioned earlier: The very idea that the world or the self has an intrinsic nature – one which the physicist or the poet may have glimpsed – is a remnant of the idea that the world is a divine creation, the work of someone who had something in mind, who Himself spoke some language in which He described His own project. Only if we have some such picture in

[11] See Hans Blumenberg, *The Legitimacy of the Modern Age*, trans. Robert Wallace (Cambridge, Mass.: MIT Press, 1982).

mind, some picture of the universe as either itself a person or as created by a person, can we make sense of the idea that the world has an 'intrinsic nature.' For the cash value of that phrase is just that some vocabularies are better representations of the world than others, as opposed to being better tools for dealing with the world for one or another purpose.

To drop the idea of languages as representations, and to be thoroughly Wittgensteinian in our approach to language, would be to de-divinize the world. Only if we do that can we fully accept the argument I offered earlier – the argument that since truth is a property of sentences, since sentences are dependent for their existence upon vocabularies, and since vocabularies are made by human beings, so are truths. For as long as we think that 'the world' names something we ought to respect as well as cope with, something person-like in that it has a preferred description of itself, we shall insist that any philosophical account of truth save the 'intuition' that truth is 'out there.' This intuition amounts to the vague sense that it would be *hybris* on our part to abandon the traditional language of 'respect for fact' and 'objectivity' – that it would be risky, and blasphemous, not to see the scientist (or the philosopher, or the poet, or *somebody*) as having a priestly function, as putting us in touch with a realm which transcends the human.

On the view I am suggesting, the claim that an 'adequate' philosophical doctrine must make room for our intuitions is a reactionary slogan, one which begs the question at hand.[12] For it is essential to my view that we have no prelinguistic consciousness to which language needs to be adequate, no deep sense of how things are which it is the duty of philosophers to spell out in language. What is described as such a consciousness is simply a disposition to use the language of our ancestors, to worship the corpses of their metaphors. Unless we suffer from what Derrida calls 'Heideggerian nostalgia,' we shall not think of our 'intuitions' as more than platitudes, more than the habitual use of a certain repertoire of terms, more than old tools which as yet have no replacements.

I can crudely sum up the story which historians like Blumenberg tell by saying that once upon a time we felt a need to worship something which lay beyond the visible world. Beginning in the seventeenth century we tried to substitute a love of truth for a love of God, treating the world described by science as a quasi divinity. Beginning at the end of the eighteenth century we tried to substitute a love of ourselves for a love of scientific truth, a worship of our own deep spiritual or poetic nature, treated as one more quasi divinity.

The line of thought common to Blumenberg, Nietzsche, Freud, and Davidson suggests that we try to get to the point where we no longer worship *anything*, where we treat *nothing* as a quasi divinity, where we treat *everything* – our language, our conscience, our community – as a product of time and chance. To reach this point would be, in Freud's words, to 'treat chance as

---

[12] For an application of this dictum to a particular case, see my discussion of the appeals to intuition found in Thomas Nagel's view of 'subjectivity' and in John Searle's doctrine of 'intrinsic intentionality,' in 'Contemporary Philosophy of Mind.' For further criticisms of both, criticisms which harmonize with my own, see Daniel Dennett, 'Setting Off on the Right Foot' and 'Evolution, Error, and Intentionality,' in Dennett, in *The Intentional Stance* (Cambridge, Mass.: MIT Press, 1987).

worthy of determining our fate.' In the next chapter I claim that Freud, Nietzsche, and Bloom do for our conscience what Wittgenstein and Davidson do for our language, namely, exhibit its sheer contingency.

---

17   Jean Baudrillard

From *The Orders of Simulcra*

Simulations, trans. P. Beitchman, Semiotexte: New York, 1983, pp 142–56.

The very definition of the real becomes: *that of which it is possible to give an equivalent reproduction*. This is contemporaneous with a science that postulates that a process can be perfectly reproduced in a set of given conditions, and also with the industrial rationality that postulates a universal system of equivalency (classical representation is not equivalence, it is transcription, interpretation, commentary). At the limit of this process of reproductibility, the real is not only what can be reproduced, but *that which is always already reproduced*. The hyperreal.

And so: end of the real, and end of art, by total absorption one into the other? No: hyperrealism is the limit of art, and of the real, by respective exchange, on the level of the simulacrum, of the privileges and the prejudices which are their basis. The hyperreal transcends representation (cf. J.F. Lyotard, *L'Art Vivant*, number on hyperrealism) only because it is entirely in simulation. The tourniquet of representation tightens madly, but of an implosive madness, that, far from eccentric (marginal) inclines towards the center to its own infinite repetition. Analogous to the distancing characteristic of the dream, that makes us say that we are only dreaming; but this is only the game of censure and of perpetuation of the dream. Hyperrealism is made an integral part of a coded reality that it perpetuates, and for which it changes nothing.

In fact, we should turn our definition of hyperrealism inside out: *It is reality itself today that is hyperrealist*. Surrealism's secret already was that the most banal reality could become surreal, but only in certain privileged moments that nevertheless are still connected with art and the imaginary. Today it is quotidian reality in its entirety – political, social, historical and economic – that from now on incorporates the simulatory dimension of hyperrealism. We live everywhere already in an 'esthetic' hallucination of reality. The old slogan 'truth is stranger than fiction,' that still corresponded to the surrealist phase of this estheticization of life, is obsolete. There is no more fiction that life could possibly confront, even victoriously – it is reality itself that disappears utterly in the game of reality – radical disenchantment, the cool and cybernetic phase following the hot stage of fantasy.

It is thus that for guilt, anguish and death there can be substituted the total joy of the signs of guilt, despair, violence and death. It is the very euphoria of simulation, that sees itself as the abolition of cause and effect, the beginning and the end, for all of which it substitutes reduplication. In this manner all closed systems protect themselves at the same time from the referential – as well as from all metalanguage that the system forestalls in playing at its own metalanguage; that is to say in duplicating itself in its own critique of itself. In simulation, the metalinguistic illusion duplicates and completes the referential illusion (pathetic hallucination of the sign and pathetic hallucination of the real).

'It's a circus,' 'It's theatre,' 'It's a movie,' old adages, old naturalistic denunciation. These sayings are now obsolete. The problem now is that of the *satellization of the real*, the putting into orbit of an indefinable reality without common measure to the fantasies that once used to ornament it. This satelliza-tion we find further naturalized in the two-rooms-kitchen shower that they have launched into orbit – to the powers of space, you could say – with the last lunar module. The banality of the earthly habitat lifted to the rank of cosmic value, of absolute decor – hypostatized in space – this is the end of metaphysics, the era of hyperreality that begins.[1] But the spatial transcendence of the banality of the two-rooms, like its cool and mechanical figuration of hyperreal-ism,[2] says only one thing: that this module, such as it is, participates in a hyperspace of representation – where each is already technically in possession of the instantaneous reproduction of his own life, where the pilots of the Tupolev that crashed at Bourget could see themselves die live on their own camera. This is nothing else than the short-circuit of the response by the question in the test, instantaneous process of re-conduction whereby reality is immediately contaminated by its simulacrum.

There used to be, before, a specific class of allegorical and slightly diabolical objects: mirrors, images, works of art (concepts?) – simulacra, but transparent and manifest (you didn't confuse the counterfeit with the original), that had their characteristic style and savoir-faire. And pleasure consisted then rather in discovering the 'natural' in what was artificial and counterfeit. Today, when the real and the imaginary are confused in the same operational totality, the esthetic fascination is everywhere. It is a subliminal perception (a sort of sixth sense) of deception, montage, scenaria – of the overexposed reality in the light of the models – no longer a production space, but a reading strip, strip of coding and decoding, magnetized by the signs – esthetic reality – no longer by the

---

[1] The coefficient of reality is proportional to the imaginary in reverse which gives its specific density. This is true of geographical and spatial exploration also. When there is no more territory virgin and therefore available for the imaginary, when the map covers the whole territory, then something like a principle of reality disappears. The conquest of space constitutes in this sense an irreversible threshold in the direction of the loss of the earthly referential. This is precisely the hemorrhage of reality as internal coherence of a limited universe when its limits retreat infinitely. The conquest of space follows that of the planet as the same fantastic enterprise of extending the jurisdiction of the real – to carry for example the flag, the technique, and the two-rooms-and-kitchen to the moon – same tentative to substantiate the concepts or to territorialize the unconscious – the latter equals making the human race unreal, or to reversing it into a hyperreality of simulation.

[2] Or that of the metal-plated caravan or supermarket dear to hyperrealists, or Campbell's Soup dear to Andy Warhol, or the Mona Lisa, since she too has been satellized around the planet, as absolute model of earthly art, no longer a work of art but a planetary simulacrum where everyone comes to witness himself (really his own death) in the gaze of the future.

premeditation and the distance of art, but by its elevation to the second level, to the second power, by the anticipation and the immanence of the code. A kind of non-intentional parody hovers over everything, of technical simulation, of indefinable fame to which is attached an esthetic pleasure, that very one of reading and of the rules of the game. Travelling of signs, the media, of fashion and the models, of the blind and brilliant ambiance of the simulacra.

A long time ago art prefigured this turning which is that today of daily life. Very quickly the work turns back on itself as the manipulation of the signs of art: over-signification of art, 'academism of the signifier,' as Levi-Strauss would say, who interprets it really as the form-sign. It is then that art enters into its indefinite *reproduction*: all that reduplicates itself, even if it be the everyday and banal reality, falls by the token under the sign of art, and becomes esthetic. It's the same thing for production, which you could say is entering today this esthetic reduplication, this phase when, expelling all content and finality, it becomes somehow abstract and non-figurative. It expresses then the pure form of production, it takes upon itself, as art, the value of a finality without purpose. Art and industry can then exchange their signs. Art can become a reproducing machine (Andy Warhol) without ceasing to be art, since the machine is only a sign. And production can lose all social finality so as to be verified and exalted finally in the prestigious, hyperbolic signs that are the great industrial combines, the ¼-mile-high towers or the number mysteries of the GNP.

And so art is everywhere, since artifice is at the very heart of reality. And so art is dead, not only because its critical transcendence is gone, but because reality itself, entirely impregnated by an aesthetic which is inseparable from its own structure, has been confused with its own image. Reality no longer has the time to take on the appearance of reality. It no longer even surpasses fiction: it captures every dream even before it takes on the appearance of a dream. Schizophrenic vertigo of these serial signs, for which no counterfeit, no sublimation is possible, immanent in their repetition – who could say what the reality is that these signs simulate? They no longer even repress anything (which is why, if you will, simulation pushes us close to the sphere of psychosis). Even the primary processes are abolished in them. The cool universe of digitality has absorbed the world of metaphor and metonymy. The principle of simulation wins out over the reality principle just as over the principle of pleasure.

18   Patricia Waugh

From *Modernism, Postmodernism, Feminism: Gender and Autonomy Theory*

Practising Postmodernism/Reading Modernism, Edward Arnold, 1992.

The discourses of feminism clearly arise out of and are made possible by those of Enlightened modernity and its models of reason, justice and autonomous subjectivity as universal categories. Feminist discourses, however, have been powerful forces in exposing some of the most entrenched and disguised contradictions and limitations of Enlightenment thought. Simply in articulating issues of sexual difference, the very existence of feminist discourses weakens the rootedness of Enlightenment thought in the principle of sameness; it exposes the ways in which this 'universal' principle is contradicted by Enlightenment's construction of a public/private split which consigns women to the 'private' realm of feeling, domesticity, the body, in order to clarify a 'public' realm of reason as masculine. In this sense at least, feminism can be seen to be an intrinsically 'postmodern' discourse. Until very recently, however, debates within feminism have tended to be ignored within discussions of Postmodernism and vice versa. Things have begun to change. Feminist theory has developed a self-conscious awareness of its own hermeneutic perspectivism based on the recognition of a central contradiction in its attempts to define an epistemology: that women seek equality and recognition of a gendered identity which has been constructed through the very culture and ideological formations which feminism seeks to challenge and dismantle. Awareness of such contradictions, in fact, start to emerge as early as 1971 with the publication by Kristeva of the essay 'Women's Time'. The concept of a 'woman's identity' functions in terms both of affirmation and negation, even within feminism itself. There can be no simple legitimation for feminists in throwing off 'false consciousness' and revealing a true but 'deeply' buried female self. Indeed, to embrace the essentialism of this notion of 'difference' is to come dangerously close to reproducing that very patriarchal construction of gender which feminists have set out to contest as *their* basic project of modernity.

Feminism of late, therefore, has developed a self-reflexive mode: questioning its own legitimating procedures in a manner which seems to bring it close to a Postmodernism which has absorbed the lessons of post-structuralism and consists at the most general level of a crisis of legitimation across culture, politics and aesthetic theory and practice. The slogan 'Let us wage war against totality', however, could be seen as Postmodernism's response to that earlier slogan of the feminist movement, 'the personal is political'. But if the latter can be seen as a rallying cry, the former implies a hostile attitude towards its implicit ideals of collectivism and community. The feminist cry situated its politics firmly within what Lyotard wishes to denounce and Habermas to affirm in modified form as the 'project of modernity'. In fact, at this point in my argument, I will have to declare my own situatedness and argue that if feminism can learn from Postmodernism it has finally to resist the logic of its arguments or at least to attempt to combine them with a modified adherence to an epistemological anchorage in the discourses of Enlightened modernity. Even if feminists have come to recognise in their own articulations some of the radical perspectivism and thoroughgoing epistemological doubt of the postmodern, feminism cannot sustain itself as an emancipatory movement unless it acknowledges its foundation in the discourses of modernity. It seems possible to me, to draw on the aesthetics of Postmodernism as strategies for narrative disruption of traditional stories and construction of new identity scripts, without embracing its more extreme nihilistic or pragmatist implications. Surely to assume otherwise is in itself to embrace a naively reflectionist aesthetic which sees representation as necessarily reflective of prior structures or ideologies. A number of questions arise out of this: can feminism remain opposed to Postmodernism's circular tendency to project itself onto the contemporary world and thus, not surprisingly, to find in that world an affirmation of its own theoretical presuppositions? Can it resist the implicitly religious vocabulary of apocalypse while acknowledging the force of its critique of Enlightenment epistemology as rooted in the instrumental domination of inert object (body, world, nature, woman), by a detached and transcendent subject (mind, self, science, man).

These issues can usefully be approached, it seems to me, through further consideration of that central Enlightenment concept, autonomy, and its role in the construction of various models of subjectivity. What the preceding discussion has suggested is that the epistemological and ethical contradictions now confronting postmodernists and feminists are fundamentally issues about identity and difference. Subjective transformation has been central to feminist agendas for political change. Similarly, over the last thirty years, the deconstruction of liberal individualism and the dissolution of traditional aesthetic conceptualisations of character have been central to postmodern art and theory. Like feminism, Postmodernism (in theoretical and artistic modes), has been engaged in a re-examination of the Enlightenment concepts of subjectivity as autonomous self-determination: the human individual as defined without reference to history, traditional values, God, nation. Both have assaulted aesthetic or philosophical notions of identity as pure autonomous essence. Ethical and epistemological contradictions have crowded onto the modern scene. Peter Berger, e.g., defined the shift from traditional to modern identity as one from a world of honour to one of 'dignity': 'in a world of honour the individual discovers his true identity in his roles, and to turn away from the roles is to turn away from himself', but in a world of 'dignity' the individual can only discover his true identity by emancipating himself from his socially imposed roles' (Berger, Berger and Kellner, 1974, p.91). We have already seen some of the contradictions involved in this, for it can only be fully accomplished through the refusal of history and institution. Even if such a self could internally formulate itself, without engagement with history or institution it could not act upon the world. Agency would exist only within a sealed aesthetic realm.

Everyone agrees that Postmodernism is much concerned with fragmentation. Either it sees the world fragmenting or it sets out to discover modes which will fracture and dissolve old and supposedly exhausted unities. Numerous examples could be offered of this, from Lyotard's competing language games to the emphasis on the local, or from Barthelme's declaration 'Fragments are the only forms I trust' to Nietzsche's proclamation of that condition of linguistic materiality which Jameson has seen, with nostalgia, as basic to the postmodern condition. One could view the impulse to fragment in psychoanalytic terms. The desire to destroy that which we cannot possess has long been recognised as a strategy of the child persisting into adult behaviour. The destruction of the other, however, cannot be accomplished without an accompanying effect of fragmentation of the self. This is the experience of the postmodern condition as expressed by Jameson:

> Schizophrenic experience is an experience of isolated, discontinuous material signifiers which fail to link up into a coherent sequence. The schizophrenic thus does not know personal identity in our sense, since our feeling of identity depends on our sense of the persistence of the 'I' and the 'me' over time. (1985, p.119).

Although Jameson draws his model of schizophrenia from Lacan, it was Melanie Klein who first showed the fragmentation of subjectivity to be a final defence against the fear of annihilation. It is preceded by a desire to destroy that which threatens to annihilate oneself: the object of desire which tantalises but can never be possessed. In my view, versions of Postmodernism which simply celebrate radical fragmentation can be seen to be a collective psychological response to the recognition that the ideal autonomy of Enlightenment cannot be possessed. Not only this, pursuit of it may have produced the worst sort of violence. Similarly, aesthetic autonomy theory may have done violence to the identities of those modernist artefacts reconstructed through it since the 1940s. As Adorno and others began to recognize earlier in the century, one of the effects of idealist philosophy has been to empty out the self into an abstract form. This may appear to confirm its transcendence. It has actually reflected its real condition of systematised negation through abstraction within the instrumental rationalism of the liberal political economy. My argument has been that the concept has functioned similarly within aesthetic discourses to suppress the historical identity of works of art, the political commitments of writers, their challenges to traditional ethics. In New Critical or later Structuralist or post-Structuralist formalisms, literature is understood as a system which allows us access to a purified autonomy for it condenses and foregrounds the existence of the linguistic sign as a reflexively self-constituting object 'purged' of reference. Thus purged: of history, ethical insights, the 'contaminations' of a debased mass cultural mode of communication, however, the literary text paradoxically becomes identified in the very terms of abstraction its existence is supposed to resist. In reaction to this, many postmodern texts flaunt their implication in and complicity with Late Capitalism by deliberately incorporating aspects of mass culture or by drawing on parodic forms which implicitly deny the possibility of pure autonomy or original self-determination (parody is always and openly parasitic upon an earlier text). Many of the discourses of Postmodernism, however, employ the more radical and desperate remedy of extreme fragmentation: a way of coping with an inability to give up a profound desire for autonomy in the pure terms of its promised Enlightenment forms. Here lies the crux of its problematic relationship with feminism.

Jameson connects this 'schizophrenic' tendency in Postmodernism with a pervasive nostalgia. In my view it is the nostalgia which produces the desire to fragment, the impossible yearning for the lost (imaginary) object of desire which issues in the frustrated and atavistic smashing of the ideal object. Although Nietzsche is often seen as the first postmodernist, he was also one of the first to connect the nostalgic impulse with nihilism. One sees in the writings of Deleuze, for example, or the fictions of Kathy Acker, the possibility of humanist affirmation destroyed by an insistent and excessive nostalgic sense of loss of pure Being (translated often from Spirit to Instinct) whose impossible realisation produces the urge to destroy altogether what can be: the representation of the human subject as an ethical, affective and effective historical agent. If things are fragmenting, let's fragment them utterly. This is the violent face of Postmodernism. Of course, it is often difficult to know if extreme fragmentation or dehumanisation is being used parodically as a mode of critique, or a extension of a fragmented and dehumanised world. Here is a description of character 'V', goal and negation of Stencil's quest in Thomas Pynch postmodern novel of that name:

> Skin radiant with the bloom of some new plastic; both eyes glass but now containing some photoelectric cells, connected by silver electrodes to optic nerves of purest copper wire leading to a brain exquisitely wrought as a diode matrix ever could be. Soleroid relays would be her ganglia, serio-actuators move her flawless nylon limbs, hydraulic fluid be sent by a platinum heart-pump through buthyrane veins and arteries (1979, p.406).

For some critics, this dissolution of human subjectivity into textual play has been seen as a means of resisting the oppressive structures of global capitalism: fragmentation into atoms becomes the means of escaping patriarchal surveillance and control of the pleasure principle. Fragmentation and dehumanisation are part of a 'postmodern' assault on the bondage of thought to regulative ideals such as 'unity' and 'truth'. But for a feminist, the first difficulty with this argument must surely be that 'V' is a woman and even if she is constructed to expose the dehumanising effects of idealistic patriarchy, she also perpetuates them in her very form. We should remember too that when Nietzsche recommended fragmentation, he represented the regulative ideals of Enlightenment thought as tied to what he saw, in fact, as phallic castration: an emasculation of the intellect which he associated particularly with emancipatory movements and especially with feminism. The idea of truth as untruth has a long history of articulation through the image of the seductive woman: a Salome who is only her veils, whose adornments cover over a gaping absence. She continues to appear with monotonous frequency in the metaphorical femininity of some postmodern writing. Her otherness is the possibility of a space of immediacy, outside language, an incitement to transgression: the postmodern version of that Romantic sublime which must forever remain outside the workings of power and history. This grotesque version of the metaphor, for example, appears in Nietzsche's *My Sister and I*: 'Truth is still elusive. However, she is no longer a young girl but an old bitch with all her front teeth missing' (1990, p.114). Before examining in more depth what such rhetorical tropes might mean for actual women, and whether, indeed, they assault the oppressive structures of Late Capitalism for women, in particular, we need to return to some of the key ideas in postmodern theory which impinge on the issue of personal identity.

Founding Assumptions: feminism and Postmodernism

Fredric Jameson is probably the best known commentator on Postmodernism to connect its insights with a radical critique of the Enlightenment ideal of personal autonomy. In his seminal 1984 essay, he argued that its most radical insight is the view that the bourgeois individual subject is not only a thing of the past but also a myth. We have never possessed this kind of autonomy: 'Rather this construct is merely a philosophical and cultural mystification which sought to persuade people that they 'had' individual subjects and possessed this unique personal identity' (1985, p.115). Yet as we have seen, this insight is far from new. One philosopher has suggested that Descartes himself had to suppress his awareness of the contradictions of self-grounding as the basis of modernity:

> Nothing, as Descartes himself seemed to realise, in the methodological identification of these internal features, in clarity and distinctness, of itself justified any metaphysical result. Being, or substance as Descartes ended up understanding it, was only the result of the application of the method, and there was no convincing reason to think that what satisfies our self-certifying criteria for what there is, what is least susceptible to certain kinds of doubt, still gets us where we wanted to go, 'back' to the world we suspended in the moment of doubt . . . Given the self-understanding of an extreme break in the tradition, of a need for a new beginning not indebted to old assumptions, and so wholly self-grounding, the modern philosophic enterprise appears locked in a kind of self-created vacuum, determining by argument or reason a method for making claims about the world, but unable to argue convincingly that what results is anything other than what the method tells us about the world, be the 'real' world as it may. (Pippin, 1991, p.25.)

Postmodernism has provided a radical critique of method both in its development of Nietzschean radical fictionality and of the idea of non-conceptualisable Being or pre-understanding from Heidegger. In the former version, the interest is in the way in which experience is aesthetically constructed and the self an ever-revisable script. In the second, the emphasis is on the possibility of recovering some immediate, primordial, authentic mode of being which is non-rationalisable and pre-conceptual and variously seen as the 'politics of desire' or 'against interpretation'. Both invoke the aesthetic as the mode of its realisation. Yet as I have tried to show, these two tendencies are derived from two modes of Romanticism which, in themselves, were powerful critiques of Enlightenment. Postmodernism, however, claims to have entirely left behind the metaphysical ground of Romanticism. But has it? The fictionality mode still reproduces a form of late Coleridgean aesthetics: self recreating itself through the (textual) imagination and still raising difficult ethical issues even as it claims to go beyond good and evil. The alternative mode, an extension of the Wordsworthian, often displaces the notion of nature with a notion of the body in a new instinctual foundationalism; or it displaces it with a notion of situatedness or tradition still effectively grounded in a sacred mysterious Being.

One hears much in Postmodernism about the subject as myth and the notion that the master narratives of history are redundant illusions. Yet, I often have the feeling, as I read postmodernist writing, that its apocalyptic nihilism about the possibility of ethical and imaginative subjective existence is still grounded in a nostalgia for the ideal autonomous self as presented in Enlightenment thought. Nostalgia rewrites history in the terms of desire. In the case of apocalyptic postmodernism, it may be that its schizophrenic fragmentation is a response to a continuing obsession with an impossible ideal. Postmodernism, in this mode, may itself have rigidified autonomy into an absolute identity. Autonomy has been a powerful concept in philosophical and aesthetic writing, but even as they ascribe to the theory most people know it cannot be lived absolutely in this ideal form. Certainly, few women have attempted to live it, because women have been more or less excluded from its applications. They have developed alternative models of self-identity. A problem for feminists in relating to Postmodernism, is that they are highly unlikely to bear this sort of relationship to history or to the ideal autonomous self central to the discourses of modernity. Those who have been systematically excluded from the constitution of that so-called universal subject – whether for reasons of gender, class, race, sexuality – are unlikely either to long nostalgically for what they have never experienced or possessed (even as an illusion) or to revel angrily or in celebratory fashion in the 'jouissance' of its disintegration. To recognise the limitations of an ideal which was never one's own is to bear a very different relationship to its perceived loss.

The decentred and fragmented subject of the 'postmodern condition' is one which has been created, at least in part, by Postmodernism itself. It is in part the consequence of an inability to rethink a self not premised in some way on the pure idealism of the autonomous subject of Enlightened thought, German Idealist philosophy and Kantian aesthetics. It is present in much postmodern writing at least as a structure of feeling. Recent feminist scholarship has shown why women are unlikely to have experienced history in this form. For feminists, therefore, the goals of agency, personal autonomy, self-expression and self-determination, can neither be taken for granted nor written off as exhausted. They are ideals which feminism has helped to reformulate, modify and challenge. Feminism needs coherent subjects and has found a variety of ways of articulating them which avoid the fetishisation of Pure Reason as the locus of subjecthood and the irrationalism born out of the perceived failure of this ideal.

Alternative Histories

Both feminism and Postmodernism have extended our awareness that one of the effects of modernity is that knowledge reflexively enters and shapes experience and is then shaped by it in an unprecedentedly self-conscious fashion. The ways in which we formulate notions of selfhood out of the models of subjectivity available to us shape our behaviour in the world and shape response to any new models consciously or unconsciously encountered. In such a climate, to talk of 'origins' is highly problematic. However, we have already examined a number of formulations of the postmodern, and seen that most of them begin to appear in the late 1950s. By the late seventies, in fact, both feminism and Postmodernism can be seen to have radically altered the way in which modern culture is understood and experienced. What I find astonishing is the fact that these discourses have had so little to say to each other. Even now, as postmodern theory increasingly draws on a highly idealised and generalised notion of femininity as 'other' in its search for a space outside the disintegrating logic of modernity, it rarely talks about (or to, one suspects) actual women or even about feminism as a political practice. I have been amazed at the number of general accounts of Postmodernism which do not even mention gender, when clearly one of the most obvious and radical shifts in late modernity has been in the relations between women and men. This shift has had all sorts of ramifications for modern concepts like nation, the aesthetic, epistemology, ethical systems, autonomy. And, indeed, there are obvious points of historical contact between Postmodernism and feminism. Both have undermined the Romantic-Modernist cultivation of the aesthetic as an auto-nomous realm and helped to expose it as a critical construction. Each assaults Enlightenment discourses which universalise white, Western, middle-class male experience. Both recognise the need for a new ethics responsive to technological changes and shifts in knowledge and power. Each has offered critiques of foundationalist thinking: gender is not a consequence of anatomy nor do social institutions so much reflect universal truths as construct historical and provisional ones. Postmodernism too, is 'grounded' in the epistemological problem of grounding itself, of the idea of identity as essential or truth as absolute.

Feminism has provided its own critique of essentialist and foundationalist assumptions. Arguably, however, even if it draws upon postmodern aesthetic forms of disruption, it cannot repudiate entirely the framework of Enlightened modernity without perhaps fatally undermining itself as an emancipatory politics. In proceeding through the demands of political practice, feminism must posit some belief in the notion of effective human agency, the necessity for historical continuity in formulating identity and a belief in historical progress. Even if people are shaped by historical forces, they are not simply reflexive epiphenomena of impersonal deep structures or of a global agonistics of circulating and competing language games. Feminism must believe in the possibility of a community of address situated in an oppositional space which can allow for the connection of the 'small personal voice' (Doris Lessing's term) of one feminist to another and to other liberationist movements. One writer producing personal confessional novels about 'women's identity' can then be seen to connect with the activity of another woman rewriting the history of slavery or one camped on the mud of Greenham Common, even as they recognise and accept each other's differences. All are ultimately engaged in practices which involve an adherence to a shared ideal of truth and justice grounded in fundamental human needs, but as the embeddedness of each of us in the world is different, so we shape different styles of living, of aesthetic expression and political action for ourselves. It seems to me that all along feminism has been engaged in a struggle to reconcile context-specific difference or situatedness with universal political aims: to modify the Enlightenment in the context of late modernity but not to capitulate to the postmodern condi-tion.

Glancing through the various postmodernisms, in fact, one can see how the full range of conceptualisations of difference has entered feminist theory and aesthetic practice. An invigorating imaginative playfulness has entered femi-nist writing: a sense of the importance of the aesthetic in the imaginative and embodied projection of alternative futures. Too often though, political claims are made for avant-garde formal disruption which are difficult to justify. One sort of disruption is assumed to be the mirror of another. Once epistemology becomes so problematic, however, such category mistakes are bound to occur. Real and fictional may be entirely conflated. Concepts are transferred unproblematically from the context of aesthetic to political practice. But surely feminists should keep in mind the centrality in his work of Lyotard's assertion that emancipatory discourses are no longer possible because there can no longer be a belief in privileged metadiscourses which transcend local and contingent conditions in order to ground the 'truths' of all first order discourses (Lyotard, 1984). According to this view, gender cannot be used cross-culturally to explain the practices of human societies. In one sense this is the state of affairs feminism is aiming for in the ideal society it imagines to be possible. It should not, however, mean that feminists abandon their struggle against sexual oppression because 'gender' as a metanarrative is necessarily a repressive enactment of metaphysical authority. Lyotard unnecessarily conflates the concept of totality with that of totalitarianism. Feminists should remember that 'totalities' such as the concept of political unity, need not mean uniformity, that they can be enabling and liberating. Globalisation may be a critical mode of knowledge as well as a functional mode of capitalism or of reigns of terror.

The postmodern concept of language games, dissensus and dispersal developed in Lyotard's reading of Wittgenstein, is one postmodern discourse often naively appropriated by an avant-garde desire to conflate artistic textual disruption with political subversion. Analogy may be confused with causality in order to claim a massive political significance for formally innovative writing. The position is as strongly identified with postmodernists like Lyotard as with feminists such as Kristeva. Its immediate impulses can be traced back to Tel Quel influences, to Barthesian jouissance and to the avant-garde manifestoes of the twenties and thirties. Critics such as Peter Bürger have argued that Postmodernism has failed to challenge the institutionalisation of modern art as autonomous practice because of the post-structuralist persistence in viewing the sign as self-reflexive (Bürger, 1984). Although I have suggested alternative ways of reading Postmodernism and of viewing the issue of aesthetic autonomy, there are implications here for feminism. I must confess to some suspicion about the way in which some postmodernist discourses have developed the concept of femininity. The dangerous use of the metaphor of 'femininity' to designate a linguistically non-reproducible 'otherness' effectively redescribes a space of the sacred. Its roots are in Romanticism. Such a 'feminine' space has always been used to deny the *material* existence of actual women. From Nietzsche through Hassan and Lacan, femininity has been used to signify an 'otherness' which has effectively been essentialised as the disruption of the legitimate or the Law of the father. This 'otherness' has been variously expressed as the repressed other; the hysterical body; the semiotic; the pre-oedipal; the ecstatic, fluid, maternal body. It is associated with the transgression of Christian mysticism. In 'Women's Time', for example; Kristeva writes:

> It seems to me that the role of what is usually called 'aesthetic practices' must increase not only to counterbalance the storage of uniformity of information by present-day mass media, data-bank systems and, in particular, modern communications technol-

ogy, but also to demystify the identity of the symbolic bond itself, to demystify therefore, the community of language as a universal tool, one which totalises and equalises . . . what I have called 'aesthetic practices' are undoubtedly nothing other than the modern reply to the eternal question of morality (Kristeva, 1982, p.53).

We have seen this argument reproduced throughout an aesthetic tradition of Enlightenment critique from Romanticism to Postmodernism. The danger is to assume that because it is often articulated through metaphors of femininity, women, in particular, will be liberated through it. It may indeed function as an agent of women's oppression. In Kristeva's own account, women have no special access to this pre-conceptual space of the 'maternal body', and even as avant-garde artists they receive little attention. It seems to be male experimental writers who can speak it. In fact, as often as not, this celebration of 'difference' goes hand in hand with an amazing *indifference* to the material and psychological circumstances of actual women. The postmodern espousal of psychotextual decentring as liberatory says little about women as beings in the world who continue to find themselves displaced and invisible even within a critique of epistemology which has supposedly, in deconstructing the centre, therefore done away with the margins to produce the possibility of a new emancipatory liminality. As in most religious discourses, Postmodernism in this 'desire' mode promises a beyond to the sense of an ending: a conversion of chronos to kairos, beyond language, concept, time. Within postmodern psychoanalytic discourse, for example, it has been described as 'the body without organs' (the small boy's view of the mother?), 'becoming woman' (the male fantasy of plenitude?) and the 'hysterical body' (the female object through which psychoanalysis first arrived at its definition of the implicitly masculine subject). It seems that as postmodernists obsessively register their sense of the collapsing legitimacy of the frameworks of Western knowledge, they are also registering, unconsciously and metaphorically, a fear specifically of the loss of the legitimacy of western *patriarchal* grand narratives. This may even share in aspects of the new forms of fear of women evident in other ways in contemporary culture: addictions to body building, violence to women, a resurgence of religious fundamentalism, new forms of pornography which present women literally in bondage to men, the popularity of films like 'Fatal Attraction' and the current cult of serial killer movies. Is it a coincidence that at the very historical moment when (male) postmodernists intensify their interest in (and master through their own discourses) a (religious) space described as the 'feminine' and nothing to do with actual women, feminists are establishing an (Enlightened modern) sense of their coherent identity as women through the very categories and discourses which postmodernists claim to have dismantled and done away with in the name of this 'femininity'. Surely this has an ominously familiar ring to it? Could one see the oppressed (women) returning in the form of the repressed (femininity) in postmodern discourse only to be worked through and mastered yet again in the language of theory?

If femininity has become, once more, a metaphor for a state beyond metaphysics, feminists should be certain that its tenor is not simply the contemporary theoretical counterpart to the Victorian parlour. If they have any suspicions then they should continue to hammer through its boundaries, those between public and private, in an assertion of their continued belief in their own capacity for agency and historical reconstruction. If Barthes writes a pseudo-autobiography to articulate the idea that 'to write an essay on oneself may seem a pretentious idea, but it is a simple idea, simple as the idea of suicide' (1977, p.56), feminists should remind themselves that the shelves of books by Barthes in libraries all over the world proclaim a confidence in his authorship even as he disclaims it. They should not be surprised then that so many women writers in the seventies articulated a desire to become 'authors of their own lives' at precisely the moment that Barthes was announcing the death of that concept. Whose death?

Jean Baudrillard's work, it seems to me, is even more problematic for feminism. For him postmodernity signifies the state of contemporary culture which exists as a simulacrum of signs where the information age has utterly dissolved identity through reflections to maskings to complete absence. In this perspective all that literature can do is to play off 'alternative worlds' in a state of pluralistic anarchy where the subject is simply a simulating machine of commercial images, the mass a silent majority and the very idea of resistance, an absurdity. Simulation replaces imagination and human beings are left with no capacity to reshape their world even in their own heads. They act like the characters in Robert Coover's novel *Gerald's Party* (1986), as dense points of transmission for all the cop and thriller and porn movies which construct their desires and which churn out incessantly throughout this text in an orgy of hedonistic sensationalism. It may be that Coover is using the parodic mode of the postmodern to offer a critique of postmodernity from within its own codes, but again one is left with the claustrophobic sense that there can be no real opposition to it because there is no place outside. In most versions of the postmodern, in fact, any claim to a substantive reality outside representation, is discredited: if signs determine reality, there can be no opposition because no space which is not already reproduced.

One difficulty in discussing Postmodernism is that the apocalypticism of the theory may have unduly affected our response to the fictional artefacts (if I may be so old-fashioned as to hang onto such a distinction). It seems to me this is an important distinction to hang onto, because it is evident that many women writers are using postmodern aesthetic strategies of disruption to re-imagine the world in which we live, while resisiting the nihilistic implications of the theory. Certainly one can see the writing of Angela Carter, Jeanette Winterson, Margaret Atwood, Maggie Gee, Fay Weldon, to name but a few, in this way. This is perhaps not so very surprising since women have, in practice, always experienced themselves in a 'postmodern' fashion – decentred, lacking agency, defined through others. Which is why, it seems to be, they had to attempt to occupy the centre in the early seventies. It is why women began to seek a subjective sense of agency and collective identity within the terms of the discourses of modernity at precisely the moment when postmodernists were engaged in the repudiation of such discourses, proclaiming the 'death of the author' and the end of humanism. Much feminist fiction of this period, therefore, was either confessional or concerned with the idea of discovering an authentic identity. If its philosophical roots are clearly anywhere it is in existentialism rather than post-structuralism. It may now appear to be philosophically naive and formally unadventurous, espousing an uncontested aesthetics of expressive realism or a simple reversal of the romance quest plot which did little to problematise ideologies of romantic love or essential identity. I have argued that perhaps feminist writers needed to formulate a sense of identity, history and agency within these terms before they could begin to deconstruct them. However, feminist writers did not subsequently rush off to embrace the postmodern – indeed they have largely maintained a cautious distance, certainly from much of the theory. This is where I shall declare my own distance as a feminist in offering some 'grand and totalising' narratives which allow us to think of subjectivity in ways which neither simply repeat the Enlightenment concept of modernity nor repudiate it in an embrace of anarchic dispersal.

Rethinking Subjectivity and Aesthetics: Alternative Feminist Positions

I want to suggest, somewhat tentatively, that despite differences in the theoretical construction of modernity and postmodernity, common to them both is the inheritance of a particular ideal of subjectivity defined in terms of transcendence and pure rationality. Postmodernism can be seen as a response to the perceived failure of this ideal. This notion of subjectivity, whether expressed through Descartes' rational 'I' and refined into Kant's categorical imperatives, or through Nietzsche's 'ubermensch' or Lacan's phallogocentric symbolic order, has not only excluded women but has made their exclusion on the grounds of emotionality, failure of abstract intellect or whatever, the basis of its identity. This position has been reproduced across philosophy, psycho-analysis and literature. In viewing this situation as fundamentally unchanged, I am, in effect, repudiating the postmodern notion that there are no longer any generally legitimated metanarratives. What I am saying is that patriarchal metanarratives function just as effectively within our so-called 'postmodern age' as in any other age and in its metaphorical play on notions of the feminine continues insidiously to function powerfully within postmodern theory itself.

Jameson has diagnosed postmodernism as the schizophrenic condition of late capitalism, but I would argue that the autonomous transcendent self of German idealism, Enlightenment humanism, European Romanticism and realist aesthetics and the impersonally fragmented self of Postmodernism are products of the same cultural tradition. Schizophrenia is clinically defined as a splitting of thought and feeling: the 'schizophrenia' of Postmodernism can be seen as a fin-de-siecle parody, or caricature, of a dualism inherent in the Western tradition of thought where the self is defined as a transcendent rationality which necessitates splitting off what is considered to be the irra-tional, emotion, and projecting it as the 'feminine' onto actual women. It is to see T.S. Eliot's 'dissociation of sensibility' from a feminist rather than a High Tory position. Freud, of course, has taught us that reason and feeling are inextricably bound up with each other, but even he believed that ego could and should master id and that impersonal reason is the basis of personal autonomy. Increasingly in this century, such a contracted 'rational' self cannot make sense of the world: whether in the fictions of Kafka or Bellow, for example, or in the aetiolated dramas of Samuel Beckett. When transcendence fails, however, the threat of disorder is seen to come from the split off (and therefore uncontroll-able) aspects of the psyche, the non-rational projected onto and thus defining women, racial minorities, so-called 'sexual deviants' or even 'the masses'.

Postmodernism may seek to locate the possibility of disruption or 'jouissance' in this space, but in continuing to regard it as 'feminine', whether it speaks of actual women or not, then it simply continues the process of projection and does little to overcome the dualism and psychological defensiveness inherent in it. Often in postmodernist fiction, for example, traditional images of the castrating female, the unknown and therefore uncontrollable woman, are overlaid in a technological age with their representation as machines which have outstripped the controlled and rational dominance of the male (one thinks of V again). The 'emotionality' thus projected onto the feminine or onto women in order to retain rationality and autonomy as the core of masculine identity produces both images of woman as the 'other' of romantic desire and woman who, thus beyond control, threatens annihilation or incorporation. If feminists wish to argue a politics of femininity as avant-garde disruptive desire they should first think about some of the meanings of, for example, V or Nurse Ratched.

In fact, in both modernist and postmodernist writing, when order conceived of as a circumscribed rationality seems no longer to cohere in either the self or in history, then it is projected onto the impersonal structures of language or of history conceived of as myth, a static and synchronic space. Despite the new 'perspectivism' which enters literary history in the early part of the century, the potential for the re-evaluation of the relations between subjectivity and objectivity, so many of the aesthetic manifestos of the time and later critical accounts of the period emphasise 'impersonality', 'autonomy', 'objectivity', universal 'significant form', 'spatial form', 'objective correlative' – even when some of the artefacts, such as *Ulysses*, clearly problematise such notions. The New Critical theorisation of literature, in particular the modernist text, as an autonomous linguistic structure, reinforced these ideas. Since then the increasing professionalisation of literature has extended the vocabulary of form and structure: defamiliarisation, systems of signs, the death of the author, the free play of the signifier, simulations . . .

One can see in much modernist literature both tne attempted assertion and the failure of Enlightened modernity's ideal of autonomy. The belief in absolute self-determination, whether that of Stephen Dedalus or Mr Ramsay, is always discovered to be dependent on the desires of others. Whereas a transcendent being could anchor desire as absolute, to express it in relation to others is always seen to produce delusion, deception, jealousy, a whole variety of epistemological crises which modernist texts offer. The possibility of Art itself as an absolute autonomous realm, however, often comes to take the place of the sacred here. Art, as religion, seems to offer precisely that illusion of utter self-determination and transcendence which relations with other mortals must always shatter. It is interesting how many of the male heroes of modernist literature achieve an apparent self-determination in aesthetic terms through a refusal of social relationship. Hence the figure of the alienated artist who affirms his own autonomy, his independence from the mediation of others at the price of the cessation of human relationship and desire: Marcel writing in his room, Ralph Touchett vicariously living through Isabel, Malone talking to himself, Mann's Leverkühn, Hesse's Steppenwolf. Art as the impersonal focus for desire displaces the possibility of human relationship because it involves no mediation through the desire of the other. Hovering behind these texts is

Nietzsche's self-creating and self-affirming artist for whom to recognise the other would be to fall into a slave mentality.

In my view it is the identification of self with an impossible ideal of autonomy which can be seen to produce the failure of love and relationship in so many texts by male modernist and postmodernist writers. Can one rethink the self outside of this concept without abandoning subjectivity to dispersal and language games? Not only do I believe that one can, I also believe that many feminist writers have done so. This is the really 'grand and totalising' part of my argument. It seems to me that autonomy defined as transcendence, impersonality and absolute independence, whether an idealised goal or a nostalgic nihilism, whether informing the aesthetics of Modernism or those of Postmodernism, is not a mode with which most feminists, nor indeed, most women, can very easily identify. Feminist theory, though drawing on anti-humanist discourses to sharpen its understanding of social processes, has emphasised that 'impersonal' historical determinants are lived out through experience. This distance from anti-humanist discourse has allowed feminist academics to connect with grass roots activists outside the academy. Their own historical experience has tended to develop in women strongly 'humanist' qualities in the broader sense of the term and feminism has always been rooted in women's subjective experience of the conflicting demands of home and work, family and domestic ties and the wider society.

Psychoanalysis, Gender and Aesthetics

Jürgen Habermas has recently suggested that modernity is not exhausted, simply unfinished. His view of this is not incompatible with some of the ideas I am trying to develop here. What he has argued is that instead of abandoning its ideals we need to modify them by redefining the model of Reason which underlies them. His work is part of a tradition of critical thinking which sees Enlightened reason failing because it is defined too narrowly in terms of an instrumental, purposive or utilitarian epistemology. He proposes instead a model of what he calls 'communicative reason', based on speech act theory and emphasising not individual autonomy but intersubjectivity (1987). Like so many theorists within the postmodern debate, however, he seems singularly unaware of many of the developments in feminist thinking over the last twenty years. It seems to me that many feminists have been working for some time with models which are not fundamentally incompatible with Habermas's whether or not they have used them in specifically theoretical ways. I will now examine some of these ideas and suggest that through them it is possible to arrive not only at an alternative definition of the aesthetic but also of subjectivity itself.

According to most psychoanalytic theories and their popularly disseminated versions, subjecthood is understood as the achievement of separation. Maturity is seen to be reached when the dependent infant comes to regard its primary caretaker (nearly always a woman) as simply an object through which it defines its own identity and position in the world. This is then maintained through the defensive patrolling of boundaries. Implicit then in most theories of identity is the assumption that the 'otherness' analysed by feminists from de Beauvoir onwards, is the necessary condition of women – certainly as long as women mother. Separation and objectivity rather than relationship and connection become the markers of identity. Freudian theory has been used to support this view. Both the liberal self and the postmodern 'decentred subject' can be articulated through Freud's notion of the unconscious, dominated by instinctual and universal drives seeking impossible gratification. In the liberal version, ego as rationality can master the drives either intrapsychically or with the help of the silent, the impersonal and objective analyst who will be uncontaminated by countertransference. In the postmodern version, rationality breaks down and the anarchy of desire as impersonal and unconscious energy is unleashed either in the freeplay of the signifier of the avant-garde text or that of the marketplace of Late Capitalism. Freud's infant hovers behind both: an autoerotic isolate, inherently aggressive and competitive, its sexuality and identity oedipally resolved only by fear, seeking to discharge libidinal energy which is necessarily in conflict with 'rational' and 'enlightened' concern for others and for society as a whole.

Can we imagine alternative models of subjectivity? If knowledge is inextricably bound up with experience then it seems that we certainly can, for this is not a description of universal experience. In fact Freud himself hints at other possibilities in less familiar parts of his writings. In the paper 'On Narcissism', for example, he says: 'A strong egotism is a protection against falling ill, but in the last resort we must begin to love in order not to fall ill and we are bound to fall ill if in consequence of frustration, we are unable to love'.[1] In fact, in the development of selfhood, the ability to conceive of oneself as separate from and mutually independent with the parent develops with the ability to accept one's dependency and to feel secure enough to relax the boundaries between self and other without feeling one's identity to be threatened. Why, then, is autonomy always emphasised as the goal of maturity? Why not emphasise equally the importance of maintaining connection and intersubjectivity? As Joan Riviere has argued 'There is no such thing as a single human being pure and simple, unmixed with other human beings . . . we are members one of another' (1986). Parts of other people, the parts we have had relationships with, are parts of us, so the self is both constant and fluid, ever in exchange, ever redescribing itself through its encounters with others. It seems to be this recognition of mediation as that which renders total self-determination impossible which so many male modernist and postmodernist writers find unacceptable. Yet much women's, particularly feminist, writing has been different in that it has neither attempted to transcend relationship through the impersonal embrace of Art as formal autonomy or sacred space nor through rewriting its own Apocalyptic sense of an ending.

Returning to psychoanalysis, however, one can see some of the reasons why the definition of subjectivity as transcendence and autonomy has been so powerful and why it has come to be seen not as a description of the experience of most white, Western males, but of universal structures of subjectivity. In psychoanalytic terms, if subjectivity is defined as separateness, its acquisition will involve radical disidentification with women in a society where women are normally the exclusive caretakers of children. This will be true even for girls

[1] Sigmund Freud, 'On Narcissism'.

who, at the level of gender, will also seek to identify with the mother. Fathers are not perceived as threatening non-identity, for in classical analysis they are seen as outside the pre-oedipal world of primary socialisation with its intense ambivalences and powerful Imagos. They are from the start associated with the clear, rational world of work and secondary socialisation. Object relations theorists like Nancy Chodorow (1978), however, have pointed out that the desire for radical disidentification with the mother will be more acute for boys since the perception of women as mothers will be bound up with pre-oedipal issues of mergence and potential loss of identity requiring a culturally rein-forced masculine investment in denial and separation. The world of secondary socialisation associated with the father comes to be seen as superior and as inherently male. Subjectivity thus comes to be seen as autonomy or as role-definition through work. Truth is defined as objectivity and transcendence. Science in the form of an instrumental technology will be overvalued and defined in terms of objectivity; philosophy comes to deal only with universal and metaphysical truths (whatever the theoretical challenges to these notions). Women (or the 'feminine') come to be identified in Cartesian or post-structuralist philosophy with all that cannot be rationally controlled and thus threatening dissolution or non-identity: mortality, the body, desire, emo-tionality, nature. Post-structuralist 'femininity' is simply another way of mak-ing actual femininity safe, of controlling through a process of naming which in post-structuralist fashion prises the term utterly away from the anatomical body of woman.

If the female sex thus represents, in Sartre's words 'the obscenity . . . of everything which gapes open' (1985), then men seem to be justified in their instrumental attitude to women and to everything, including nature, which has been 'feminised' and which must therefore be distanced, controlled, aesthet-icised, subdued (one might call this the Gilbert Osmond syndrome). Women appear threatening in this way because they carry the culture's more wide-spread fear of the loss of boundaries, of the uncontrollable, more threatening because unconsciously split off in order to retain the purity of a subjectivity, a human-ness defined as autonomy, pure reason and transcendence. Cartesian dualism thus persists along with strict empiricism in science and impersonality and formalism in literary theory and criticism.

What I have tried to argue here, therefore, is that an examination of alternative feminist models of identity can add a further and important dimension to the debates considered earlier about the construction of Modern-ism in terms of formal autonomy. The exclusion of gender from postmodern discussions has left its theorists largely blind to the possibilities of challenging autonomy through a relational concept of identity. If women's identity has tended, broadly and allowing for differences across this, to be experienced in terms which do not necessarily see separation gained only at the expense of connection, one would expect some sense of this to be expressed in discourses other than the theoretical and psychoanalytic. Women's sense of identity is more likely, for psychological and cultural reasons, to consist of a more diffuse sense of the boundaries of self and their notion of identity understood in relational and intersubjective terms. I am certainly not claiming that this is exclusive to women, for clearly gender is a continuum, and there are several theoretical models often invoked in the postmodern debate which articulate a similar sense of identity. It provides a further perspective on the Woolf passage. Certainly, I believe that Woolf's work has been so important for feminists because both formally and thematically it articulates a critique of patriarchal institutions through its exploration of the relatedness of subjects and objects. Beyond this, however, she offers a critique of the exclusive identification with relational modes of identity as they have functioned within patriarchy. She shows their negative as well as positive potential in characters such as Mrs Ramsay and Clarissa Dalloway. In a society where women are perceived as culturally inferior, relationality as the basis of identity has often reinforced their desire to please, to serve others and seek definition through them, internalising any anger about this as a failure of (essential) femininity. Mrs Ramsay's desire for autonomy, her travels in the imagination, remain a dark core. If it could rise to the surface, tempered by a relational sense of connection to others, then it might no longer hover as a suicidal impulse. It could fully realise the sense that human beings are fundamentally bound to and produced through each other as well as fundamentally separate. Indeed, the recognition of the co-existence of these states might be essential for the survival of the human race. If ego is the product of culture, as Freud argued, and if ego may only be defined in terms of separateness, impersonality, containment and pure reason, then culture has produced only divided and deformed human beings. Feminist discourses suggest that the dissolution of containment into irrational desire or the dispersal of jouissance are not the only alternatives to a discredited Enlightenment. My hope is that these perspectives may be fairly represented in future accounts of the postmodern debate and the condition of late modernity.

SECTION FIVE

Reading Postmodern Artefacts

This reader concentrates on postmodern theory, but in viewing it as an analytic strategy with its roots in an aesthetic tradition of thought, it would be a serious omission if there were no discussion whatsoever of postmodern art. I have therefore included short extracts from books on postmodern poetics by Linda Hutcheon and Brian McHale. As with theory, postmodern aesthetic forms draw on modes of irony, parody, fragmentation and multiplicity and are similarly, therefore, part of and subject to the general crisis of legitimation. The virtue of the critics represented below, however, is that they neither offer sweeping generalisations which dismiss postmodern art as straightforwardly and thoroughly co-extensive with the depthless surfaces of Late Capitalism, nor do they proclaim it as a liberation of desires and intensities which can overthrow internalised and external oppressions. Each, however, engages in a careful and detailed analysis of literary postmodern texts. In my view, to offer an analysis of an aestheticist theoretical mode without engaging with works of art themselves (even if the distinction is supposed to have been deconstructed) is inadequate. If Postmodernism opposes the violence of the concept and the totalising mode of theory, it is necessarily, as an 'analytics' (Foucault's term), bound to articulate its own position in the very terms of its object of critique. If Rorty is correct in arguing that literature can avoid this because it is a form of non-totalising, embodied, contingent and particular representation, then any consideration of postmodern theory should engage with postmodern art. Certainly postmodern literature uses a variety of strategies which explore the same problems of representation and foundationalism as postmodern theory (see Waugh 1992), but because literature is self-consciously fictional and self-consciously particular from its very inception, its examination may enhance understanding of the theoretical preoccupations of postmodernists.

The first excerpt is taken from Hutcheon's *The Poetics of Postmodernism* (1990). In this she extends an earlier interest in modern uses of self-reflexive forms such as parody to a defence of their political potential in postmodern writing. Parody is viewed as a perfect postmodern form because it always acknowledges implication in that which it criticises, implicitly asserting that if there can be no position outside culture from which to oppose it, there can be critique from within. So she extends her earlier work on parody as repetition with critical distance which allows an ironic signalling of difference at the heart of similarity. The second excerpt is from McHale's *Postmodernist Fiction* (1987). The basic argument of this book is that Postmodernism can be distinguished from Modernism because it draws on strategies which produce an effect of ontological problematisation as opposed to the concerns of the latter with epistemological issues. Whereas modernist texts foreground questions such as 'How do I interpret this world?', postmodern ones raise questions such as 'Which world is this?' McHale does not comment on the broader cultural implications of the postmodern debate and his work is taxonomic rather than evaluative, but he does suggest that the postmodern concern with ontological transgression may ultimately be bound up with issues of security of existential identity. He suggests that in foregrounding the question of the existence of worlds, Postmodernism allows us to imagine our own non-existence. It thus constitutes a new *ars moriendi*. Again, therefore, although not engaged with broader philosophical and political issues thrown up by the debate, the implication of McHale's argument is that the aesthetic has profound existential implications. It has entered debates about ethics and knowledge and can no longer be ignored by philosophers or political scientists. Whether we like it or not, we cannot simply turn our backs on Postmodernism.

---

19   Linda Hutcheon

From *A Poetics of Postmodernism*

Routledge, 1988, pp 195–200.

It is comparatively recently that the perception and definition of the field of the 'political' has undergone a radical expansion beyond the traditional ghetto of party politics and considerations of 'class struggle' to now include, amongst other things, considerations of sexuality.

Victor Burgin

As Wolf's *Cassandra* shows, the ex-centric or the different has been one of the postmodern forces that has worked to reconnect the ideological with the aesthetic. Race, gender, ethnicity, sexual preference – all become part of the domain of the political, as various manifestations of centralizing and centralized authority are challenged. While some French poststructuralist theory has argued that the margin is the ultimate place of subversion and transgression,[1] another branch has shown how the margin is both created by and part of the center,[2] that the 'different' can be made into the 'other.' As we have been seeing, postmodernism tends to combat this by asserting the plurality of the 'different' and rejecting the binary opposition of the 'other.' Though *Cassandra*'s paradigm is clearly male/female and thus unavoidably binary, its model is an expanded one (like Engels's, in which the marital relationship and its inherent inequality is the model for class conflict). For

[1] Kristeva, Julia, *Desire in Language*, trans. Thomas Gora, Alice Jardine and Leon S. Roudiez (Oxford Blackwell; New York: Columbia University Press, 1980).
[2] Foucault, Michel, *The Order of Things: An Archaeology of the Human Sciences* (New York: Pantheon).

Wolf, the gender opposition is the model for national (Greek/Trojan or east/west today) and class power relations.[3] Her Cassandra makes contact with all the socially and ethnically heterogeneous minority groups around the Trojan palace, and in so doing, loses any privileges of centrality her birth grants her. This is the destiny of the ex-centric.

Postmodern metafictions have looked to both the historiographic and fictional accounts of the past in order to study the ideological inscriptions of difference as social inequality. In *A Maggot* the twentieth-century narrator fills in the background of the eighteenth century's sexism and classism as it is needed in order to explain his characters' actions – such as the 'crudely chauvinistic contempt'[4] of the middle-class English lawyer, Ayscough, for his poor Welsh witness, Jones. We are told that the roots of such contempt lie in the real religion of the century, the 'worship, if not idolatry' of property:[5] 'this united all society but the lowest, and dictated much of its behaviour, its opinions, its thinking,[6] including its notion of justice. Like many other postmodern fictions, this one is not content to say something about the past and stop at that. Like *Cassandra*, this novel forges a link with the present:

> Jones is a liar, a man who lives from hand to mouth . . . [yet] he is the future and Ayscough the past; and both are like most of us, still today, equal victims in the debtors' prison of History, and equally unable to leave it.
>
> (1985, 231)

The overt didacticism of Fowles's novel(s) is, in the work of others, replaced by a more indirect satiric mode, but the ideological implications of the representations of the marginal and the different are just as clear. Ishmael Reed's *Mumbo Jumbo* is as much an attack on the present as on the Harding years, for the simple reason that there has been little but stasis in terms of the white American establishment view of black consciousness as subversive and alien.[7] In *The Terrible Twos*, the satiric attack on the economic and political situation of 1980s America is vehicled by what is called, in the text itself, 'the right metaphor':[8] white America is like a 2-year-old child. It is demanding and harbors 'cravings that have to be immediately quenched'.[9] The list of its qualities builds up as the novel progresses: 2-year-olds 'have very bad taste'[10] and 'Life to them is a plaything anyway'.[11] 'Two-year-olds are what the id would look like if the id could ride a tricycle',[12] we learn. The reader is 'hailed' (in Althusser's sense) into the text as 'you' in order for her/him to recognize America in this guise: 'You know how two-year-olds are. Their plates will be full but they'll have their eyes on everybody else's plates'.[13]. The narrative

---

Foucault, Michel, *op. cit.*, p. 230.

[4] Fowles, John, *A Maggot* (Toronto: Colins, 1985).

[5] Fowles, John, *op. cit.*, p. 227.

[6] Fowles, John, *op. cit.*, p. 228.

[7] Martin, Richard, 'Clio Bemused: The Uses of History in Contemporary American Fiction', *SubStance* 27 (1980), pp. 20–1.

[8] Reed, Ishmael, *The Terrible Twos* (Garden City, NY: Doubleday, 1982), p. 106.

[9] Reed, Ishmael, *op. cit.*, p. 24.

[10] Reed, Ishmael, *op. cit.*, p. 82.

[11] Reed, Ishmael, *op. cit.*, p. 82.

[12] Reed, Ishmael, *op. cit.*, p. 28.

[13] Reed, Ishmael, *op. cit.*, p. 115.

fleshes out the image of a greedy, egocentered, demanding, and dangerous society.

Reed uses the metaphor both to illustrate and to undercut the power of the center. 'Machotots' are what he calls the 'Competitors for the Great Teat whose conversations revolve around themselves. Bully the blacks, bully the women'.[14] But the second-person address by the black narrator and that 'hailing' of the reader implicates us, even if it becomes clear that the 'you' being addressed is a male, white lawyer, married and with a 2-year-old child, a former 1960s radical who does not find black people 'interesting' any more. We may not fit the description, but we cannot fail to get the point of our implication in the satiric attack on the 1980s as 'grand times for white men'.[15] The narrative's ideological inscription of both difference and inequality covers both past and present and includes race (native and black), gender, and class.

Reed uses his metaphor of the 'terrible twos' in much the same way as Grass had used little Oskar's refusing to grow beyond the size of a 3-year-old. While the allegorical nature of both the image and the wildly imaginative satiric plot is clear in Reed's novel, it is somewhat more problematic in Grass's. As Patricia Waugh has asked: 'Is Oskar . . . a "real" midget . . . or is he an allegorical reflection, in an otherwise realistic fiction, of the anarchic, destructive, libidinous infantilism of Danzig society as it partakes in the rise of Nazism?'.[16] I would question if it really is 'an otherwise realistic fiction,' given the intensely metafictive nature of the text: we are always aware of Oskar's (later) writing – and fictionalizing – of his past. Nevertheless, the general point stands. How are we to interpret Oskar? Probably in the same way as we interpret the insomnia plague in *One Hundred Years of Solitude*. In other words, clearly fictional creations they may be, but this does not mean that they do not have ideological implications for the 'real,' as Waugh's second interpretation, in fact, suggests. The insomnia plague is a lesson in the dangers of forgetting the personal and public past, as is the more obvious revisionary history that wipes out Macondo's experience of economic exploitation ending in massacre.

Those in power control history. The marginal and ex-centric, however, can contest that power, even as they remain within its purvey. Ishmael Reed's 'Neo-HooDoo Manifesto' exposes these power relations in both history and language. But in several ways, he reveals the inside-ness of his inside-outsider marginalized position. On the one hand, he offers another totalizing system to counter that of white western culture: that of voodoo. And, on the other hand, he appears to believe strongly in certain humanist concepts, such as the ultimately free individual artist in opposition to the political forces of oppression. This is the kind of self-implicated yet challenging critique of humanism, however, that is typical of postmodernism. The position of black Americans has worked to make them especially aware of those political and social consequences of art, but they are still part of American society.

Maxine Hong Kingston's articulation of this same paradoxical positioning is in terms of Chinese Americans. When these ex-centrics visit China, she claims,

---

[14] Reed, Ishmael, *op. cit.*, p. 108.

[15] Reed, Ishmael, *op. cit.*.

[16] Waugh, Patricia, *Metafiction: The Theory and Practice of Self-Conscious Fiction* (London and New York: Methuen), p. 141.

'their whole lives suddenly made sense. . . . They realize their Americanness, they say, and 'You find out what a China Man you are'.[17] This is the contradictory position too of Wiebe's Métis, Rushdie's Indian, Kogawa's Japanese-Canadian, and of the many women, gays, hispanics, native peoples, and members of the working class, whose inscription into history since the 1960s has forced a recognition of the untenable nature of any humanist concepts of 'human essence' or of universal values that are not culturally and historically dependent. The postmodern attempts to negotiate the space between centers and margins in ways that acknowledge difference and its challenge to any supposedly monolithic culture (as implied by liberal human-ism).

Feminist theories have clearly been among the most potent decentering forces in contemporary thought, and their rhetoric has been largely opposi-tional (gender's binary oppositions are perhaps not that easily surmounted). Witness the opening of Judith Fetterley's *The Resisting Reader*: 'Literature is political. It is painful to have to insist on this fact, but the necessity of such insistence indicates the dimensions of the problem'.[18] Feminisms have, in fact, almost replaced the more traditionally political concerns (such as nationalism) in places like Quebec, where women artists and theorists are rearticulating power relations in terms of gender and language. Historiographic metafiction has participated in this politicizing process in typically postmodern ways, insisting on both the history of the ideological issues and their continuing relation to art and society. The heroine of Susan Daitch's *L.C.* receives her political education through the aesthetic and the personal. The novel is set in Paris in 1848, so the public dimension is overt. But it is the personal relations which the fictive Lucienne Crozier has with various artists, including the historical Delacroix, that teach her both about the role of art in politics and about the marginalized role of women in both domains: they are muses, models, observers, diversions. The novel's complex framing relates Berkeley 1968 to Paris 1848 (equally marked as revolutionary contexts). But the conclusions of both story and frame – outside of those marked contexts – question the patriarchal values underlying (male) revolutions, but offer no positive substitute. Just as Cassandra must beg to have her story told, so Lucienne's journal manuscript is used and abused by those whose political and economic interests it can serve.

In historiographic metafiction, this kind of exposition is often directly connected to that of other similarly unequal oppositions, such as race and class. In Michael Coetzee's *Foe*, as we have seen in other chapters, the enabling conceit of the text is that Defoe's *Robinson Crusoe* was indeed a real tale told to its author, but the teller was a woman, Susan Barton, and the tale somewhat different from the one we have come to know. In this novel, however, her awareness of the inequalities of gender do not save Susan from other ideologi-cal blind spots: she berates Cruso [sic] for not teaching Friday how to speak: 'you might have brought home to him some of the blessings of civilization and

[17] Kingston, Maxine Hong, *The Woman Warrior: Memories of a Girlhood Among Ghosts* (New York: Knopf, 1976), p. 295.
[18] Fetterley, Judith, *The Resisting Reader: A Feminist Approach to American Fiction* (Bloom-ington and London: Indiana University Press, 1978), p. xi.

made him a better man'.[19] The narrative's exploration of these 'blessings' and of Friday's status in their regard makes it another of the challenges to the liberal humanist – and imperialist – heritage that lives on in Coetzee's South Africa, as elsewhere. Like Susan, Friday cannot tell his own story, but it is not because he has been silenced by a controlling male writer: here it is the white slave traders who literally and symbolically have removed his tongue. Susan shares the assumptions of her age, but her gender helps her see a little, at least, of her own ideological motivations:

> I tell myself I talk to Friday to educate him out of darkness and silence. But is that the truth? There are times when benevolence deserts me and I use words only as the shortest way to subject him to my will.

> (1986, 60)

Language paradoxically both expresses and oppresses, educates and manipulates. Though the writer, Foe, denies her charge, she asserts that his ignoring of her 'true' castaway story of Cruso is comparable to the slavers' robbing Friday of his tongue.[20] What she learns is to question the humanist assumptions underlying her own ironic claim that she is 'a free woman who asserts her freedom by telling her story according to her own desire':[21] her sex, like Friday's race and Foe's class, conditions her freedom.

In Puig's *Kiss of the Spider Woman*, the protagonists' freedom (or rather their lack thereof) is literally determined by their sexual and political roles in Argentinian society. But the revolutionary politics of Valentin and the sexual politics of Molina are as closely connected as are the fates of the two very different men who share a prison cell. There is, in this novel, a set of paratextual footnotes to psychoanalytic theories of domination operative in patriarchal society that makes us aware of the double political repression the narrative works to combat: that of gay sexuality and that of women. Molina sees the female as the opposite of all that is evil and unjust in society and persists in referring to himself with feminine pronouns. He teaches Valentin the parallel between the struggle for class liberation and the struggle for sexual liberation, and he does so as much by his narration of illustrative movie plots as by his acts of kindness and didactic lessons.

In terms of theory, the work of feminists, Marxists, and black critics, among others, have argued this kind of interaction of the discourses of the marginalized. They have done so in such a powerful way that many feel today that they have created a new cultural hegemony, in the Gramscian sense of a new set of values and attitudes which validates what is now a dominant class in its power. But within each group there is little sense of unity or power: some claim that feminism is the discourse of the white, middle-class woman. Alice Walker calls her fiction 'womanist' to set it apart from this discourse.[22] But there is a black feminist discourse, a Marxist feminist discourse, and, of course, a humanist feminist discourse. From a metatheoretical point of view, it is this

---

[19] Coetzee, J.M., *Foe* (Toronto: Stoddart, 1986), p. 22.

[20] Coetzee, J.M., *op. cit.*, p. 150.

[21] Coetzee, J.M., *op. cit.*, p. 131.

[22] Bradley, David, 'Novelist Alice Walker: Telling the Black Women's Story', *New York Times Magazine* (8 January, 1984), p. 35.

plurality of feminisms that makes the postmodern valuing of difference possible. Though no acceptable non-totalizing alternatives may be available, the
questioning of the existing order should not cease for that reason. The
interrogations of the ex-centric form their own discourses, ones that attempt to
avoid the unconscious traps of humanist thought, while still working within its
power-field, as Teresa de Lauretis has recently been arguing.[23] Like feminists,
post-colonial theorists and artists now have their own discourse, with its own
set of questions and strategies.[24] Black and gay critics now possess quite a long
discursive history. And all of these marginalized ex-centrics have contributed
to definition of the postmodern heterogeneous different and to its inherently
ideological nature. The new ideology of postmodernism may be that everything is ideological. But this does not lead to any intellectual or practical
impasse. What it does is underline the need for self-awareness, on the one
hand, and on the other, for an acknowledgement of that relationship –
suppressed by humanism – of the aesthetic and the political. In E.L. Doctorow's words: 'a book can affect consciousness – affect the way people think
and therefore the way they act. Books create constituencies that have their own
effect on history'.[25]

---

20 Brian McHale

From *Chinese-Box Worlds*

Postmodernism Fiction, Methuen, 1987, pp 112–19.

ACHILLES: That's quite a bit to swallow. I never imagined there could be a world
            above mine before – and now you're hinting that there could even be one
            above that. It's like walking up a familiar staircase, and just keeping on
            going further up after you've reached the top – or what you'd always taken
            to be on the top!
CRAB: Or waking up from what you took to be real life, and finding out it too was
            just a dream. That could happen over and over again, no telling when it
            would stop.
                              (Douglas R. Hofstadter, *Gödel, Escher, Bach*, 1979)

Suppose it were decided to film a novel of forking paths – John Fowles's *The
French Lieutenant's Woman* (1964), let's say. How would one go about it? One
might choose to preserve the self-contradictory structure of the original, with

---

[23] de Lauretis, Teresa, 'The Technologies of Gender', course, International Summer Institute of Structuralism and Semiotics (Toronto, 1987).

[24] Bhabha, Homi, K., 'Difference, Discrimination and the Discourse of Colonialism' in Barker, Francis, *et al* (eds), *The Politics of Theory* (Colchester: University of Essex, 1983).

[25] Trenner, Richard, (ed.) E.L. Doctorow: Essays and Conversations (Princeton, NJ: Ontario Review Press, 1983).

its violation of the law of the excluded middle, producing something like Resnais's and Robbe-Grillet's *L'Année dernière à Marienbad* (1961) – a movie of forking paths. Or one might choose to do what Harold Pinter and Karel Reisz actually did when they made their film of *The French Lieutenant's Woman*, and transform one type of ontological structure into a different but related type with greater chance of being grasped by the average film-goer. Pinter and Reisz recast the double ending of Fowles's novel as a film-within-the-film, locating the unhappy ending (the hero loses the heroine for good) at the level of the film's 'real world,' the happy ending (hero and heroine reconciled) at the level of the film-within-the-film. This ingenious transformation suggests something like a functional equivalent between strategies of self-erasure or self-contradiction and strategies involving recursive structures – nesting or embedding, as in a set of Chinese boxes or Russian *babushka* dolls. Both types of strategy have the effect of interrupting and complicating the ontological 'horizon' of the fiction, multiplying its worlds, and laying bare the process of world-construction.

A recursive structure results when you perform the same operation over and over again, each time operating on the product of the previous operation. For example, take a film, which projects a fictional world; within that world, place actors and a film crew, who make a film which in turn projects its *own* fictional world; then within *that* world place another film crew, who make another film, and so on. This, as Douglas Hofstadter has demonstrated, is a basic structure of thought, occurring in mathematics, computer software and, of course, natural language. In Hofstadter's exemplary recursive dialogue, 'Little Harmonic Labyrinth' (from *Gödel, Escher, Bach*), Achilles and the Tortoise distract themselves from a tense predicament by reading a story in which two characters called Achilles and the Tortoise enter an Escher print, in which they read a story in which two characters called Achilles and the Tortoise are lost in a labyrinth.[1] We can describe this recursive structure most easily in terms of the metalanguage of narrative levels which Gérard Genette has taught us to use.[2] Hofstadter's dialogue projects a primary world, or *diegesis*, to which Achilles and the Tortoise belong. Within that world they read a story which projects a *hypo*diegetic world, one level 'down' from their own. The characters of *that* world, in turn, enter the hypo-hypodiegetic world of the Escher print; and so on, an additional 'hypo' being prefixed for each level as we descend 'deeper' into what Hofstadter calls the 'stack' of narrative levels.

Each change of narrative level in a recursive structure also involves a change of ontological level, a change of world. These embedded or nested words may be more or less continuous with the world of the primary diegesis, as in such Chinese-box novels as *Wuthering Heights*, *Lord Jim*, or *Absalom, Absalom!*; or they may be subtly different, as in the play-within-the-play of *Hamlet*, or even radically different, as in Hofstadter's dialogue. In other words, although

---

[1] Douglas R. Hofstadter, 'Little Harmonic Labyrinth,' in *Gödel, Escher, Bach: An Eternal Golden Braid* (Harmondsworth, Penguin, 1980), 103–26.

[2] Gérard Genette, 'Discours du récit,' in *Figures III* (Paris, Seuil, 1972), esp. 238–43. Actually, the use of the prefix 'hypo-' to designate embedded narrative levels follows a recommendation of Mieke Bal's; Genette prefers to use 'meta-', for which, however, both Bal and I have other uses; see Bal, *Narratologie* (Paris, Klincksieck, 1977). Genette defends his terminological preferences in *Nouveau discours du récit* (Paris, Seuil, 1983).

there is always an ontological discontinuity between the primary diegesis and hypodiegetic worlds, this discontinuity need not always be foregrounded. Indeed, in many realist and modernist novels, such as *Wuthering Heights*, *Lord Jim*, or *Absalom, Absalom!*, it is rather the epistemological dimension of this structure which is foregrounded, each narrative level functioning as a link in a chain of narrative transmission. Here recursive structure serves as a tool for exploring issues of narrative authority, reliability and unreliability, the circulation of knowledge, and so forth.

So if recursive structure is to function in a postmodernist poetics of ontology, strategies obviously must be brought to bear on it which foreground its ontological dimension. One such strategy, the simplest of all, involves *frequency*: interrupting the primary diegesis not once or twice but *often* with secondary, hypodiegetic worlds, representations within the representation. *Hamlet*, with its single interruption by the play-within-the-play, is unproblematic in its ontological structure; the relatively frequent interruptions of the primary diegesis by the film-within-the-film in *The French Lieutenant's Woman* make it somewhat more problematic; while still more problematic are such postmodernist novels as Claude Simon's *Tryptique* (1973), Gilbert Sorrentino's *Mulligan Stew* (1979), or Italo Calvino's *If on a winter's night a traveller* (1979), where the primary diegesis is interrupted so often, by nested representations in such diverse media (novels-within-the-novel, films-within-the-novel, still-photographs-with-the-novel, and so on), that the fiction's ontological 'horizon' is effectively lost.

Other such foregrounding strategies are a good deal more complex, involving logical paradoxes of various kinds. Recursive structures may raise the specter of a vertiginous infinite regress. Or they may dupe the reader into mistaking a representation at one narrative level for a representation at a lower or (more typically) higher level, producing an effect of *trompe-l'œil*. Or they may be subjected to various transgressions of the logic of narrative levels, short-circuiting the recursive structure. Or, finally, a representation may be embedded within itself, transforming a recursive structure into a structure *en abyme*. The consequence of all these disquieting puzzles and paradoxes is to foreground the ontological dimensions of the Chinese box of fiction.

Towards infinite regress

Among the forms of textual infinity proposed in 'The Garden of Forking Paths' (1941), apart from infinite bifurcation and infinite circularity, Borges also mentions infinite regress, exemplified by the night of the *Arabian Nights' Entertainment* when Scheherazade begins to narrate her *own* story which, if continued, would eventually bring her to the night when she began to narrate her own story, and so on, *ad infinitum*.[3] The specter of infinite regress haunts every recursive structure in which narrative worlds have been 'stacked' beyond

---

[3] The examples of Scheherazade's infinite regress – or rather, *potential* infinite regress – recurs in Borges's essay, 'Partial Enchantments of the *Quixote*' (from *Other Inquisitions 1937–1952* translated by Ruth L.C. Simms (Austin and London: University of Texas Press, 1964), 43–6, where it is coupled with examples from the Ramayana and, of course, *Don Quixote* Part Two.

a certain depth of embedding. Some recursive structures, such as those in modernist texts like *Lord Jim*, evade this disturbing possibility; others court it, including many postmodernist texts.

How deep does a recursive structure need to go before the tug of infinite regress begins to be felt? Certainly we feel it in John Barth's *tour-de-force* of recursively nested narrative, 'Menelaiad' (from *Lost in the Funhouse*, 1968), in which Menelaus narrates how he once narrated to himself how he told Telemachus and Peisistratus how he told Helen how he told Proteus how he told Eidothea (Proteus's daughter) how he reminded Helen of what Helen herself had said to Menelaus himself on their wedding night – a Chinese-box structure totaling seven narrative levels. But do we already begin to feel the possibility of infinite regress in a recursive structure of only three levels, such as the chapter 'Wind Die. You Die, We Die' from William Burroughs's *Exterminator!* (1973), where a man in a waiting-room reads a magazine story about a man reading a magazine story about a man reading a magazine story? If the specter of infinite regress does get evoked here, it is not so much by the depth of the recursive structure as by the vigor and explicitness of its foregrounding. Burroughs allows one of his magazine-readers to reflect upon the multi-leveled ontology in which he himself is sandwiched:

> Quite an idea. Story of someone reading a story of someone reading a story. I had the odd sensation that I myself would wind up in the story and that someone would read about me reading the story in a waiting room somewhere.[4]

Where a modernist text might pass over its recursive structures in silence, these postmodernist texts flaunt theirs. Our attention having thus been focused on recursiveness *for its own sake*, we begin, like Borges, to speculate: why stop the recursive operation of nesting worlds within worlds at any particular level of embedding? Why stop at all, ever?

Infinity can also be approached, or at least evoked, by repeated *upward* jumps of level as well as by *downward* jumps. Thus, for example, the fictional author in Barth's 'Life-Story' (also from *Lost in the Funhouse*), who is writing about an author who is writing about an author, and so on, also suspects – quite rightly – that he himself is a character in someone else's fictional text. But why stop there? If there is a *meta*-author occupying a *higher* level than his own, just as there is a hypodiegetic author occupying a level below his, then why not a meta-meta-author on a meta-meta-level, and so on, to infinity?[5] Caught between two infinities, two series of recursive nestings regressing toward two vanishing-points. Barth's fictional author breaks down, abandoning his project

---

[4] William Burroughs, *Exterminator!* (New York, Grove Press, 1973), 41. Actually, by my calculation, Burroughs is mistaken here. *This* magazine-reader has *not* read a 'story of someone reading a story of someone reading a story': he has only read a 'story of someone reading a story.' In other words, this reader claims to be aware of more levels of embedding than Borroughs has provided for! These words should have been attributed to the *next* reader, the one located one 'story' (level) *above* the present one.

[5] cf. the dialogue 'Little Harmonic Labyrinth,' *Gödel, Escher, Bach*, 110–15, where Hofstadter also includes an example of recursive meta-levels, a genie who depends for his authority upon a meta-genie, who in turn depends upon a meta-meta-genie, and so on, to GOD – not the divinity, but an infinitely recursive acronym which may be expanded as 'GOD Over Djinn, Over Djinn, Over Djinn,' and so on for as long as one has the patience to continue.

and beginning again with what he hopes will be a simpler structure. This, in fact, is a general pattern in postmodernist multilevel texts: complexity increasing to the point where levels collapse, as if of their own weight, into a single level of diegesis. It also happens, for instance, in Raymond Federman's *Double or Nothing* (1971). Here the 'intramural setup' of the text initially involves four narrative levels – protagonist, narrator, recorder, and 'fourth person' (i.e. author) – but as the text proceeds these levels begin to lose their initial clarity of definition, and the four distinct roles in the narrative structure merge into a single quasi-autobiographical figure. Setting up an elaborate hierarchy of levels, only to allow it to break down before the reader's eyes, is, of course, one means of foregrounding the ontological dimension of recursive structure. There are other variants on this strategy, to which I shall return shortly.

Trompe-l'œil

Douglas Hofstadter has shown that the human mind is capable of handling recursive structures quite readily and confidently, and that it does so all the time. 'It is not too uncommon,' he tells us,

> to go down three levels in real [radio] news reports, and surprisingly enough, we scarcely have any awareness of the suspension. It is all kept track of quite easily by our subconscious minds. Probably the reason it is so easy is that each level is extremely different in flavor from each other level. If they were all similar, we would get confused in no time flat.[6]

No doubt this is true, so far as everyday recursive structures and their processing are concerned. What is striking about many postmodernist texts is the way they *court* confusion of levels, going out of their way to *suppress* the 'difference in flavor' that, as Hofstadter says, we depend upon for keeping levels distinct in our minds. Postmodernist texts, in other words, tend to encourage *trompe-l'œil*, deliberately misleading the reader into regarding an embedded, secondary world as the primary, diegetic world. Typically, such deliberate 'mystification' is followed by 'demystification,' in which the true ontological status of the supposed 'reality' is revealed and the entire ontological structure of the text consequently laid bare. In short, *trompe-l'œil* functions in the postmodernist context as another device for foregrounding the ontological dimension.

Jean Ricardou has called this the strategy of 'variable reality,' that is, the strategy whereby a supposedly 'real' representation is revealed to have been merely 'virtual' – an illusion or secondary representation, a representation within the representation – or vice versa, a supposedly virtual representation is shown to have been 'really real' after all.[7] An example of variable reality is the *in medias res* beginning of Pynchon's *Gravity's Rainbow* (1973): a nightmarish evacuation of a big city, from the viewpoint of one of the evacuees. 'Nightmarish' is the operative word here: the episode is dream-like, but not *so* dream-

---

[6] Hofstadter, *Gödel, Escher, Bach*, 128.
[7] Jean Ricardou, 'Réalités variables, variantes réelles,' in *Problèmes du nouveau roman* (Paris, Seuil, 1967), 23–43.

like that it couldn't pass for real; yet it proves retroactively to have been a dream of Pirate Prentice's, a nested representation, one level 'down' from reality. Now, this is certainly a disorienting way to begin a novel; but even more disturbing is the way *Gravity's Rainbow* ends. For the *trompe-l'œil* strategy of variable reality, of pushing the representation back into a secondary plane, is repeated on the novel's last page, but this time on a global scale. The entire world of *Gravity's Rainbow* is retroactively revealed to have been the world of a movie-within-the-novel, hypodiegetic rather than diegetic:

> The screen is a dim page spread before us, white and silent. The film has broken, or a projector bulb has burned out. It was difficult even for us, old fans who've always been at the movies (haven't we?) to tell which before the darkness swept in.[8]

'The screen is a dim page' – or is it, the page is a dim screen? Either way, the difficulty is that the nested world of *Gravity's Rainbow* has the same 'flavor' (as Hofstadter would say) as diegetic, first-order reality. Can the reader really be expected to mentally reprocess the entire fictional world, dropping it all down one level in his mind? Is it even possible for a reader to accomplish such a 're-vision,' or has *trompe-l'œil* triumphed over demystification, for once?

Other examples of variable reality occur in Claude Simon's *Les Corps conducteurs* (1971) and *Tryptique*, Federman's *Double or Nothing*, John Fowles's *Mantissa* (1982), and throughout William Burroughs' fiction. Many of these examples involve erotic or luridly melodramatic or horrifically violent materials. The function of such materials in recusive structures is equivalent to their function in self-erasing structures: here, as there, they intensify ontologi-cal instability, titillating or horrifying the reader (it works equally well either way) so that she or he will resist having to 'surrender' the reality of these materials when they are erased or, in the case of recursive structures, dropped down one narrative level.

A notorious example is the Orgasm Death Gimmick from Burroughs's *Naked Lunch* (1959). The Gimmick, appearing in a blue-movie-within-the-novel, involves sex-murder by hanging – one of Burroughs's nastier obsessions – followed by cannibalism. While this episode may not be pornographic, concludes David Lodge about the Orgasm Death Gimmick, neither is it what Burroughs himself claims it is, namely a satire on capital punishment. Lodge argues that the representation is simply too unstable in this text generally for the reader either to respond appropriately to pornographic solicitation, or to discover the norms necessary for satire. 'It would seem to be a general rule,' he writes, 'that where one kind of aesthetic presentation is embedded in another, the "reality" of the embedded form is weaker than that of the framing form,'[9] thus corroborating Hofstadter's intuition about the different 'flavors' of dif-ferent levels in a recursive structure. However:

> The context in which the passage under discussion is embedded (both the local context and the whole book) is no more 'realistic' than the passage itself: indeed *it is in many ways less so*. That is to say, although the events reported in this passage are 'impossible,' the style in which they are reported is clear, lucid and for the most part

[8] Thomas Pynchon, *Gravity's Rainbow* (New York, Viking, 1973), 760.

[9] David Lodge, *The Modes of Modern Writing: Metaphor, Metonymy, and the Typology of Modern Liberature* (London, Edward Arnold, 1977), 37.

[10] ibid., 37–8.

of the kind appropriate to descriptions of actuality. . . . when we come to the Orgasm Death Gimmick, no norms have been established by which its nauseating grotesquerie can be measured and interpreted in the way intended by Burroughs.[10]

In other words, the realistic representation of such hair-raising material at the embedded level of a movie-within-the-novel has the effect of disorienting the reader and undermining the ontological status of the primary diegesis. Now, insofar as disorientation is undesirable both in pornography and satire, Lodge is right to consider Burroughs a poor pornographer and worse satirist; nevertheless, he is a superior postmodernist.

In addition to these strategies for soliciting the reader's involvement in 'unreal,' hypodiegetic worlds, there are other devices designed to encourage him or her to mistake nested representations for 'realities.' Among the simplest is the device of the missing end-frame: dropping down to an embedded narrative level without returning to the primary diegesis at the end. Hofstadter illustrates this in his 'Little Harmonic Labyrinth': Achilles and the Tortoise go down three 'stories,' but only come back up two; the apparent resolution of their adventures is actually a suspension, since events on the level of the 'Real' – the diegesis – remain in a kind of limbo, stranded one level *above* the level of the text's ending. It requires an attentive reader to notice this, however, for, as Hofstadter observes, 'When you pop out of a movie-within-a-movie you feel for a moment as if you had reached the real world, though you are still one level from the top.'[11]

Beckett, as we saw in Chapter 1 (see p. 12), does this in *Malone Dies* (1951/6), where the text actually ends one level down from the world in which Malone presumably dies. The same deception is practiced on a more local scale by Robbe-Grillet in *Projet pour une révolution à New York* (1970). His elegant sleight-of-hand involves simply omitting the end-quotes from a character's quoted discourse – *literally* a missing end-frame! Robbe-Grillet thus makes it impossible for the reader to determine whether, or even *if*, a nested narrative ends. In effect, the text never rejoins the primary, diegetic level; or, to put it differently, the distinction between diegesis and hypodiegesis can no longer be safely maintained.

Another *trompe-l'œil* device violates the implicit contract with the reader even more outrageously. In this device, a nested 'still' representation is transformed before our eyes into an 'animated' sequence with every appearance of belonging to first-order reality. Undoubtedly the best-known example of this type of transparent deception is the etching of the 'Defeat of Reichenfels' near the beginnings of Robbe-Grillet's *Dans le labyrinthe* (1959). Here a still representation of a bar-room scene is described in implausibly fine and verisimilar detail, gradually acquiring movement and 'liveliness' to the point that it becomes an apparently independent episode:

> The contrast between the three soldiers and the crowd is further accentuated by a precision of line, a clarity in rendering, much more evident in their case than in that of other individuals the same distance from the viewer. The artist has shown them with as much concern for detail and almost as much sharpness of outline as if they were sitting in the foreground. But the composition is so involved that this is not apparent

[11] Hofstadter, *Gödel, Escher, Bach*, 184.

at first glance. Particularly the soldier shown full face has been portrayed with a wealth of detail that seems quite out of proportion to the indifference it expresses. . . .

He has finished his drink some time ago. He does not look as if he were thinking of leaving. Yet, around him, the cafe has emptied. The light is dim now, the bartender having turned out most of the lamps before leaving the room himself.

The soldier, his eyes wide open, continues to stare into the half-darkness a few yards in front of him, where the child is standing, also motionless and stiff, his arms at his side. . . .

It is the child who speaks first. He says: 'Are you asleep?'[12]

At this point the text seems, impossibly, to have rejoined the diegetic level that it left when it began describing the details of the etching.

This pattern recurs in Robbe-Grillet's *La Maison de rendez-vous* (1965), where, for example, a magazine-cover illustration in the hands of a Chinese street-sweeper develops into an apparently 'real' scene at Lady Ava's luxurious villa; in Burroughs' *Cities of the Red Night* (1981), where the etching 'The Hanging of Captain Strobe' becomes animated and develops into an action sequence; and throughout Simon's *Les Corps conducteurs*. Even more spectacular, perhaps, are the *trompe-l'œil* effects in Robbe-Grillet's *Projet pour une révolution*. Here the girl Laura deceives a voyeur by holding a lurid book-jacket in front of the keyhole through which he is peeping – literally *trompe-l'œil*. When, much later in the text, the voyeur returns with others to break into the house, they interrupt the scene on the book-jacket, which proves not to be a nested representation but a 'real' event – seen, however, not directly but reflected in a mirror, which supposedly accounts for its slight air of unreality!

As in other types of *trompe-l'œil*, here too demystification often follows deliberate mystification: dynamic episodes which have evolved illicitly from static representations often collapse back into 'stills,' thus abruptly reminding the reader that he or she has been at the hypodiegetic level all along. This effect parallels the 'freeze-frame' or 'stop-action' device of film and television. Thus, for example, the action of *Dans le labyrinthe* which has developed from 'The Defeat of Reichenfels' freezes into an etching once again:

> The soldier hesitates to leave the busy care where he has come to rest for a moment. It is the rain he is staring at through the large window with its pleated curtains and its three billiard balls on the other side of the glass. The child is also watching the rain, sitting on the floor close to the window so that he can see through the thin material. It begins to rain much harder. The umbrella in its black silk sheath is leaning on the coat rack near the furlined overcoat. But in the drawing there are so many other garments hanging on top of each other that it is difficult to make out much of anything in the jumble. Just under the picture is the chest with its three drawers.[13]

Similar stop-action or freeze-frame effects occur in *La Maison de rendez-vous*, *Projet pour une révolution*, Simon's *Corps conducteurs*, and elsewhere. The ultimate result, in every case, is to foreground the ontological dimension of the recursive structure.

---

[12] Alain Robbe-Grillet, *In the Labyrinth*, in *Two Novels by Robbe-Grillet*, trans. Richard Howard (New York, Grove Press, 1965), 152–3. See Christine Brooke-Rose's admirable account of *Dans le labyrinthe*, 'The real as unreal: Robbe-Grillet,' in *A Rhetoric of the Unreal* (Cambridge, London, New York, Cambridge University Press, 1981), 291–310

[13] Robbe-Grillet, *In the Labyrinth*, in *Two Novels by Robbe-Grillet*, 271.

Select Bibliography

Adorno, Theodor 1986: *Negative Dialectics* tr. E.B. Aston. London: Routledge Kegan Paul.

Allen, D.M. and Tallmann, W. *The Poetics of the New American Poetry*

Allen, J. and Young, I.M. 1989: *The Thinking Muse: Feminism and Modern French Philosophy* Bloomington and Indinapolis: Indiana University Press.

Anderson, Perry 1984: *In the Tracks of Historical Materialism*. London: Verso.

Antin, David 1972: 'Modernism and Postmodernism: Approaching the Present in American Poetry', *Boundary* 2, 2, 1, pp.98–133.

Arac, J. 1987 *Critical Genealogies: Historical Situations for Postmodern Literary Studies*. New York: Columbia University Press.

Barth, John 1969: *Lost in the Funhouse*. New York and London: Secker and Warburg.

Barth, John 1967: 'The Literature of Exhaustion', *The Atlantic* 220, 2, p.29–34.

— 1980: 'The Literature of Replenishment: Postmodernist Fiction', *The Atlantic* 245, 1, pp.65–71

Bataille, Georges 1985: *Visions of Excess*. Minneapolis: Minnesota University Press.

Baudrillard, Jean 1975: *The Mirror of Production*. St. Louis: Telos Press.

— 1983a *Simulations*. New York: Semiotext(e).

— 1983b *In the Shadow of the Silent Majorities*. New York.

— 1987: *Forget Foucault*. New York: Semiotext(e).

— 1988 *The Ecstacy of Communication*. New York: Semiotexte.

Bell, Daniel 1973 *The Coming of Post-Industrial Society*. New York: Basic.

— 1976: *The Cultural Contradictions of Capitalism*. New York: Basic Books.

Benhabib, S. and Cornell, D. 1987: *Feminism as Critique*. London: Polity.

Benjamin, A. (ed.) 1989: *The Problems of Modernity*. London and New York. Routledge.

Bennington, G. 1988: *Lyotard: Writing the Event*. Manchester: Manchester University Press.

Berman, Marshall 1982: *All that is Solid Melts into Air*. New York: Simon and Shuster.

Borges, Jorge Luis 1970: *Labyrinths*. Harmondsworth: Penguin.

Brennan, T. (ed) 1989: *Between Feminism and Psychoanalysis*. London and New York: Routledge.

Bürger, Peter 1984: *Theory of the Avant-Garde*, tr. M. Shaw, Mineapolis: Minnesota University Press.

Burgin, Victor 1986 *The End of Art Theory: Criticism and Postmodernity*. London: Macmillan.

Butler, C. 1980: *After the Wake*. Oxford: Clarendon.

Calinescu, Matei 1987: *Five Faces of Modernity*. Durham: Duke University Press.

Callinicos, Alex 1990: *Against Postmodernism: A Marxist Critique*. Cambridge: Polity.

Caramello, Charles 1983: *Silverless Mirrors: Book, Self and Postmodern American Fiction*. Florida State University Press.

Cassirer, Ernst: 1951: *The Philosophy of the Enlightenment*, tr. F. Koellen and J. Pettegrove. New Jersey: Princeton University Press.

Chodorow, Nancy 1978: *The Reproduction of Mothering: Psychoanalysis and the Sociology of Gender*. Berkeley and London.

Collins, J. 1989: *Uncommon Cultures: Popular Culture and Postmodernism*. New York and London: Routledge.

Connor, Stephen 1989: *Postmodern Culture*. Oxford and New York: Blackwell.

Couturier, M. 1982: *Representation and Performance in Postmodern Fiction*. Proceedings of the Nice postmodernism Conference.

Debord, Guy 1976: *The Society of the Spectacle*. Detroit: Black and Red.

Deleuze, Gilles 1983: *Nietzsche and Philosophy*. New York: Columbia University Press.

— and Guattari, Felix: 1983 *Anti-Oedipus*. Minneapolis: Minnesota University Press.

De Man, Paul 1971: *Blindness and Insight*. London and New York: Oxford University Press.

Derrida, Jacques 1989: 'Structure, Sign and play in the Human Sciences', repr. in Philip Rice and Patricia Waugh *Modern Literary Theory: A Reader*. London: Edward Arnold.

— 1976: *Of Grammatology*. Baltimore: John Hopkins.

— 1981: *Margins of Philosophy*. Chicago: Chicago University Press.

— 1984: 'Of an Apocalyptic Tone in Recent philosophy', *Oxford Literary Review*, 6, 2.

Descartes, R. 1970: *The Philosophical Work of Descartes*, (ed.) E.S. Haldane and G.R.T. Ross. London: Cambridge University Press.

Diamond, I. and Quinby, L. 1988: *Feminism and Foucault*. Boston: Northeastern University Press.

During, Simon 1987: 'Postmodernism or Post-colonialism Today', *Textual Practice*, 1, 1, pp.32–47.

Eagleton, T. 1986: *Against the Grain*, London: Verso.

— 1987: 'The Politics of Subjectivity', in ICA Document: *Identity*, (ed.) L. Apignanesi. London.

— 1990: *The Ideology of the Aesthetic*. Oxford: Blackwell.

Fekete, J. 1988: *Life After Postmodernism*. London: Macmillan.

Felski, R. 1989: *Beyond Feminist Aesthetics*. London: Hutchinson.

Flax, J. Thinking Fragments 1990: *Psychoanalysis, Feminism and Postmodernism in the Contemporary West*. Berkeley: California University Press.

Fokkemma, D. 1984: *Literary History: Modernism and Postmodernism*. Amsterdam: John Benjamins.

— and Bertens, H. 1986: *Approaching Postmodernism*. Amsterdam: John Benjamins.

Foster, Hal 1985: *Postmodern Culture*. London and Sydney: Pluto.

— 1985b: *Recodings: Art, Spectacle, Cultural Politics*. Washington: Bay Press, Port Townsend.

Foucault, M. 1974: *The Order of Things*. London: Tavistock.

— 1977: *Language, Counter-Memory, Practice*. (ed.) D. Bouchard, Oxford: Blackwell.

— 1980: *The History of Sexuality*. New York: Vintage.

— 1986: *The Uses of Pleasure*. New York: Vintage.

— 1986: *The Foucault Reader*. (ed.) P. Rabinow. Harmondsworth: Penguin.

— 1988a: *The Care of the Self*. New York: Vintage.

— 1988b *Technologies of the Self*. (ed.) L.H. Martin, H. Gutman, P.H. Hutton. London: Tavistock Press.

Gadamer, Hans-Georg 1975: *Truth and Method*, (ed.) G. Barden and J. Cumming. New York.

Gass, William 1970: *Fiction and the Figures of Life*. New York: Alfred Knopf.

Giddens, Anthony 1981: 'Modernism and Postmodernism', *New German Critique*, 22, pp.15–18.

Gelpi, Albert 1987: 'A Coherent Splendour' *The American Poetic Renaissance 1910–1950*. New York: Cambridge University Press.

Graff, Gerald 1979: *Literature Against Itself*. Chicago and London: Chicago University Press.
Grosz, E. 1989: *Sexual Subversions*. Sydney: Allen and Unwin.
Habermas, Jurgen 1981: 'Modernity versus Postmodernity', in Foster (ed.) 1985: *Postmodernism Culture*. London and Sydney: Pluto.
— 1984, 1987: *Theory of Communicative Action*, vols. 1, 2. Boston: Beacon Press.
— 1987 *The Philosophical Discourses of Modernity*, tr. F.G. Lawrence. Oxford: Polity.
Harvey, David 1989: *The Condition of Postmodernity*. London: Blackwell.
Hassan, Ihab 1971: *The Dismemberment of Orpheus: Towards a Postmodern Literature*. New York: Oxford University Press.
— 1975a 'Joyce, Beckett and the postmodern imagination', *Triquarterly*. 34.
— 1975b: *Paracriticisms: Seven Speculations of the Times*. Urbana, Chicago and London: Illinois University Press.
— 1980: *The Right Promethean Fire*. Urbana, Chicago, London: Illinois University Press.
— 1987: *The Postmodern Turn*. Columbus.
Heidegger, Martin 1962: *Being and Time*. New York: Harper and Row.
— 1972: *On Time and being*. tr. J. Stambaugh. New York: Harper and Row.
— 1975: *Poetry, Language, Thought*. tr. A. Hofstadter. New York and London: Harper and Row.
— 1977: *The Question Concerning Technology*, tr. William Lott. New York: Harper and Row.
Horkheimer, M. and Adorno, T. 1972: *Dialectic of Enlightenment*. New York: Seabury.
Hoffman, G., Horning, A., and Rudinger, K. 1977: '"Modern", "Postmodern" and "Contemporary" as Criteria for the Analysis of Twentieth Century Literature', *Amerika Studien*. 22, pp.19–46.
Howe, I. 1959: 'Mass Society and Postmodern Fiction', *Partisan Review*, 26, p.420–436.
— 1971: *Decline of the New*. London: Gollancz.
Hutcheon, Linda 1989: *The Politics of Postmodernism*. London and New York: Routledge.
— 1990: *A Poetics of Postmodernism: History, Theory, Fiction*. New York and London: Routledge.
Huyssen, Andreas 1988: *After the Great Divide: Modernism, Mass Culture and Postmodernism*. London: Macmillan.
Jaggar, A. 1983: *Feminist Politics and Human Nature*. Brighton: Harvester.
Jameson, Fredric 1971: *Marxism and Form*. Princeton: Princeton University Press.
— 1972: *The Prison House of Language*. Princeton University Press.
— 1981: *The Political Unconscious*. New York: Cornell University Press.
— 1984: 'Postmodernism, or the Cultural Logic of Late Capitalism', *New Left Review*, 146, pp.53–93.
— 1985: 'Postmodernism and Consumer Society', in Foster (ed.) 1985: *Postmodernism Culture*. London and Sydney: Pluto, pp.111–126
— 1989: *The Ideologies of Theory: Essays 1971–86*. New York.
— 1989: 'Periodising the Sixties', in *The Ideologies of Theory*.
Jardine, Alice 1985: *Gynesis: Configurations of Woman and Modernity*. Ithaca and London: Cornell University Press.
Jencks, Charles 1987: *The Language of Post-Modern Architecture*. London: Academy.
Josipovici, Gabriel 1971: *The World and the Book*. London: Macmillan.
Kant, Emanuel 1952: *Critique of Judgement*, tr. J.C. Meredith. Oxford: Oxford University Press.
— 1984: 'What is Enlightenment?', in David Simpson, (ed.) *German Aesthetic and*

Literary Criticism: Kant, Fichte, Schelling, Schopenhauer, Hegel. Cambridge: Cambridge University Press.
Kaplan, A.E. 1988: *Postmodernism and its Discontents*. London: Verso.
Kauffmann, Walter 1974: *Nietzsche: Philosopher, Psychologist, Antichrist*. New Jersey: Princeton University Press.
Kearney, Richard 1988: *The Wake of Imagination*. Minneapolis: Minnesota University Press.
— 1991: *Poetics of Imagining*. London: Harper Collins.
Kellner, Douglas 1989a: *Jean Baudrillard: From Marxism to Postmodernism and Beyond*. Cambridge: Polity.
— 1989b: *Postmodernism/Jameson/Critique*. Washington D.C.: Maisonneuve.
Kermode, Frank 1966: *The Sense of an Ending*. Oxford: Oxford University Press.
— 1968: *Continuities*. London: Routledge, Kegan and Paul.
— 1988: *History and Value*. Oxford: Oxford University Press.
Kolb, David 1986: *The Critique of Pure Modernity*. London: Chicago University Press.
Kramer, Hilton 1985: *The Revenge of the Philistines: Art and Culture 1972–1984*. New York: Free Press.
Kroker, Arthur 1986: *The Postmodern Scene*. New York: St. Martin's Press.
— and Kroker, Marilouise 1988: *Body Invaders: Sexuality and the Postmodern Condition*. London: Macmillan.
Kristeva, Julia 1982: 'Women's Time', in Keohane, N., Rosaldo, M., and Gelpi, B.C. 1982: *Feminist Theory: A Critique of Ideology*. Brighton: Harvester.
Laclau, E. and Mouffe, C. 1987: 'Post-Marxism Without Apologies', *New Left Review*, 166, pp.79–106
Lash, Scott 1985: 'Postmodernity and Desire', *Theory and Society*. 14, 1, pp.1–33.
Levin, D.M. 1988: *The Opening of Vision: Nihilism and the Postmodern Situation*. London: Routledge.
Lovibond, S. 1989: 'Feminism and Postmodernism', *New Left Review*, 178, pp.5–28.
Lyotard, Jean-Francois 1974: *Economie Libidinale*. Paris: Minuit.
— 1985: *The Postmodern Condition*. Manchester: Manchester University Press.
— 1988: *The Differend*. Manchester: Manchester University Press.
— 1989: *The Lyotard Reader*, (ed.) Andrew Benjamin. London and Cambridge, Mass.: Blackwell.
— and Thebaud, J.L. 1985: *Just Gaming*. Minneapolis: Minnesota University Press.
Mandel, Ernest 1975: *Late Capitalism*. London: New Left Books.
Marcuse, Herbert 1964: *One-Dimensional Man*. Boston: Beacon Press.
MacIntyre, Alisdair 1985: *After Virtue: A Study in Moral Theory*. London: Duckworth.
— 1990: *Three Rival Versions of Moral Enquiry*. London: Duckworth.
— 1991: *A Short History of Ethics*. London and New York: Routledge.
Mazarro, Jerome 1980: *Postmodern American Poetry*. Urbana: Illinois University Press.
McHale, Brian 1987: *Postmodernist Fiction*. London and New York: Methuen.
Meese, E., and Parker, A., (eds) 1989: *The Difference Within: Feminism and Critical Theory*. Amsterdam/Philadelphia: John Benjamins.
Megill, A. 1985: *Prophets of Extremity: Nietzsche, Heidegger, Foucault, Derrida*. Berkeley and London: California University Press.
Merquior, J.G. 1986: 'Spider and Bee', in *Postmodernism*. London: ICA Documents 4, 5, pp.16–18.
Nehemas, A. 1985: *Nietzsche: Life as Literature*. Cambridge, Mass. and London: Harvard University Press.
Newman, Charles 1985: *The Postmodern Aura*. Evanston: Northwestern University Press.
Nicholson, L. 1990: *Feminism/Postmodernism*. New York and London: Routledge.
Nietzsche, Friedrich 1966: *The Birth of Tragedy*. New York: Vintage.

— 1956 *The Birth of Tragedy and the Genealogy of Morals*, New York: Archer.
— 1954: 'Thus Spake Zarathustra', in *The Portable Nietzsche*. New York: Viking.
— 1973: *Beyond Good and Evil*. Harmondsworth: Penguin.
— 1979: *Philosophy and Truth: Selections from Nietzsche's Notebooks of the Early 1870s*, tr. D. Breazeale. New Jersey: Humanities Press.
— 1979: *Ecce Homo: How One Becomes What One Is*. Harmondsworth: Penguin.
— 1967: *The Will to Power*. New York: Random House.
— 1990: *My Sister and I*. Los Angeles: Amok Books.
Norris, Christopher 1985: *The Contest of Faculties: Philosophy and Theory after Deconstruction*. London and New York: Methuen.
— 1990: *What's Wrong With Postmodernism*. Brighton: Harvester.
Olson, Charles 1984: 'Human Universe' and 'Projective Verse', in Allen and Tallman, (eds) pp.147–58, 161–74.
Pippin, R. 1991: *Modernism as a Philosophical Problem: On the Dissatisfactions of European High Culture*. Cambridge, Mass. and Oxford: Blackwell.
Poster, Mark 1990: *The Mode of Information: Post-structuralism and Social Context*. Cambridge: Polity Press.
Roberts, J. 1990: *Postmodernism, Politics and Art*. Manchester and New York: Manchester University Press.
Rorty, Richard 1980: *Philosophy and the Mirror of Nature*. Oxford: Blackwell.
— 1989: *Contingency, Irony and Solidarity*. Cambridge: Cambridge University Press.
Russell, Charles 1985: *Poets, Prophets and Revolutionaries: The Literary Avant-Garde from Rimbaud through Postmodernism*. Oxford: Oxford University Press.
Sarup, M. 1988: *An Introductory Guide to Post-Structuralism and Postmodernism*. Brighton: Harvester.
Schiller, J.C.F. 1967: *On the Aesthetic Education of Man, in a Series of letters*. Oxford: Oxford University Press.
— 1988: 'On Naive and Sentimental Poetry', in David Simpson, (ed.) *The Origins of Modern Critical Thought*, p.148–177.
Simpson, David 1984: *German Aesthetic and Literary Criticism*. Cambridge, Cambridge University Press.
— 1988: *The Origins of Modern Critical Thought*. Cambridge: Cambridge University Press.
Silverman, H.J. 1990: *Postmodernism: Philosophy and the Arts*. New York and London: Routledge.
Smythe, E.J. 1991: *Postmodernism and Contemporary Fiction*. London: Batsford.
Sontag, Susan 1966: *Against Interpretation*. New York: Farrar, Strauss and Giroux.
Spanos, William 1972: 'The Detective at the Boundary: Some Notes on the Postmodern Literary Imagination', *Boundary 2*, 2, 1, pp.147–68.
— 1979: *Martin Heidegger and the Question of Literature*. Bloomington and London: Indiana University Press.
Stevens, Wallace 1951: *The Necessary Angel: Essays on Reality and Imagination*. London: Faber.
Stratton, Jon 1990: *Writing Sites*. Ann Arbor: Michigan University Press.
Wilde, Alan 1987: *Modernism, Postmodernism and the Ironic Imagination*. Philadelphia: Pennsylvania University Press.
Wittgenstein, Ludwig 1978: *Philosophical Investigations*. Oxford: Blackwell.
Wolin, R. 1984–5: 'Modernism and Postmodernism', *Telos*, 62, pp.9–29
Woolff, J. 1990: *Feminine Sentences: essays on Women and Culture*. Cambridge: Polity Press.

Index